THE VIRTUAL WEAPON AND INTERNATIONAL ORDER

THE
VIRTUAL
WEAPON
AND INTERNATIONAL ORDER

LUCAS KELLO

YALE UNIVERSITY PRESS
NEW HAVEN AND LONDON

For information about this and other Yale University Press publications, please contact:
U.S. Office: sales.press@yale.edu   yalebooks.com
Europe Office: sales@yaleup.co.uk   yalebooks.co.uk

Set in Adobe Caslon Pro by IDSUK (DataConnection) Ltd
Printed in Great Britain by TJ International Ltd, Padstow, Cornwall

Library of Congress Cataloging-in-Publication Data

Names: Kello, Lucas, author.
Title: The virtual weapon and international order / Lucas Kello.
Description: New Haven, [CT] : Yale University Press, [2017]
Identifiers: LCCN 2017022267 | ISBN 9780300220230 (alk. paper)
Subjects: LCSH: Cyberspace operations (Military science) |
    Cyberspace—Security measures. | Cyberspace—Government policy. |
    Security, International.
Classification: LCC U167.5.C92 K46 2017 | DDC 355.4—dc23
LC record available at https://lccn.loc.gov/2017022267

A catalogue record for this book is available from the British Library.

10 9 8 7 6 5 4 3 2 1

JAN - 4 2018

To Stanley Hoffmann

Contents

PART III PROBLEMS OF STRATEGY AND POLICY

Tables

Acknowledgments

An author who writes a book on cyber issues at Oxford University is in a fortunate place. He has access to a vibrant network of thinkers in multiple disciplines. At his disposal are the intellectual resources of established scholarly initiatives, including the Cyber Studies Programme, the Centre for Doctoral Training in Cyber Security, and the Oxford Internet Institute. Many universities today recognize the necessity for cyber studies. Some have established research projects in this field of study. But few operate, like Oxford, an organized network to coordinate their varied efforts. I have benefited more than I can recount from the intellectual companionship of this extraordinary community of scholars.

I wrote this book under the auspices of the Cyber Studies Programme at Oxford University's Centre for Technology and Global Affairs. The program has developed a multidimensional procedure for the stimulation of ideas. This procedure involves a seminar series, specialized workshops, and irregular but ongoing meetings with affiliated faculty, visiting fellows, external practitioners, and students. The program, the center, and the Department of Politics and International Relations that houses them have provided unobtrusive administrative support in the preparation of the manuscript. Other institutions also supported this work. Chapter 9 on active defense in the private sector grew out of a workshop sponsored by U.S. Cyber Command and hosted by Stanford University's Center for International Security and Cooperation.

The generous advice of many experts provided guiding lights when exploring unfamiliar – sometimes uncharted – intellectual terrains. Andrew Martin and Ivan Martinovic helped me to navigate the technical world of machines. Richard J. Harknett was especially helpful in identifying and wading through the pitfalls of prevailing theory and strategy. James Sherr and Alex Pravda aided my journey through Russian history and doctrine; Katy Minshall helped in the collection of primary sources. Richard Caplan, Dave Aitel, Max Smeets, Florian Egloff, Jamie Collier, James Shires, and Benjamin Daus-Haberle all read parts of the manuscript. Their generous advice saved me from errors of fact and interpretation. Discussions with practitioners helped me to fill gaps in the public record. I profited in particular from discussions with Sorin Ducaru, Christian-Marc Liflander, Marina Kaljurand, Nick Alexander, and David Pickard. Each of them contributed a crucial resource without which a book of this sort would be impossible: a sense of the practical dimensions of new security challenges and of attempts to overcome them. The job of these men and women is unenviable: they must defeat relentless threats even as new technology undermines the assumptions of their actions. I am grateful to Karen Motley of the Harvard Kennedy School and to Taiba Batool and Melissa Bond of Yale University Press for their extremely helpful editorial guidance.

I owe a special debt of gratitude to Venkatesh Narayanamurti and Kalypso A. Nicolaïdis – the former for encouraging me (with uncommon zeal) to fuse modern technology and political science, the latter for helping me to erect in Oxford an institutional shelter in which to pursue this vocation. The inspiration of Stanley Hoffmann, a late mentor to whom this book is dedicated, permeates these pages. Hildengard's support was vital; more so her unflagging patience and gentle understanding.

Introduction

A Permanent Revolution

Every historical era begins with a revolution: it comes of age when revolution becomes the new normal. The Reformation began when a disaffected Augustinian friar asked, What authority has the Pope? It achieved its peak when the schism in Christianity became a source not of religious war but of stable social structures. The Romantic period started with the philosophical challenge, What is a state if not also an integral nation? It matured when nationalism in Europe became less a cause of violence than of political cohesion. The present era, too, can be defined by a revolutionary question, one rooted in technology: what limits has space? For cyberspace, a defining motif of our era, smashes the constraints of geography on the speed and range of human action. Never before has technology permeated society so completely or influenced the dealings of states and peoples so intricately as in the present. Yet despite significant experience with the related technology, the cyber age remains in a revolutionary condition. We have yet to master the forces of change that define our times.

The distinguishing feature of revolution is that it challenges not just the rational but also the moral order. Contemporary observers struggle to make sense of both sets of problems as they relate to the virtual weapon of cyberspace – malicious computer code designed to manipulate the functions of machines or else seize, corrupt, or disclose their sensitive data. This lag in understanding is especially acute in the study of international relations, a realm of inquiry whose intellectual fashion is to reject deep change in the states system as an outcome before it is even conceived as a theoretical premise.

Consider, first, the shock to the rational order of interstate relations. The virtual weapon is a recent addition to the arsenal of states, although some nations already regard it as "an integral part" of their armory.[1] Its meaning for interstate strategic dealings is difficult to decipher. Only a limited record of events exists to orient this laborious learning process. The new capability, moreover, is scientifically complex and highly volatile. Even computer specialists do not fully grasp its behavioral properties or the consequences of its use, which may devastate modern society even if they fall below the traditional criterion of interstate violence on which the conventions of international law and diplomacy rest. There is also the problem of the technology's sheer speed of action. Released from the restrictions of the physical laws of motion, security crises transpire at a pace (often measurable in milliseconds) that even seasoned statesmen find difficult to manage.

Second, and more fundamental, is the disturbance of the moral order. Cyberspace empowers states whose basic goals – sometimes grounded in a revolutionary domestic ideology, other times in the perverse visions of despots – are incompatible with the fundamental purpose of international society: the preservation of a minimum measure of order and peace. More elementally, the technology also empowers nontraditional players – proxy militias, political hacktivists, private corporations, extremist militant groups, and even lone agents – who may seek to undermine the political order, who may reject or fail to understand the complex conditions of peace and stability among states co-existing in the international jungle, and whom the traditional apparatus of diplomacy struggles to absorb because such players are not recognized state entities. New entrants onto the international scene who were traditionally barred from geopolitics are now able to disrupt it, at times decisively, via cyber politics.

Tendencies of chaos among the new players compound familiar problems of anarchy among the old: how to stem the development and proliferation of arms, how to tame their use by an arsenal of rules and norms, how to develop stable expectations of behavior out of uncertainty – in short, how to impose order upon turmoil. The sum result of these shocks to the international order is that a cyber conflict may be difficult to model, regulate, and terminate even among rational state contenders bent on avoiding it.

Despite the peculiar features of security in our times, the tendency of international relations specialists has been to bring the virtual weapon to the rule of conventional statecraft – to deny the existence of the cyber revolution. Skeptics invoke that unfailing servant of intellectual reactionism in the field of international security studies: Carl von Clausewitz.[2] The school of skepticism takes various forms. It elaborates a paradigm of security and conflict that continues to prioritize the physical over the virtual world, interstate violence over sub-threshold conflict, the interests and capabilities of states over unconventional actors. The temptation of political thinkers has been to integrate the new technology into familiar doctrines – the laws of armed conflict, the principles and methods of interstate coercion and conquest, the machinery and logic of military warfighting. The academic enterprise of security studies is far behind the times.

The resulting lag in understanding is not for lack of experience with the related technology. Cyberspace is not a recent invention.[3] It emerged and grew in a series of uneven and partly coinciding stages beginning in the first half of the twentieth century. More than seventy years have passed since the advent of computers (one possible starting point of the cyber age); fifty since the invention of the Internet (a truer point of origin); twenty since the explosive global growth of this information skin, which now envelops almost all aspects of society: governmental, financial, social, even military. Two decades have also elapsed since the first significant malware incident – the Morris worm, which in 1988 impaired thousands of computers and led network operators to partition the Internet[4] – awoke computer specialists to the technology's harmful potential (international relations theorists remain in a deep slumber). Whatever point of origin one selects – and the point is debatable – the current cyber age is well past its first generation of contemporaries. Possibly we are its fourth.

Gaps in security doctrine nevertheless persist at the most elemental level. Is cyberwar possible (a question first posed in 1993)?[5] How can nations deter each other from carrying it out (2001)?[6] What measures can mitigate the intensity of a cyber conflict if private citizens attack foreign government targets (2007)?[7] For future generations of practitioners, the persistence of old policy puzzles is prophetic of still vaster difficulties, for cyberspace only grows in complexity and reach. Will the so-called Internet of Things compound existing defensive vulnerabilities? How will religious extremist groups employ the Internet to radicalize, recruit, and direct agents in distant lands that are unreachable physically but are easily penetrable virtually? What meaning has security if unknown adversaries, domestic and foreign, permanently reside within society's most prized computer infrastructures, such as financial exchange systems, nuclear facilities, and military weapons systems? The cyber age has given rise to an expanding field of technical specialists (who today has not heard of the "cybersecurity expert"?) but no true sages, students but few qualified theoreticians, policymakers yet scarcely any accomplished statesmen – it has, in brief, produced no masters. In this basic sense, then, the technology remains "new."

What accounts for the endurance – so far – of this masterless era? Three sources of difficulty are notable. One involves the sheer scale of change. Some observers regard the advent of cyberspace as the greatest transformation in security affairs since the invention of nuclear arms. For all the symbolic enormity of the explosions over Japan in 1945, this comparison is wrong: it inflates the relative significance of the atom bomb.

The comparison of these two strategic revolutions is in a sense correct: both were driven by new technology and both were consequential in their own times. But the transforming potential of the cyber revolution is on a scale much deeper and broader than that of its older technological cousin. The nuclear era marked a revolution in the horrors of war and, thus, attempts to prevent it. The cyber age has subtler yet more disruptive features – the expansion of nonphysical threats to national security, the growing ability of nonstate actors to instigate diplomatic and military crises, the deep penetration of critical computer systems by undetected agents. The nuclear and cyber revolutions are similar in source: both sprang from advances in technology. But the moving force of the cyber revolution – the disruptive power of information – is closer to the drivers of the Reformation or the Romantic period. Subversive ideas were the means by which individuals and groups in those eras strived to subvert political and social orders. The virtual weapon works in much the same way, for malware is at bottom pernicious information stored as electrons. But rather than influence the ideas of humans, it manipulates the "minds" of machines. Indeed, Alan Turing, the inventor of modern computers, wrote about machines as if they were animate perceiving objects. Marvin Minsky, the conceiver of artificial intelligence, went further, arguing that *humans are machines.*[8]

This, then, is the chief transforming feature of security in our times: information has become a weapon in the purest sense. Information to be sure has always been a source of power in history. Knowledge about the intentions and capabilities of adversaries conferred tactical and strategic advantages. Misinformation could affect behavior with similar results. Yet information never exerted more than an indirect influence on human affairs, because harnessing its power required some intervening human action: for example, stealing an adversary's military secrets to achieve vital tactical surprise on the battlefield. Before the era of Turing's machines, it would have been futile to measure the destructive capacity of information because there was no means to bring its power to bear directly upon the physical world. Or as a maxim of von Clausewitz conveys, to achieve important affects, "information must become capability."

Cyberspace has dramatically altered this situation. Information is no longer just a source of power; it has become force *itself.* The virtual weapon's payload, which, like all computer code, consists of just 0's and 1's in the form of electrons can travel through cyberspace to destroy nuclear enrichment turbines, paralyze the operations of large firms, incapacitate tens of thousands of workstations at large multinational firms, or disrupt stock-trading platforms. Crucially, the weapon can achieve these effects without ever exiting the minds of machines; machine functions have replaced human intermediation. The new capability, therefore, is "virtual" in two common meanings of this adjective: most obviously, because it entails the use of data stored in machines or traveling the Internet; less obviously, but no less distinctively, because it is close to being materially real without actually being so – that is, essentially massless particles of data can direct machines to inflict harm in the physical world.

Machines are both the necessary vehicles and, in many instances, the final object of cyberattack. The virtual weapon works by manipulating their functions (Minsky would say thoughts). Without an intermediary object that is manipulable by computer code, there can be no such thing as a cyberattack. The critical intermediary object – cyberspace – is simultaneously the delivery vehicle and the target of attack. And because machines and networks of them pervade modern society, security threats permanently reside at its core. States and other actors use cyber-space to penetrate each other's most basic infrastructures. Often, breaches are unknown to the defender even after an attack has begun. Here, then, is another splendid reversal of the established security paradigm: in the past, the enemy's presence in essential domestic terrains signaled the failure of security policy; today it is a starting axiom.

A second difficulty that sustains the cyber revolution concerns the technology's scientific complexity. The correct interpretation of cyber phenomena by strategists presupposes a strong technical understanding of a capability that is highly esoteric, more so than the nuclear revolution – the twentieth-century's great technological current in security affairs. When in the 1940s nuclear physicists conceived of the fission bomb, even the most eminent among them could not foresee its manifold effects on human biology, social structures, or the environment. Ingenious speculators even believed that a nuclear explosion risked igniting the Earth's atmosphere. Within a decade, however, the nuclear attacks on Hiroshima and Nagasaki, as well as successive atmospheric tests, revealed to a high degree of certainty the broad range of effects associated with fission (and later fusion) explosions. By contrast, the virtual weapon's behavioral properties are far more elusive to scientists who wish to model them with certainty – for two reasons. First, it is difficult to ascertain the weapon's direct effects, in other words those that unfold within the logical environment of the target machine complex, because of the intricacy of modern hardware and software. Second, the weapon's indirect effects, namely, those that hinder activity beyond the logical perimeter of the compromised computer host,[9] are even more difficult to ascertain, because modern society's reliance on complex computer systems for core functions of government and the economy, and the interconnectedness between both these systems and the functions they support, mean that a cyberattack can produce cascading effects that affect essential activities across a range of sectors and jurisdictions. These indirect effects are largely unknowable before attack – and possibly afterward as well.[10] The vast range of unknown and inadvertent effects impedes the interpretation of probable consequences of cyberattack. Three decades after the virtual weapon's birth, scientific knowledge of its behavioral properties and effects remains rudimentary.

A third complication concerns the volatility of change: the problem of how to dominate a technology whose technical features change far more quickly than strategists' ability to identify, much less comprehend them. The growth of technological ability is rapidly outpacing the design of concepts to interpret it. Threats in cyberspace are widely discussed yet rarely foreseen; opportunities to enhance national welfare and power are recognized yet often unrealized. The life cycle of some advanced malware strains can be measured in minutes. Many can update themselves instantly upon activation. Contrast this situation with the relative technological stability of nuclear arms. Major alterations in the design features of nuclear weapons often occurred in periods of several years or decades, whether because the weapons' capital-resource intensity imposed extremely high costs on developers, or because test-ban treaties set an artificial freeze on redevelopment. The cyber arms race suffers no such hindrances. What a few years ago was considered a sophisticated capability, such as a distributed denial-of-service attack, may today be obsolescent. Regimes of cyber arms control have been proposed; none has gone far. Further, there is enormous volatility in the proliferation of arms, including among nontraditional players, many of whom do not obey, or exist beyond, the influence of diplomatic instruments. Consequently, even if international law could arrest the development of states' offensive tools, the speed with which other actors can acquire them compounds the analyst's difficulty of formulating stable conflict models. Volatility exists not only within cyberspace itself – the technical plane of action – but also, more fundamentally, outside it: in the purposes that inspire the weapons' use.

Every historical epoch in international affairs begins with the appearance of a new genus of political action and security competition. The resulting challenge of strategic adaptation is great even when relevant state contenders share an identity of purpose. It is greater when divergence of values among them is high. It is greatest when new entrants into the international system dilute the main units' traditional supremacy. For the theorist, revolution in international affairs presents an intellectual challenge: how to adapt existing concepts to new dangers. The decision-maker's difficulty is the reverse and graver: how to apply potentially outmoded axioms to reduce the measure of peril.

The problems of strategic interpretation of new threats are not unique to the cyber age. Previous generations of thinkers and practitioners grappled with similar challenges. But today the problems of interpretation are amplified by the scale, scientific complexity, and volatility of modern technology – so much so that categories of thinking may permanently, though to varying degrees, lag behind the pace of change.

Aims and Argument

This book seeks to provide the basic elements of a conception of the cyber revolution in the international system. Its purpose is to ask a series of questions: what have we learned, or rather what should we have learned, from previous experiences adapting to technological revolution? How can concepts of international relations, and in particular the international security studies field, neither of which has been especially adept at merging technology into theory, clarify or confuse understanding of contemporary phenomena? How can theoretical and empirical analysis yield strategic insight? What policy courses can help reduce or mitigate new threats?

It is important to realize that this book is a work of political science and not computer science. It paints a broad picture of the virtual weapon's consequences for stability and order in the international system, while largely eschewing technical arcana, except where necessary to contextualize specific points. The book covers the cyber question in its various cross-cutting dimensions: (1) *technological* – the origins, proliferation, and behavioral properties of cyberweapons, a topic that is rightly the preserve of technical specialists but on which the professional student of international affairs will have a particular view; (2) *doctrinal* – problems of strategic adaptation to rapid technological change, such as the challenges of deterrence and risks of crisis escalation following a failure to deter, which will be a special concern to makers of policy; (3) *regulative* – difficulties of achieving international consensus on rules, laws, and institutions to govern cyber conduct, a dimension that may appeal to both theorists and practitioners; (4) *agent-level* – the empowerment of nontraditional and dissatisfied actors who can disrupt interstate dealings, a subject that many theorists omit from their security frameworks; and (5) *conceptual* – how these disruptive forces affect prevailing models of conflict and cooperation in global politics. In addressing these dimensions, this study draws from and adapts concepts in the discipline of international relations, identifying the strengths and weaknesses of contending theoretical approaches.

Few studies of this sort exist. One of the central premises of this book is that cyberspace has a growing – indeed decisive – importance for world affairs and not just, as many people already know, personal and commercial life. Yet there is only a modest commitment within the international relations community to explore the subject. True, a growing number of works – some masterful – address the strategic, tactical, legal, ethical, and economic aspects of the cyber question. There is, for example, Lawrence Lessig's foundational (and superbly written) book on the interrelation of cyberspace, law, and social norms;[11] Gregory Rattray's analysis of "strategic information warfare," one of the earliest attempts to conceptualize the effects of information systems on strategic affairs (as distinct from issues of crime and espionage);[12] Jack Goldsmith and Tim Wu's deflation of high aspirations of a borderless Internet beyond the state system's clutches;[13] Martin Libicki's sober study of the limits and possibilities of hostile conquest or his examination of the challenges of deterrence in the new domain;[14] Jason Healey's comprehensive historical account of cyber conflict;[15] Michael Schmitt's volume on the legal and ethical travails of international cyber conduct;[16] or Adam Segal's review of how nations, small and large, use the Internet to achieve strategic and tactical ends outside cyberspace.[17]

On this basis, some scholars claim, rather cavalierly and complacently, that in international relations the field of cyber studies is flourishing.[18] It is not. For the existing literature betrays an important gap: it barely, and sometimes not at all, integrates the virtual weapon into the theoretical matter of international relations. Notable exceptions to this trend of neglect exist, to be sure – for instance, Joseph Nye's work on "power diffusion" in the cyber domain and its implications for global power structures; or Nazli Choucri's exploration of "cyber politics" as a new manifestation of anarchic international relations, drawing explicitly on the discipline's theoretical debates and frameworks.[19] But the analysis of other foundational concepts and questions remains primitive. Scholars have not systematically addressed how cyberspace affects notions such as international order and stability; institutions and regimes; identity, norms, and ideology; and the balance of power – which are the discipline's prime units of intellectual currency. Security studies thinkers in particular have barely begun to apply their conceptual toolkits to clarify, model, or explain developments in the new domain. In a realm of study that should be theirs, they have provided no school – so far.

The current scholarship gap inhibits the intellectual progress of international relations. Rivalrous cyber phenomena occur with incessant frequency. Yet there are few or no theories to interpret and explain them. This situation erodes the explanatory capacity and policy relevance of the profession. The inability of prevailing paradigms to explain important aspects of the cyber question only worsens the problem of "change" in international relations; it confirms the charge that the discipline has a recursive but not transforming logic.[20]

This book's chief intention is to resolve the growing gap between the emerging omnipresence of technology and the limited grasp most thinkers have of its impact on interstate dealings. The book seeks to prevent or at least arrest this process of intellectual decay: it provides international relations specialists with a conceptual apparatus on which to build a new field of cyber studies. The growing number of important books on cyber issues provides valuable entry points to general audiences.[21] This work will go further. It will develop and apply international relations theory to derive orderly propositions that reduce complex new realities to a manageable simplicity. Different to existing academic efforts, the study will create new benchmarks to analyze the broader relationship between technological revolution and international order. Where cyber activity fits the frame of prevailing conflict models, especially rationalist theories, which assume players are unitary actors who pursue objective goals efficiently, the study applies such models to explain it. Here, the focus is on problems of *instrumental* instability, whereby accidents and misinterpretation of new technology destabilize the interactions even of rational states. Where the technology disturbs these rigid models, however, the work draws from alternative concepts to refine them. The chief concern in these cases is with problems of *fundamental* instability, in which the empowerment of revolutionary states or, worse, actors that are alien to the states system, undermines strategic stability – a situation that rational-choice theory struggles to elucidate. The book clarifies how technological change affects foundational concepts such as "anarchy," "order," and "international system" to guide theorists in the formulation of ordered research questions as well as in the selection of variables when answering them.

The preliminary step in filling the scholarly void is to identify its possible sources. Largely, it is the outcome of two forms of skepticism. The first concerns methodology: some thinkers believe that the technology's sheer complexity as well as problems of data collection and reliability inhibit cyber studies. The second involves intellectual preconceptions: some scholars question the significance of cyber phenomena to security studies because the new weapon lacks an overtly physical quality or because it is not a useful instrument of interstate coercion, conquest, and warfighting.

This book challenges these two attitudes. It argues, first, that cyber studies is both possible and indispensable to the intellectual progress and policy relevance of international relations and security studies.[22] While problems of data reliability are real, they do not confine cyber studies to ahistorical abstraction. At most, data gaps reduce the degree of certainty of hypotheses. Correspondingly, this book seeks to maximize the leverage of its findings by avoiding single-case inferences and by drawing, where possible, on a variety of observable cases. Where only single relevant cases are observable, however, the analysis will seek to derive from them insights about broader trends, even if these insights are not fully determinate because the conceivable universe of action is much wider.[23] For its qualitative data, the study draws upon a diverse mix of sources that includes publicly available government documents outlining current strategy and regulations as well as data available from news reports and published forensic analyses of recent cyber events (including systems vulnerabilities manipulated in these events). Furthermore, the book generates new data from interviews with senior public and private officials in selected countries and regional organizations.

A further preliminary note on methods is warranted. It comes as a warning about the dangers of what one might call "scientism," or the idolization of quantitative inference over qualitative analysis in the discovery of reality. Here, the problem that arises is twofold: the observable realm of cyber incidents, while varied and rich, does not reveal the full scope of real action, because of the many obstacles of data secrecy; moreover, in building data sets on observable cases, the invocation of potentially outmoded concepts of interstate violence and conquest may lead thinkers to ignore nontraditional but relevant incidents and actors. The sum effect of these two tendencies may be to diminish or altogether neglect new trends in security affairs. The quest for large datasets is a symptom of the reluctance of some analysts to consider the need for new theoretical departures. Worse, it is an abdication of strategic learning if theorists substitute the defense of prevailing theory

for the interpretation of novelties that the old thinking leads them arbi-
trarily to neglect. This book assumes, as a core methodological principle,
that in a new realm of strategic action involving a largely untested technology, sometimes the most important events in theory construction are
those that did not occur but may plausibly happen.

This book eschews the tendencies and fashions of scientism that
prevail within certain quarters of security studies. By pursuing a deep
analysis of single cases, not always or even primarily involving traditional national defense purposes, this work strives to provide broader
and truer insights about the nature and scope of the contemporary cyber
revolution than would be possible through the canvassing of a large
number of data points that represent only narrow segments of a much
vaster and varied world of action (both proven and plausible).

Second, the book argues that understanding the cyber question
requires a new paradigm of security commensurate with it, one that
privileges not just physical but also nonphysical threats and that elevates
nonstate actors to a higher level of theoretical existence than the traditionalist viewpoint allows. This work is a sequel to the few existing
political science books on cyber issues, but it strives to avoid repeating
errors of conviction and omission: of obstinately applying old security
paradigms to the study of new problems, while neglecting alternative
theoretical lenses that may yield a truer picture of present trends.
The book's main argument is that cyber politics exhibits two states of
nature. One is the traditional system of states locked in familiar contests
for security, but featuring a largely untested weapon whose use is difficult to model and regulate even among rational contenders. The other
is a chaotic "global" milieu comprising nontraditional players whose
aims and motives may be subversive of national or international order
and who may not accept or even understand (seasoned statesmen often
fail to grasp it) the delicate political framework of the anarchic states
system.

Therein lies the book's main theoretical contribution: it presents a
framework that clarifies how these two universes converge and collide.
On the one hand, the study shows how the wide diffusion of cyber
capabilities enables new modes of coordination between state and
nonstate players who share certain goals and adversaries. An example of
this phenomenon is the reported collusion between Iran and company
insiders at Saudi Aramco, the Saudi Arabian national oil firm and the

largest firm in the world, to incapacitate tens of thousands of the firm's machines in 2012. On the other hand, there are also dangers of collision – a cyber event in which nonstate activity encounters the high stakes of interstate competition, as we saw in the Estonian crisis, in which cyberattacks by Russian private culprits prompted officials in Tallinn to consider invoking NATO's collective defense clause. The analysis explores the potential for private actors to produce both convergence and collision. Take, for example, the question of civilian cyber militias. These actors furnish governments with the option of plausible deniability in a cyberattack. Furthermore, they provide a means to harness society's technological prowess while avoiding the cumbersome organizational structures and costs of traditional military formations. But they may also generate pressures of instability. In the midst of a heated interstate conflict, there is no guarantee that the proxies will remain obedient to their parent capitals. What was conceived as a device for states to avoid retribution could become a cause for its invitation. These and other disruptive forces defy established assumptions of rational-choice theory: for example, the notion that states conduct their foreign policy as unitary actors pursuing objective goals. A new conceptual framework is required that combines the peculiarities of international affairs in the cyber age with conventional notions of interstate rivalry in a way that is useful – in fact necessary – for future scholarship.

To impose conceptual order upon these disparate trends, the book develops benchmarks of "technological revolution" that distinguish between three basic sets of disruptive forces. They are (in growing degree of severity): third-order revolution, or *systemic disruption*, which involves the appearance of a new technology that disturbs the regularized interactions of rational state contenders (because, for example, it alters the balance of offensive and defensive forces); second-order revolution, or *systemic revision*, which occurs when a new invention empowers revolutionary states (such as North Korea) within the system, thus causing a rupture in the social order; and first-order revolution, or *systems change* – the severest form of revolution, which arises when new players (hacktivists and technology firms, for instance) challenge the traditional supremacy of states, thus altering the system's very building blocks: the units. The first two orders of revolution, then, occur within the conventional Westphalian system; they reveal that even on the interstate plane, important distinctions must be drawn in comprehending technological revolution. The third variety of revolution transpires within the wider global system – or rather, it represents an intrusion upon the Westphalian order by forces from below. Although the book applies this framework only to the current cyber revolution, its benchmarks are applicable to the study of technological revolution broadly.

The cyber revolution expresses all three orders of technological revolution in different degrees. First is the role of cyberspace as a driver of systemic disruption. Here, it is important to recognize limits. The virtual weapon is not reconfiguring the balance of power among large nations, is only an imperfect tool of coercion, and has not altered the nature of territorial conquest. Nevertheless, the new capability fuels systemic disruption because it deprives states of clear "if-then" assumptions on which to carry out a restrained contest for security. Although it does not alter the balance of power or transform the nature of war, the cyber domain is a perfect breeding ground for strategic instability. The new capability evolves faster than analysts can divine its properties and effects; it obfuscates the "signature" of power because adversaries can often mask their identity and location; its offensive dominant nature aggravates the security dilemma of anarchic politics; and it greatly expands the "depth" of power: adversaries can use it to affect each other's intimate political affairs and core interests remotely. Second, the virtual weapon is a driver of systemic revision: it empowers revolutionary states. The clearest example of this trend is North Korea. This small nation, peculiar for its combination of bizarre ideology and military prowess, is able to use cyberspace to challenge the basic political purposes of international society. Importantly, it can use the new technology to sow chaos without ever resorting to war. The third order of the cyber revolution is the most notable of all: it challenges the supremacy of the system's established units – states. To be sure, states retain their primacy. They possess the intelligence and other resources necessary to mount the most sophisticated cyber actions. Thus the emergence of new actors does not mean that states are becoming irrelevant. Yet in important ways their supremacy is challenged by actors residing outside the conventional system. States are no longer the sole or even the main sources of national security threats; some nontraditional players can cause surprising degrees of harm. States are not the only or even, in some cases, the primary national security providers. Also, the traditional units can no longer maintain full control over the dynamics of conflict among them. Other actors can disturb the fragile political framework of interstate dealings. States, in short, are no longer the sole masters of international security.

The skeptics would ask us to suspend analysis at the conceptual bounds of systemic disruption; the search for revolution ceases before it has truly begun. They cannot grasp the cyber revolution because their concepts act as blinders to its existence. The conventional model of the international system, to be sure, is a good basis on which to measure the degree of change wrought by new technology. But by itself it is a poor and incomplete indicator of change. By defining three distinct kinds of technological revolution, two of which transcend the conventional model, and by integrating their disruptive trends into the study of international relations, this book will add new theoretical content to the view – derided by traditionalists – that the contemporary world confronts an enormous cyber danger.

Beyond building concepts, the book seeks to guide the laborious task of strategic interpretation of new technology. In other words, it strives to benefit not merely theory but also statecraft. The necessity of this book arises from the novelties and urgencies of the cyber danger and the difficulties for practitioners of international politics in dealing with them. Western intelligence agencies rate the cyber threat higher than or equal to that of global terrorism.[24] They warn of the potential for a calamitous cyberattack. Many of the major developments in domestic and international politics – for example, the possibly decisive intervention by Russia in the 2016 U.S. presidential election – are incomprehensible unless one grasps the role of new technology in enabling them. Yet makers of policy have little time to interpret the strategic implications of the transforming technology because the pressures for action are immediate. There is little consensus on how to reduce the new threat. Does "declaratory ambiguity" deter attacks or merely increase the chances that the prospect of retaliation will be underrated? What dangers does a policy of cross-domain deterrence that includes escalation to conventional force pose for the management of a cyber crisis? What signaling procedures and confidence-building measures could halt an exchange involving nonstate actors from accelerating beyond the ability of states to control it? With what mechanisms can private actors be coopted into the national cyber establishment so that states can leverage civilian resources for strategic gain? NATO's Supreme Allied Commander Europe (2009–13), Admiral James Stavridis, captured the anguish of practitioners when he observed that understanding of cyber interactions is in a similar state of development as was the early theory of flight.[25] The growth of cyber arsenals, in short, is outpacing the design of doctrines to limit their risks.

Amid these growing pains of statecraft, scholarly attention to the cyber question is necessary to preserve the policy relevance of the international security studies field. Removed from the pressures of having to defeat the new threat, yet possessing concepts necessary to analyze it, theorists are in a privileged position to resolve its strategic quandaries. The deductive models of theorists have in the past served as a basis on which to develop strategy: for example, the influence of game theory and other rational-choice models (some ported from microeconomics) on the development of strategies to prevent conflict and enhance cooperation among states.[26] Similarly, this book proposes new avenues of thinking – conceptual frameworks, empirical analyses, and doctrinal reviews – that can assist practitioners in the reevaluation of strategic axioms on which the efficacy of security policy ultimately rests.

Overall, the book addresses the concerns of scholars, practitioners, and laypersons – not always equally, because the work's emphasis is on theory and strategy, not policy or technical arcana, though often in tandem. The emphasis in Part I on elaborating conceptual benchmarks will appeal especially to international relations scholars. Students in other disciplines may also derive valuable insights. Computer specialists in particular may find this analysis useful in framing nontechnical questions, for example, meanings of cyber "security" and "attack" that concern assets beyond cyberspace, or a conception of "threats" that emphasizes not lines of code but the human agents who employ it. Part II on degrees of the cyber revolution may appeal to a wide audience of observers wanting to make sense of the contemporary cyber danger. Part III may interest security professionals and practitioners most directly, for it engages in a task that is often crucial but always perilous for theorists: the application of concepts to policy guidance. Overall, then, the book strives to cast a wide net of interest. Technologists will find in it a perspective on the cyber question that is distinct but complementary to theirs; business analysts and consultants, a new criterion on which to build and refine risk models; national security experts, a comprehensive analysis of threats that affect nations in various regions of the world in equal measure, but that require responses attuned to the specific political and institutional restraints of each society.

Plan of the Book

The remainder of this volume is organized into three parts. Part I deals primarily with theory and concepts. It contains three chapters. Chapter 1 explores the interdisciplinary character and disciplinary boundaries of cyber studies, sketching the sometimes ambiguous contours of an emergent "Congress of Disciplines." It provides comprehensive groundwork on the cyber question – its novelties and complexities, its central theoretical debates and contending positions within them. In addition, the chapter reviews the technical and conceptual rudiments of cyber activity from the perspective of the international relations specialist. In the process, the analysis will draw important conceptual distinctions, some of which contravene prevailing understandings.

Chapter 2 dispels the view – popular among traditionalist thinkers – that the cyber threat is largely a myth. The analysis examines five major defensive costs: offense unpredictability, defense denial, complex defense surface, defense fragmentation, and supply-chain risks. It draws on observable cases of cyberattack and exploitation to illustrate the defensive gap. Moreover, it introduces a new concept – the state of *unpeace* – to characterize the new range of rivalrous activity that falls between the binary notions of war and peace, which together do not adequately capture the full spectrum of cyber activity.

Chapter 3 develops a conceptual framework appropriate for the analysis of technological revolution in international relations. It defines an ideal type of international system – the Conventional Model – as a basis for distinguishing the three degrees of the cyber revolution examined in this book, each with varying implications for stability and order in the system. Along the way, the discussion will refer to historical cases of rapid change in weapons systems to derive "test" principles on the general relationship between technological revolution, international order, and strategic adaptation.

Part II applies these frameworks to identify and clarify the virtual weapon's implications for international order. Chapter 4 analyzes third-order problems of systemic disruption, principally the risks of unwanted or accelerating cyber crises among rational state adversaries. In order to illustrate these problems, the chapter reviews past cyber incidents, such as the Stuxnet operation against the nuclear facility at Natanz in Iran.[27]

Chapter 5 reviews the potential for cyberspace to aggravate second-order problems of systemic revision. Here, the plight of the analyst and policymaker is especially acute, for they must decipher problems of a rational but also an ideological nature. The cyber domain is a perfect breeding ground for political subversion; more so when the source of subversion is a powerful player such as North Korea that repudiates elements of the world consensus and which possesses potent instruments to pursue its deviant ideals.

Chapter 6 explores first-order problems of systems change – namely, the threat that nonstate actors will use cyberspace in ways that subvert international order (or national order, with similar effects). The discussion analyzes proliferation dynamics: these mark the difference between first-order technological revolution and lesser orders. The analysis designs conceptual typologies that clarify the relative capacities of nontraditional players to acquire and employ cyber instruments and their motives for doing so. It examines manifestations of fundamental instability in the states system – such as the danger that new players will crash foreign computer systems without their own government's direction or even sanction.

Part III focuses on applied aspects of strategy and policy. Chapter 7 examines problems of deterring a major cyberattack in the absence of viable measures to repulse it. It considers two classical techniques of deterrence: denial and punishment. The virtual weapon spoils the logic of each. Another mechanism – entanglement – may be more effective at explaining deterrence in the new domain; it is not, however, failsafe. The chapter also analyzes the challenges of preventing mid-spectrum cyberattack and proposes a new approach to overcome them: *punctuated deterrence*, which prescribes a response to a series of actions and cumulative effects, rather than individual actions and particular effects. Chapter 8 reviews Russian innovations in the methods of information warfare. It explores the cyber operations that disrupted the U.S. presidential election process in 2016 and threatened to subvert liberal democracy. These occurrences reveal an important truth about security in our times: the nonviolent methods of unpeace can be more potent sources of national power and influence than the overt violence of Clausewitzian war. Chapter 9 explores the possible strategic and other consequences of private sector active defense (e.g. intrusion and incapacitation of attacking machines) in foreign jurisdictions. The analysis evaluates the challenges and opportunities of convergence in the new domain between the world of states and the world of citizens – traditionally treated as separate universes by international relations theorists – and the dangers associated with a collision of these two universes.

Chapter 10, the concluding discussion, summarizes the book's argument and explores ongoing evolutions in the threat landscape. For example, it asks: will the emergence of the Internet of Things and universal quantum computers exacerbate the cyber curse of modern society?

PART I

THEORY AND CONCEPTS

CHAPTER 1

The Quest for Cyber Theory

The Clash of Conceptions

Cyber studies is a clash of conceptions. Few thinkers know about this clash because few venture outside their home field of learning. The clash involves not the arcane quarrels of theorists within a specific discipline, which is the ordinary activity of science, but a more elemental divide among entire professions, which occurs only rarely, when a subject arises of such magnitude and complexity that it convulses established jurisdictions of learning. Many scientific disciplines touch on the cyber question. Each imposes upon it its own ideal type, a perception of the essence of the related technology or its effects on the political and social world. Some ideal types end at the perimeter of cyberspace; others begin there. Thus there is no single criterion of relevance to frame security problems and their solutions uniformly. Only if one understands this crucial point can one grasp not merely the obstacles to the development of a new field of intellectual endeavor in international relations but also its opportunities.

Most attempts to define the limits and delineate a theory of cyberspace emerged out of the discipline that created the technology: computer science. Here, the chief concern is the technical plane of action, that is, the workings of cyberspace itself – the systems that store and process data, and the infrastructure of networks, routers, domain name servers, and other network components that bind these distributed systems together.[1] Because it emphasizes mechanical functions rather than human dealings, and because technical analysis is not the same as strategic learning, a technical criterion will not always seem appropriate to international relations specialists. It may, in fact, impede learning because absorption with the virtual weapon's technical complexity obscures the purposes that drive its use. And then there is the scope of the policymaker's conception: the translation of *both* technical knowledge *and* political axioms into policies to defeat relentless threats. The clash of conceptions and the absence of bridges to join them renders the task of statesmanship even harder than if its problems were solely technical or solely political. Thus whether technical mastery obstructs strategic learning, whether strategy inhibits policy, depends on a resolution of the contest of views within the academy.

But a resolution of what kind and at what price? Three broad approaches are possible. One is multidisciplinarity. This recognizes the necessity for diverse viewpoints without, however, seeking to organize them into a harmonious school of learning. Each profession is left to pursue its own solitary path of knowledge. Another is interdisciplinarity. Similar to the first approach, it respects the integrity of distinct viewpoints, but it strives to fuse their teachings into shared insights, though without elevating any single one above the others. The third approach is unidisciplinarity. This strives to absorb alternative conceptions: in computer science, to subsume the laws of human behavior within the logic of computer programming; in political science, to reduce technological phenomena to the imperatives of governments and their peoples – in short, to deny that machines and humans have separate essences.[2] This approach is the natural temptation of each discipline in dealing with the fashions of other disciplines, for scientific professions define themselves not by tearing down walls of learning but by building esoteric bodies of knowledge within them; not by recognizing and reconciling external differences but by immersing in internal divisions. These internecine quarrels are often so fierce that they destroy opportunities to cross the quiet but much deeper divide that separates professions from each other. Or else, if the internal diversions can be set aside, what may emerge is a "bridging" discipline,[3] a field of study that is so vast in scope and so pluralistic in methods – strategic studies, for example, which combines insights from perspectives as diverse as philosophy and geography – that it is not a definable discipline.

There exists, then, a continuum of resolution: segmentation, synthesis, and absorption. Segmentation, or multidisciplinarity, suffers the common deficiency of halfway measures; it recognizes the problem without supplying a lasting solution. Because it preserves divisions without adjudicating between them, the approach may instigate further clashes of understanding. Unidisciplinarity by way of absorption – the natural intellectual reflex – also hinders learning, for no single discipline can answer all relevant questions. Even computer specialists recognize that cybersecurity is not primarily a technical issue but a challenge to political and social, even philosophical, understandings. Equally, the conceptualization of nontechnical problems and the framing of solutions rely on a correct interpretation of the underlying technology. To accept that humans and machines have separate essences is not to deny that the technical and social planes affect each other. Another kind of unidisciplinarity, one striving for a "master" discipline of cyber studies, would result in *adisciplinarity*, or the absence of a defined scientific perspective: either a pure policy science eschewing theory or a universal field that preserves all subforms in their original state, which is in fact no different to multidisciplinarity, but with a catch-all label that gives the impression – false, unless it is understood to be superficial – of a fusion.[4]

Synthesis is the superior method of resolution. So many academic professions – computer science, political science, law, anthropology, and so on – can contribute insights to the cyber question that each side must identify its strengths (and limits) and conserve its own conception; other forms are neither superior nor inferior, merely different, to be judged according to the standards of their parent disciplines. Yet a distribution of competencies is vital.[5] In its absence, the disciplines will not distinguish clear boundaries of expertise. Competing pressures to assimilate will intensify. Thinkers will pose questions beyond their analytical remit. Or else they may use similar terms to analyze very different aspects of the same problem. The inevitable result is conceptual confusion and congestion.

Take, for instance, the term "information security." Computer scientists ordinarily define it as the protection of computer data from unauthorized access, but international relations analysts think of it as the control of domestic channels of information flow.[6] Place these two groups of specialists at the same table to discuss, say, Chinese Internet censorship, and you are likely to witness a spectacle of cross-disciplinary confusion of the kind native speakers of two related languages sometimes experience: the use of the same words bearing different meanings.

Meanwhile, the policymaker at the table – a native speaker of neither language who must nevertheless master the fundamentals of each – would struggle to know which set of lexicons is valid or how to reconcile them when translating their insights into policy. Thus in so crowded a disciplinary realm, mutual awareness of other conceptions is indispensable to avoid confusion; it may even lead to new shared insights – for example, the observation that technical data protection methods can provide viable means to defeat politically motivated censorship policies.

A division of competencies will not emerge automatically, however. For the interdisciplinary arena does not open naturally. Recall that the inclination of the disciplines is to dig chasms, not erect bridges. Above all, the quest for shared knowledge requires that all relevant disciplines stake their claim to the subject. Serious disciplinary work is an essential complement – indeed, precondition – to meaningful interdisciplinarity. Erecting bridges requires that theorists first build up their own discipline's substantive plank – that is, a foundational plunge into *disciplinarity*. For students of international relations, including, if only distantly, the analytical and policymaking layperson, this common view is our theory – the body of concepts and orderly propositions that select and organize the complex phenomena that we study. Yet despite a growing number of important works on cyber issues, there are few systematic efforts of this sort to guide inquiry. Much less is there a sense of how technical concepts relate to familiar categories of thinking about international rivalry and conflict.

Cyber studies, in sum, suffers from two deep structural flaws: different states of preparedness among relevant disciplines; and the absence of a unifying charter to avoid misconceptualization and give their various labors coherence.

This chapter explores the origins and state of this emergent field of study, both as a broad realm of intellectual endeavor and as a largely neglected subject within international relations, in which the impression exists that to discuss cyber issues is to risk confusion or – worse – boredom. It argues that evasion of the cyber question by international relations theorists only defers difficult questions and produces larger puzzles; hence the need to test our models against it. This crucial assignment belongs to us. We cannot relinquish it to other professions no more than a computer specialist should cede to us the crafting of complex code.

The Congress of Disciplines

What, then, is cyber studies? Few international relations thinkers have posed the question, though there exist glimpses of an answer. Computer specialists have supplied detailed responses, but in the only way they can: for themselves. Let us nevertheless search for a comprehensive answer. It helps here to invoke a metaphor.

Imagine a large concave chamber. Around an empty central rostrum sit delegates from a bevy of disciplines – computer science, political science, engineering, law, business, philosophy (especially ethics), economics, criminology, sociology, and so on. In the gallery behind them stand the players who dominate the world outside the chamber – representatives of government, private industry, and civil society. Depending on the substance of the debate, delegates speak or not. Sometimes members of one delegation dominate; other times a loose coalition of factions speaks; still other times the discussion is level and wide-ranging. In places, an empty section of benches can be spotted. No delegates materialize, though, oddly, the bill on the table affects their profession's core interests. This congress assembles only occasionally and irregularly, rarely as a full plenum, and always in the absence of a guiding constitution on which to define priorities, designate competencies, identify relative strengths and weaknesses, and set the bounds of discussion beyond the urgent supplications emanating from the gallery, whose voices often sound loudest because of the clashes – real clashes of policy and their consequences – unfolding outside this esteemed setting.

Such is the academic realm of cyber studies: more a medley than a unison; more confusion than consonance. Within the normally established disciplines – that is, within the delegations – a sense of familiarity among members binds them in a joint enterprise. A common intellectual currency restrains the clashes of conception among them and reduces, at least partly, the air of confusion that prevails inside the chamber generally. Forget for a moment the uncertainty produced by the technology, the object that is always on the agenda but which the delegates often do not understand and rarely (except on the technical benches) control. Deeper sources of discord arise from the partial vacancy of seats and the absence of a unifying charter, so that even when the aims of discussion seem identical or complementary, the methods each side legitimately pursues in satisfying its constituent interests may confound other parties.

The uneven attendance sheet and disarray within the chamber reflect the fact that cyber studies is both very old and very young. The field is old in the sense that computer specialists have strived to understand the behavior of machines and their ability to enhance (or degrade) human activity ever since Alan Turing first laid down the principles of computing in a seminal paper published in 1936.[7] Famously, Turing proved that it was theoretically possible to invent a machine that could solve finite mathematical problems by interpreting simple symbols – 0's and 1's.[8] According to the "Church-Turing thesis," every conceivable computer program can be written as a Turing machine program, in other words as a particular kind of mathematical function. There flowed from this realization a series of engineering quests of vast proportions. Almost immediately, in the early 1940s, inventors applied the Turing principle to create machines that could solve pressing problems of military tactics, such as the tabulation of ballistic trajectories or the decryption of German cyphers during the Second World War. The principle has since been applied to address a limitless array of economic and social problems: the prediction of climatic patterns, the facilitation of global financial transactions, the collection of citizen data by governments, and so on. Almost any human task can be rendered as a mathematical function. Consequently, no aspect of contemporary public or private life is beyond the reach, in some way, of Turing machines.

The field is also old in the sense that technical specialists have long reflected on the security problems that arise from the invention of machines that are controllable by abstract data. The benefits of cyberspace apart, there is a basic truth to Turing's invention that generations of technicians have been unable to escape: because there is no absolute standard for the interpretation of code, no computer program in the world is perfectly secure. A phrase by Kenneth Thompson immortalized the problem: 'How to trust trust?'[9] If no amount of scrutiny can protect you against imperfectly trusted code, if the only software worthy of trust is that which the machine operator wrote totally (and even here human error may occur), and if computer programs contain code from multiple coders – sometimes hundreds or thousands of them – then actions in cyberspace always entail some measure of misplaced trust in the correct workings of machines, in the benign intentions of their inventors, or in machines' ability to interpret correctly those intentions. When malicious code abuses that trust and alters computer behavior, it would be wrong to say that the compromised machine "misbehaved." Machines interpret data fed into them according to a stored program. They have no moral faculty to discern the correctness, from a human standpoint, of task orders. For this reason, all computer functions are inherently manipulable by human operators; that these functions are also *remotely* manipulable via the Internet lends problems of computer security a special uniqueness and, since the information skin's rapid expansion in the last twenty years, urgency.

The field of cyber studies is young, however, if one takes it to mean the organized study of a vast array of observable phenomena that tries to discover the technology's effects on the behavior, laws, and institutions of political units – that is, if one takes the field to mean the investigation not of cyberspace but of the cyber *domain*. Such efforts at social science theory as opposed to technical theory are more recent; they have not gone as far. True, in those quarters of the social sciences where cyber studies has an easily discernible relevance to the resolution of policy puzzles, that is, where the yells from the gallery are loudest, the field has attracted notable scholarly attention. Legal scholars, for instance, have explored in detail questions such as the government's appropriate role in Internet governance or the constitutional implications of compelled decryption;[10] criminologists, new methods of theft and their pressures on policing tactics;[11] economists, problems of collective action in malware markets;[12] public policy experts, the ability of cyberspace to enhance the provision of public services.[13] But in more theoretical quarters, such as international security studies, where the chief concern of inquiry is to develop conceptual lenses and models that serve to interpret, explain, or predict interstate behavior rather than design policy to affect it, thinkers have shown remarkable apathy in the face of the cries from the gallery for the development of such knowledge.

In sum, the Congress of Disciplines – let us give it a label – has evolved this far: most disciplinary professions affected by its problems have sent delegates; no delegation, however, has a clear sense of the priorities and interests that attach specifically to itself in relation to the concerns of others. Worse, some professions – notably, international relations and security studies – have barely begun even to define their own questions and priorities. For these disciplines, the promise of theory is greater than the accomplishments. And the promise is real, if we can only put skepticism aside.

Schools of Skepticism

It is superfluous – almost – to state that security studies scholars are skeptical of the existence of a cyber danger: they have barely acknowledged the issue, as reflected in the scant relevant literature. There has been little systematic theoretical or empirical analysis of cyber issues from their perspective.[14] What accounts for this scholarly void? The question is important: cyber studies can thrive only if the factors – primarily intellectual, but also institutional – that inhibit it are overcome. There are not one but two schools of skepticism, one intrinsic to the cyber question, the other inherent in the intellectual fashions of security studies.

First, some thinkers – call them deep skeptics – evade the subject because of methodological obstacles, especially the related technology's scientific complexity. There is a sense in some quarters of political science that cyber studies is fraught with intellectual obstacles. Holders of this view emphasize two major obstacles.

One concerns the paucity of cases available to propose, test, and refine theoretical claims about empirical phenomena. Paradoxically, this problem reflects a combination of too much and too little data. Reports of hostile cyber events are profuse, with governments and private industry registering incidents, separately and mostly disjointedly, on an ongoing basis. At the same time, the tendency of governments to over-classify information has produced a data gap that complicates these tasks. The most important tactical maneuvers in cyberspace remain shrouded in secrecy,[15] complicating scholarly investigation of cyberattack as an instrument of foreign and defense policy. Archival material of the kind security studies thinkers have often relied on to uncover the motives and aims of conflict will likely remain inaccessible for many years still. Thus it is often difficult to ascertain the relevance of cases to security studies, given either poor techniques of data collection or the lack of suitable metrics to codify the events. A recent comment by a British official illustrates the data paradox. Asked about breaches of government machines, he stated, "Sixty-eight cyber incidents from all types of organisations were voluntarily reported to the National Cyber Security Centre (NCSC) in its first month of operation (1–31 October 2016)," to which followed the obfuscation, "These incidents vary in scale, nature and target," on which there was no clarification: "For security reasons the Government does not comment on specific details of cyber security attacks."[16] Other factors magnify the problem. The private firms that operate the majority of critical computer systems are often reluctant to report damaging cyber incidents because of their potential to create reputational and other costs.[17]

Nor is that all. Deep skeptics also cite a more fundamental problem with cyber studies: they claim that rather than being merely unknown, the properties of cyber phenomena are *unknowable*. Stephen Walt stated: "[T]he whole issue is highly esoteric – you really need to know a great deal about computer networks, software, encryption, etc. to know how serious the danger might be."[18] It is possible, in other words, that the barriers to scholarship are intrinsic to the new technology, which is so specialized as to bar entry to laypersons.

A second form of skepticism concerns the threat scale. Lesser but still influential skeptics, mainly adherents of the Clausewitzian school of war, invoke traditional notions of interstate violence to dismiss the virtual weapon's significance and transforming potential. They pose the question on which much of security studies pivots: where are the disturbances to the interstate military balance? Then, not finding any, they dispose of the new danger. They claim that cyber operations are not directly violent. Nor do they create significant collateral damage. Thus the new phenomena do not qualify as acts of war.[19] Moreover, skeptics argue that insofar as some cyberattacks can cause physical destruction, they nevertheless will be rare owing to their high costs of preparation.[20] Finally, some analysts challenge the common wisdom that the virtual weapon confers asymmetric power on weak states – for instance, Joseph Nye's claim that "small states can play a significant role at low cost."[21] The United States and other large nations, they contend, are "well ahead of the curve" when it comes to "military-grade offensive [cyber] attacks." The consoling and predictive title of an important and influential work by Thomas Rid sums up skeptics' perception of threat inflation: "Cyber War Will Not Take Place."[22]

Deep skeptics reject the very possibility of cyber theory. Substantive skeptics discard new realities to preserve old models. Both viewpoints would ask thinkers to submit to the intellectual conventions of Clausewitz, whether his general reluctance to examine the implications of technology for strategic affairs (as an excellent biography by Sir Michael Howard notes),[23] or the conviction that the precepts and forms of interstate war are eternal – or insofar as new departures are possible, they are inconsequential to the timeless verities of anarchic rivalry. Cynics among the skeptics have proffered an explanation for the prevalence of the cyber threat "myth" within government circles that would make even some anarchists blush: "There's a power struggle going on in the U.S. government right now," remarked the distinguished computer security expert Bruce Schneier. "It's about who is in charge of cyber security, and how much control the government will exert over civilian networks. And by beating the drums of war, the military is coming out on top."[24] Inflated notions of the cyber threat, in brief, are not just popular but also *official* myth.

The inevitable result of these two forms of skepticism is considerable neglect of the cyber question. First, the presumption of the inscrutability of cyberspace has created a sense of resignation: the new threat – if real – lies beyond the ability of political scientists to understand. Among some observers, there is a sense that the cyber question is fraught with intellectual danger: its intricacies will overwhelm anyone who attempts to master it. Second, the perception of threat inflation makes a direct appeal to the preconceptions of security scholars, arguing that threats which appear to lack an overtly physical character or do not rise to the level of interstate violence are intellectually uninteresting.[25] To the question of whether the cyber issue merits investigation it is tempting to answer: perhaps not, because its hazards are not of a magnitude considered relevant to theory – the familiar theory of states competing for territory and influence with the technologies of war. This view contains an element of intellectual conceit. Its adherents claim to perceive a truth that somehow eludes practitioners who possess greater experiential insight and privileged facts on the matter. Paradoxically, the Clausewitzian perspective supplies substance for debate while possibly reinforcing the very skepticism that inhibits it.

These two viewpoints cannot logically coexist. The thesis of threat inflation presupposes that the scale of danger can be accurately assessed, thus defeating the notion that the cyber question is incomprehensible. Yet the absence of any systematic account of why this question is beyond our grasp suggests that the two views coexist in the minds of some observers. This posture is untenable: either both positions are wrong – as this book argues – or only one, the notion of threat inflation, is accurate. (As a matter of principle, both viewpoints could be correct, but in the presence of the first, the second cannot be validated.) The next section assesses the price paid for the scholarly void that is a consequence of the prevailing skepticism.

Costs of the Scholarship Gap

States and other actors will continue to employ code as a weapon regardless of theorists' reluctance to merge it into their thinking. Therefore, the withdrawal of scholars from cyber realities, whether as the result of perplexity or indifference, risks eroding the crucial relationship of theory to science – that is, the relevance of our theoretical concepts to ongoing technological transformations. Unless theorists subject the cyber question to serious appraisal, the gap between the study and practice of security affairs will grow. The consequences for the security studies craft and its relevance to policy guidance are profound. Let us weigh two main sets of costs.

First is the intellectual damage of scholarly neglect. When the range of empirical topics that theory is able to elucidate narrows, the academic enterprise inevitably enters a process of internal corrosion, which reveals itself in one or both of two ways – a loss of conceptual fertility or a reduced capacity for explanatory analysis, each of which inhibits intellectual progress in the study of international relations.[26] As a starting point of theory, the study of international security relies on concepts that reduce complex empirical facts to a manageable degree of simplicity.[27] Foundational notions such as "anarchy," "order," and "international system" guide the formulation of ordered research questions as well as the selection of dependent and independent variables when answering those questions. These guiding concepts are especially important when thinking about rapid technological change in weapons systems because they mediate the relationships among the new technology, its effects on international relations, and scholars' explanatory theories. At the same time, conceptual frameworks can be altered by the very technology that scholars seek to interpret, possibly leading to theoretical breakthroughs.

Accordingly, past generations of thinkers have tended to respond to technological revolution by testing their concepts against it. Consider, for instance, nuclear studies. In a seminal work written when nuclear weapons did not yet travel in space, Henry Kissinger exposed the flaws of a deterrence strategy – dominant at the time – that rested on the promise of "massive retaliation" for any use of the weapons, calling instead for a "weapon system which permits the *tactical* employment of nuclear weapons and enables us to fight *local* wars"[28] – that is, the doctrine of limited nuclear war. Kalevi Holsti's analysis of the new technology's implications for the notion of "power" is another example of conceptual fertility. By then, the study of international relations had begun to crystallize into an organized field, but it had not yet acquired the obsession – common today – with abstract universal principles. Lamenting the ambiguous meaning of power, especially the treatment of Hans Morgenthau (an early expounder of hallowed truths about international politics), Holsti set out to elaborate the notion's core elements, invoking the implications of nuclear weapons to illustrate them.[29] This great tide of nuclear theory, as much destructive of old paradigms as creative of new ones, did not cease at the shores of the technology's early creation. Rather, it gained strength and overwhelmed more ridges as new generations of weapons came into being. A few decades after Kissinger and two after Holsti, Robert Jervis popularized the slogan of a nuclear "revolution" by expounding the transforming effects of Mutual Assured Destruction (MAD) on superpower statecraft. Regardless of the passage of time, at no point did the current of theory disperse into slack waters. The earliest spokesmen of nuclear theory, in fact, often revised their principles to account for new dangers on the international scene. In 2007, for example, Henry Kissinger reversed his earlier view that nuclear deterrence enhanced peace. "In a world of suicide bombers," he observed, "that calculation doesn't operate in a comparable way."[30]

All of the central trends in security studies, by contrast, seem arrayed against the technological motif of the present age. As we saw in the preceding chapter, the analysis of foundational notions remains primitive. The implications of cyberspace for international anarchy and order have barely been explored, even though practitioners repeatedly warn of global chaos. The conceptual apparatus of international relations is behind the times.

Consequently, we are witnessing an explosion of incidents in the absence of theories to give them coherence. Security studies scholars have barely begun to apply their theoretical toolkits to explain, model, or predict competition in the cyber arena. In a realm of study that should be theirs, they have provided no school. This scholarship gap has two dimensions. It is *fundamental* inasmuch as the void reflects the partial irrelevance of existing models. For example, if the dispersion of cyber power away from states distorts the Westphalian mold in which dominant theories are cast, then the mismatch between theory and cyber activity only worsens the charge often levied against international relations: that it can explain recurrent but not new modes of security competition.[31] Intellectual stagnation can also take an *applied* form. Here a novel phenomenon that is in principle explainable remains unexplained; intellectual progress is inhibited even where extant theory applies. Whatever its form, the dilatoriness of scholars devalues the stock-in-trade of security studies, which, as an eminently empirical science, is to elucidate major trends in contemporary security relationships.

The second set of costs involves statecraft: scholarly neglect of the cyber question degrades the capacity of security studies for policy guidance. This is a perfect situation – if it be the object of scholars to allow policy to practice itself. Many thinkers, however, regard the notion of the irrelevance of theory to policy as repugnant. Stephen Walt expresses this general view: "There is no reason why policy relevance cannot be elevated in our collective estimation."[32] This exhortation applies to the cyber question as well – especially because of the prevailing uncertainty over its associated dangers, some of which skeptics regard as a mirage. The possibility that practitioners, who hold the wealth of facts of events but not the luxury of time to analyze them, could be wrong in their estimation of the cyber danger does not make scholars' withdrawal into the cloistered halls of academic life acceptable. On the contrary, it increases the need to challenge governing misconceptions – if such they are – as an essential step toward developing sensible security policy.

Therein lies the central premise on which the necessity to establish a field of cyber studies within the profession rests: policy succeeds or fails based on the correctness of the theory it presupposes. A policy based on flawed assumptions is doomed to fail unless rescued by good fortune; one drawing on sound theory can be defeated only in its execution. The theory–policy nexus is especially close in our era of rapid technological change, in which threats and opportunities arising from a new class of weapons produce pressures to act before the laborious process of strategic adaptation concludes (if ever it does). Consequently, axioms are applied that may have outlived their validity. Historically, bad theories of new technology have been behind many a strategic blunder. In 1914,

British commanders failed to grasp that modern submarines had rendered their magnificent surface fleet obsolescent. In 1940, French strategic doctrine misinterpreted the lessons of mechanized warfare and prescribed no response to the Nazi tank assault. In the opening stages of the First World War, the misinterpretation of new weapons kept the British Royal Navy largely sequestered in port. During the Second World War, it helped to cause the defeat – in a period of just six weeks – of what was then regarded as the world's mightiest army, the French. But for bad theory of new technology, the tragedies of the North Sea and Dunkirk may both have been averted.[33]

Against this backdrop, scholars have a duty to decipher the meaning of the cyber revolution for strategy and policy. For our own times are no exception to the historical problem of a lag in strategic adaptation to new technology. Joseph Nye observed that in comparison with the early nuclear era, "strategic studies of the cyber domain are chronologically equivalent to 1960 but conceptually more equivalent to the 1950s."[34] Circumstances in the lead-up to the U.S. offensive cyber operation that destroyed uranium-enrichment centrifuges in Natanz, Iran, vividly demonstrate the problem.[35] The custodians of the worm (named Stuxnet by its discoverers) grappled with three sets of doctrinal quandaries. One involved ambiguities regarding the tactical viability of cyberattack to destroy physical assets. The worm's developers could not have high assurance that it would reach the target computer system, for the Natanz facility had no Internet connection. Even if the worm penetrated the wall of air, they could plausibly expect that it would not function as they intended. When dealing with so complex a target system (a Siemens-built programmable logic controller, or PLC, governing thousands of centrifuges) and so intricate a malware artifact (15,000 lines of code),[36] the possibility that the weapon will malfunction or produce inadvertent effects is always real.[37] Proliferation presented another worry. The advanced code could reach weaker opponents who might reengineer it to strike back at one's own facilities. Other anxieties concerned the dangerous precedent that the operation would set. Would lesser powers replicate the secrets of this genial code? Would it embolden adversaries to unleash their own virtual stockpiles?

Later chapters will revisit these quandaries. It suffices here to note that they were real enough to Stuxnet's handlers. The U.S. President Barack Obama and his team of advisers were the kind of decision-makers who, recognizing that a new genus of conflict was in the offing, proved inordinately obstinate in searching for satisfactory answers to the hazards it portended. Nevertheless, in the race against Iran's development of a nuclear bomb, they decided to act. It still remains for security studies scholars to develop a theoretical scheme to address the quandaries of cyber conflict for the future.

The torments of decision-making faced by practitioners are an opportunity for scholars. Whatever aspect of the cyber question one considers – its strategic, tactical, or moral problems – there is in it a chance to demonstrate the merits of academic insight in the resolution of pressing policy challenges. The impression of a cyber danger seems only to intensify at the highest strata of government as new threats come to light – from the destruction of corporate networks at Sony Pictures Entertainment to the infiltration of politicians' personal files during national elections (to which we will return later). So long as it persists, the reluctance to assess the defining revolution of our times risks nourishing practitioners' preconception that security studies is, as one U.S. diplomat put it, "irrelevant" and "locked within the circle of esoteric scholarly discussion."[38]

Conceptual and Technical Rudiments for Cyber Studies

So, can a field of cyber studies flourish? Contra the deep skeptics, who perceive opportunities for inquiry as hazards, methodological obstacles do not severely inhibit scholarship. These problems are smaller than they have been made out to be. Orderly investigation of cyber issues is possible – a crucial point for those who think it is also necessary. Let us shatter two barriers that might otherwise dissuade even the intrepid student from making incursions into a field where so few have sought to shine: the scarcity of cases to analyze and the technology's scientific complexity.

Filling the Data Gap – But Beware the Dangers of Scientism

Much noise has been made about obstacles of data collection. The problem arises, as we saw, because government classification policies conceal many of the most important events in cyberspace, inhibiting investigation of their underlying motives and aims. Moreover, the private firms that operate the majority of critical computer systems are often reluctant to report cyber incidents because of their potential to damage the companies' reputation and create financial, legal, and other costs.

Yet cyber studies is not confined to ahistorical abstraction. There are comparatively more cases to examine than in other technological domains, such as the nuclear and biological, in which a paucity of events has not prevented fields of study from thriving. At most, the data gap reduces the degree of certainty of claims but does not prevent reasoned debate about grave and partly observable problems. While the shroud of government secrecy shrinks the pool of observable cyber events and reduces available details about them, this is true of all national security activity. Furthermore, the cyber research community has the unique advantage that the very technology which governments are eager to conceal is itself capable of piercing the veil of secrecy. The diffusion of the Internet means that, once released, many malware agents will eventually replicate to third parties, thereby raising the chances of eventual detection. As the Stuxnet operation reveals, this can occur even in connection with covert operations involving "air-gapped" computer systems (i.e. those not joined to the Internet).[39] Stuxnet also shows that the consequences of a successful cyberattack can be difficult to hide, particularly if they contain a destructive element. In addition, legislative efforts are under way in a number of countries to give private industry incentives to report network breaches that escape public detection because of their subtle impact.[40] Finally, the common reluctance of officials to discuss offensive cyber operations is easing as the need for public debate on its strategic quandaries intensifies. For instance, in 2013 the British Secretary of State for Defence, Philip Hammond, admitted that his government was "developing a full spectrum military cyber capability, including a strike capability" – the first official recognition of Britain's advanced cyber arms program.[41] Similarly, in 2016, U.S. Secretary of Defense Ashton Carter announced that his country's military was unleashing "cyber bombs" against the Islamic State militant group in Syria and Iraq. "We are using cyber tools, which is really a major new departure," remarked Carter. "I'm talking about attacking the ability of someone sitting in Raqqa to command and control ISIL forces outside of Raqqa or to talk to Mosul ... So these are strikes that are conducted in the warzone using cyber essentially as a weapon of war just like we drop bombs. We're dropping cyber bombs."[42] The universe of observable pronouncements and cases grows steadily.

Yet attempts at empirical inquiry may misfire if theorists succumb to the idolatry of scientism: the exaltation of quantitative inference as the only viable or most worthwhile means to uncover reality. Two dangers specific to cyber studies arise here. First, a large-case investigation will distort as much as elucidate if the observable universe does not accurately reflect the true scope of actual or possible action and effect. Before the attacks by Al-Qaeda on September 11, 2001, terrorism scholars could have conjured large datasets spanning many countries to posit that jihadists would not inflict thousands of deaths in a single operation against the West. On this basis, they may have dismissed the gravity of the real threat posed by terrorist groups to the United States. A second cause of misguided conjectures is the use of outmoded concepts to select explanatory variables and relevant cases. Some theorists missed the novel features of global jihadism because the phenomenon did not fit established notions of thinking in international relations – namely, the political contests of rational states armed with conventional means of war.[43]

Attempts at cyber theory within international relations have faced similar dangers. One study that is skeptical about a cyber revolution marshaled a diverse array of "evidence and rigorous data" on cyber incidents to dismiss competing qualitative accounts as "grand statements with little connection to actual processes."[44] The implicit methodological assumption is hard to miss: a quantitative survey can reveal these processes more accurately than a qualitative review of single cases.

Yet there is strong reason to believe that much relevant cyber activity occurs beyond the ability of researchers to analyze or even observe. The vast majority of intrusions of computer systems are probably not known to them – or, for that matter, to defenders of affected systems. Consider that the intelligence-gathering phase of the Stuxnet operation did not become known until as late as five years after it started. Note, also, that some governments habitually report thousands of attacks, about which little knowledge is publicly revealed. A senior British military official has claimed that the Ministry of Defence experienced "hundreds if not thousands" of serious attempts to penetrate or disrupt its computer systems *every day*.[45] As the head of the British intelligence service MI5 recently remarked, Russia is conducting "high-volume activity out of sight with the cyber-threat."[46] The U.S. Department of Homeland Security reported 50,000 intrusions of or attempts to intrude on U.S. computer systems in one recent six-month period.[47] South Korea's Cyber Investigation Unit recently disclosed that North Korean agents penetrated 140,000 machines in 160 public and private organizations.[48] Soon after, officials in Seoul announced the penetration of 3,200 more machines.[49] In 2016, the French repelled 24,000 "cyberattacks" against military and defense systems.[50]

At these orders of magnitude, case numbers lose their meaning. There is perhaps no other domain of security in which researchers know so little about so much activity. The plethora of reported incidents on which governments have revealed few facts cannot all be significant, for if they were, Britain would lack a functioning military and South Korea a working economy. Yet at least some, if not many, of these unobservable incidents may be significant enough to affect the validity of inferences derived from quantitative analysis, which relies on an accurate picture of a whole universe of events rather than on deep knowledge about any single event.

These problems complicate the statistician's three main analytical tasks, which are, for coding each event, to ascertain its nature, intent, and effects (e.g. Was it a disruptive or merely intelligence-gathering activity?); its possible interrelation with other events (Are intrusions single or combined actions and are they unique or replicated instances?); and the adversary's profile (Was it a single actor, say, a foreign government, or a combination of culprits, such as a nation colluding with criminal syndicates?). Only then is it possible to draw an accurate and meaningful picture of the heaps of incident data that distinguishes disruptive attacks from snooping operations, separates stand-alone or replicating incidents from larger operations comprising multiple stages and targets, and identifies linkages among distinct human and organizational agents acting in concert.

Barriers of data collection hinder quantitative study more than qualitative review. Moreover, they favor the perception of real danger over the thesis that it has been inflated. Researchers more commonly discover new, more damaging facts about known events or facts about altogether new harmful events than they learn that previously reported harm did not occur. In the hundreds of thousands of partly disclosed or unknown cases, there are likely to lurk major effects about which the research community does not yet know. Analysts are continuously behind the empirical curve. Short of a real cyberwar, which may never occur, wherever the claim has appeared that in the cyber domain a stable peace will prevail or that no events more damaging than heretofore will occur, history has corrected the lapse into optimism.

But even assuming full knowledge of the empirical record, the absence of more severe cyberattacks does not prove the unlikeliness of major conflict or the impotence of the new weapons. Rather, it may be an indication of great peril if fear of retaliation or blowback are the cause of restraint. Moreover, the aforementioned quantitative study selected variables and cases on the basis of conventional benchmarks of interstate rivalry. Notably, it omitted cyberattacks by nonstate actors or even state-sanctioned proxies, thus evading cases – even known ones – that may challenge the central finding of continuity in security relationships within the cyber domain.

Theory, it is important to understand, does not emerge merely from the sum of past events. It takes shape also from inferences about present and emerging trends that may be only partially known yet plausibly inferred by contemporary observers. Sometimes, the most important events in strategic theory construction are those that did not occur but may plausibly transpire. This is especially true of a new technological domain in which the trajectory of proven action has few clear limits. The problem of scientism is that it does not sufficiently recognize that cyber studies entails an inevitable element of conjecture about an unprecedented technology. Perhaps in no other arena of modern conflict is the gulf between the visible and the conceivable universes so wide. Paradoxically, a broad survey of the case record may obscure more than it reveals the horizon of possibility if it causes theorists to prioritize events that conform to conventional statecraft. A deeper analysis of single cases may yield truer propositions about the virtual weapon's nature and effects on international order if it can identify trends that breach (or may breach) the scope of familiar conduct.

The stubborn – at times dogmatic – quest for large datasets appears to be as much an imaginary requirement of political "science" as it is a compensatory device of some traditionalist theorists who strive to preserve old postulates in the face of sharp anomalies in the historical record. The dangers of scientism are evident in other quarters of political science, too. Consider the failure of statistical models to predict the Conservative Party's outright victory in the British parliamentary election in 2015; or the victory of Donald Trump, who repeatedly denounced data driven models, over Hillary Clinton, whose campaign spent nearly $1 billion on them, in the U.S. presidential election in 2016. These two analytical fiascos illustrate the dangers that can arise if observers apply natural science methods to evaluate disruptive political currents that qualitative techniques can perhaps more accurately explain. Insofar as the elevation of "large-n" studies above all other modes of inquiry causes some thinkers to defend established security models because they have neglected new trends that the old theories cannot anticipate or that statistical models cannot decipher, then the tendencies of scientism will inhibit rather than promote strategic learning.[51]

The Need for a Congress of Disciplines

The cyber question is scientifically complex: no one familiar with the workings of code can deny it. The sense of inscrutability among some skeptics reflects the natural intellectual stress of laypersons who are suddenly tasked with interpreting the strategic consequences of an unfamiliar technology; suddenly confronted with a broadening field of political effects resulting from its use; and, moreover, suddenly asked to integrate its arcane features into theories and models of uncertain relevance. The deep skeptics convey a sense of insecurity about our professional performance as a scientific community of analysts.

Yet cyber studies does not require a miracle of learning. Only the minimum degree of technical acuity is needed to reveal the scope of maneuver in the new domain. The international relations theorist is not called upon to craft weaponized code – this is a task for technicians – or even to prescribe tactics for its use – a realm in which practitioners hold the advantage. Although he can contribute important insights to both tasks, the theorist's proper role is to decipher the technology's influence on international security relationships and to examine critically official strategies to affect them. The hesitant theorist caught in the sway of deep skepticism should draw inspiration from the record of nuclear studies. Its founding architects of theory and strategy were not natural scientists. True, this rule has had notable exceptions, theorists of the natural order who for reasons of moral or political conviction effectively developed a second, parallel career oriented to resolving problems of national security and international order. Take, for instance, Paul Doty. A biochemist who worked on isotope separation in the Manhattan Project, he served as a consultant to President Dwight Eisenhower on nuclear arms control and founded what became the leading journal in the field of international security and military affairs.[52] Or Herman

Kahn, a trained physicist and mathematician who elaborated so fine and believable a picture of graduated nuclear holocaust that detractors named him "the futurist everyone loves to hate."[53]

Yet the most common intellectual font of breakthroughs in strategic learning lay in the social sciences and humanities. Consider the following luminaries: Bernard Brodie, the original nuclear strategist who in the words of one admirer resisted "idiot savants who confuse technological banalities with intellectual and political profundities,"[54] was a student of international relations;[55] Albert Wohlstetter, an innovator of nuclear deterrence strategy, a mathematician with a natural proclivity to military matters.[56] Henry Kissinger, who refined the theory of limited nuclear war only to renounce it decades later, a political historian;[57] Robert Osgood, another expounder of limited war, a student of government;[58] Thomas C. Schelling, the initiator of nuclear game theory, an economist.[59] In brief, the early sages of the nuclear age were likelier to have been schooled in British naval history or the diplomacy of Metternich than the arcana of isotope separation.

In our own times, mastery of coding is not a prerequisite for cyber strategy any more than intimate knowledge of atomic physics was for nuclear strategy. Indeed, a technical mindset may in fact hinder strategic learning if it leads the analyst to assume a false preeminence of technical over human and behavioral forces, or to conflate events in cyberspace with occurrences in the cyber domain (more on this distinction in the next section).

So far, however, the analysis of cyber issues has effectively been ceded to the technologists. Consequently, public perceptions display the following tendencies: a propensity to think of "cyber threats" as pernicious lines of code – instead of focusing on the human agents who utilize them and their motives for doing so; an inclination to conceive of "security" as the safety of a computer system or network – without paying sufficient attention to the safety of critical activity (e.g. nuclear enrichment) that is beyond cyberspace but reliant on computer functionality; and the habit of labeling any hostile cyber action – from the theft of personal data to the destruction of nuclear turbines – as an "attack," ignoring the potentially serious connotations of that term in an international context.[60]

All these tendencies involve aspects of international relations that technologists are unequipped to address, for technical virtuosity is not identical to strategic insight: it can illuminate the properties of a new class of weapon yet contribute little to explaining the purposes that inspire its use. In this new and complex domain, we are all laypersons – even the craftiest computer technician. For political scientists to stake a claim in cyber studies is to acknowledge that even the technical experts are novices – to assert that interpreting the contests of international anarchy demands its own kind of "technical" skills that only the initiates in political science possess.

Common Technical Concepts

What cyber studies in international relations requires is a selection of common technical concepts that lays out the most salient aspects of the subject for the discipline. Such a schematization can perform four important functions for this delegation at the Congress of Disciplines. The first is to frame the complex scientific properties of cyberspace in a manageable way. So long as the misperception pervades that strategic learning requires coding ability, some political thinkers will not dare enter the chamber. Inasmuch as the basic technical markers of strategic behavior remain unclear, those who enter will feel themselves strangers in a house discussing magical (to them) occurrences.

The second function is to identify the most relevant features of the technology and its related phenomena while eliminating activity that does not rise to the level of national or international security. Not all cyber actions are of a kind that delegates to the congress will regard as relevant to their theory. Some are the business of other benches; others, though they are primarily a subject for other benches, may nevertheless be new and legitimate topics of inquiry.

The third function is to orient theory development, enabling scholars to organize and codify data collected after a cyber event becomes known, search for causal chains linking determining factors to the event, and establish conceptual benchmarks for evaluating competing explanations of it. Until, for instance, the different meanings of intelligence-gathering activity and a cyber "attack" become common wisdom or unless analysts recognize that there has been no such thing as a "cyberwar," theorists may put forth propositions or design models whose starting assumptions are flawed.

A fourth function concerns the clash of conceptions within the chamber: a clarification of concepts can help to sort out discrepancies in the meaning of core notions and common terms as well as allocate priorities of investigation among professions other than international relations.

All of these functions can help to address the rhetorical hysterics and conceptual convulsions that prevail in much of the public perception of cyber issues. Errors of rhetoric such as "Cyber Pearl Harbor!" or "Cyber 9/11!" or "Cybergeddon!" misrepresent the essence of cyber threats no less (perhaps more) than skeptical disbelief. They make the task of theoretical and strategic adjustment harder than if it involved merely the analysis of phenomena about which observers know nothing at all. Cyber studies, in other words, parts from a basis worse than zero knowledge; it must begin from *negative* knowledge.

The schematization below fills the conceptual void and clarifies prevailing misconceptions. It contains the following six elements: cyberspace and cyber domain, cybersecurity, malware and cyberweapon, cybercrime, cyberattack, and cyber exploitation and "kompromat."[61]

1. *Cyberspace and cyber domain.* Cyberspace is the most elemental concept in the new field: it establishes the technical markers within which the virtual weapon can operate. One common definition construes cyberspace as all computer systems and networks in existence, including air-gapped systems.[62] Another excludes isolated nodes.[63] For the purposes of this study, the first definition is appropriate. Total isolation of computer systems is rarely feasible today. The ubiquity of computing devices, ranging from removable drives to personal laptops – each a potential carrier of malware – has multiplied the access vectors through which an attacker can bridge an air gap. Moreover, the computer systems likeliest to be shielded by air (e.g. nuclear facilities) are ordinarily of high significance to national security and therefore should not be excluded from the plane of action. Cyberspace can thus be conceived as comprising three partially overlapping terrains: (a) the Internet, encompassing all interconnected computers, including (b) the World Wide Web, consisting only of nodes accessible via a URL interface; and (c) a cyber "archipelago" comprising all other computer systems that exist in theoretical seclusion (in other words not connected to the Internet or the web and thus not to be confused with the "Dark Web," or the compartments of the public web whose interactions are not known to an outsider because they transpire behind authentication controls).[64] This conceptualization reflects an important consideration in security planning: not all threats propagated through the web can transmit via

the Internet and those that are transmissible cannot use the Internet to breach the cyber archipelago. On these terms, there are two basic kinds of target: remote-access and closed-access, each of which is susceptible to different methods of approach in a cyberattack.

Some observers have contested the definition of cyberspace as comprising only machines and networks. They argue that it also encompasses "technicians, network operators, vendors, regulators, and institutions."[65] Although there is no axiomatic definition of cyberspace – the meaning of the term is disputed – there are strong reasons to resist conflating the technical and the social planes in a single, catch-all term.[66] We already possess a suitable term for the expansive notion: cyber domain, which encompasses the bevy of human and institutional actors that operates and regulates cyberspace itself. The two notions, it is important to realize, are distinct. Cyberspace is a technical plane comprising machines and networks whose uniform feature is manipulability by code; by contrast, the cyber domain is primarily a political and social plane subject to wholly different interventions and behavioral rules. We require separate concepts to capture their separate essences.[67]

2. *Cybersecurity*. Cybersecurity consists of measures to protect cyberspace from hostile action. It can also be conceived of as a state of affairs: the absence of unauthorized intrusion into computer systems and their proper functioning. Crucially, the concept also encompasses measures to protect the cyber domain from threats emanating from the technical plane: i.e. it means the safety and survivability of functions operating beyond cyberspace but still reliant on a computer host, to which they are linked at the logical or information layer.[68] Insofar as measures of security are the purview of the military or impinge on military capabilities, they constitute cyber defense.

As we saw above, an alternative conception of cybersecurity, often labeled "information security," involves government protection of channels of information flow in domestic society (e.g. Internet censorship). This area of concern dominates cybersecurity planning in authoritarian nations. The Chinese government, for instance, operates a vast array of Internet surveillance and suppression techniques – the so-called Great Firewall. Officials often utilize these controls to stem activity that Beijing regards as subversive, such as social media postings by the Uighur Muslim minority who represent 40 percent of the country's Xinjiang region's population.[69] As one important study found, Chinese censorship does not silence all anti-regime information; merely that which appears to "represent, reinforce, or spur social mobilization, regardless of content."[70] Russian authorities, too, have taken steps to erect a grand virtual glacis of information security. Its technical core is "SORM" (System of Operative Search Measures), a scheme of universal data collection that dates back to the 1990s and is presently in its third life cycle. Surveillance is not the only measure of information control in Russia. The Kremlin has also employed disruptive cyberattacks against political dissidents – for example, the DDoS (distributed denial-of-service) campaign in December 2011 directed against the election-monitoring organization Golos, which planned to divulge information about violations in the Duma parliamentary elections that month.[71]

Information security is not the preserve only of illiberal nations. Western democracies also harbor concerns about malicious information flows. Examples include attempts to stanch the exchange of child pornography or efforts to combat the flow of fabricated news items during a heated national election. The priority that Western officials have traditionally ascribed to the functionality of computer systems and networks has not diminished, but recent attempts to subvert democratic voting procedures via the Internet (which we will discuss in future chapters) have elevated concerns about information security in Washington and European capitals.

But there is a crucial difference in the motives behind the practice of Internet censorship in authoritarian nations and in the West. In the former it expresses a desire to preserve the public legitimacy and existence of regimes that may not otherwise survive the sowing of discontent. In the latter, by contrast, it strives to maintain an open and secure (to vulnerable members of society) arena of political expression. To the autocrats, information security is a means to ensure the continuity of a political *regime*; to the liberals, a method of conserving the political system *itself*.

Such differences of interpretation of the meaning of cybersecurity have hindered efforts to establish international regimes of rules and norms of cyber conduct, particularly among nations such as the United States or Britain that espouse Internet freedom as a basic right and those such as China or Russia which as a matter of national policy curtail that right.[72]

3. *Malware and cyberweapon.* Malware denotes software designed to interfere with the functions of a computer or degrade the integrity of its

data. It encompasses the gamut of malicious code – viruses, worms, Trojans, spyware, adware, and so on. Malware exploits known vulnerabilities that the victim has not patched in his system, or else "zero-day" vulnerabilities that are known only to the attacker or to software vendors that have not publicly disclosed them. Malware can take two basic forms. It can be designed as penetration code that opens an avenue of access to a target computer system. Or it can be designed as a payload that affects the functionality, services, or information of a computer to achieve the attacker's objective. That objective may be data capture or destruction, impairment of workstations, incapacitation of nuclear centrifuges, and so forth.[73]

Many penetration methods employ malware. But not all: DDoS attacks, for example, access targets directly via the Internet. Although many DDoS operations use malware to recruit zombie machines, participants can also be mobilized to download attack tools onto personal machines voluntarily. Here, it would be misguided to regard the Internet as an element of the weapon itself. Instead, it is a medium to reach the target – that is, a feature of cyberspace, the technical plane on which attack code travels.

An attacker can also gain access to a computer system by using "phishing" techniques, which rely on deception to cause a legitimate computer user to reveal sensitive data (such as passwords) that the attacker can use to enter it or another target. For this purpose the attacker may use an email designed to deceive unsuspecting users into clicking on a link that takes them to a dangerous website. For example, the malicious emails that members of the Democratic National Committee received in 2016 asked recipients to visit a website that was expertly crafted to resemble a legitimate Google Gmail page. Visitors who entered their account credentials into this website unwittingly revealed their login information to the Russian state hacking group Fancy Bear.[74] Thus although these virtual features of a phishing attack are elements of the weapon, they themselves do not affect machine behavior. They affect humans.

Payloads, too, come in different forms. The most advanced is customized code that executes a command – often exploiting a zero-day vulnerability – on the target system. But some payloads do not involve the use of malware. Again, DDoS attacks are an example. The payload consists of floods of data requests that deny legitimate computer users access to the targeted services. Thus what makes the torrents of DDoS packets harmful are not their contents, which in lower quantities are harmless, but their intense volume.

We arrive at a thorny conceptual question: should malware be labeled a "weapon" at all? It is reasonable to impose limits on this language. After all, two of the defining features of weaponized code (we shall see in Chapter 2) are its intangible payload and effects, which are often nonviolent and which have not caused fatalities.

Not all forms of malware are weapons from an international relations perspective. In particular, we may question whether intelligence-gathering code merits the label. Some forms of it do not because they have innocuous aims: an undisruptive intrusion into a machine to detect harmful agents in it does not paint a convincing picture of a weapon. But at least two kinds of intelligence agents may be regarded as such. One is exploitative code that produces harm which impinges on national security – e.g. an artifact that seizes military or industrial secrets or else sensitive information about politicians in the midst of a national election. Another example is code that gathers systems' relevant data which the attacker later uses to customize a disruptive payload.

The crucial definitional criterion of a virtual weapon lies in its intended and possible effects. On these terms, the vast majority of malware is from a national security perspective uninteresting. It involves criminal actions at the low end of the spectrum of effects: credit card fraud, identity theft, web defacement, and so on. These forms of malware uses are not weapons from an international relations perspective because their possible effects are not of a magnitude that states would regard as relevant to their core interests. Other forms of code potentially meet this criterion of relevance: the destruction of nuclear enrichment centrifuges, the incapacitation of financial infrastructures, the crippling of governmental networks, the theft of prized military and commercial secrets, the capture of personal data whose public divulgence influences the outcome of national elections, and so on – actions that may damage the political, economic, or military security of nations.

A further question concerns physical objects: can they be elements of the weapon? Attackers sometimes embed backdoors into hardware components – for instance, a hardware Trojan, or a maliciously modified circuit that enables an intruder to monitor or modify the circuit's contents and transmissions.[75] Or they use USB drives and portable computers to deliver payloads to the target. We may be tempted to treat these excipients as an element of a virtual weapon – for example, a delivery vehicle. This treatment is misguided. It means that thousands of innocuous machines could become weapons, thus degrading the label's meaning. Moreover, this usage conflates the weapon with the domain. On the basis of the definition of cyberspace above, a physical object carrying malware is a compartment of the technical plane of action rather than the weapon itself.[76] As a general rule, it makes sense to restrict the label of "weapon" to the virtual elements themselves – executable code, malicious emails and web links, torrents of data requests, and so forth. But there may be limited exceptions in cases where the hardware's express purpose is to assist in an offensive operation: for example, a machine or group of machines that commands and controls botnets in a DDoS attack.

Sometimes, intangible weapons other than 0's and 1's travel via cyberspace to harm humans outside of it. Or more accurately, they travel cyberspace in the form of computer code but upon leaving it undergo a conversion into another state of being: ideas that directly affect human behavior. Examples of such a conversion include the use of social media channels to disseminate extremist views that motivate once law-abiding humans to behave nefariously; or, more peculiarly, the delivery of a video which if played emits a blinding strobe light that prompts an epileptic viewer to fall into a seizure.[77] Based on the terms proposed in this chapter, neither of these threats qualifies as a virtual weapon, because it does not alter the behavior of computers or seize their data. Strictly speaking, the only way to "weaponize" information – to convert knowledge into force itself – is to package it into electrons which can manipulate the minds and functions of a machine.

The label "virtual weapon" represents a stretching of the standard meaning of a weapon in international affairs, which ordinarily invokes the imagery of the horrors of war. Conceivably, computer code can cause effects that mirror real war. This has not yet occurred. The label is nevertheless appropriate in view of the fact that some forms of code can cause significant political and economic harm even if they are nonviolent. It draws attention to a central truth that Chapter 2 will discuss: despite its nearly massless properties, the virtual weapon can be a potent instrument in an international conflict.

4. *Cybercrime*. Cybercrime entails the use of a computer for an illicit purpose under the existing penal code of a nation. It includes credit card

fraud and transmission of prohibited data such as child pornography – hence its substance overlaps with the notion of information security. Because domestic criminal law is unenforceable against states, cyber-crime prevention focuses on private agents prosecutable in national jurisdictions. For this reason, it is the least contentious aspect of the cyber question at the intergovernmental level. Also for this reason it is the only dimension expressly regulated by treaty, the 2004 Council of Europe Convention on Cyber Crime, which regulates computer-related fraud and some intellectual property infringements. Tellingly, the treaty omits items that many nations agree are vital areas of concern but which raise fierce clashes of interest: strategic cyberattack and intelligence gathering.[78] In the usage proposed here, cybercrime lacks political or strategic intent; therefore, it rarely has an impact on national or inter-national security. Cybercrime is a topic that the international relations specialist can often but not always avoid in analysis. It belongs mainly to the legal and technical benches, whose members explore it assiduously.

5. *Cyberattack.* Cyberattack refers to the use of code to interfere with the functionality of a computer system for a political or strategic purpose. The first significant cyberattack reportedly occurred in 1982, when a so-called logic bomb caused a Soviet oil pipeline to explode.[79] Cyberattacks are characterized by the attacker's desire and capability to disrupt computer operations or destroy physical assets via cyberspace. Thus if the defender unnecessarily ceases computer operations as a consequence of misinformation or misinterpretation, the incident does not constitute cyberattack.

Neither the goal nor the effects of a cyberattack need be contained in cyberspace. The final object may be to incapacitate the computer system itself or to degrade social, economic, or government functions dependent on its proper operation. Accordingly, two main types of cyberattack effects can be identified: direct effects, which unfold within the logical environment of the target machine complex (e.g. destruction of nuclear centrifuges by manipulating their industrial controller);[80] and indirect effects, which hinder activity or functions that lie beyond the logical habitat of the compromised computer system but which rely on that system (e.g. interruption of the chemical process of uranium isotope separation necessary for the material's weaponization).

This description of the effects of a cyberattack departs from common understanding, which situates the effects boundary at the physical frontier of logically tied machines.[81] Consider, for example, the Stuxnet operation. The custom-built Stuxnet worm was designed to attack the logical environment of the Siemens S7-315 PLC at the Natanz nuclear facility in Iran. The attack sequence injected malicious code into the PLC to alter the behavior of IR-1 centrifuge cascades controlled by it.[82] Commentators ordinarily describe the effects on the PLC as direct and those on centrifuges as indirect, because the latter effects were "transmitted" via the PLC. This standard definition is nonsensical from the perspective of strategic analysis because it unnecessarily discriminates between effects exerted on an industrial controller and those on its constituent machines. By contrast, the usage proposed above assumes a more general perspective: it separates effects occurring within a unitary logical environment such as the Natanz facility from those affecting, say, Iran's ability to purify uranium – a far more useful distinction for strategic analysis. Moreover, because malware manipulates the logical unison of a computer system to execute a payload, treating effects within that system as direct and those beyond it as indirect makes more sense.[83] In short, the interesting segmentation of cyberattack effects lies at the boundary between cyberspace and the cyber domain, not between physical compartments of cyberspace.

If the effects of a cyberattack produce significant physical destruction or loss of life, the action can be labeled cyberwar, a term that should be used sparingly (this book does not apply it to describe any known case) given that no cyberattack to date meets this criterion.[84] If the attack is perpetrated by a private actor for political or ideological purposes, it is an example of "hacktivism."[85]

Cyberattacks can be customized or generalized. In a customized attack, the payload is designed to manipulate only machines within a specific logical habitat, such as the Natanz facility's PLC. In a generalized attack, no machine reachable via the Internet is in principle spared. An example of this phenomenon is the DDoS attacks that paralyzed computer systems in Estonia in 2007. Herbert Lin, Susan Landau, and Steven Bellovin describe these attacks as "discriminate," or customized, because they used "weapons that have been carefully targeted and, for various reasons, have not caused significant damage beyond the original target."[86] In a strict sense, yes, these attacks were discriminate because they targeted a set list of web services. But the malware that recruited and directed zombie machines was indiscriminate in target selection; moreover, the attackers were able to alter the target list with ease and speed. Thus the main difference between a customized and generalized artifact is the difficulty or ease, respectively, with which the weapon can be turned upon other targets.

6. *Cyber exploitation and "kompromat."* Cyber exploitation refers to the penetration of an adversary's computer system for the purpose of exfiltrating (but not defiling) data. One of the first major acts of cyber exploitation occurred in 1986 with a foreign breach of military and government computers in the United States. Another notable incident was the seizure by Chinese agents of several terabytes of secret U.S. government data in 2003. Essentially an intelligence-gathering activity, cyber exploitation relies on stealth and undetectability; thus disruption of the host system, which can lead to discovery and closure of access, defeats the purpose of exploitation. One objective of exploitation may be to seize a nation's military or industrial secrets, an activity known as cyber espionage. The technique can also be employed to acquire knowledge of an adversary's computer systems to plan future cyberattacks, in which case exploitation is an element of a multistage cyberattack.[87]

The goals and methods of exploitation are expanding. No longer does it involve merely the theft of military and commercial secrets. It increasingly also entails the Russian tactics of "kompromat": the release of sensitive information about a public official or organization that is timed specifically to influence and possibly alter the shape of an adversary's government or foreign policy; or else to undermine public confidence in an institutional or alliance system to which the nations of targeted officials belong. Examples of this behavior include the public disclosure of seized emails from officials at the Democratic National Committee and the hacking of machines in the offices of German legislators and political parties, which some observers describe as an attempt by Russia to influence, respectively, the U.S. presidential election in 2016 and the German national election of 2017. Here the virtual weapon may constitute just one email linking to a malicious website that obtains the user's login credentials. But this simple method may enable the attacker to disrupt and possibly even alter the course of a large nation's internal politics and foreign policy – without ever resorting to an act of war.

Acts of cyber exploitation are often conflated with cyberattack.[88] From a strictly technical standpoint this makes sense. In cyber exploitation, the target computer system is itself subjected to "attack," because access to privileged data usually requires aggressive measures to over-come computer defenses – hence the tendency for the conflation of terms within the technical community. Cyber exploitation "isn't passive anymore," argues Bruce Schneier. "It's not the electronic equivalent of sitting close to someone and overhearing a conversation. It's not passively monitoring a communications circuit. It's more likely to involve actively breaking into an adversary's computer network ... and installing malicious software designed to take over that network." For this reason, he continues, "Cyber-espionage is a form of cyber-attack. It's an offen-sive action."[89] From a tactical perspective, moreover, differentiating cyber exploitation from cyberattack can be difficult because both rely on the presence of a vulnerability and the ability to manipulate it; only the nature of the payload, which may not be immediately evident to the defender, varies. Moreover, a multistage cyberattack by an "advanced persistent adversary"[90] may involve preliminary rounds of exploitation to gain knowledge of the target, further obscuring the two forms of action.

These technical and tactical ambiguities, however, should not conceal an essential difference: cyber exploitation and cyberattack invite very different policy and legal consequences. As a form of espionage, exploita-tion by itself does not exert adverse direct effects and is not prohibited by international law. By contrast, a high-impact cyberattack could consti-tute a use of force or even an armed attack under treaty obligations. The use of unmanned aerial vehicles (UAVs) highlights the difference. Similar to code, UAVs can be employed to conduct remote sensing or they can be fitted with Hellfire missiles to strike ground targets (or both). Like a computer operator, a defender on the ground may not know the precise nature of the weapon until the operation is well under way. Yet it would be senseless – politically, legally, and strategically – to label the use of a UAV for strictly reconnaissance purposes a "drone attack." Fusion of the terms cyber exploitation and cyberattack could, however, produce such misidentification. From the perspective of international security, there-fore, the common conflation of labels inhibits rather than aids understanding of cyber issues.

The protection of military, industrial, and political assets from hostile cyber action is a key preoccupation of national security policy. These threats have been expanding in variety and rising in scale recently. Exploitation now involves the politically and ideologically subversive techniques of kompromat. The threshold of proven cyberattack effects also has been rising steadily, as later chapters will discuss; it now includes physical destruction of essential infrastructure. In addition, the virtual weapon in all its advanced forms poses enormous defense challenges while disturbing interstate strategic stability. Whether security scholars grasp these implications of the cyber revolution for international security depends on their ability to break free from their preconceptions as to what constitutes a serious threat.

The Necessity for Theoretical Departures

What of the Clausewitzian skeptics? The tendency of theorists is to dismiss the peculiar features of security in our times: to reject the thesis of a cyber revolution as myth. The main interest of the school of skepticism is to conventionalize the virtual weapon within familiar theories. This approach is largely grounded in traditional notions of interstate war, as conveyed in Walt's definition of security studies as "the study of the threat, use, and control of military force."[91] This viewpoint emphasizes the eternal relevance of the Clausewitzian philosophical framework.[92] It emphasizes three factors: military force and effect, rational and restrained rivalries, and state centrism. Yet the distinguishing features of contemporary security are the reverse: the expansion of nonphysical threats to national security, the dangers of unwanted or accelerating crises even among rational contenders, and the growing ability of private actors to disturb familiar political orders.

Skeptics are correct in noting that cyberweapons so far have not produced physical destruction and loss of life equivalent to war. Nevertheless, the new capability can have potent political, social, and economic effects. Examples of this are not hard to find. Cyberattacks have convulsed a small nation's financial and governmental activities (Estonia cyberattack); paralyzed a country's central bank and communications infrastructure (Georgia attack); destroyed hundreds of nuclear centrifuges (the Stuxnet operation against Iran); incapacitated tens of thousands of machines at the world's largest oil firm (Saudi Aramco attack); and crippled three-fourths of computers and servers at a major U.S.-based corporation (Sony Pictures hack). These cases display new degrees of potency. Experts warn of graver consequences to come. There is no room for complacency about the cyber threat: it may get worse before it gets worst.[93]

The traditionalist lens of interstate violence reveals merely what the cyber issue is *not*: it is dissimilar to armed attack, military conquest, physical coercion. The other half of the analytical puzzle – What, then, is it? – remains largely unanswered. Clausewitzian dictums are unlikely to solve it, as other chapters of this book will show. For the capacity of cyber arsenals to affect the military equation is not their main contribution. Rather, the virtual weapon is expanding the range of harm *between* the polar notions of war and peace, with important consequences for national and international security. Skepticism grounded in traditional thinking about war fails to acknowledge the broader security studies agenda, which encompasses issues such as the protection of essential governmental and financial infrastructures against intrusion and breakdown.

There is, moreover, the problem of inadvertent war. Tactical and strategic ambiguities impede the design of escalatory models for the full spectrum of conceivable conflict even among unitarily rational states. A low-grade cyber conflict could intensify into a major exchange – possibly one involving the use of military force, as some nations have promised could occur. Consider, for instance, the "equivalence principle" of current U.S. military doctrine, which stipulates that a major cyberattack may elicit a conventional military reprisal – without clarifying thresholds for such a response. Because the application of equivalence is not clear, it is possible that the punished party will perceive the conventional reprisal – whatever its form – as excessive. The resulting grievance may induce a further unreasonable counter-response, possibly in kind. And so on: what began as a contest in cyberspace intensifies into a familiar clash of armies. Thus a cyber event can occur that does not meet the traditional definition of war but nevertheless elicits a military or other grave reprisal. Even cyber exploitation, which does not seek to disrupt computer functions, could cause a crisis if the defender misconstrues the intrusion as a prelude to an act of aggression.

The dispersion of power away from states presents further problems. Clausewitzian skeptics emphasize the centrality of states: their political purposes and competitions. Indeed, as we saw, some studies within international relations omit other actors altogether unless they are integrated into state structures or act on behalf of governments.[94] States, to be sure, remain the principal players in the cyber domain; they possess the means to conduct the most sophisticated offensive actions. But states are no longer the only relevant actors in international relations in the cyber age. Other players – corporations, criminal syndicates, militant groups, hacktivists, even lone agents – can inflict significant harm. They may do so in ways that propel a crisis beyond the control of governments. In Estonia in 2007, for instance, the world witnessed the potential for hacktivists to precipitate a major diplomatic showdown involving Russia and NATO, and Estonian officials considered involving NATO as their essential infrastructures crashed. Thus by confining the problem of conflict escalation to state interactions, skeptics omit a central and peculiar feature of security in our times.

The Clausewitzian paradigm, in sum, supplies only a narrow frame of concepts against which to assess the scale, nature, and implications of the contemporary technological revolution. Old theory can inhibit rather than enable necessary policy adjustments if it causes officials to believe that familiar axioms apply to the resolution of new security problems that make them obsolete. Much depends, therefore, on theorists' criterion of what counts as "revolutionary" change, and especially its technological dimension, in international affairs.

CHAPTER 2

The Cyber Curse
COMPLICATIONS OF DEFENSE

The Question of Threat Inflation

Is the cyber threat real or inflated? It is superfluous to explore the virtual weapon's revolutionary potential without first answering this question. For if the threat is but a mirage – as some skeptics claim[1] – then there is little need to expend energy assessing its problems for theory and statecraft. Alternatively, the need for analysis exists merely to puncture the threat inflation and the associated presumption of a technological revolution that pervade in the highest strata of governments. The gravity of the threat, if real, does not by itself signify a technological revolution, but the virtual weapon cannot be revolutionary unless its threat to society is also grave. The thesis of cyber danger therefore logically precedes the thesis of cyber revolution.

Policymakers and security planners have answered this question unequivocally: the contemporary world confronts an enormous cyber threat. U.S. President Barack Obama defined the threat as "one of the most serious economic and national security challenges we face as a nation."[2] Former U.S. Director of National Intelligence Michael McConnell warned that a "full-blown cyberwar" may produce effects similar to nuclear war.[3] Official policy documents reflect the severity of these statements. The U.S. intelligence assessment rates the cyber threat higher than that of global terrorism.[4] French policymakers rank it alongside the threats of terrorism, nuclear attack, and biological pandemics.[5] Britain classifies it as a "Tier 1" threat, that is, equal in priority to a terrorist attack with weapons of mass destruction and above the threat of a conventional attack by another state. The public perception broadly reflects official attitudes; it is likely shaped by them as well. According to a recent poll of attitudes in the United States, interstate cyberattack is the second most feared scenario after a large-scale terrorist attack by Islamic State.[6] Media commentators and experts routinely warn of real disaster. As noted in Chapter 1, among the fashionable slogans one hears are warnings of a "Cyber Pearl Harbor!" or "Cyber 9/11!" or "Cybergeddon!" or "Cyber Fort Hood!"[7]

These judgments are a sore point for traditionalists in the security studies field, for whom interstate violence is the highest concern of theory.[8] If the popular perception of a cyber danger is to be translated into orderly concepts and propositions, then we must break it down into three main assumptions.

First is the degree of vulnerability to cyberattack: the security of cyberspace is a condition of the survival of modern society. In the developed world and many developing countries, most essential infrastructures – from nuclear power plants to civilian transportation networks to government communications systems – rely on the proper functioning of computers and networks. Second is the steady growth of offensive capabilities. Security planners repeatedly warn that a cyberattack could inflict severe economic and social damage. The disruption of financial exchange systems could convulse the banking industry. The derailment of trains carrying hazardous materials could cause severe environmental damage and mass casualties. The interruption of civilian energy supplies could result in urban chaos and large-scale loss of life. A third assumption concerns the offense–defense balance: officials repeatedly warn that, in the cyber domain, the attacker holds the advantage; thus it is extremely difficult to thwart a high-impact cyberattack.[9] Together, these three assumptions supply a nearly complete formula of urgent danger – acute vulnerability, high adversarial capability, and low defensive ability. Only the absence so far of a firm motive to cause harm among the strongest contenders – the United States, Britain, China, and Russia, or the advanced persistent adversaries – contains the measure of peril. Yet as any student of international anarchy knows, reliance on the benign intentions of opponents provides only a flimsy edifice of security.

Skeptics challenge two of these assumptions. On the first count, alarmists and disbelievers largely agree: the dependence of modern society on cyberspace is extremely high and growing. Disagreement exists, however, over the second and third points. Some doubters question the ability of weaponized code to cause significant harm. The proven consequences of cyberattack, they note, are limited. Despite the elevation by some strategists of the threat of cyberattack above that of conventional war, critics claim that cyberattack does not rise to the level of interstate violence because it never directly produces major physical damage or loss of life.[10] Skeptics have also disputed the assumption of offense dominance. They point out that a high-impact cyberattack is very costly to mount; thus they consider its likelihood to be low.

This chapter argues that both of these skeptical arguments are misguided. Cyberattack can cause enormous harm to national security even if its effects are nonphysical. And while it is true that mounting a high-impact attack requires a significant effort, this conclusion is only half complete. It neglects the other half of the strategic picture: the enormous costs of defense, which are higher still.

The Potency of Cyberweapons

We begin with a concession to the skeptical viewpoint: innumerable cyberattacks occur each day; yet to date none has produced fatalities.[11] This observation is both undeniable and important. Human death is the highest form of physical damage – ethically, legally, politically, and theoretically. It matters to established security studies debates, many of which pivot around the notion of fatality. For many theorists, it supplies a criterion of relevance below which events do not register. Take, for example, the debate over the "democratic peace." Liberal thinkers, drawing from the inspiration of Immanuel Kant, hold that liberal democratic nations do not engage in war against each other.[12] Political thinkers dispute the precise criterion of a "war" that would falsify this hypothesis – possibly the closest thing to a universal law of behavior in political science – yet virtually everyone agrees that some loss of life is a necessary condition of the criterion.[13] Thus the occurrence of a fatal cyberattack among liberal democratic states would present a momentous blow to liberal theory; its reverberations would be felt within broad quarters of the international relations community.

The reason for the absence of a cyber death is not hard to fathom. It inheres in the uniquely virtual method of harm. To reach its target, a traditional weapon has to traverse a geographic medium: land, sea, air, or outer space. Upon arrival, it inflicts direct material results: the piercing of flesh by an arrow's tip, the detonation of an explosive charge of TNT against the hull of a ship, the fusion of uranium isotopes in the atmosphere, and so on. Traditionally, then, overt violence was the only method of harm that weapons could inflict. Even if they produced no political or economic effects, the weapons' methods of operation were still inherently violent. There is no such thing as a nonviolent attack in conventional domains of conflict. Militaries, to be sure, commonly employ means of "psychological" and "information" warfare to supplement their tactical operations, but these nonviolent actions are not commonly regarded as attacks, for information itself does not directly inflict damage upon the physical world.

The cyber revolution has dramatically altered this situation. Malware can travel the vast information skin of the Internet. It obeys the protocols of TCP/IP, not the laws of geography.[14] It is little constrained by space and obliterates traditional distinctions between local and distant conflict. The payload is an intangible: it operates through complex coding, which means that the weapon's charge – a series of malicious 0's and 1's – is not the most proximate cause of damage. Instead, the payload requires a remote object – such as a programmable logic controller, or PLC, a machine that automates industrial processes – which can be manipulated. Information is no longer just a supplement of national power; it has become force *itself.* The virtual weapon – information stored as electrons – can inflict harm upon the political and social world without ever exiting the intangible minds of Turing's machines. Machine functions have replaced violent charges in the behavior of weapons.

The absence of death and the intangibility of most direct effects are not convincing grounds to refute the virtual weapon's potency, although theories wedded to the notion of violent loss of life may lead us toward that conclusion. Cyberattack need not result in physical destruction to pose a serious danger to society. "It may not be a bomb coming down our middle chimney of our house," Jonathan Zittrain explained, "but it could be something that greatly affects our way of life."[15] Or as General Martin Dempsey, Chairman of the Joint Chiefs of Staff, stated, "The uncomfortable reality of our world is that bits and bytes can be as threatening as bullets and bombs."[16] Moreover, the new capability's indirect effects – those occurring outside the logical bounds of the compromised computer system – can be powerful, even catastrophic.

The cyberattacks against Estonia and Georgia illustrate the point. According to NATO's Supreme Allied Commander Europe, Admiral James Stavridis, these cases provide a "glimpse of this future [of conflict]" by demonstrating the potent indirect effects of nonviolent and generalized cyber weapons.[17] The distributed denial-of-service (DDoS) attacks on Estonia in the spring of 2007 froze the country's governmental and financial activities for approximately three weeks.[18] There was no physical wreckage or loss of life; hence the label of cyberwar does not apply. Yet the incident was far graver than just a "large popular demonstration," as Thomas Rid portrayed it.[19] Rather, the cyberattacks on Estonia represent a wholly new type of social and economic disturbance.

Three factors explain why traditional analogies of political disturbance do not apply to the characterization of the Estonian crisis: the perpetrators resided mostly outside the affected territory; the torrents of attack data crossed multiple national jurisdictions via the Internet with awesome speed; and identifying and punishing the perpetrators proved very difficult because of Moscow's refusal to provide legal assistance to Estonian investigators, who possessed log files of affected machines revealing that many of the culprits had operated out of Russia.

The cyberattacks on Georgia in the summer of 2008 further demonstrate the potency of nondiscriminating cyberweapons. The DDOS attacks, which were carried out by nonstate agents including Russian criminal syndicates, occurred against the backdrop of Russia's military ground incursion into Georgia. A detailed study of the case concluded that the attacks tactically benefited the Russians in two important ways. First, it crippled the Georgian government's communications infrastructures, hindering Tbilisi's ability to coordinate domestic civil defenses. Second, it paralyzed the operations of the National Bank of Georgia, which impeded procurement of war materiel from private industry that was essential in the government's effort to conduct defensive actions.[20] Although these same tactical effects could have been achieved using conventional arms, it is important to note that the new weapon offered a feasible and superior substitute. The capability did not directly implicate Russia's military services, was cheap and readily available to nonstate actors, and proved impervious to conventional defenses.

The direct effects of cyberattack can be potent even if the indirect effects are not. Consider the so-called Shamoon virus that hit computer systems in Saudi Aramco – the world's largest oil firm – in the summer of 2012. The virus operated by a combination of two processes: a reporter module, which conveyed information to the attacker, and a wiper module, which corrupted the master boot records of workstations that were seemingly randomly selected.[21] By some estimates, the attack incapacitated approximately ten thousand employee workstations. The operation's indirect effects were limited, because the virus did not disrupt the industrial control systems of machines involved in oil refining. Had it done so, the indirect damage to global economic activity could have been significant: the company refines approximately four million barrels every day. Analysts recognize the potential of a cyberattack to hinder oil-refining machinery. Thus Shamoon's failure to impair refining activity does not signify the new technology's impotence; merely the desire of the attackers (Iranian agents, by some accounts) to limit the severity of the impact, possibly to escape a punishing retaliation.

Until recently, in fact, the ability of code to damage physical facilities remained entirely in the realm of theoretical speculation. The Stuxnet operation changed that. The direct effects of this operation, as revealed in a report by the International Atomic Energy Agency, included the decommissioning of approximately 984 IR-1 uranium enrichment centrifuges at Iran's Natanz facility during a three-month period. The indirect effects of the attack are subject to dispute, but they were almost certainly greater than this figure suggests. Indeed, the most powerful effect may have been psychological. Discord and mistrust within Iran's nuclear establishment, arising from paranoia that a rogue scientist was among its ranks, and fears of intrusion elsewhere in the nation's cyber archipelago, may have slowed Iran's ability to acquire the bomb by as much as two years – significantly longer than the time required to replace the impaired centrifuges.[22] The disruption, possibly by sophisticated malware, of operations in twenty-seven distribution stations and three power plants in eastern Ukraine in December 2015, which cut energy supplies to more than 200,000 civilians,[23] provides a warning of the possible indirect effects of cyberattacks against physical infrastructures.

The above cases illustrate five difficulties in conceptualizing cyber-attacks by conventional measures. First, the actions lack a proximate cause of injury and may not even be violent. Second, the conception of war as the use of armed force sets high thresholds in terms of scope, duration, and intensity that cyber actions may not meet.[24] Third, the perpetrators of a cyberattack can be nonstate parties who are not typically considered subjects of international law and thus not subject to its restraining procedures. Fourth, an offensive cyber operation by non-traditional players, such as that conducted against Estonia, need not involve the strategic purposes of states or their militaries. Fifth, at least in the case of a generalized cyberattack, the important distinction between military and civilian targets dissolves due to the broad diffusion of computer systems in society and their interdependencies.

Despite a long record (from 1988) of dealing with major disruptive cyber incidents, the difficulties of conceptualization continue. Leading politicians are given to passionate and incautious depictions. In 2016, Ted Cruz, a leading contender in the U.S. Republican Party's presidential primary campaign, warned that Russia and China were waging "cyber war" against the United States, although the hostile activity he had in mind – espionage – produced no intentional direct effects and was not prohibited under international law.[25] Similarly, John McCain, the incoming chairman of the U.S. Senate Armed Services Committee, floridly decried the Sony Pictures attack as an "act of war,"[26] chiding President Obama for describing it as an act of "vandalism." "The president does not understand that this is a manifestation of a new form of warfare," said the senator. "When you destroy economies, when you are able to impose censorship on the world, and especially the United States of America, it's more than vandalism. It's a new form of warfare."[27] Such reactions may in the future embarrass those who articulate them; today, however, they pervade the public perception.

Clearer-minded officials have struggled to correct persistent mischaracterizations. U.S. Defense Secretary Ashton Carter rejected the description of Chinese cyber espionage as an act of war. The White House declared that while the Sony Pictures attacks amounted to "a serious matter of national security," they did not meet the criteria of an act of war. Obama himself publicly repudiated the "cyber war" label, sending a message to Washington as much as to Pyongyang that his administration would not respond with conventional force. Were it not for the seniority of the speakers, these corrective statements might have been lost among the melee of gross simplifications that often ensues after a major incident. These statements, though rare, are revelatory of the current state of thinking. They show that at least some officials have filled in an important part of the analytical puzzle: what the cyber question is *not*; that is, it is not (or is not yet) a matter of traditional war. We have yet to figure out, however, the other side of the puzzle: what, then, is it?

On this question the accumulation of unsatisfying concepts intensifies. Carter described Chinese espionage as "cyber misbehavior." Obama referred to the Sony Pictures attacks as "cybervandalism." Observers have applied the label of "sabotage" to describe the Stuxnet worm's destructive effects.[28] These are all empty concepts: they have no precise definitions in this or other domains of conflict. The use of such terms adds little to the resolution of prevailing conceptual problems. The terms merely convey what we already knew: that cyber actions hinder national security, that they therefore merit some policy response, but that this response must fall below the threshold of war because the attack itself does so. Because of their ambiguity, these terms do not help us fill the terminological vacuum. Another possible analogy to cyberattack – sanctions – is also misleading. Sanctions are an exercise in negative power; they operate through the denial of gain rather than the direct infliction of loss. Yet offensive code clearly exerts positive effects; it initiates harmful activity that otherwise would not occur and causes direct injury to machines.

The "equivalence" principle that underpins American, British, and NATO cyber defense policy represents an attempt to resolve the conceptual muddles attached to the cyber question. It maintains that the direct and indirect effects of cyberattack, not its method, should determine the manner and severity of retaliation – including conventional force. Yet it does not identify specific thresholds for such a response. The deliberate declaratory vagueness of this principle is an attempt to adapt the doctrine of "calculated ambiguity" to the peculiar conditions of the cyber domain.[29]

It is tempting to see in this a crude treatment of cyberattack as a form of war. Yet the equivalence principle reflects a willingness to reinterpret and transcend, on a case-by-case basis, the limitations that traditional concepts of violence place on the retaliator. It leaves open the possibility of a forcible response even if the initial cyberattack is not construed as an act of war. As one American soldier put it rather cavalierly, "If you shut down our power grid, maybe we will put a missile down one of your smokestacks."[30] The implications of this principle for international security are potentially serious: a cyber event can occur that does not meet the traditional definition of war but nevertheless elicits a reprisal of commensurate severity.[31]

The known cases of cyberattack display an almost sequential accretion of harm that exposes the tenuity of skeptical thinking about the scope of technological possibility. Estonia proved the technology's ability to convulse the economic affairs of a small nation; Georgia, the ability to hinder civilian defense during a military invasion; Stuxnet and the Ukrainian malware incident, physical infrastructural damage; Saudi Aramco, systems-wide computer malfunction in a large corporation. Yet these cases, however alarming, do not convey the limits of possibility of cyber conflict. Scientists and experts widely recognize the potential for graver consequences. Officials at the U.S. Department of Homeland Security, for instance, have identified sixty-five facilities in the United States against which a single cyberattack could cause "catastrophic harm," which they defined as "causing or having the likelihood to cause $50 billion in economic damage, 2,500 fatalities, or a severe degradation of our national security."[32]

In the future, war by malware may occur if a cyberattack results in a similar number of deaths or level of physical destruction as a major kinetic strike. "I believe that what is termed an act of war should follow the same practices as in other domains because it is the seriousness, not the means of an attack that matters most," stated Carter. "Malicious cyber activities could result in death, injury or significant destruction, and any such activities would be regarded with the utmost concern and could well be considered 'acts of war.'"[33] War-like scenarios are not difficult to conjure. Based on extrapolations of a cyberattack simulation conducted by the National Academy of Sciences in 2007, penetration of the control system of the U.S. electrical grid could cause "hundreds or even thousands of deaths" as a result of human exposure to extreme temperatures.[34] Such an attack would be all the more damaging because, at least initially, officials would be unable to detect the source of the problem. Other calamitous cyberattack simulations involve the derailment of trains transporting hazardous chemical materials or the contamination of public water supplies.[35] The absence to date of more severe cyberattacks, therefore, does not prove the impotence of the new weapons. It may instead indicate their severity if fear of retaliation and blowback are restraining factors. To the question of where are all the catastrophic cyberattacks?, the easy and obvious response is: where are all the nuclear attacks? To make sense of such an eventuality, traditional concepts of interstate warfighting are useful.

The trajectory of proven potency has few clear limits. We should not seek to impose them on so novel and volatile a capability. We must not be complacent about the virtual weapon: it may yet produce devastating surprises. At any rate, physical catastrophe does not exhaust the spectrum of conceivable cyber conflict; although the gravest concern, it may be the least probable danger.

The capacity of cyber arsenals to augment military force is not their main significance, however. Rather, the new weapons expand the available methods of harm that do not fit established conceptions of war but may be no less harmful to national security. The ability of a cyberattack to inflict economic and other damage without resort to traditional violence affords the virtual weapon a special utility: it expands the choice of actions and outcomes available to the strategic offense.

Again, Stuxnet underscores the point. This operation was part of a broader campaign to deprive Iran of the ability to produce weapons-grade uranium. The United States and Israel agreed on this objective but differed on how to achieve it, with Israel eventually favoring airstrikes on Iranian nuclear plants. Officials in Washington agonized over the potential consequences of such a move, fearing that it could ignite a regional conflagration and only intensify Tehran's resolve to obtain the bomb. The Stuxnet worm offered the two countries at least a temporary solution to their differences: it promised to deliver some of the tactical results of a military strike while avoiding certain retaliation. Thus the fact that the worm's direct effects were not comparable to the scale of destruction possible in an air attack was the new weapon's principal appeal. The worm alone could never totally prevent development of an Iranian bomb, but it could at least delay enrichment while averting a regional war. Tehran's response to the Stuxnet operation so far as we know has been muted.[36]

This demonstrates that the phenomenon of cyberattack merits strategic analysis as much for the consequences it avoids as for those it produces. Indeed, it is tempting to conclude that cyberweapons promote international security – after all, their use may avert traditional forms of war.[37] Although this argument may have some merit in specific cases, it is too simplistic as a general observation; gains to the offense produce enormous losses in defense as well as conditions for strategic instability.

Complications of Defense

Security planners repeatedly warn that, in the cyber domain, the offense holds the advantage.[38] Some skeptics seek to dispel this notion by emphasizing the high costs of staging a destructive cyberattack. They cite Stuxnet to make their point: the operation required years of meticulous planning, involved a preliminary intrusion into the Natanz PLC to gain knowledge of the target, manipulated no less than six vulnerabilities in the PLC environment[39] – each an expensive technical feat – and required a skilled operative on site or nearby to deliver the worm across the air gap. Moreover, once the worm's coding secrets were revealed, systems operators were able to patch the programming defects that the worm exploited, rendering knowledge of these weaknesses useless to aspiring proliferants.[40] For these reasons, skeptics assert, the defense, not the offense, has the advantage.[41]

This conclusion is only half complete, however. It ignores or downplays the other half of the strategic picture: the enormous costs of defense against a cyberattack. Four such costs in particular are notable.[42]

First, there is the problem of offensive unpredictability. The use of code to achieve destructive direct effects requires the manipulation of vulnerabilities in the target's computer system. By definition, the defender is unaware of such zero-day weaknesses – hence their name. The universe of unknown and manipulable weaknesses renders a cyberattack difficult to predict or even imagine, complicating the design of measures to repulse it. Incomplete knowledge of defensive weaknesses also hinders remediation of intrusion post facto, because this requires understanding the zero-day vulnerabilities that the offensive payload exploits. Furthermore, the abundance of zero-day flaws and other possible access vectors that an attacker can utilize complicates the interception of malware in transit. True, malware is often easier to detect and neutralize when it is traveling across computer nodes – for example, via the Internet – toward its destination than when it is already lodged within it. Again, however, this is merely a relative statement: it says nothing about the defender's absolute costs (which are often high) in conducting a successful interception.

The Stuxnet operation demonstrates these points. Stealth was a genial feature of this multistage operation. The method of access, which may have involved the use of infected removable drives, was unanticipated. For three years, the Stuxnet worm and its antecedents, which acted as "beacons" for the offense, resided in the logical environment of the target PLC – that is, the PLC, the machines used to program it, and the machines it governed – without the plant operators noticing their presence. Remarkably, the worm was able to mask its damaging effects from the controllers even after the attack sequence had begun. Only a few months later did the Iranians determine, with outside assistance, the source of the centrifuge malfunction. "These guys know the centrifuges better than the Iranians," said Ralph Langner, an expert on Stuxnet and the first to divine its geopolitical intent. "[They] know everything. They know the timing, they known the inputs, and they know it by heart."[43]

The second cost of defense concerns the problem of offense undetectability. Perhaps the most worrisome feature of the cyber strategic landscape is the possibility that attack code will reside undiscovered in a defender's computer system. Even after the attack sequence has begun, detection of the threat can be slow if the defender does not realize that malware is the cause of the mechanical malfunction.[44] The difficulties of detection are especially complicated when dealing with a complex defensive terrain comprising multiple nodes and entry points – that is, the most prized kinds of systems: for instance, the financial exchange systems that process electronic securities trades or the systems that manage a city's civilian power supply.[45] According to a report by Verizon, private firms take an average of 240 days to spot network intrusions.[46] The problem of detection lag also applies to the most sensitive governmental quarters of cyberspace. Examples of the lag abound. In April 2014, computer security specialists discovered the presence of exploitative malware in the computer network of the Office of Personnel Management (OPM); one year later, they discovered a second intrusion in OPM's network, concluding that the intrusion was not just "historical, but an ongoing breach."[47] By the time the breach was seemingly defeated, the intruders had exfiltrated millions of secret personnel files, including the sensitive records of security clearance applications by federal government employees. In July 2014, computer experts discovered an intrusion in JPMorgan Chase's network that compromised eighty-three million customers; the breach had begun one month earlier.[48] In November 2014, officials confirmed that hackers had penetrated the unclassified email system of the U.S. State Department; three months later, the authorities were still trying to expel the intruders.[49] The Pentagon's weapons tester concluded: "The continued development of advanced cyber intrusion techniques makes it likely that determined cyber adversaries can acquire a foothold in most [military] networks, and could be in a position to degrade important [Department of Defense] missions when and if they choose to."[50] In February 2016, the FBI warned that state-sponsored hackers had penetrated "various government and commercial networks" since at least 2011.[51] Ominously, even the computer systems of firms such as Kaspersky Lab, which develop front-line defenses against malware, have been successfully penetrated by techniques that were previously unknown to them.[52]

Four events in particular demonstrate the ease with which attackers can penetrate sensitive computer systems and the difficulties that the defenders face in spotting the intrusions.[53] The hackers who penetrated the email accounts of executives in the Democratic National Committee in 2016 may have roamed the machines undetected for a period of eleven months.[54] In September 2016, Yahoo employees discovered that in the previous year culprits had stolen the personal data of 500 million users of the company's Internet services. Three months later Yahoo learned that a separate breach had compromised the data of one billion users three years earlier.[55] Most famously, exploitative code may have resided in the Natanz nuclear facility for between three to five years before the attack phase began.

By definition, cases of delayed detection account only for *known* intrusions. But the most sophisticated intrusions may be known only to the attacker. Therefore, it is plausible to assume that some form of attack code permanently resides undiscovered within much of the public and private sectors' essential computer infrastructures, or that at any given moment at least some of these infrastructures are compromised.

The prospect of permanent intrusion of the defender's infrastructure represents a reversal of the classical security paradigm. Previously, the primary aim of security planning was to prevent the enemy's presence in the home terrain. In the new domain, it must be a starting assumption of strategy that the enemy is already inside. One often hears FBI Director Robert Mueller's famous refrain: "There are only two types of companies: those that have been hacked and those that will be hacked."[56] It is more accurate, however, to distinguish between organizations that know they have been hacked and those that do not know – and might never find out. The ability of advanced adversaries to reside permanently within essential infrastructures proves a maxim paraphrased from British politician Stanley Baldwin's remark about strategic warfare in the 1930s: malware will always get through.[57]

A central task of security policy, then, is to detect the enemy's presence in the defender's computer terrain. The failure to do so raises enormous dangers, because residency within the logical habitat of a machine complex affords the invader means to deprive the defense of the ability to manage its own protection in at least two ways. One is peer-to-peer monitoring, which allows an attacker to adjust the attack sequence remotely and in real time. Another is the use of an intelligent malware agent with self-adaptive capacities that enable it to learn and override defensive acts. The attackers of Natanz, for instance, intercepted security updates to the facility's PLC. The Stuxnet worm would identify and co-opt these updates before the PLC operators could implement them.[58] The ability of malware to generate multiple versions of itself means that the threat variants during a cyberattack are theoretically limitless.

Nevertheless, a permanent breach of a computer system need not entail permanent insecurity if the defensive terrain can be organized in concentric zones of access so that the most prized nodes are quarantined from less secure compartments. This approach, however, runs counter to the very purpose of "information" technologies, namely, to ease transmission of data between machines. Therein lies the root dilemma of cybersecurity: an impregnable computer system may be inaccessible to legitimate users, while an accessible machine is inherently manipulable by pernicious code.

The difficulties of detecting the foe's presence complicate the task of "compellence," which Thomas Schelling described as the act of convincing an opponent to withdraw from territory that he has invaded.[59] To be sure, the penetration of a machine with intangible code does not equate to the seizure of physical territory. A remote operator's ability to manipulate the behavior of a machine will always be limited compared with what an equally skilled operator can achieve in situ. Thus the seizure of computer terrain cannot achieve the full effects of physical conquest. Yet, crucially, virtual conquest may enable the defender to achieve results that previously only physical conquest could deliver. Moreover, some forms of virtual conquest are more costly to the defender than physical conquest. Compare China's seizure of the Joint Strike Fighter Jet's (F-35) secret engine designs,[60] which the People's Liberation Army used to build a similarly sophisticated stealth jet, the Shenyang J-31, at far lower cost (see below), with China's seizure of uninhabited areas of the Spratly and Paracel Islands in the South China Sea to which it lays claim.[61]

The problem of the permanent residency of malware is by itself a revolutionary development within strategic theory. To be sure, spies have long infiltrated the societies and even the governments of foreign nations; or else native citizens who fell under the sway of foreign money or ideology willingly rendered their services to a hostile power. Yet the *scope* of infiltration via cyberspace, which may affect computer systems in *all* departments and agencies of government, and its *scale*, which can involve the seizure of millions of files in a single action, are likely impossible to achieve by means of conventional espionage. Equally important, the nature of the enemy's presence in the home terrain has changed. No longer does it involve a human agent who, if caught, can be subjected to the full penalties of the domestic legal code (and, in wartime, shot). Rather, the "spy" exists in a virtual state of being, a package of pernicious information stored in the form of nearly mass-less electrons whose handlers are frequently beyond reach of the courts because they reside in a foreign jurisdiction. No more is the nature of the threat one merely of information seizure. Information *itself* has become the threat because it has the capacity to disrupt the operations of or destroy vital computer infrastructures.

A third problem concerns the complexity of the defense surface. Computer systems and networks are becoming more intricate at all stages of design and use. As software and hardware complexity increases, so do the costs of customizing weaponized code. This increases the work factor of the attacker, who requires greater resources of manpower and intelligence to tailor the payload. At the same time, the costs to the defender, who has more node interdependencies to map and greater vulnerabilities to patch, also increase exponentially. The result is a fundamental offense–defense imbalance. Whereas the attacker only needs to understand the procedures of entry and attack that it decides to employ, the defender must continuously protect the entire network surface against the vast universe of conceivable attacks. The growing tendency to connect critical computer systems to the Internet is multiplying the available points of entry for use in customized cyberattacks. Moreover, society's mounting reliance on interconnected computer systems to support basic economic and social functions is increasing the opportunities to cause harm through a generalized cyber-attack. The expanding network surface provides conditions for a shock offensive or, as John Mearsheimer puts it, "the ability to choose the main point" – indeed, multiple points simultaneously – "of attack for the initial battles, to move forces there surreptitiously, and to surprise the defender."[62]

Fourth, supply-chain risks present a major challenge to defenders. Computer systems rely more and more on off-the-shelf and offshore manufacturers for components, introducing vulnerabilities into the supply chain. Foreign agents or private contractors could preload soft-ware or hardware components with malware, whether for attack or exploitative purposes. Apple security experts, for example, reportedly worry that the company's cloud services, "iCloud," have been compro-mised by vendors who have installed "back door" technologies for the purposes of government spying.[63] In 2009, Britain's Joint Intelligence Committee warned that Chinese-stocked components of British Telecom's phone network could be preloaded with malware or zero-day weaknesses, giving Beijing the ability to interrupt the country's power and food supplies. A "sleeper" payload of this kind could be remotely executed to achieve a preferred outcome in a future diplomatic or mili-tary crisis. In 2012, the U.S. House of Representatives Intelligence Committee warned that machine parts supplied by Huawei, a Chinese company founded by a former officer of the People's Liberation Army, could be used to exfiltrate data from government computers. Supply-chain risks are also a concern of the West's adversaries. The Chinese government, for example, recently banned the use of the Windows 8 operating system in its computers.[64] Protection against such risks requires government-wide and industry-wide coordination, yet such efforts have barely begun.[65]

None of the above observations is axiomatically true, for the cyber revolution continues to advance faster than our ability to interpret it. In combination, however, these four points underscore the immense disadvantages of defense against cyberattack. Nothing in the available historical record suggests that defensive costs are low or diminishing – certainly not Stuxnet, a case cherished by skeptics who challenge the common wisdom of offense dominance. The enormity of the defender's challenge is convincingly illustrated by the successful penetration of computer systems at Google, RSA, and Yahoo – three companies that represent the quintessence of technological ability in the cyber age.[66]

The thesis of defense dominance misses an essential truth: the offense–defense equation is relative. Thus the absolute measurement of offensive costs has meaning only in reference to the expenses of the defender.[67] At most, the current high price of mounting a high-impact cyberattack limits the ability of traditionally weak players to harness cyberspace for asymmetrical gain. It does not eliminate the significant tactical advantages of a possessor of advanced code. Moreover, the absolute costs of cyberattack are diminishing. "What was considered a sophisticated cyber attack only a year ago," warned Iain Lobban, chief of Britain's GCHQ, "might now be incorporated into a downloadable and easy to deploy Internet application, requiring little or no expertise to use."[68] The former U.S. Director of Central Intelligence, George Tenet, summarizes the defender's anguish: "We have built our future upon a capability we have not learned how to protect."[69]

The State of Unpeace

As already noted, some theorists argue that cyber threats are overblown. They contend that cyber actions have no intrinsic capacity for violence – at least not on a scale of intensity and destruction that analysts peering through the Clausewitzian prism deem relevant to theory. This strategy to puncture the perceived threat inflation works by conceptual fiat: because the method of harm lacks similarities with interstate armed conflict, by definition there can be no such thing as cyber "war."

In a sense the skeptics are correct: so far, the virtual weapon has not produced an unequivocal act of war. At the same time, this skepticism, grounded in traditional thinking about war and peace, fails to acknowledge the broader agenda of international security studies, which encompasses issues such as the protection of political, economic, and social interests against both state and nonstate threats that fail to satisfy the rigid criteria of war. The conventional security paradigm misses the essence of the cyber danger and conceals its true significance: the virtual weapon is expanding the range of possible harm and outcomes between the concepts of war and peace, with important consequences for national and international security.[70] Of course, the impact of cyberspace on military affairs is an important concern. For some thinkers this will be a starting point of theory. But it is not a point of terminus. The disanalogy between cyber actions and war conveys only what the new activity is not; it does not reveal the true meaning of the danger and may even conceal it. An appraisal of the cyber revolution in its fuller dimensions and new concepts to explain it are therefore needed.

If not war, then what label attaches to the current state of incessant cyber hostilities? Peace is the obvious alternative term. Some observers have proclaimed a state of "cyberpeace" in the world. They celebrate the emergence of an "international consensus stabilized around a number of limited acceptable uses of cybertechnology – one that prohibits any dangerous use of force."[71] Where others see war, these skeptics find a tolerable state of comity.

Such a view misunderstands the nature of the contemporary peril. The notion of a cyber "peace" is unsuitable for two main reasons. First, the harmful consequences of sub-threshold cyber action – hostile activity that falls below the recognizable criteria of war – are greater than any previous peacetime competitions in our history. In fact, the damage to national and economic security from cyberattack and cyber espionage is conceivably greater than even some acts of war or uses of force could achieve. Yet they do not neatly fit the definition of either war or force.

Compare the following scenarios. On the one hand, on August 20, 1998, the United States launched a cruise missile attack against the Al-Shifa industrial complex in Sudan, which Washington suspected was processing VX nerve gas for Al-Qaeda. This incident unambiguously fulfilled the terms of an act of war by virtue of its modality – a cruise missile attack – and direct consequences – physical destruction of the factory and one death. By many accounts, the attack's indirect effects were limited. Although it reduced the supply of anti-malarial medicines among the local population, there were no cascading effects beyond the local economy and society.

Now consider, on the other hand, the threat of customized cyberattack against crucial financial infrastructures. In 2014, Russian intelligence services reportedly inserted disruptive malware into the central servers that operate equity trades in the NASDAQ, the second largest stock exchange in the world. The malicious code bore the signs of a sophisticated adversary: it exploited two zero-day vulnerabilities, each of which is ordinarily expensive to acquire. According to U.S. government investigators, the code was not designed to destroy machines in the fashion of the Stuxnet worm, but it could have interrupted the network's functions by overpowering them.[72] Were an attack of this sort to occur, its indirect effects could be momentous: it could erode public confidence in the integrity of equity exchanges, the lifeblood of modern advanced economies. Yet because neither the modality nor the direct effects of the attack are violent, the action would likely fall below the bar of war.

Consider as well the theft by China of fifty terabytes of secret military data from the computers of private defense contractors and the U.S. government in 2013. The data included the design secrets of the stealth radar and engine of the F-35, the most advanced fighter jet in history. Two decades in the making, this weapon's program has been the costliest in U.S. history. Yet analysts suspect that China used the stolen designs to produce, at much lower cost and higher speed, the rival stealth plane J-31, which by some accounts equals the F-35 in aerodynamic performance.[73] The theft and replication of U.S. technological prowess via cyberspace prompted the Director of the U.S. National Security Agency, General Keith Alexander, to characterize such actions as "the greatest transfer of wealth in history."[74] The implication of Alexander's remark is obvious: the scale and costs of the nonviolent seizure of data by remote computers are greater than what was ever achieved by the violent seizure of land and peoples by armies.

Never before has the international contest for security in the absence of war so imperiled nations or drained their intellectual, industrial, and political resources as in the cyber age. Yet because these actions are not acts of war, the instruments of foreign policy enter a state of doctrinal paralysis when prescribing a response. Because the Clausewitzian notions of war and peace are polar binaries, denying that a major cyber action is warlike is to affirm that it is peacelike. "If Chinese or Russian spies had backed a truck up to the State Department, smashed the glass doors, tied up the guards and spent the night carting off file cabinets, it would constitute an act of war," quipped Jim Lewis, a researcher at the Center for Strategic and International Studies. "But when it happens in cyberspace, we barely notice."[75]

Second, for this reason, the notion of peace fails to capture the essence of our strategic problem. The absence of war no longer means the existence of peace – if peace means not merely the silence of guns but, more fundamentally, a state of affairs to which statesmen can generally aspire as the maximal condition of coexistence within the system of international anarchy. In the past, nations willingly exited a state of peace when the perceived gains of war or the desire to preempt its losses were greater than in peacetime, but always the situation of peace – whatever its final shape – was a *prima facie* desirable object of statecraft. Thus we intuitively know that a given state of affairs violates the conceptual limits of peace when some of the system's main units no longer accept it as a desirable or even bearable state of affairs.

Much of cyber activity is neither recognizably war nor recognizably peace; it falls between the definitional bounds of these two binary concepts without satisfying either one. It is symptomatic of this reality that the comments of public officials and writings of analysts abound with statements conflating the meanings of the two notions. "Russia and China see cyber operations as a part of a warfare strategy during peacetime," stated the U.S. Republican Party in its 2016 electoral platform.[76] One commentator similarly depicted cyber activity as "warfare during peacetime."[77] Another wrote about "Waging war in peacetime."[78] In these depictions of the contests in the new domain, it has become difficult to distinguish a situation in which nations are at war from when they are at peace; peace can become a form of war.

How many more conflations of elemental concepts can the design of strategy tolerate? The thesis of "war in peacetime" has intuitive appeal because it conveys the essential truth that much of cyber activity is neither peace nor war. Yet because the view merges elements of each of these two notions, it violates them both. It contains an obvious logical fallacy: because there is neither real peace nor real war, there is therefore both. The main result of these utterances is further confusion in the public perception. Again their effect is to neglect the real and difficult analytical question before us: if neither peace nor war, then what to call the new phenomena?

Let us leave at the wayside the two oppositional notions of war and peace, neither of which captures the essence of the contemporary situation. Let us resist, too, the urge to discard the distinction between war and peace. Instead, let us refer to the costly but nonviolent, incessant though often imperceptible hostilities in the new domain as a new state of affairs – a situation of *unpeace*, or mid-spectrum rivalry lying below the physically destructive threshold of interstate violence, but whose harmful effects far surpass the tolerable level of peacetime competition and possibly, even, of war.

By focusing so much attention on the important observation that major cyber actions are not war, analysts and politicians have lost sight of an equally important reality: neither are they peace, at least not peace as statesmen have come to know and tolerate the condition. One might also apply the label "nonwar" to describe mid-spectrum activity. Unpeace is a better term because the vast majority of sub-threshold cyber incidents do not even remotely approximate the criterion of physical destruction in war. In other words, their nonviolent modality is closer to peace, though their effects are distinctly not peaceful.

The notion of unpeace is in our context similar in essence to colloquial usage of the term – the case of a tragically "unpeaceful marriage," for example. A couple in this situation is not at "war" because the two parties are still wedded. That is, they have not divorced, that final severance of relations that frequently brings forth fierce exchanges of legal blows in court. Yet neither is the situation one of peace, for the shaky union may experience severe flare-ups of treachery and abuse which (even if physical violence does not occur) can inflict far more psychological and emotional damage upon the parties than skirmishes on the judicial battlefield. Now, refine the plane of deception and misdeeds such that the husband holds – secretly – the login credentials of his wife's banking, social media, as well as work and personal email accounts; the keys to the parent-in-law's house; and remote access to the mobile devices of them all. The man's opportunities to cause his spouse harm and misery without crossing the judicial threshold of nuptial war multiply exponentially.

Trapped in rigid mental reflexes, some skeptics will dismiss the label of unpeace as theoretical conjuring. Minds that are enchanted by old concepts do not easily adopt new ones. But other, more flexible minds may find in this term a welcome means to escape the conceptual tangles of the peace–war binary that so blights popular characterizations of the new realm of action. Let us continue to strive for new breakthroughs in concepts that are better suited to capturing the unprecedented trends of security in our times.

CHAPTER 3

Technological Revolution and International Order

The Challenge of Technological Revolution

What is a technological revolution? If the answer to this question rested in the technology itself, we would not need political thinkers to remedy the causes of revolution or to grasp its consequences. Its study could recede into esoteric quarters of learning: into the technical minds of inventors unconcerned with the affairs of states and their peoples. Because this concept of revolution begins and ends in the technical realm, laypersons would not have to trouble themselves with its problems. Engineers and natural scientists could define lines of inquiry as if by decree, possibly in consultation with specialists in other scientific professions, but never seeking their approval on matters that after all lie outside their remit. The Congress of Disciplines would be unnecessary: it could disband under a system of one-party rule.

A historical perspective reveals a different answer, however. The revolutionary potential of technology resides not in the invention itself but in its political and social effects. On this basis, a new technology is never more than an *enabling* force of change. Even when technology is a primary driver of transformation, even when new forms of political dealing are inconceivable without it, it alone can never be *the* revolution (unless one is a technologist, which will be discussed further below). To believe otherwise is to confuse revolutionary resources with revolutionary aims; to conflate physical means with the social agents who wield them; in short, to neglect a central truth: ideals, beliefs, and habits are what define a revolutionary situation in the political system.

As important as the nature of a new technology, therefore, are the nature and purposes of its possessors. Confronted with a potentially transforming invention, international relations specialists must ask not only whether it alters the physical power of states – a question that links their concerns with the applied knowledge of engineers – but also whether it affects states' ability to realize revolutionary ideals. Even more fundamentally, analysts must ask: does the technology significantly diminish the supremacy of the main units – states – such that the international system's very structure is in peril?

These questions demand of traditional international relations theory more than it can honestly give. Surprisingly little has been written about the general relationship between new technology and international order.[1] True, analysts have long sparred over the impact of specific technological breakthroughs on strategic affairs – the influence of nuclear arms on superpower rivalry,[2] the effects of bombers and cruise missiles on the logic behind deterrence,[3] the implications of advances in robotics on war and warriors,[4] and so on. Yet the investigation of how technology affects foundational questions of system, order, and anarchy remains rudimentary. Theorists show a natural reverence for such questions; if they do not invoke them, then they do not believe that the questions apply. Thus the gap in thinking betrays a sense of skepticism – more visceral than analytical – about the transforming potential of new technology, one that features in contemporary debates about cyberspace. New inventions may influence ordinary international contests involving interstate coercion and territorial conquest, but they are not normally a menace to the international political order, much less a threat to the state system's very constitution.

To this school of technological doubters one can attach a by now familiar label: Clausewitzian skepticism. It displays the core tenets of intellectual reactionism in security studies – a focus on the dealings of states (usually only large ones), an emphasis on the technologies of military conflict, and an assumption of states' unitary rationality. This fixation with mechanical interstate dealings reflects the broader Westphalian mold in which established theories are cast. It derives from a rigid model of "system" that does not allow much possibility for deep change in the units' basic purposes or composition. The absence of an organized theory of technological revolution, then, does not signify the absence of a dominant opinion on the subject. Rather, it means that the skeptical position enjoys such a high appeal among theorists that they see no need to articulate its main assumptions.

The simplified Clausewitzian scheme serves as a useful starting point to analyze technological revolution in international affairs. The phenomenon has mattered most when it has affected the military balance among major powers. Rational calculations largely explain states' responses to major advances in the technologies of conflict. States have largely barred other actors from enjoying the strategic and tactical benefits of new inventions. At a basic level, the standard paradigm has been true throughout modern history – from the improvement of gunpowder in the seventeenth century to the development of mechanized weapons and thermonuclear bombs in the twentieth.[5]

Yet this paradigm suffers notable deficiencies. It neglects the potentially important effects of new technology on non-military forms of security and conflict. It fails to recognize the ability of technology to alter not only rational interactions, but also the basic purposes of the dominant units by strengthening others whose aims may be subversive. It ignores pressures of change from *outside* the states system that arise from the growing relevance of alien players that the main units do not ordinarily recognize as legitimate, but whose influence on the preservation of order among them may nevertheless be decisive. The traditional paradigm can explain the effects that new technology can produce *within* an existing political system, such as differential growth rates among nations pursuing familiar goals.[6] But it cannot account for factors that give impetus to a *new* political system: one that features new state purposes and the means to achieve them; or, more elementally, one that houses an altogether different species of relevant units. The paradigm's sway with theorists confirms the charge that the international relations profession faces a problem explaining – indeed, envisaging – deep change in the political system of international anarchy.[7]

The design of a post-Clausewitzian paradigm of technological revolution appropriate for the cyber age makes a special demand on theorists. It requires them to relax the preconception that technology can produce only limited systemic disruption. It asks for an admission that the international system is susceptible to evolution not only in the material order, but also in its social fabric and even its main building blocks, the composition of units. It demands self-criticism – a willingness to accept that our conception of revolution is in fact the problem.

This chapter develops concepts to build a new paradigm of techno-logical revolution. Drawing from international relations theory and historical experience, it proposes benchmarks that will help to distinguish between varieties of international revolution and will guide analysis of technology's role in producing them. The discussion proposes "test" principles to identify and contrast the presence of three broad forms of revolution in the international system – systemic disruption, systemic revision, and systems change; clarifies the effects of each on the international order at different stages of revolutionary change; and identifies the techniques by which a revolutionary condition in international relations can end. Along the way, the discussion will draw lessons and insights from historical cases of technological revolution in weapons systems, such as mechanized warfare and the nuclear revolution, to derive lessons and insights for the contemporary era.

The Conventional Model of the International System

The first and basic step in the analysis of revolution is to establish a concept of the states system against which to measure the degree of change within it. The basis of the Clausewitzian security paradigm is an ideal type of system that reflects fairly constant attitudes among theorists. Let us plainly call it the Conventional Model. It involves three sets of basic assumptions.

One set concerns the system's *organizing principle*. This concept defines the makeup of the international system in the most basic sense: its units. The organizing principle is close to Kenneth Waltz's "ordering principles"[8] and Hedley Bull's "constitutional normative principles,"[9] which establish the relative importance of different types of actors in the system – nation states, citizens, an imperial hegemon, World Leviathan, etc.[10] Thus the organizing principle is logically prior to the system's structure and procedures; it identifies the units that possess independent authority to act and whose actions most directly influence their security and welfare (and that of their subjects). Other factors, such as the goals and relative capabilities of the units, reside within the parameters of a given set of organizing tenets. Ordinarily, states are the main and – crucially – irreducible units to which all other agents, domestic and international, are subordinate.

A second set of assumptions relates to *structure*: those features of the international system that cannot properly be comprehended as properties of units because they apply across all or a group of them.[11] Structure has both social and material elements. The social element reflects the common (though not always explicit) assumption among theorists that the competing units share a basic interest in survival and the preservation of order, which moderates the intensity of rivalry among them, especially the resort to violence. For this reason, some political thinkers describe international politics as comprising not only a mechanical system of rational interactions – the world, writ large, of John Stuart Mill's detached *Homo economicus* who prioritizes defined ends according to their numerical value[12] – but also a "society of states" – Immanuel Kant or Woodrow Wilson's realm of players whose values, ideologies, and passions always shape and sometimes displace selfish conveniences. In the words of E. H. Carr: "No political society, national or international, can exist unless people submit to certain rules of conduct."[13] The existence of a society does not mean that the units share common interests at all times; merely that when these interests diverge, sometimes greatly, the units commonly accept the contenders' right to protect their own interests even if in certain instances the clash involves an outbreak of limited violence. This common social fabric defines the basic parameters within which states respond to the system's material structure, such as the balance of power or international commercial flows, which define the context, and often the drama, in which the units pursue basic goals without, however, altering their essence.

Third are the system's *procedures*: the rules, laws, norms, and institutions that help to sustain this temperance of behavior and facilitate cooperation even in the absence of a central authority to suppress the will of the units. Views on the importance of the system's procedural machinery (such as international organizations or normative conventions) in averting conflict and preserving order diverge widely. Some scholars depict institutional mechanisms as tools that large powers use to seize the distributional advantages of cooperation. Others portray them as necessary conditions for cooperation to occur. For one side, institutions are a device of anarchic power politics; for the other, they are a means to overcome its crudities.[14] Whatever one's position in these debates, procedural reform is largely a means to cope with, rather than a manifestation of change in, the system's organizing principle and basic purposes.

The Clausewitzian security paradigm is a specialized subset of this ideal type of system, from which it never strays significantly. The paradigm's core tenets may be summarized as follows. It emphasizes the centrality of supreme sovereign units – states – that coexist in a condition of anarchy that produces incessant uncertainty, rivalry, and suspicion about the true intentions of adversaries even when these intentions are known. It holds that the units share a thin pluralism of basic purposes, the chief of which are self-preservation, the maintenance of a minimum of order, and the avoidance of generalized violence, which could imperil the very existence of the system. Thus the paradigm accepts the inevitable recurrence of war, but only as a regularized method of competition for limited ends. It urges the creation of institutions, rules, norms, and other procedures that can support the attainment of these ends. It holds that armed force is the *ultima ratio* of international affairs and exalts the view that the state, in particular its military apparatus, is the principal agent in ensuring that the system functions as it should, so that if rationality loses its battle with ideology – if social man overpowers economic man – the result is not a total contest among savages bent on each other's destruction but a finite battle among cavaliers who wish to preserve society even as they occasionally mar it. The paradigm is in short state-centered, socially recursive, and oriented to military power.[15]

Varieties of Revolution: A Conceptual Framework

Observers frequently discuss the impact of new technology in terms of a revolution. Yet this concept has not been satisfactorily defined. It can mean significant change within an established international political order. Or it can mean a transition among distinct orders. Consequently, another basic question in the analysis of revolution is conceptual: a revolution of what kind and to what extent? Only after answering this question can we probe the ability of new technology to bring it forth.

In general, there are – to coin new terms – three broad benchmarks of international revolution (in increasing magnitude of change): third-order revolution, or *systemic disruption*; second-order revolution, or *systemic revision*; and first-order revolution, or *systems change*. The extent of change implied by each criterion may be gauged according to the degree of variation or continuity that it implies in one or more of the above aspects of the Conventional Model.

Third-Order Revolution: Systemic Disruption

Third-order revolution refers to important adjustments within the sharp limits of the states system. It involves a major disturbance to the regularized interactions of states sharing basic purposes of survival and stability in their relations. It does not signify a disturbance of the moral order or organizing principle. Thus despite its label, the essence of third-order revolution is continuity: all forces of change, however disruptive, work to preserve rather than overthrow the existing structure. Thus while third-order revolution disrupts the conduct of units, sometimes disastrously, it does not challenge the system's constitutional structure; in fact, the units interact in a way that preserves their supremacy over all other actors. We can apply to this kind of revolution the label *systemic disruption*. Two kinds of change fit this notion.

The first and most obvious involves change in the system's physical properties – the material ingredients of power. This is the form of change that most concerns rational-choice theorists. In the neorealist view of states locked into a contest for physical survival, it denotes the replacement of one or a group of dominant states in the system by another, such as the shift from multipolarity to bipolarity after 1945, which ushered in the Cold War, or from bipolarity to unipolarity after 1991, which cemented the era of so-called Pax Americana.[16] In the neoliberal view of states enacting the rational tenets of economic man, the label of systemic disruption may attach to major alterations in the international commercial order, such as the appearance in Europe of a Single Market and Currency Union,[17] or in the emergence of globalized financial exchanges.[18] The label "revolution" does not apply, however, to strictly procedural changes, such as a rearrangement of alliances or the formation of integrative bodies, unless they themselves produce dramatic effects – for example, the eradication of war in Western Europe, in which case the rationally minded theorist has strayed into a historical and ideological terrain that his axioms may not have led him to conceive was possible.

Systemic disruption affects the dealings of self-interested states pursuing imperatives of survival and welfare. The notion's central concerns relate closely to some aspects of existing concepts of change. Robert Gilpin, for instance, provides a notion of revolution – if it is that – that centers on units that seek "to change the international system in a way that will enhance the states' own interests,"[19] thus "calculations regarding expected net benefits of changing the system are profoundly influenced by objective factors in the material and international environment."[20] Systemic disruption is always purely instrumentalist, because the goal of foreign policy is to maximize the national interest. Gilpin instructs: "Calculations regarding expected net benefits of changing the system are profoundly influenced by objective factors in the material and international environment."[21] That is, systemic disruption reflects the interests and distribution of power among the dominant units.[22]

Systemic disruption in this conception ends at the borders of the material order. As the basis for a theory of revolution, it reflects the common view of "ontological objectivism": the assumption that the system's social properties are fixed throughout time and place.[23] This view obeys a social constant that Waltz conveyed in his famous claim about the "socializing" effects of international anarchy, whereby the absence of world government (an immutable material fact) fashions states into "like units" pursuing physical security – hence his explanation of major trends in international politics on the basis of the distribution of military power among nations.[24] And because it is constant, the system's social element quietly slips away from theory construction, no different than the natural scientist who, assuming a fixed law of gravity, explains the varying motion of stellar objects only in reference to differences in their relative size and position. Underpinning this view is the rational-choice assumption that states seek to maximize materially conceived ends and are impeded in doing so only by physical constraints. The remarkable consequence of this theoretical approach is a fusion of perspectives among the natural and social sciences. As Arnold Wolfers put it, states are "billiard balls."[25] In this view, contrary to the Kantian philosophy of history that perceives ideas as a potent force of history, international affairs is reduced to the caroms of a physical process in which the growth or displacement of one ball shifts all other balls from their station.

To restrict the meaning of revolution in this way is to impose upon it severe limits. Neorealists such as Gilpin assume that no single state will ever dominate completely, for if it did there would be no states system to speak of, only a World Leviathan – a replication on the world stage of the scene in which individuals have sprung out of their state of nature to establish a government. Any resulting change in the power structure will conform to the higher organizing principle of anarchy – that is, the preservation of quarreling state sovereignties. When one state grows too strong, others will seek to check its power. When a player with the arsenal to achieve world domination emerges, such as Germany's rapid rise in the 1930s, the other powers, fearing for their own survival against the rising behemoth, will combine to resist it. In this way, the end result of systemic revolution, no matter how rapid its pace or extreme its extent, is a restoration of the constitutional order – even if an epic clash of armies is the necessary waypoint on the journey to this destination.

A second form of systemic disruption involves the social element: rules, norms, and principles. This form of change is a central concern of social theories of international relations such as classical liberalism and constructivism.[26] Here, too, strict limits apply. Normative change involves only a thin layer of the political framework of international anarchy: its norms and rules, which affect the players' pursuance of basic ends without, however, altering their essence. Indeed, historically, normative change in international relations rarely rises to a level that affects the system's social character. Ethical restraints on armed intervention have not yielded a program of global pacifism.[27] The doctrine of "responsibility to protect," which prescribes military intervention to stop gross human rights violations and that was invoked to justify the intervention against Muammar Gaddafi's Libya in 2011, has not produced a universal imperative to defeat repressive regimes by armed intervention.[28] In international affairs, norms and principles of behavior have a mainly procedural character; they serve to reinforce habits that are conducive to the preservation of the eternal purposes of ordinary states in the Conventional Model. Often, the most significant form of social change occurs not at the systems level but in the units: for example, the domestic rehabilitation of Japan and Germany after the Second World War.[29] Yet domestic revolutions do not qualify as international revolutions unless they yield systemic shockwaves: for instance, if the revolutionary state shatters the ideological cohesion of the units because it pursues an expansionary project, as in the case of Napoleonic France or Hitler's Germany.[30] But as Stephen Walt has observed, the impact of domestic revolution on international order is historically limited.[31]

Moreover, many social theories of international relations are wedded to the organizing principle of state sovereignty. True, some ascribe important moral value to the individual citizen. An example is Bull's notion of a "world society," which encompasses "transnational social bonds that link the individual human beings [across national borders]."[32] This more solidaristic conception of the social order addresses ethical obligations and political relationships in which the citizen is the focal point of moral concern, yet a world society is still an international society in the sense that it ascribes to the individual only moral relevancy, not political primacy.[33] The "world society of individual human beings exists only as an ideal, not as a reality," explained Bull.[34] World society exists morally above but politically below international society; it is a moral guidepost, not a political call for citizens to dismantle the international system's Leviathans and crawl back into their original state of nature. The state remains the principal political agent; it has ultimate power and responsibility in the protection of individual rights. World society in brief does not imply a world *system*.

Within the broad category of systemic disruption we may also include shocks to strategic theory: changes in the patterns and methods of international rivalry and conflict that challenge the axioms of interstate behavior prevailing in any given historical moment. This form of change need not involve a shift in the distribution of power, although it may facilitate such a transition. Instead, it involves the appearance of a new form of competition in the system that enables one or another contender to gain significant advantages or to inflict major losses that the oracles of strategy previously considered impossible or unlikely.

In sum, systemic disruption may involve a disturbance in the distribution of power among the units, a change in the regulative norms and principles that guide their behavior (but do not define their identities), or new methods of rivalry that upset established assumptions of strategic theory. In all instances, the essence of systemic disruption as a benchmark of revolution is the preservation of the Clausewitzian skeptics' prized affection for the Conventional Model. Revolution influences – sometimes decisively, but never transformatively – the stakes, rules, methods, and consequences of security competition among units pursuing national interests within a thin political framework of common, though not always reconcilable, goals of survival and order. Systemic revolution respects – indeed reinforces – the recurrent patterns of behavior that mar but also make tolerable political life in the international jungle. "[A]n underlying continuity characterizes world politics," concludes Gilpin, invoking from the classical world a famous adherent of the belief in historical continuity: "The history of Thucydides provides insights today as it did when it was written in the fifth century B.C."[35] It is no small irony that third-order revolution is in fact a concept of elemental constancy in international affairs.[36]

Second-Order Revolution: Systemic Revision

Second-order revolution implies a sharp fissure in the moral order. It springs from the ascent of a state or a group of states that repudiates the shared basic purposes of the units and rejects the accepted methods of achieving them, in particular restraints on the objectives and means of war. That is, it involves the appearance of a program to alter the social character of international society – the underlying political framework that binds states into a primitive community of common ends. But second-order revolution is also limited: it leaves the system's organizing principle, or state supremacy, intact. It is the most meaningful form of change that can occur within the Conventional Model short of its obliteration. We can label it *systemic revision*.

Basic purposes are logically prior to and therefore determining of actor instrumentality. Consequently, the implications of systemic revision for patterns of interstate conduct are profound. The point is important: it means that a transformation of international relations can occur even within the bounds of a given organizing principle (e.g. a system of states). The point is often overlooked by theorists of international revolution, most notably by Martin Wight in his description of "revolutionism" as involving an all-or-nothing reformulation of the system's organizing blocks. Closer to the notion of systemic revision is Bull's understanding of revolution, which he suggests need not be usurpatory of states. Although Marx and Engels envisaged the disappearance of the state, and thus of the system of states, the political strivings of revolutionaries such as Lenin or Trotsky reflected a desire to release the working classes from imperialist oppression "so as to achieve justice *within* states, and the revolt of oppressed nations, so as to achieve justice *among* them: demands for the abolition of the state itself, or of the nation, do not figure in these prescriptions [my italics]."[37] But the liquefaction of the state within a global proletariat did not feature in the Soviet program of change. It was an end point more imaginable than realizable, less a command to political action than a topic for sedate discussion among theoreticians.[38] Yet Moscow's pursuance of "world revolution" in the form of a sustained campaign to refashion, often by force of arms, other nations in the figure of its own domestic image represented a direct challenge to the Westphalian credo of ideological pluralism in the states system – an immoderate quest to mold a *global* identity of purpose.[39]

Another historical example of systemic revision is the contemporary project of European union, at least in its deeper political purposes. Following the cataclysm of the Second World War, the leaders of West Germany, France, Italy, Belgium, the Netherlands, and Luxembourg – "the Six" – sought to secure permanent peace on the Continent. This aim had enjoyed a long history in European political thought, existing, as Andrew Hurrell noted, as an "imaginable political reality" since at least the seventeenth century.[40] Most famously, it formed the principal concern of Kant's system of international ethics and was the basis of his assault on Grotius and other pluralists as "sorry comforters."[41] Political movements agitating for lasting peace proliferated well before the Second World War, emerging in Britain already in the eighteenth century.[42] But at no point prior to 1939 did the aim acquire a sustained following among leaders in positions of national authority within a core group of countries – no less France and Germany, on whose soil Europe's most sanguinary battles were fought. The peace aim represented a major departure from the dogma of power politics, which accepted as legitimate only the avoidance of generalized war among the great powers because it could jeopardize the continuance of the states system itself. Limited war, by contrast, was deemed permissible in proportion to balancing needs, as often arose. What is more, in the logic of power politics, the aspiration to permanent peace seems pernicious, because to eradicate the use of force is to remove the final means in the preservation of the balance of power. It is an invitation to universal conquest: permanent peace at the cost of permanent subjugation – and after much violence. On these terms, the logic of power politics deemed only a transitory peace attainable or even desirable; peace was a contingent but not an absolute goal. On the contrary, European federalists extolled peace as the final end of statecraft, as an advocation for absolute security. They devised supranational techniques of statecraft – themselves a major departure from the regulatory principles of power politics – to secure their aim. At the same time, the leaders of the Six did not strive to dissolve the nation state within a single European entity. Their program of federalism preserved the Conventional Model's central organizing tenet.[43]

In brief, whereas systemic disruption concerns itself with the almost mechanical interactions of rational state units, or else with the influence of norms and rules of behavior upon these interactions, systemic revision is a project of deep ideological reform. It involves change in the common ends that motivate, guide, and restrain the anarchic contest for security among sovereign units.[44] Analysts who question the influence of ideas in history may be tempted to characterize an instance of systemic revision as systemic disruption. This conflation of concepts is misleading. Nazi Germany's mastery of mechanized warfare technology and the country's rapid growth in military power relative to other contenders were not the most important cause of the collapse of the international order in the 1930s. Rather, the main destabilizing force was the new regime's pernicious ideology and its craving for foreign territory. Thus changes at the systemic level became, on account of the revolutionary state they empowered, forces of systemic revision.

First-Order Revolution: Systems Change

As the label implies, first-order revolution, or *systems change*,[45] is the most extreme form of conceivable revolution because it involves modification of the very building blocks of the system – the units. It occurs when alien players challenge the supremacy of the dominant units, states, whose purposes the new entrants may reject or else not even understand, but whose affairs they nevertheless significantly affect. This situation need not imply, however, the complete eradication of the old units, although this is more than a sufficient condition. Rather, systems change means that the units have lost their customary supremacy relative to other actors, at least in areas of activity that affect the core interests of the system's former masters. Systems change is best described not as a change in the Conventional Model, but as the appearance of an altogether new ideal type of international system.

In assessing the emergence of a new organizing tenet, then, we must consider a spectrum of importance in unit agency: *supremacy*, *primacy*, and *relevance*. Supremacy denotes a measure of influence over other actors which is so elevated that they are irrelevant to an account of how states secure their core interests or of the forces that drive their interactions within the system. In this fashion, some theorists – neorealists such as Kenneth Waltz, for example – presume that the influence of nonstate actors on international affairs does not rise to a level of significance that is relevant to theory. Hence they customarily expel them from their security models. Primacy has a partly related meaning: it signifies that the main units are the foremost agents in the system such that they deserve a special place in theory construction, but they are not so dominant that theorists can legitimately bar other kinds of actor entirely from explanation. Relevance, of a kind that is lower than supremacy and primacy, implies that the influence of secondary actors (which are not "units," for this term of distinction applies only to the dominant subjects) is sufficiently high that no systemic theory can be complete without them.

Liberal theory illustrates the difference between primacy and relevance. It acknowledges the important influence of nonstate actors in the dealings of states. For example, liberal thinkers point to the role of private corporations in cultivating commercial ties among nations that increase the costs of war, thereby helping to avert it.[46] They stress the role of transnational nongovernmental organizations in agitating against certain forms of warfighting.[47] Or they emphasize the important function of international institutions in reducing the uncertainty and sometimes fear that inhere in anarchic interactions. Yet these observations do not amount to an argument that new players have usurped the ability of governments to manage their own affairs or that the players are more relevant than governments in the resolution of national security problems. Sharing authority does not mean usurping it; relevance does not yield primacy. Thus liberal theorists admit nonstate actors into the Conventional Model as relevant actors – *quasi* units, one might say – but the thinkers do not forgo the central assumption that states retain their primacy, even if they are not absolutely supreme.

The spectrum of systems change, therefore, begins on the low end with the state's loss of supremacy, which has become primacy, and the rise of erstwhile irrelevant new actors, who have become relevant. At the middle is a situation where new actors' acquire primacy – thus becoming units in their own right – against the state's mere position of relevance. On the high side of the spectrum is the relegation of the state to a position of irrelevance, whether because another unit has become supreme or because (the anarchist's dream) government has ceased entirely to serve its function. The low side of the spectrum, such as the growing relevance of nonstate actors in liberal accounts, is not a sufficient condition of systems change, although some theorists have suggested such a mischaracterization by describing this trend as "system transformation."[48] Instead, let us set the bar at the attainment by alien players of primacy or supremacy, for it is here that the Conventional Model begins to encounter an existential danger.

The concept of "world system,"[49] an underdeveloped notion of the English School of international relations, is especially useful in unlocking the potential of an ideal-type of system that is not based on state supremacy or primacy. Hedley Bull describes the world system as a "world-wide network of interaction that embraces not only states but also other political actors, both 'above' and 'below' it."[50] He gives the example of the influence of Catholic and Protestant groups in the sixteenth and seventeenth centuries, whose relations with each other, with their state, and with foreign powers cut across state boundaries and at times superseded state institutions in importance.[51] From this historical backdrop there emerges another example of systems change: the appearance of the modern states system after the 1648 Treaty of Westphalia – what one student of revolution called the "symbolic origin" of contemporary international society.[52] This transforming settlement provided the legal and political foundations for the emergence, over time, of a system of sovereign states that challenged two central features of the medieval feudal order which preceded it: the role of the individual Christian soul as the principal moral object and the spiritual and temporal authority of the Pope (an organizing principle). Both features had provided for a political system in Europe in which the state, in whatever stage of rudimentary development, was not dominant.[53]

Historically, systems change has also appeared in the form of a political program of change: for example, Napoleon's and Hitler's quests for universal empire. Both programs sought to smash the European nation state and erect in its stead a structure based on single-state dominion. The difference between these two examples and the Communist revolution helps to illustrate the difference between systemic revision and systems change. Whereas Napoleon and Hitler were sincere in their repudiation of the principle of state sovereignty, as we saw the Soviet leadership, whose creed also proclaimed a vision of the "withering away of the state," was not. Soviet foreign policy was revolutionary only in the second order. It attempted to redraw foreign nations' domestic societies in the image of Communism and create a system of subservient satellite states. It nevertheless accepted the right of these other states to an independent existence. Moreover, it obeyed the necessity to preserve a minimum of order in East–West relations, eschewing on several occasions the impulse of other despotic regimes toward universal domination at all cost.

Another conjectural, more theoretical example of systems change is Wight's notion of "revolutionism," or the emergence of a fully developed world system in which nonstate actors are the supreme political agents. Revolutionism, in Wight's words, "[seeks] to revive, or to perpetuate, the minority medieval idea of a single human republic, an *imperium mundi* (Dante), or to harden international society into a world-state, to define it and constitute it as a super-state."[54] Here is a splendid conceptual irony: the notions of World Leviathan and World Democracy assume the same organizing principle, for they each imply the complete fusing of the domestic and international political systems. That is, they both entail the elevation of the individual citizen – whether under a despotic or a liberal regime – as the basic unit of political action within a single universal polity.

The notion of systems change does not enjoy a high reputation among international relations specialists. Many thinkers consider scenarios of nonstate dominance difficult to conjure. Succeeding chapters of this book, however, will discuss precisely such an ideal-type conception in the context of the cyber revolution.

The Question of Technological Determinism

Before assessing the ability of new technology to bring forth the varying degrees of revolution, it is important to revisit the question that launched this chapter: is technological change itself revolutionary?

Again, the answer will depend on one's intellectual upbringing. To a technician whose principal concern is technological affairs, the answer may well be Yes. Merely the achievement of nuclear fission by British and Irish scientists in 1932 revolutionized understanding of the field of theoretical physics.[55] It confirmed Ernest Rutherford's bold theory of the atom and set up the discovery, in 1934, of the phenomenon of nuclear chain reactions.[56] The purification of uranium isotopes into fissile material in the secret city of Oak Ridge, Tennessee, in 1942 revolutionized the field of nuclear engineering. It proved that human endeavor could manipulate the abstractions of Rutherford and his students for applied purposes. Ignoring for a moment its implications for the Manhattan Project's success, the feat paved the way for breakthroughs in civilian life – for example, the use of nuclear radiation in cancer treatment.[57]

Yet neither of these achievements was by itself of a scale that could transform the international system's power structure, moral order, or constitutional makeup. Only the development of a fully deployable fission bomb by the United States in 1945 and by the Soviet Union in 1949 could rise to that level of significance. Even then, the strategic significance of nuclear weapons inhered not in the underlying technology that made them possible but in their impact on the interstate contest for security – its substantiation of two poles of power, East and West, whose ideological contest henceforth played out under the shadow of mutual annihilation, a prospect that affected not merely the logic of nuclear war but also all other forms of conflict.

In brief, from the standpoint of the international relations specialist, new technology is revolutionary only insofar as it affects the main elements of the Conventional Model. Technological change does not by itself represent a revolution but can *enable* it. Let us state once again: equally important as the properties of a new technology are the ends that its possessors seek to achieve with it. What marks the difference between systemic disruption and systemic revision is not the nature of the technology but the nature of its creator and owner.

Importantly, this point leads neither to technological determinism nor to technological indeterminacy.[58] The question of whether the inherent properties of technology define its political and strategic effects (the determinist view: technology is an independent causal variable) or whether politics and strategy define the development and use of technology (the indeterminist view: technology is a dependent variable) is immaterial to the observation that what counts in measuring technology's revolutionary impact is how it shrinks or expands the scope of human action. The question of technological determinism matters only, though still greatly, when considering the ability of its possessors to generate, control, and suppress this impact.

In assessing the influence of new technology in human affairs, it is necessary to separate *secondary* and *primary* roles. A secondary technological revolution is one in which technology gives impetus to, but does not by itself cause, an international revolution. In other words, technology catalyzes rather than instigates revolution. The influence of technology is felt in its ability to shape or accelerate the march of a preexisting revolution whose main drivers may in fact reside outside the technological realm.

Consider, for example, the relationship between mechanized warfare and Nazi Germany. Mastery of the tank's strategic potential allowed the Germans to achieve stunning victories on the battlefield in the terrible spring of 1940, a period that saw a succession of democracies – Denmark, Belgium, the Netherlands, and France, including the latter's possessions in northern Africa – fall to the tyrant in Berlin. Yet the technologies of Blitzkrieg did not themselves launch the Nazi revolution or define its political aims. Instead, they defined its strategic limits; they carried the agents of revolution to Paris, the shores of the English Channel, and the gates of Moscow. In the hands of an ordinary power, the new arsenals might have solidified rather than disturbed the international order. We will return to this case below when discussing technological empowerment of the revolutionary state.

In a primary technological revolution, by contrast, technology is the principal instigating cause of change. This does not mean that technology is the only force of change; merely that the political revolution is not possible without it. Sometimes, for this reason, the new invention gives its name to revolution. Take the nuclear revolution. It is difficult, though not impossible, to conceive of a "cold" war among major contenders in the absence of the atom's awesome destructive power. True, even in a world of nuclear zero, economic entanglement may cause some nations – say, China and the United States – to avoid the enormous financial and commercial penalties of a direct war.[59] Yet the restraining influence of economic destruction, whose costs some decision-makers may find psychologically difficult to conjure, cannot match the easily imagined horrors of nuclear obliteration.

A consideration of the relationship of new technology – whatever its degree of effect – to political dealings requires that we separate the technological life cycle into different stages. We must distinguish between *technology-in-the-making* and *technology-in-being*. The ability of humans to influence the shape and effects of technology for some political or strategic purpose may be greatest at the technology's point of inception or soon after it. As Eugene Skolnikoff has pointed out, "Technological change comes about as a result of human decision and is in that sense a dependent variable."[60] Technology is in a stage of "making" if humans are able to define its main properties or control the effects of its applications in society.

The early development of nuclear arms is a fine example of this point. The first manipulation of the atom at Los Alamos in 1942 occurred in the context of and for the purposes of the American war effort in the Second World War. Similarly, the Soviet Union's acquisition of the fission bomb and the test by the United States of the first fusion device in 1952 were largely driven by the intensifying rivalry between those two nations. It is unlikely that the fission and fusion bombs, and the subsequent wide civilian applications of nuclear technology, such as in energy, would have emerged in the absence of the political and strategic contexts that gave rise to them.

Yet it would be erroneous to assume that technology is always subservient to political imperatives.[61] Even conceding that the initial selection of technology is preordained, its future swings and effects do not always obey the expectations or intentions of developers. Much less, for this reason, does a new technology submit readily to attempts by policy-makers to govern its future direction. A lot of the history of nuclear proliferation can be interpreted as an attempt to grapple with this reality: the regulation of nuclear weapons technology is today far less susceptible to the influences of the United States than was its initial discovery.[62] Technology achieves a stage of "being" if its main features are largely beyond the ability of humans – even the original inventors – to manipulate with any degree of decisiveness.

The evolution of the ARPANET, the precursor to the modern Internet, illustrates this point. Established in 1969 with funds from the Department of Defense, one of ARPANET's primary purposes was to enhance the reliability of military communications. Although various civilian objectives, such as the facilitation of academic collaboration, also resulted, its driving reason was strategic. That logic has since frayed owing to evolutions in the Internet's design that ARPANET's originators could neither anticipate nor arrest. They defined the medium's architecture before its eventual uses in society became known. The design questions were largely technical. How would machines identify themselves to each other? How would data travel between them? Debates over these questions consumed much thinking within the small and esoteric community of scientists who used the network during the 1970s and 1980s. Vinton Cerf and Robert Kahn, two Internet pioneers, proposed the TCP/IP protocols: one to parcel out and transmit data content as streams of packets, the other to provide a "gateway" that would read envelopes of data.[63] In 1982, this loosely governed community of scientists decided that henceforth, all civilian communications would employ TCP/IP. Adherents of the main competing protocol, NCP, resisted the move, but relented after Cerf threatened to cut off their connections. By this singular act of coercion, the Internet became essentially a technology-in-being.

Later, these early design decisions provided the technical basis for the inherent insecurity of Internet communications. The TCP/IP protocols prioritized the successful delivery of packets over accounting of the sender's identity and their content. David Clark explained: "[S]ince the network was designed to operate in a military context, which implied the possibility of a hostile environment, survivability [of communications] was put as a first goal, and accountability as a last goal."[64] But the nonmilitary functions such as commercial activity that today predominate in the network "would clearly place these goals at the opposite end of the list."[65] That it would have been better if the Internet's founders had prioritized accounting over delivery is something about which many computer specialists would agree. But in a world in which so many social and economic functions rely on the original architecture, this is a statement of retrospective lament and not of current possibility. Thus without knowing how to think about basic security problems, the Internet's insular community of custodians wielded the powers of creativity and coercion to establish a universal communications syntax, one that enabled a "consolidation period" during which the Internet grew to connect tens of thousands of users. As Chapter 4 will discuss, the Internet has become a medium through which threats to military systems can propagate; its architecture confers advantages to the offense over the defense.[66]

It is remarkable that the Internet's early designers were able to predict some of its wide uses in society; not the least that the technology has long ceased being a creature of their control.[67] Thus, contra John Ruggie, who argues that political forces become "preponderant" only *after* a technology's emergence, the Internet is proving far more difficult to control now than at its stage of creation, when political goals were supreme.[68]

Even in its deterministic stage, however, technology can be but one among several important factors that shape the scope of possible political action. And it may not even be the most significant. It would be wrong to presume that technology can operate entirely beyond reach of the political forces that motivate its development and guide its consequent uses.[69]

Technological Revolution: Pathways of Impact and Control

The conceptual benchmarks above allow us to distinguish varieties of technological revolution. Together, they give a series of "test" principles to identify third-, second-, and first-order revolutionary effects arising from new technology.

Third-Order Technological Revolution: Pathways to Systemic Disruption

The first six test principles relate to third-order technological revolution. New technology can produce systemic disruptions which destabilize the instrumental dealings of self-interested states coexisting under conditions of anarchic uncertainty or that challenge the starting axioms of strategic theory. These changes are shocks to the rational, not the moral, order.

Alteration of the Balance of Power

Perhaps the most obvious and important consequence of new technology is its ability to affect the balance of power within the Conventional Model.[70] Shifts in the balance of power can drastically affect the character of the international order. As Thucydides so baldly stated in one of the most celebrated pronouncements on international affairs (from which much of contemporary theory flows), "increasing Athenian greatness and the resulting fear among the Lacedaemonians [Spartans]" was what made the Peloponnesian War inevitable in 431 B.C.[71] Until then, a rough equipoise of power between Athens and Sparta – a situation of bipolarity – had sustained peace between these two preeminent units of the ancient Greek system of city states. Thereafter, the gradual consecration of Athens as a regional empire, and the fear this caused in Sparta, prompted Sparta to seek to preserve the equilibrium of power by war, Thucydides' account goes.

This pathway of change may take at least two distinct forms. First is differential growth rates in national industrial capacity: that is, in military potential. Significantly, it the *implied* rather than actual military power of Athens that inspired Sparta's fear. Yet new technology was not the decisive factor in that ancient Greek drama, showing that technological revolution is not a necessary precondition of systemic disruption.[72] In other cases of power transition, however, technological change was a crucial driving factor. One prominent example is the role of new manufacturing methods in Britain's rise to a position of global dominance during the nineteenth century. New technology was a precursor to the Industrial Revolution. The mechanization of spinning, for example, increased British manufacturing output in that sector by a factor of three or four. These and other manufacturing leaps fashioned Britain into the "first industrial nation," enabling it to dominate world trade.[73]

Second, changes in the balance of power may arise more directly from new advances in weapons systems. Here technology plays a more direct role in systemic disruption because it involves the technologies of conflict and thus affects nations' relative fighting capacity. The most prominent recent example of this phenomenon is the crucial role of nuclear weapons in the elevation of the United States and the Soviet Union to "super-power" status after the Second World War.[74] To be sure, these two nations would likely have attained positions of dominance within their respective regions even without nuclear arms. But it is debatable whether the degree – or, to use Waltz's term, "purity" – of deterrence and bipolarity would have been as severe as it was in the absence of the new capability, which gave the two superpowers the ability to annihilate each other and all other military contenders.

This is especially true of the Soviet Union after the Second World War and of Russia after the Union's collapse. Moscow's vast nuclear arsenal allowed it to preserve its position of relative strength even under conditions of deep economic and institutional malaise – even, that is, between 1960 and 1989, when Soviet economic growth was the lowest in the world,[75] or between 1992 and 1998, when the Russian economy declined on average almost 7 percent per year.[76] In the absence of nuclear weapons, the post-1945 bipolar order would have been less pure in the sense that the two superpowers would have been less able to influence their interactions both with each other and with their respective smaller partners. In the post-1991 period of American preeminence, it may have led to the absorption – peacefully or forcefully – of all fifteen former Soviet Republics (and not just Estonia, Latvia, and Lithuania) into the Western security architecture.[77]

It is important to note, however, the limits of the nuclear revolution in this regard: it has not equalized large and small states. Acquisition of the bomb has not consecrated Israel, North Korea, Pakistan, or even India as global powers equal to the larger nuclear states – the United States, Russia, and China – even if the elevated status of the lesser powers would be inconceivable without their nuclear arsenals. In other words, the expansion of systemic disruption via the proliferation of nuclear arms has not given rise to a multipolar order, although it may have increased the scope of maneuver of the nuclear powers over all others.

Technological Volatility

A new technology may contribute to instability among rational states because it complicates the task of evaluating the true balance of military capabilities among them. This can occur if the pace of technological development is faster than strategic planners' ability to measure its effects on the means of war; or if these effects are hidden or so scientifically complex that the contenders cannot decipher them.

The emergence of submarine warfare illustrates the first instance. In the early twentieth century, British military commanders regarded the submarine as a strategic relic even though they perceived its potential effects on naval strategy. Submarine warfare, in the words of one British admiral, was "underhand, unfair, and damned un-English."[78] Military planners regarded the beloved Dreadnoughts – the colossal "castles of steel" – as tactically superior to submarines. As a result, the Royal Navy invested heavily in the production of surface ships in whose ultimate superiority over submersible vessels they firmly believed.[79] Reality proved otherwise. At the start of the First World War, few viable means existed to detect the presence of enemy ships below water. Even if their detection was possible, viable defenses against them were slow to develop.[80] Consequently, during the opening months of the war, the Royal Navy lost four capital ships – three of them in a single action – to German U-boats. The development of this new form of warfare outpaced the ability of military commanders to learn the lessons of defense (or, for that matter, offense).[81]

The early stages of the nuclear revolution illustrate the second problem. Consider, for instance, nuclear fallout – the chief collateral effect of nuclear explosions. When in 1952 the United States detonated the first megaton hydrogen bomb, few scientists correctly anticipated the degree of fallout, even though the phenomenon was well known to them.[82] Technical analyses of the effects of the first Soviet thermonuclear test in 1953 also ranged wildly. The Chairman of the European Atomic Commission, Lewis Strauss, observed that individuals injured by the blast were recovering swiftly from the effects of radiation.[83] This finding disturbed A. H. Sturtevant of the California Institute of Technology, who claimed that the pathological effects (e.g. permanent genetic mutations) endured beyond the first generation of victims.[84] General Curtis LeMay, the founding director of U.S. Strategic Command, which held responsibility over nuclear forces, expressed the contraposition to these concerns, testifying that a person could avoid deleterious health effects by lying under three feet of dirt![85] For ten years the fallout debate raged and hindered the development of nuclear strategy. It obscured understanding of the extent of civilian deaths, the uninhabitability of populated areas, the contaminability of food and water supplies – questions that were at the core of political, doctrinal, tactical, even ethical debates about the management of this new genus of warfare. The scientific debate waned only in 1963 with the signing of the Partial Nuclear Test Ban Treaty, which prohibited testing in outer space, the atmosphere, and below water, and thus placed an artificial freeze on the pace of technological development. In this way, a procedural device in international law enabled strategic knowledge to match scientific realities; it helped to control the destabilizing effects of the nuclear revolution.

Obfuscation of the Signature of Power

A new technology may increase instability if it complicates the defender's ability to identify correctly and credibly the attacker's location or identity – in other words, if it obfuscates the "signature" of power. Most important, this mask of obscurity diminishes the assailant's expectations of punishment for the attack. Thus it weakens the logic of deterrence by punishment, whereby a conflict is averted because the adversary calculates that the retaliatory cost of the initial attack is higher than the resulting gains. In this way, problems of attribution may increase the chances of a conflict.

Concerns over clandestine nuclear attack illustrate the potential of new technology to produce this problem. A nation that could carry out a secret nuclear attack could inflict massive damage on an adversary while escaping the penalties of nuclear or other severe retaliation. During the 1950s, U.S. military planners anguished over the possibility that the Soviet Union would carry out a nuclear attack whose point of origin would be untraceable: for example, by smuggling a bomb through customs as a commercial artifact, by using a civilian aircraft or merchant ship, or by smuggling pieces of a nuclear device onto national soil that secret agents would then assemble and detonate.[86] Or else, more ingeniously, U.S. officials worried that the adversary would guilefully misattribute the source of its nuclear strike to a rogue unit commander acting independently, thus complicating the moral, diplomatic, and political grounds for retaliation.[87]

As Chapter 7 will discuss, this point reflects a truth about conflict prevention that statesmen who have suffered the anguish of anarchic uncertainty can confirm: deterrence has a psychological and not only a physical element. Not all adversaries are equally willing to run risks. Those whose toleration of risk is higher may find that the obscurity of action that a new technology affords makes the decision to enter into a conflict more attractive than the desire to maintain peace – even if the adversary's physical power of retaliation is great, even if his commitment to use it is unequivocal. In some areas, the psychological interest in initiating a hostile action will be high because the stakes matter to the attacker a great deal. In other areas, the interest of the other side will be so high that the adversary does not attack because he believes that not even uncertainty of attribution will prevent a reprisal. In the case above, for example, because the stakes for the United States were enormous, and the gains for the adversary not nearly so great, it could reasonably expect that any clandestine nuclear attack would produce a general war regardless of the attack's obscure signature.

Alteration of the Offense–Defense Balance

The development of new weapons systems may alter the balance of offensive and defensive forces, with important implications for the security dilemma of anarchic international politics. In a penetrating analysis, Charles Glaser and Chaim Kauffman show that when the ratio of the costs of the attacker's weapons relative to the costs of the defender's weapons is lower, war is more likely. When the opposite situation holds true, war can be averted.[88] Thus advances in weapons systems need not be destabilizing if they create or are perceived to create (the effect is the same) advantages for the defender. One finds in the six major areas of technological impact that Glaser and Kauffman identify as decisive – mobility, firepower, protection, logistics, communications, and detection – a reminder, if ever one was needed, of the emphasis that the Clausewitzian paradigm places on the military applications of new technology.

The clearest example of the destabilizing effects of offensive weaponry is when the perceived advantages of attack are so high and so firmly entrenched in the observers' minds that a "cult of the offensive" arises. Often, the main sources of the cult are cultural and ideological, rather than technological. At the turn of the twentieth century, German military commanders such as Alfred von Schlieffen and Helmuth von Moltke exalted the offense as an absolute virtue. Only a clannish, almost mystical commitment to offensive philosophy could produce the famous dictum, popularized by Schlieffen and widely ingrained in German society, "offense is the best defense."[89] So powerful, in fact, was the dictum's sway in Germany and elsewhere that it annihilated the verities of technology. Different to French Marshal Joseph Joffre's account, for instance, the machine gun in reality aided the defense, not the offense.[90] Terrain, too, mattered: the vast open spaces separating Poland from Nazi Germany gave German Panzer units, in 1939, a fertile ground on which to inflict a swift offensive blow. Switzerland's jagged Alpine wall, by contrast, was penetrable only at great cost, thus diminishing the offensive advantages of mechanized warfare.[91]

Yet in other contexts new technology may be the main trigger of offensive cravings. Hitler was more willing to invade neighboring nations when he perceived that the offense dominated.[92] During the Cold War, American and Soviet strategists sought to acquire for themselves, while denying it to the other side, a nuclear "first-strike" capability that was able to neutralize in a single surprise blow the adversary's ability to respond. Such a prospect, analysts worried, could precipitate a major nuclear conflict, whether because the stronger party decides to realize the expected gains of offense dominance, or because the weaker party launches a preemptive strike before the adversary has deployed the nuclear first strike (assuming knowledge of its imminent creation is not secret).

Increase in the Depth of Power

National security policy strives to protect citizens and their interests from foreign threats. This program of activity has three basic aims: to reduce foreign adversaries' influence in the organization of domestic affairs; to prevent or repulse a remote act of aggression; and – the final aim – to prevent the enemy's presence in the home terrain. New technology that increases the ability of its possessor to inflict harm swiftly and suddenly in the heart of an adversary's society may upset these finely wrought concepts of national security. It may alter logics of conflict in ways that confound analysts and enable strategic surprises.

The emergence of strategic air bombing illuminates the problem. Before the 1930s, warfare had often been confined largely within battle-fields outside of large cities. Ordinarily, urban centers confronted its direct horrors only as a consequence of occupation following the defeat of the defending forces in distant locations. The development of bomber technology during the 1930s dramatically changed this situation. It brought the horrors of industrial-scale warfare to the heart of urban population centers. Worse, during the first decade of this new form of warfare, which the German Luftwaffe and Japanese Imperial Army inaugurated, respectively, over the cities of Guernica in 1937 and Chongqing in 1938, there existed few viable defenses against bomber forces. As the famous maxim of British politician Stanley Baldwin conveyed: "The bomber will always get through." Here, again, is a splendid example of a lag in understanding of new strategic realities born of technological change. Between 1940 and 1941, the Luftwaffe subjected British cities to fierce bombing raids against which the defenders had developed no viable doctrines or means to repulse. Consequently, Germany nearly won the Battle of Britain that raged in

British skies. Only the secret and timely development of a counter-vailing technology – principally the radar, which enabled the British defenders on the ground to detect German aircraft from a distance of up to 120 miles at an altitude of 30,000 feet – by British scientists under the direction of Oxford physicist Frederick Lindemann turned the tide of the epic struggle over Europe's destiny.[93]

Together, or individually, the preceding five pathways of systemic disruption can aggravate the security dilemma of international relations, a perversity of anarchic politics in which the uncertainty produced by the security of one actor provides for the certainty of insecurity in others.[94] Consider, again, the rivalry between Athens and Sparta. It did not matter that the two Ancient powers were bound by a treaty of peaceful arbitration; in the absence of a central authority to oversee the settlement of differences through dialogue, Sparta feared that in the future Athens would possess the means to impose its will by force or threat of arms. Thus the Spartan leaders decided that they had no recourse other than to attack Athens first.[95] The fear of coercion arising from an imbalance of power, the misinterpretation of the principles of war, the anticipation by defenders of nearly anonymous strikes, the temptation of attackers to seize instant gains through offensive action, the prospect for all that adversaries will penetrate deeply into the home terrain – all these factors will cause the relative security of members of the international jungle to rise and fall in ways that increase the chances that the state of nature will collapse into a state of war despite the common interest of all participants to moderate their competition.

Increase in Commercial Flows

Not all forms of technologically induced systemic disruption concern the security dilemma. For example, technology may significantly affect the intensity of economic relations among states. As Robert Keohane and Joseph Nye explained, behind much of the unprecedented rate of economic growth in the developed world were "the remarkable advances in transportation and communications technology, which have reduced the costs of distance."[96] Greater economic interdependence, we saw, can increase the costs of war and reduce the chance that it will break out.

Second-Order Technological Revolution: Pathways to Systemic Revision

New technology can help to drive systemic revision if it significantly strengthens the hand of revolutionary states in the international system; or else if it gives impetus to new forms of interaction among the established units, which give rise to fundamentally new goals and principles among them. The former variety of systemic revision concerns the properties of individual players in the international state of nature; the latter, the properties of the broader system, because it involves beliefs that are held widely among the players.[97]

Empowerment of Revolutionary States

Normally, revolutionary states are born into the ruthless international jungle weakly. Frequently, this position of vulnerability derives from the fact that revolution emerged out of an implosion of the domestic order without which the champions of change could not have seized power. A new technology may be the catalyzing factor behind domestic revolution's internationalization if it empowers the revolutionary state in this moment of weakness or if the technology increases the state's opportunities for subversion after it has secured a place in the states system whose basic principles it spurns.

Consider the French Revolution. For all the muscularity of France's radical foreign policy after 1789, the first years of the Revolution were in fact perilous for the new regime. Evildoers within the leadership bathed their nation and each other in blood as one clique fell to another in a tragic succession of terror and turmoil. Foreign powers intervened militarily to stanch the flow of ideological ferment near their borders. Only the emperor Napoleon's ruthless political guile and military genius – which included masterful use of new technologies of war, such as artillery guns[98] – prevented a victory of counter-revolutionary forces; more than that, his sweeping battlefield conquests thrust Republican values (under the mantle of Empire) upon millions of hapless Europeans who had known only the crude repressions of the *ancien régime*.

Recall, also, the case of Nazi Germany and mechanized warfare. The rise to power of the Nazi Party in January 1933 created a revolutionary threat to international order because the new government in Berlin repudiated the system's basic goals of sovereign coexistence and the limitation of violence. It was the regime's radical ideology, which derived from anti-Semitism and anti-Slavism the justification for a campaign to smash the European states system by military conquest, that defined the revolutionary condition of the epoch. But the threat of Germany's ideological defection from international society was still only theoretical – even if it flashed its face of defiance in the country's withdrawal from the League of Nations as early as October 1933 – for the revolutionary power had few practical means to realize its plan of conquest. It could repudiate but not overturn the prevailing order. Germany's rapid rearming and its superior grasp of mechanized warfare drastically changed that situation.[99] During the early stages of the Second World War, Germany's tank units were able to operate with awesome speed and deliver shock offensives. By contrast, the French perception was full of inhibition: it regarded the tank merely as an adjunct to infantry forces, not as a means of war worthy of independent development.[100] A similar attitude of technological complacency prevailed in Britain. In 1916, Lord Kitchener – Britain's strategic superplanner – dismissed the new invention as "a pretty mechanical toy," adding that "the [First World War] will never be won by such machines."[101] The impression stuck in the preparation for future wars. Although Britain had created, in 1919, the world's first tank regiment, its military commanders shared their French allies' misapprehension of the tank's strategic potential. In 1936, one year after Germany created its first Panzer divisions, the British Army's sole anti-tank weapon was in the hands of a platoon commander who stored it in a truck at headquarters. One injudicious observer held that barbed wire would repulse a tank thrust.[102] French and British military planners failed to decipher both the new strategic realities of mechanized warfare and the strategic and ideological ends to which Germany put it to use. In this way, even though British and French tank forces outnumbered Germany's, Germany was able to defeat the French Army, which many analysts regarded as the world's mightiest military, in just six weeks.[103]

Although domestic political forces, not technology, may be the primary cause of ideological defection in the international system, new technology nevertheless may be a determining secondary factor in the emergence or success of the revisionist program of change. Therefrom stems an important lesson for the ages: more important than superiority in military equipment is superiority in the doctrines and principles that orient its use. Or in language closer to the fashions of our own era: strategic *software* is more important than strategic *hardware*.

Germination of a World Society

Another technological pathway to systemic revision concerns the system's moral order: a technological invention can intensify flows of new ideas and beliefs among political leaders or citizens such that the units' basic purposes and ideals change notably.

An example of this phenomenon is the fostering of a global civil society in which governments consider it a legitimate duty to protect the human rights and interests of individuals abroad. This process of moral awakening may depend not only on the prevalence of such a view in official circles but also on the awareness among citizens of abuses in distant lands. Greater awareness of atrocities and deprivation of rights may itself be an agent of moral change. New technology may increase the level of awareness by intensifying the flow of information and what Barry Buzan and Richard Little call "interaction capacity" among citizens in different nations.[104] Some observers credit the telegraph, for example, with the emergence of an early wave of "moral" globalization that rapidly raised awareness of atrocities in Cuba, Africa, and Asia, and thus elevated the reprehensibility of war during the late nineteenth and early twentieth centuries.[105] Or else the effect could be the reverse: the congealment of close-minded communities of thinking that communicate across national boundaries.

First-Order Technological Revolution: Pathways to Systems Change

Finally, we arrive at the most fundamental phenomenon: technological courses toward systems change, or the reordering of the system's organizational units into a new hierarchical arrangement in which the traditional players are no longer dominant. In the contemporary international context, systems change means the erosion – completely or partly, but still significantly – of the organizing principle of state sovereignty. A technological revolution of the first order may occur in at least three ways.

Creation of a World Leviathan

One concerns advances in weapons systems that alter the balance of power among units so radically that one of them is able to subjugate all contenders completely. This scenario, it is important to realize, is different to unipolarity or world hegemony, in which the hegemon's power and influence are preponderant but not limitless. A hegemon enjoys a position of preeminence in many important areas of international life, such as Britain's dominance over world trade during the eighteenth and nineteenth centuries, but lesser powers have not entirely lost their influence in the management of their own affairs or even the hegemon's. Gangs of Davids can still resist the influence and even subvert the affairs of the Goliath. Without the lesser powers' acquiescence on at least some important matters, the giant cannot govern the international state of nature; at any rate, its sway never extends to all or even most aspects of life in the jungle. Instead, what concerns us here is World Leviathan *à la* Hobbes: a single unit's climb atop the hierarchy of power so high that all other players are not sovereign in the sense that they can define their internal and external dealings free from foreign influence – that is, a loss of the condition of "natural equality" that drives men toward power and competition, a concentration of power within a single player so pure that it is meaningless to speak of all other actors as "units" in the system.

No single technological development has produced this outcome; probably no single invention could ever do so. Yet the phenomenon of the World Leviathan may be observed, at least partly, in the rise of the Roman Empire and its near-total conquest of all other societies in the known world, thus bringing to a close the fractious system of anarchic tribal groupings of fluid and uncertain boundaries that had prevailed on much of the Continent, in northern Africa, and western Asia.[106] Mastery of the principles of military technologies such as siege engines enabled the Roman armies to conquer a vast territory, while innovations in non-military technologies such as the aqueduct helped them to retain it.[107] The prospect of Nazi Germany's acquisition of the atom bomb before the United States once raised the specter of totalitarian world government. In 1939, Nazi Germany initiated a secret nuclear weapons program under the informal direction of Werner Heisenberg following the discovery of nuclear fission by scientists the previous year. The program stalled after 1942 owing to the German scientific community's preference for small research groups and Berlin's focus on short-term weapons development.[108] It is a wondrous question of counterfactual history: how different would the course of international politics and the fate of Western liberal society in particular be had Nazi Germany acquired a deployable nuclear bomb first? Some analysts have answered the question, all direly.[109] Such speculation is not entirely idle: atomic supremacy would have brought the prospect of a World (or a European) Reich closer to realization than real history allowed.[110] We pose the question because it illuminates the difference between, on the one hand, a hegemonic order comprising a large power and lesser sovereign states, and, on the other, a centralized order consisting of a master government and subservient Protectorates, or *Reichskommisariats*.

Creation of a World System

New technology can give rise to a new organizing principle in the modern states system if it empowers alien players to a degree that calls into question the main units' supremacy in the management of their own affairs or in their dealings with each other. In this way, new technology could give impetus to the development of a true *global* system in the sense captured by Hedley Bull's notion of a world system, a milieu that encompasses not merely states but also citizens, nongovernmental groups, transnational entities, and other players who reside outside of the Westphalian machinery.[111] In such a system, not only the interests and actions of states, but also the claims and interventions of other players matter in determining the character and stability of international relations. International order (if states exist at all) can endure in the absence of global order, but because it is never more than a minor subset of global order, there is always a risk that contact between states and other actors will produce disruption rather than complementarity.

Here the nuclear revolution is again instructive. So far, as we saw above, nuclear weapons technology has proven transformative only in the sense of second- and third-order revolution. It empowered revolutionary states and transformed the interstate strategic equation without altering the basic ordering principle of international anarchy, sovereignty, which defines how nuclear powers – even revolutionary states such as the Soviet Union – compete for survival. By contrast, ongoing efforts to deprive terrorist groups of the bomb are motivated by a desire to avert a transformation of the international system's very constitution, because this eventuality would elevate nonstate groups to a position of primacy and possibly supremacy over the state in some core aspects of national security.

Contemplating this scenario does not require a flight of reason. In the summer of 2001, Al-Qaeda leader Osama bin Laden received blueprints of a nuclear weapons program from a Pakistani specialist in uranium enrichment.[112] Were a single extremist militant group to obtain one or two deployable warheads, or just one-tenth of 1 percent of the U.S. and Russian nuclear arsenals,[113] this development would launch a new phase in the nuclear revolution. In the words of Graham Allison, "A single [terrorist] nuclear bomb in a single American city would be a nation-altering event."[114] Conventional logics of deterrence, crisis prevention, and conflict reduction would instantly become obsolescent. Nuclear security would cease to be a matter only of international security; it would also become one of global security.

The main problem for theory posed by terrorists is not that they repudiate (or fail to understand) the basic purposes of international society in the preservation of stability and order. Rather, it is that they do not fit the agent frame of conventional state actors: their leadership structure, organizational relationships, operational habits, geographic locations, communications methods, and avenues of resource acquisition are so fundamentally different from the attributes of states that the traditional apparatus of diplomacy struggles to address them. The threat posed by these players is of a kind that challenges traditional understandings and mechanisms of deterrence, conflict prevention, and conflict termination within the Conventional Model.

Technologically Induced Holocaust

Another conceivable technological shock involves the obliteration of the modern states system through sheer force of violence. This may occur purposefully or accidentally if the awesome power of nuclear weapons is unleashed by their possessors. At present, there are 15,000 deployed nuclear weapons in the world dispersed among nine nations, two of which, the United States and Russia, own 90 percent of the global arsenal. According to a recent scientific study, even a regional nuclear war featuring one hundred nuclear explosions – less than 1 percent of the global arsenal – would release five teragrams of soot into the stratosphere.[115] This is a sufficient amount of debris to screen the sun's light, producing a sudden plunge in the Earth's temperature and damaging one-quarter of the planet's ozone layer.[116] Mass migration and global famine would ensue. In addition, these events may produce the dis-integration of internal state structures. Territorial boundaries would become indistinguishable, national jurisdictions would be rendered meaningless, and local or transnational authorities may become the new agents of a chaotic system of global politics.

Theory in Revolutionary Times

The primary goal of theory in a period of revolution is to normalize it. Until and unless analysts form a clear concept of the nature of the change, strategic quandaries will persist. Worse, they will become graver as the continuance of old policy dogmas extends beyond their period of usefulness. Mastery of the current cyber revolution, therefore, requires a paradigm that clarifies the transforming effects of cyberspace on inter-national order and that orients the design of policy to manage them.

The quest for such a paradigm immediately invites the obstacles of intellectual reactionism: the temptation of international relations specialists to subsume irregular events within familiar abstractions. For theory, like policy habits, has an inertial quality. Intellectually the most fashionable stance is to defend rather than tear down conventional models; to analyze a disturbance of the order in terms of set formulas instead of taking it on its own merits; in short, to normalize revolution by conceptual fiat. One might say of theory what Alexander Herzen said of Russian reactionism: it operates on the confidence that the forces of change will subside in a familiar orderly outcome that only conservatives can foresee. Or as the brilliant scholar of intellectual revolution Thomas Kuhn put it: "The source of resistance [to new theory] is the assurance that the older paradigm will ultimately solve all its problems."[117]

The consequences of theoretical rigidity for the resolution of security problems are profound. The cyber revolution can be mastered only if it is recognized. The criterion of revolution supplied by the Clausewitzian philosophical framework emphasizes changes in the material order, especially the balance of power and the methods of interstate war. This viewpoint can elucidate change within an estab-lished international order of rational states: for example, the effects of nuclear arms on U.S.–Soviet bipolarity and its consequences, in turn, for global security contests. It cannot, however, provide benchmarks to analyze how new technology may profoundly alter the system beyond the rigid parameters of the Conventional Model, that is, the basic purposes of the units or their supremacy next to other players.

This chapter has outlined a more expansive revolutions framework. It distinguished changes in scale from changes in kind. Not all revolutions are equal in transforming potential; in fact, some reflect a basic continuity in international affairs because they leave untouched the established model's defining assumptions. The least severe form of revolution – if it is that – is systemic disruption, or third-order technological revolution. It transpires within the material and social confines of the state-centric universe. A more fundamental form of change, systemic revision, or second-order technological revolution, implies a deep internal reform of this universe. It occurs if new technology empowers a state or group of states that repudiate the basic ends that the dominant units regard as legitimate and which, in the analyst's eye, seemed "rational." Systems change – first-order technological revolution – is the most radical form of transformation, because it affects the system's basic constitution: the traditional supremacy of states over other actors. It happens when technology gives rise to a new class of actors whose motives and aims the units are unable to grasp and whose actions they are unable to control even as they are greatly affected by the alien players. The next part of the book will elaborate on these distinctions as they apply to the contemporary cyber age.

PART II

DEGREES OF THE CYBER REVOLUTION

CHAPTER 4

Third-Order Cyber Revolution
PROBLEMS OF INADVERTENT CONFLICT

Limits of the Revolution

The virtual weapon is a force of systemic disruption in international affairs. The new capability is disturbing regularized patterns of rivalry among rational, self-interested state contenders. There are the problems of instrumental instability: a disturbance of the conventional states system featuring familiar contests for security by the appearance of a largely untested weapon whose use is difficult to model and regulate. Yet even within the narrow bounds of this type of change, the least transforming of the three orders of technological revolution, these effects are limited. They are not of a magnitude that matches the change implied by the great systemic dislocations of the twentieth century – that is, the emergence of two superpowers and the subsequent disintegration of one of them – or of the nineteenth century – the appearance of a German colossus on the world scene.

Thus when speaking about the cyber revolution's third-order effects, it is important to recognize at the outset what this revolution is *not*. We may thereby clarify the true extent of change and in this way correct common misconceptions of the cyber revolution thesis. In other words, we must begin the analysis with three concessions to the skeptical viewpoint.

First, and most important, the virtual weapon is not reconfiguring the balance of power among states. It does not meet the first test principle of systemic disruption that was discussed in Chapter 3. Few new technologies can give secondary impetus to a reconfiguration of the balance of power (mechanized warfare in the early twentieth century is one rare example) and fewer still can cause it primarily (nuclear weapons are an even rarer instance).[1] So far, cyberspace is neither kind of driver of power transition.[2] True, the new capability provides means for a rising nation such as China, a resurgent great power such as Russia, or an aspiring middle power such as Iran to obtain prized industrial and commercial secrets that close the power gap with the preeminent military player in the international system, the United States. Yet the technology is neither the necessary nor even a principal cause of the shifting balance. Other factors such as China's native industrial prowess or Russia's concerted military rearmament efforts are more important. Thus the influence of cyberspace on the balance of power is both secondary and nonessential to it. Nations whose climb up the hierarchy of power is already in train are not likely to benefit from the technology significantly, nor is it likely that waning powers will be able somehow to reverse their relative descent by harvesting cyberspace for strategic gain.

Second, the virtual weapon is an imperfect tool of interstate coercion – a lesser but still important concern of international relations specialists. Paradoxically, the new technology expands the arsenal of mild coercive means that fall short of armed attack, but it has proven only partly effective at forcing adversaries to rethink their policy courses. By averting a possible Israeli airstrike against nuclear enrichment plants in Iran, the destructive Stuxnet operation against the Natanz facility in 2009 may have influenced Iran's decision to sign a nuclear accord five years later; the attacks may have kept open the space for political maneuver among the contenders.[3] The attacks against Estonia in 2007 failed to reverse the country's decision to relocate a Soviet war memorial. Similarly, the blow against Sony Pictures' computer infrastructure in 2014 did not convince the company to suspend the release of a film that personally offended North Korean leader Kim Jong-un; in fact, the strike may have increased viewership of the film.[4]

A third limitation concerns the virtual weapon's effects on the nature of war and conquest – cherished notions, as we saw in Chapter 2, of the Clausewitzian skeptics. Nothing is more damaging to the debate about the existence or not of a cyber revolution than the misreading of the thesis of revolution. Some skeptics have mischaracterized the thesis to mean that cyberspace has revolutionized war. "According to proponents who help construct the discourse of cyber politics in this debate, international interactions are shifting due to the advent of cyber technologies," two analysts claimed, citing this book's author. "The rising fear of cyber combat and threats has brought about a perceived *reorientation in military affairs*."[5] Similarly, they wrote that revolutionists claim that the world is "seeing or will see a proliferation in *cyber war* because digital society will be a logical extension of the security domain."[6]

This is not an accurate portrayal of the cyber revolution thesis. For one thing, there has never been, and possibly there never will be, a true act of cyberwar. For another, let us state plainly (as this author has stated elsewhere)[7] that so far as we can tell, malware is a largely ineffective tool of military victory. Cyberattack can augment but not replace traditional military power. Even in conventional war settings, such as Russia's invasion of Georgia in 2008, it can achieve only partial tactical results. True, some military planners warn that cyberattack could incapacitate advanced weapons systems. For example, initial tests on the U.S. F–35 – the most advanced contemporary fighter plane – showed that this weapon system is vulnerable to some forms of cyberattack.[8] Similarly, Des Brown, the former British Defence Secretary, warned that the country's Trident nuclear submarine fleet was susceptible to an incapacitating cyberattack – despite the naïve comments of some detractors, who observe, for instance, that because the Royal Fleet's command and control functions do not go through the Internet, "I am very comfortable saying that our ... [nuclear] control system is insulated from cyber-attack because it doesn't go into any place the cyber world would intrude."[9] The tactical viability of computer code to impair other weapons systems, however, remains largely unproven. A nation bent on seizing an adversary's physical terrain will find in weaponized code a largely irrelevant instrument. Code is an intangible: it cannot hold any more than it can occupy ground.

Based on the above allowances, we can summarize the skeptical view in the form of a syllogism: the distribution of power among states and their ability to conquer and coerce other states are the maximum concerns of theory. The virtual weapon does not significantly alter these aspects of international rivalry. Hence the cyber revolution is a myth – at least on the narrow conceptual terms supplied by the Conventional Model of the international system.[10]

Let it be stated once and again: theory serves the purpose of understanding empirical realities; these do not serve the purpose of defending theoretical dogmas. According to their own lights, the skeptics are correct in their assessment of essential continuity in interstate strategic dealings. Yet the notion of technological revolution neither begins nor ends logically with the traditionalist syllogism of interstate rivalry. There are still the dangers of accelerating crises and inadvertent conflict. In other words, we must consider not only problems of crisis prevention but also the difficulties of controlling crises that may produce unwanted conflict. Crucially, these dangers exist even if we accept, as we must within the definition of third-order revolution, a central skeptical premise: the unitary rationality of states, or the notion that states seek to maximize their individual gains – primarily in physical, but also in economic security – and that they do so in the character of coherent rational units.[11] Admiral James Stavridis enunciated this concern, referencing the advent of aviation in 1903: "In the world of cyber, we are at the beach at Kitty Hawk. We are just at the beginning. We don't have 100 years [of experience] in cyber [conflict] . . . We have to take steps today to bring order to [this] chaotic world."[12]

This chapter elaborates practitioners' apprehensions about international chaos. Here the concern is not artificial irrationality arising from the intrusions of ideological fervor into decision-making (this is a topic of Chapter 5) or the interventions of unrecognized players (Chapter 6). Instead, the focus is on the problems of the bounded rationality of levelheaded officials struggling to discern "the national interest" among a bevy of possible policy courses in conditions of partial but perpetual uncertainty.[13]

This set of concerns invokes a theme familiar to the theoretician: the nature and requirements of order under conditions of international anarchy – most important, the stability of strategic interactions among states. Everyone knows that international politics transpires in the absence of a constraining authority, which produces incessant rivalry and occasional violence among actors competing for security. The interesting feature of anarchy, however, is not the recurrence of conflict – that is obvious – but its regularity. Although conceptions of national interest differ, even quarreling states recognize the need to preserve order in their security relationships. This recognition underpins states' acceptance of common purposes as well as rules and principles of conduct; it helps to sustain the constancy of anarchic interactions and makes the permanent "state of war" tolerable because its contests for security are in the main regularized.

The cyber revolution upsets this political framework of relations by depriving states of clear "if-then" assumptions that are necessary to conduct a restrained rivalry. The problem is one of third-order technological revolution, whereby accidents and misinterpretation of a new technology destabilize the dealings even of rational state adversaries.[14] Even if it does not alter the balance of power or transform the nature of war, cyberspace is a perfect breeding ground for political and strategic instability. It meets the criteria of four test principles of systemic disruption – those involving technological volatility, the signature of power, the offense–defense balance, and the depth of power.

Technological Volatility

Technology itself is a destabilizing factor: cyberweapons are so novel and the vulnerabilities they seek to manipulate so inscrutable as to impede interpretation of the probable effects of their use. Put simply, it is difficult to know how pernicious code will behave.

One difficulty concerns collateral damage. A poorly designed cyberweapon can cause far-reaching effects beyond the intended target if it infects a large number of third-party machines. The danger of collateral damage is due to the ease and rapidity with which malware travels the Internet. It also arises from the intertwining of many military and communications networks. In the lead-up to the NATO air campaign to depose Muammar Gaddafi in 2011, American officials reportedly weighed the option of using weaponized code to blanket Libya's government communications systems. They decided against the move because this infrastructure was closely entwined with civilian systems.

One important means of limiting collateral effects and of concentrating the force of the blow upon a single system is to customize the malware. The Stuxnet worm illustrates this design feature. It altered the rotor speed of IR-1 centrifuges that were joined to Siemens S7-315 and S7-417 industrial controllers, which governed respectively the plant's Centrifuge Drive System and the Cascade Protection System.[15] The worm's handlers had hoped it would not escape the air gap that enveloped the facility. But like a fish in an open-top tank that is dipped in the sea, the artifact travelled speedily beyond its designated logical habitat, infecting tens of thousands of other machines in more than one hundred countries in less than one year.[16] Newly infected systems included industrial controllers that the worm did not affect because they did not match the precise configuration at Natanz. Thus although the propagation technique (it could infect almost any machine running a Windows operating system) was not customized,[17] the payload that caused physical damage to Natanz's centrifuges was closely tailored to their controller.

Malware customization only partly resolves the problem of unintentional civilian harm. Although it reduces the scope of direct effects beyond the target machine, the attack's indirect consequences can still be enormous if the affected machine (or the secondary activity, such as power generation, that it governs) supports essential social and economic functions. These indirect effects are difficult to model or predict. But the effects of technical errors in stock-trading systems offer a glimpse of the chaos that a major cyberattack on these systems might produce. In the famed "flash crash" incident of May 2010, a design flaw in the "sell algorithm" of a trading house seeking to sell 75,000 mini-contracts prompted a spiraling trade volume and loss of liquidity that saw the value of the Dow Jones fall by nearly 1,000 points in a matter of a few minutes.[18] Two years later, a software error caused the equities trading company Knight Capital Group to issue faulty orders, resulting in losses of $440 million.[19] In July 2015, the New York Stock Exchange halted the trading of $28 trillion worth of equities for nearly four hours because of the discovery of a coding error.[20] None of these technical crashes points to an impending scenario of financial Armageddon, as some alarmists have warned. Yet they reveal the fragility of the underlying technology of modern financial infrastructures. What an inadvertent technical error can cause, a highly customized weapon can multiply several times over. A major and intentional interruption of stock-trading platforms could create psychological reverberations that undermine public confidence in the entire financial system.

A related difficulty is the potential for blowback: the possibility that the negative effects of a cyberattack will be felt by the attacker or its allies, whether through the self-propagative tendencies of malware (causing direct effects on home computer systems) or through cascading economic damage (indirect effects on one's home society).[21] Part of the problem arises because of the interconnectedness of computer systems and networks. Take down servers in Iraq's financial and banking sector and you might also disrupt cash dispensers far away in Europe. This was a real concern of U.S. Air Force military tacticians who rejected a planned cyberattack during the opening stages of the invasion of Saddam Hussein's Iraq in 2003. The problem, Pentagon officials discovered, was that the banking and financial systems that supplied the dictator with cash were joined to a financial communications hub located in France.[22] That same year, in a public show of frustration about the tactical uncertainties of a cyber conflict, the Air Force Chief of Staff, General John Jumper, commented ironically: "Anybody who thinks they've got their arms around information warfare and information operations, please stand up. I'd like the briefing right now."[23]

In the Libyan and Iraqi cases, concerns about collateral damage and blowback were a cause for tactical restraint: the handlers of worms and viruses decided not to unleash them in order to spare civilian populations and allied nations the weapons' indirect effects. Now the petulant skeptic who dismisses the cyber revolution thesis will protest: "The shared norms of anarchic society, the basic concern to impose order out of chaos, these moderating influences prevailed over forces of instability!"

This is true if one considers only the especially restrained character – *extrarational*, if one has to label it – of the Bush and Obama administrations, which though they presided over a rapid expansion of arms, nevertheless heeded the warnings of unwanted escalation associated with their use. The Stuxnet operation we will see below did not provoke Iran to climb the escalation ladder, but it may have accelerated its entry into the new domain with enormous effects in unrelated cases, such as the cyberattacks that devastated tens of thousands of workstations at the oil firm Saudi Aramco three years later. Then there are the conjectural but worrisome dangers of a spiraling conflict following an act of cyberwar that unambiguously satisfies the Clausewitzian criterion – a scenario that the United States has stated may evoke a conventional military reprisal. The absence of clear "conversion tables" to orient interpretation of this so-called equivalence principle could prompt an excessive response from a victim of an attack; a lack of agreed standards of proportionality may produce further unreasonable counter-responses; and all the while, the lack of iterated learning and confidence-building measures could hinder attempts to de-escalate or terminate the crisis. What may begin as a low-intensity cyber exchange could intensify into a major showdown, possibly of conventional proportions.

Another problem concerns the rapid pace of arms development. Advanced malware strains typically have very short life cycles. Some strains have the capacity to update themselves almost instantly upon release. Initially, malicious code featured single, predefined attack vectors. Recently, however, coders have begun to design malware – the so-called compound threat – that is self-adaptive and which combines elements of multiple attack vectors. Adaptability may have several aims, including detection avoidance, attainment of new objectives, the defeat of competitors, and self-preservation against defensive adaptations.[24] Even if the strains of code did not evolve, they would still be enormously diverse. In 2010, the computer security firm McAfee identified ten million unique malware strains.[25] Three years later, the number was ten times higher; on average, a new malware strain appeared every second.[26] Thus it is difficult to foresee what future stages of virtual arms development, even a few years down the line, will herald for defenders seeking to prepare for them or for contenders who do not wish to fall behind in the technological arms race.

Compare this situation with the life cycle of nuclear weapons, which some nations measure in ten-year cycles.[27] In the nuclear realm, the contenders restrained the technology by imposing treaty limitations upon it. The first major accord, the Partial Test Ban Treaty (PTBT) of 1963, prohibited all nuclear detonations above the ground – that is, in the atmosphere – below water, and in outer space. Lest a cunning developer seek to mask a weapons test as a civilian nuclear exercise, the treaty banned *all* explosions that produced radioactive debris. A flurry of other accords ensued, such as the Threshold Test Ban Treaty, which limited the yield of underground explosions to 150 kilotons.[28] The PTBT did not reduce nuclear stockpiles, halt their proliferation, or limit their use in wartime. Indeed, one year after the treaty's signing, China, which still has not signed the accord, conducted 596 explosions. The treaty did not even achieve a reduction in the absolute number of explosions among the signatories. In the ten years following ratification, the United States conducted 408 nuclear explosions, compared to 268 in the preceding decade (the number of Soviet detonations declined to 157 from 218).[29] Nonetheless, the nuclear arms-control regime slowed the development of some new weapons. Although the regime did not seriously impede the superpowers' development of small-yield tactical weapons, it slowed the development of entirely new classes of weapon.[30]

Consequently, nuclear warheads today are not much different or powerful than they were in the 1970s. The United States, in fact, has not introduced new nuclear weapons designs since 1991.[31] Furthermore, some recent innovations in nuclear weapons technology have tended to reduce the yield and potential collateral effects of its use. For instance, the United States' revitalization of the B61 bomb, originally designed in 1963, will reduce its yield by as much as fifty times the explosive power of the bomb detonated over Hiroshima.[32]

The technological freeze mandated by international treaties does not apply easily to the new domain. Cyber arms verification – the chief prerequisite of successful arms control – confronts enormous challenges. The intangibility of the weapons, which exist as information stored in the form of electrons, complicates their detection. In faithful observance of the logic of the security dilemma of international anarchy, parties who agree a meaningful reduction in weapons cannot be certain that one party will not breach the arrangement until it is too late to neutralize the threat of more powerful arms. Weaponized code can be stored in almost any digital device. Thus it is impossible to verify the absence of weapons. And what does weaponized code even look like? Frequently, the presence of a malicious artifact becomes known only after the activation of the payload. Even if inspectors gained precise knowledge of the totality of cyber arsenals, it would be impossible to measure their destructive capacity, for the measurement process itself would reveal the underlying vulnerabilities in the target system that the weapon was designed to exploit. Another complication of arms control relates to test bans. Testing in a simulated environment is essential to build confidence that new code can achieve its intended tactical effects. Before delivering the Stuxnet worm to the Natanz facility, the worm's inventors first tested its effects against a replica of the plant's Siemens-built industrial controller. The test itself was air-gapped; no visible signatures outside the simulated environment were reported. Detection of cyber arms development, therefore, is much harder than in the nuclear realm, in which Soviet Premier Nikolai Bulganin once remarked that an immediate agreement was possible because "any explosion of an atomic or hydrogen bomb cannot . . . be produced without being recorded in other countries."[33] For all these reasons, presently no international limitations exist on the production of offensive cyber artifacts. No such regulatory framework has yet been foreseen.

A further and possibly more significant source of technological volatility concerns not the weapons themselves but the technical terrain in which they operate – cyberspace. Traditional domains of conflict comprise natural terrain that is largely beyond the ability of humans to manipulate. For centuries during the Middle Ages, defenders constructed mounds of dirt or moats of water around prized positions to fend off attackers, but they could not move mountains or relocate seas. Today, China is altering the shape – largely through the movement of sediment from the seabed to reefs – of small, contested islands in the South China Sea that it seeks to possess. But Chinese engineers cannot alter the reach of the Continental Shelf any more than China's competitors in the region can relocate the islands closer to their home shores. Military engineering, in short, is the science of negotiating, not altering or creating, tactical terrain.

Cyberspace, by contrast, is a man-made terrain: it is in principle wholly susceptible to human design. Its configuration in the form of machines and networks as well as society's reliance on them constantly change by force of human intervention in ways that are difficult for strategic planners to divine. Who would have said during the advent of social media in the early twenty-first century that within ten years transnational terrorist groups such as Islamic State would utilize it to recruit, finance, and organize tactical operations in distant lands? And yet no-one today can turn back the dial to the period when social media and its nefarious applications did not exist. As we saw, even more difficult is the task of re-architecting the Internet so that its chief communications protocols – TCP/IP – prioritize security (i.e. the accounting of users and data packets) over the delivery of packets.

Cyberspace, then, exhibits a peculiar combination of features of different stages of the technological life cycle. On the one hand, the technology is in certain respects in the making, because some of its technical properties and social applications constantly evolve in ways that humans control, even if they do not always foresee or understand the implications of these developments for society, politics, and international affairs. On the other, the technology is already in being, because some of its technical features are effectively unalterable. At this point the engineer whose profession excels at shattering the limitations of human endeavor will object, for every engineer knows that any feat is possible – so long as you can pay for it. Yet despite much exaggerated discussion about "re-architecting" the Internet, the design decisions of past generations of technology developers regarding the network's communications protocols, and their underlying security problems, are beyond the ability of policy and institutions to change. Even ingenious venturers such as U.S. Senator Lindsey Graham who eschew email because "they are ahead of their times" may find it impossible to extract themselves wholly from the digital information skin and its security threats.[34]

Cyberspace, and in particular the Internet, exhibit simultaneously the new possibilities of an evolving technology and the old perils of an established technology. Some aspects of this constructed space lie within the realm of practical engineering. Social media, the Internet of Things, machine learning – all of these areas of software and hardware development are susceptible to design changes that can significantly influence patterns of human activity. Other aspects of cyberspace, by contrast, are beyond the practical ability of humans to refashion. Internet communication protocols and the priority they give to the delivery of data packets over their security – these are problems that even the most moneyed engineers struggle to solve.

The Signature of Power: The Attribution Problem

The signature of power in the cyber domain is opaque. Authentication of the location, identity, and motives of an attacker is ordinarily difficult. Often it is impossible. It is not necessary here to review in detail a problem that others have discussed so well elsewhere.[35] A summary of five salient sources of the attribution problem will suffice.

First is the ease of proliferation of cyberweapons (on which more in Chapter 6). Except in the case of the most sophisticated offensive actions, such as the Stuxnet and Sony Pictures attacks, which required the intelligence and other resources of a large state apparatus, the number of plausible assailants is unquantifiable. Second, proving the identity or location of any one of these assailants can be a huge challenge, because cyberspace affords an attacker an inordinate degree of anonymity. Third, where attribution is possible, it may not be of the right kind to organize a punitive response. Knowing the IP address of an attacking machine – the most basic form of technical attribution – does not necessarily reveal the identity of its human handler. Even if it does, this does not mean that the identity and motives of the sponsoring party (e.g. a government or private organization), if there is one, will be divulged.[36] Fourth, because malware crosses multiple national jurisdictions with ease, obtaining forensic evidence in the aftermath of an attack is difficult without effective international cooperation. The distributed denial-of-service (DDoS) attacks against Estonian computer systems in 2007 traveled via machines in more than one hundred nations. A large number of the attacks originated from machines located inside Russia. Two months after the attacks, Estonian officials invoked a bilateral Mutual Assistance Treaty with Russia to seek its help in the forensic investigation of possible Russian assailants. The Russian government, however, rebuffed the request. To date, only a single person has been successfully prosecuted and punished for this incident.[37] Fifth, even if all of these complications are resolved, it is still possible that attribution will not be prompt enough to organize a timely retaliation. By the time their identity and location are known, the perpetrators may have relocated beyond the ability of the victim to respond.

One important consequence of the attribution problem is that it weakens deterrence by reducing an assailant's expectation of unacceptable penalties.[38] Moreover, because reprisal in the absence of convincing attribution incurs legitimacy costs for the retaliator, acceptable options following a failure to deter may be limited. Another notable consequence is that the defender may misattribute the source of aggression to a machine that is in fact not involved because the attacker employs spoofing software that alters the attack indicators (e.g. the IP address), or because the defender correctly attributes the source or transit point of the attack but the identified machine is in fact innocent since the attacker has hijacked it (e.g. if the attacker uses malware to recruit "zombie" machines in a botnet). Chapter 7 of this book will revisit in greater detail problems of deterrence in the new domain.

A further complication arising from attribution difficulties concerns political opportunism: it gives skillful political insurgents room to maneuver when for reasons of self-interest they wish to question credible claims of authorship of an operation.

As Chapter 8 will discuss, in July 2016 the media reported that unknown agents had hacked the email servers of the Democratic National Committee (DNC). The intruders released on the Internet the records of communications involving the DNC's chairwoman,

Debbie Wasserman Schultz. Although Schultz's function demanded strict neutrality with respect to the candidates in the party's presidential race – a heated contest between establishment figure Hillary Clinton and insurgent Bernie Sanders – the leaked emails revealed Schultz's salacious and derogatory remarks about Sanders' staff members.[39] The accuracy or not of this impression did not matter. Nor did the veracity of the statements in the email contents (sharp observers have noted that the intruders could easily alter them). For the impression stuck among many Sanders sympathizers that the party's leadership was partial to Clinton and thus tarnished its image among millions of potential supporters of Clinton in her subsequent presidential campaign against Donald Trump.

Regardless of whether this embarrassing episode tipped the scales of the race in favor of Trump, the impression also stuck in many quarters that the hacking operation represented an unprecedented subversion of the U.S. electoral process by a foreign power. The U.S. intelligence community roundly affirmed that Russian state agents, in particular the GRU, a military intelligence unit, perpetrated the hack to enhance the chance of victory of the Republican Party candidate, whom the Kremlin viewed as potentially friendlier toward Russia than Clinton.[40]

Yet Trump immediately invoked the common difficulties of attribution to undermine public confidence in their findings. In January 2017, the incoming president claimed to have intimate knowledge of hacking. He emphasized the difficulties of identifying culprits.[41] As he said during the presidential campaign, they could have been Russian or Chinese agents, or "lots of other people" – even a single person operating out of his bedroom.[42] It was simply impossible to know who seized the DNC email records. He repudiated, moreover, the intelligence agencies' account of the motives of the operation.[43] Thus a political novice but skillful insurgent threw the public perception into doubt about a matter that intelligence analysts had firmly resolved.

More fundamentally, the attribution problem hinders the emergence of stable processes of strategic learning. In a groundbreaking analysis of international cooperation drawing on game theory, Robert Axelrod showed that sustained cooperative patterns can evolve under conditions of anarchic uncertainty if the players, which he assumes are rational, engage in iterated "tit-for-tat" games. These games allow players who doubt or do not know each other's intentions and habits to learn, imitate, and select certain forms of behavior that prove mutually rewarding. Over time, a lasting structure of cooperation can appear that limits the potential for miscalculation and unwanted conflict – not to the point that the players have eradicated all trace of the security dilemma, because in the system of international anarchy this is not possible, but nevertheless to a sufficient degree that their cooperative dealings are notably improved. This logic of iterated cooperation has produced, for example, fewer arms races, localized conflicts, and trade wars.[44] Crucially, the learning pathways require that the players know each other's identities, on which they build reputations. Reciprocity is another important mechanism of the learning process: it enables players to build durable expectations of future conduct. As Axelrod puts it, "For cooperation to prove stable, the future must have a sufficiently large shadow. This means that the importance of the next encounter between the same two individuals must be great enough to make defection an unprofitable strategy when the other player is provocable. It requires that the players have a large enough chance of meeting again and that they do not discount the significance of their next meeting too greatly."[45] Axelrod's brilliant exposition of the logic of cooperation by the accumulation of experience was also reflected in the thinking of two other celebrated strategic thinkers, Thomas Schelling and Morton Halperin, who theorized that contenders caught in the incertitudes of anarchic life often reach a tacit understanding of acceptable behavior rather than agreeing formal accords.[46]

The ordinary obscurity of the players' behavior in the cyber domain complicates the crafting of stable reputations and the implementation of reciprocity. In effect, the murky signature of power dissipates the shadow of the future of interactions. Possibly, a partial version of iterated games can develop on the basis of imperfect certainty of attribution for cyber conduct. But any such cooperative dynamic will constantly face the problem that at any given time, players can find ways to violate the relationship that do not implicate them even partially – for instance, if a "defector" (in the language of game theory) convincingly spoofs his identity to make the victim of attack believe that the defector is in fact another player. Paradoxically, in a nascent cooperative scheme, the higher than normal expectation of mutual cooperation may increase the chances of defection if it leads players to believe that the climate of cooperation will diminish the likelihood of accusations of defection for actions that can be only imperfectly attributed.

The Offense–Defense Balance

For reasons enumerated in the preceding chapter, the offense holds the advantage over the defense in the cyber domain. This has brought about a revolution in the preservation of strategic stability among state contenders. This dimension of revolution can be understood only if one notes a number of important distinctions.

We can distinguish *degrees* of offensive advantage: it can come in the form of superiority or dominance. If the offense holds a notable but not overwhelming advantage, then its position over the defense is ascendant only to a degree; it is superior but not wholly dominant. The attacker may reasonably expect (or unreasonably deny) but cannot be certain that an attack will succeed. Minor interventions by the defender or extraneous circumstances may foil it. The same might be said of the defense: its relative position is superior if the defender can expect with some but not full confidence that it will thwart an attack. This situation of ascendancy is illustrated, in this case in favor of the defense, by the U.S. Patriot missile system: it achieved a success rate of approximately 60 to 65 percent against Iraqi missiles targeting Israel and Saudi Arabia, respectively, in the 1991 Gulf War.[47]

If, however, the degree of advantage is clearly overwhelming, then the position of the offense is dominant. The attacker can estimate with a total or high degree of confidence that the attack will prevail regardless of the defender's moves or external factors. Similarly, the defensive position is dominant if both sides of the conflict can reasonably anticipate with a high measure of confidence that the defender will prevail in a confrontation.[48] The situation of dominance is demonstrated, again for the defense, by Britain's radar-guided weapons, consisting of the SCR 584 radar and 90mm gun, which neutralized 95 percent of German V–1 cruise missiles during the Second World War.[49]

The *type* of advantage also matters. At one end of the spectrum are tactical advantages: those that may produce success in a limited offensive action. In 1428, the Earl of Salisbury obliterated the walled defenses of Orléans with siege cannon, yet his forces failed to conquer the French city due to the arrival of substantial French reinforcements. The advantage of cannon over walls was in this case tactically significant but strategically negligible. At the other end are strategic advantages: those that by themselves (or largely by themselves) may enable victory in a setting that transcends the immediate terrain of battle.[50] In the spring of 1940, German Panzer divisions under the command of General Heinz Guderian ripped through France's northern defenses with awesome speed and shocking surprise, helping to produce the defeat – in just six weeks – of what many contemporary military observers regarded as the mightiest army in the world. In both of these cases, the offensive technology in question enjoyed overwhelming advantages over the defense. Yet in the first case the advantage conferred only a tactical gain of little strategic value; in the second, it enabled a succession of tactical victories that yielded a decisive blow in a global clash of nations.

One must also consider the *persistence* of the advantage (whether superiority or dominance). The attacker's position of advantage may be tenable because the offensive capability is so novel that defenders struggle to understand how to craft viable defenses against it or because the implementation of this knowledge in the design of defenses is slow. During the mid-1930s and early 1940s, as we saw in Chapter 3, strategic bombers enjoyed a brief period of dominance against ground and air defenses, as testified by the reduction of Chongqing, Guernica, and numerous English cities to rubble by Axis air forces. These tactical wins did not evolve into strategic victories for Japan or Germany, however, for the dominance of offensive bombers was short lived. Technological advances in radar and fighter planes and their integration into British defensive doctrine by military planners such as Air Chief Marshall Hugh Dowding – an early champion of fighter squadrons – reversed this situation in favor of the defense. In other cases, however, the position of advantage is perishable because viable defenses are quick to materialize or because the usefulness of the offensive tactic itself is quick to expire. We must distinguish, further, the position of advantage held by a *whole class* of weapon and the position of advantage enjoyed by a *specific* deployed instrument. As a class of offensive weapon, nuclear weapons have broadly enjoyed an advantage over the defense during their entire existence – hence the robustness of the stabilizing logic of mutual assured destruction. Yet over time, the advantage of specific kinds of nuclear systems has expired: for instance, the B-36 Peacemaker, a U.S. propeller-driven strategic bomber, was almost impossible to intercept until Soviet-built MiG fighter jets rendered it obsolescent in the 1950s.[51]

What degree, type, and persistence of advantage does cyber offense enjoy? The advantage is dominant, strategic, and perishable. Some forms of advanced malware are dominant because there exist few – possibly no – viable defenses against them. Most security experts recognize that even the ablest defender cannot neutralize, if he can even detect, the actions of advanced persistent adversaries. Recall that a unique feature of the virtual weapon is its ability to inhabit a computer system undiscovered, thus enabling the attacker to outmaneuver the defender even on his own terrain. At the same time, many attack tools are offensively weak. The UK National Audit Office estimates that simple defensive measures by individual users, such as routine changes of account passwords and the updating of virus definitions, can neutralize 80 percent of low-grade actions, such as some "phishing" attacks, which seek to obtain users' sensitive data by masquerading as a friendly or harmless agent or by using "brute force" techniques to decipher account passwords.[52] Thus it would be wrong to assign a degree of offensive dominance to the virtual weapon as a class of weapon. Notably, however, the offense enjoys a position of dominance where it matters most to international relations specialists: in the realm of sophisticated attacks by state players.

The type of advantage is strategic: states may employ cyberweapons to achieve or facilitate momentous gains in foreign policy. For example, the destruction of almost one thousand uranium-enrichment centrifuges in the Stuxnet operation may have decisively influenced Iran's decision to sign, in 2016, a nuclear pact with the P5+1 nations (i.e. the five permanent members of the UN Security Council – the United States, Russia, China, Britain, and France – plus Germany), by which the country effectively suspended its native ability to produce nuclear weapons.[53]

Again, the querulous skeptics will voice complaints. The Stuxnet operation, they will observe, did not significantly curtail Iranian nuclear enrichment. In fact, it may even have enhanced the activity because it caused Iran to replace the antiquated IR-1 centrifuges with a superior model.[54]

This view is correct; it is also misguided. The fixation on Stuxnet's limited direct effects should not obscure its greater indirect effects, which included the fear in Tehran that Iran's nuclear establishment had been deeply penetrated by enemy agents, real or virtual. By some accounts, these indirect effects may have retarded the Iranian bomb by as much as three years. They may also have eased Iran's path to the negotiating table in a moment of sharp international tension. To be sure, these kinds of strategic gains do not rise to a level that significantly influences the global balance of power. Nonetheless, they may confer on the attacker benefits that carry over to political and diplomatic arenas, as in the Iranian case, whose significance far transcends cyberspace.

The advantage enjoyed by advanced cyberweapons is generally durable but specifically perishable. Remember that nothing in the observable record credibly suggests that defensive costs are diminishing. This advantage, however, applies to advanced computer code in the abstract; it may not carry over to specific weapons such as the Stuxnet worm. Indeed, all three main components of weaponized code – knowledge of zero-day vulnerabilities, access vectors, and the payload – ordinarily have a narrow window of usefulness. The defender may discover the target system's vulnerabilities and entry points before the attacker deploys the weapon. Or else another attacker may exploit the weaknesses before the original attacker. Alternatively, the defender may simply upgrade his system with software and hardware components that no longer feature these weaknesses, rendering the customized payload obsolete. Moreover, there is the problem that once the attacker has used the weapon, the target system's weaknesses will become known to the defender or to a third party, who will patch them. The virtual weapon, therefore, is often a single-use capability.[55]

This peculiar combination of characteristics – dominance, strategic usefulness, and perishability – exacerbates the security dilemma of international anarchy in at least three ways.[56] First, the recognition of offense dominance has instigated an arms race as states seek to avert strategic upsets in the new arena of conflict. According to some accounts, possibly based more on deductive conjecture than on verifiable intelligence, the fifteen largest militaries are developing advanced cyber weapons systems.[57] The true figure may be far higher. For who can tell how many nations possess or are developing advanced virtual stockpiles? Recall that the capability is an intangible. Because it is nearly massless, it has almost no physical signature to aid detection. Even when it penetrates the defender's terrain, he may not know of its existence.

Second, the perceived advantages of offensive use elevate the chances that those in possession of an advanced virtual weapon will actually employ it. As more cases of successful high-impact cyberattack become known, its gains will become a matter of proven record rather than reasoned conjecture. Other nations will have taken note of the tactical and strategic returns of Stuxnet. They may consider similar policy adventures in the future. In fact, the general reluctance of the Bush and Obama administrations to disclose or claim offensive actions may reflect a desire to conceal the strategic returns of a still largely unproven capability to which the American economy and society are immensely vulnerable.[58] Before Stuxnet struck in 2009, Iran's arsenal of weaponized code was vacant or negligible. The Iranian cyber army's chief capacities were in the area of surveillance. Its main preoccupation was the monitoring and interception of the "Green Movement," a popular uprising that engulfed the nation's urban centers in 2009. The dazzling spectacle at Natanz altered these priorities and activities. Within three years, in the summer of 2012, Iranian agents reportedly disrupted U.S. financial operations with DDoS attacks, which some American officials regarded as a muted retaliation for Stuxnet.[59] Later that year, Iranian agents crafted the "Shamoon" virus that incapacitated about thirty thousand machines at Saudi Aramco, the world's largest oil firm. Thus it was not long before the despair and embarrassment of Natanz evolved into a recognition that the new technology's offensive dominance afforded its possessors a new capacity for potent action in foreign policy.

A third and graver problem concerns the use of active defense, a class of proactive measures that involves preemption or prevention of cyberattack by infiltrating or disrupting an opponent's computer systems (Chapter 9 will discuss this problem further).[60] Cyber artifacts are most easily detected in transit, by which time it may be too late to neutralize them. Therefore, the existence of a wide defensive gap has produced a tendency among the most capable players toward the persistent and absolute penetration of adversaries' computer systems. Both the American and British governments operate mass surveillance programs. Officials at U.S. Cyber Command have boasted that they can penetrate almost any computer system in the world. The revelations of covert surveillance programs by Edward Snowden in 2013 show that Washington has put this claim to wide practice abroad. In 2016, the British Parliament passed the so-called Snoopers' Charter that will expand the foreign surveillance powers of the electronic spy agency, Government Communications Headquarters (GCHQ).

Some observers like to claim that such systematic programs of privacy infringement show that the state has become dominant in private life. This is a mischaracterization of the current situation. The compulsion to engage in surveillance is a reflection of the defender's anguish. It gives credence to the presumption that "malware will always get through" (to purloin Stanley Baldwin's claim about strategic bombers) – hence the necessity to know at all times and in all places the adversaries' intensions, capacities, and moves.

Active defensive measures obscure the offense–defense boundary in weapons systems. The problem inheres in the multistage character of advanced offensive operations. These require deep knowledge of design vulnerabilities in the target system. Unless the attacker can purchase them in the arms market, which though common is not always possible, he will have to seize them by exploitative action – the initial stage of the offensive campaign.

Yet the defender may fail to distinguish the final purpose of exploitation. Is it solely intelligence gathering? Is it to "prepare the battlefield" for future offensive action? Is it to prepare the home terrain to deny an attack? The defender may not know. As U.S. Director of National Intelligence, James Clapper remarked: "Foreign actors are reconnoitering and developing access to US critical infrastructure systems, which might be quickly exploited for disruption if an adversary's intent became hostile."[61] Intelligence gathering by itself is neither offensive nor defensive. A defender cannot read intent clearly from exploitative code. An opponent who has entered your network may have done so for reconnaissance, espionage, or preparation for defensive or offensive operations.

Only the nature of the payload can reveal the true tactical intent of the action. But when the defender uncovers the exploitation code, the attacker may not yet have inserted the payload into the target machine. Alternatively, the payload may already have arrived but remains undetected. Consequently, a defender who discovers an intelligence-only exploitation operation may misconstrue it as the preliminary stage of an overt attack, producing pressures for an accidental exchange of blows. "Think of this in terms of the Cuban missile crisis," one senior American defense official intoned following the discovery by FireEye, a cybersecurity company, of a systematic cyber espionage outfit in China targeting U.S. technology developers, military contractors, and energy firms. "[T]he last thing we would want to do is misinterpret an attack and escalate to a real conflict."[62]

The Depth of Power: Conflict at the Speed of Electrons

Strategic depth in the new domain barely exists: the time between the detection and impact of a hostile action is ordinarily extremely short.

The speed at which code can travel and execute eliminates temporal limitations to the infliction of harm across national borders. The new capability pushes the upper speed of weapons systems from Mach 20, the speed of the fastest intercontinental ballistic missiles, to the velocity of electrons.

Consequently, the interaction domain of a cyber conflict unfolds in milliseconds – an infinitesimally narrow response time for which existing crisis-management procedures, which move at the speed of bureaucracy, are not adequate. The attacker, to be sure, also faces bureaucratic encumbrances. But he has the advantage of being able to preselect the initial, and possibly decisive, moves in the conflict before it begins. This is particularly true of a multistage cyberattack involving the preliminary intrusion of the defender's terrain. The longer the enemy resides inside the target system undetected, the more information on its design and the defender's habits he is able to obtain and the greater will be his opportunities to derive tactical gains in the actual battle. The defender, by contrast, faces immediate policy hurdles. Who has the tactical capacity to respond? To whom does the authority to initiate the response belong? What retaliatory action, if any, is adequate?

In answering these questions, traditional precedents that regulate the role of government agencies in the conduct of national defense can be difficult to interpret in a cyber emergency. And even where the necessary tactical action is known, the authority to initiate it may be unclear; or else the ability of operational and command structures to implement it may not exist. To illustrate, the U.S. National Security Agency (NSA) has authority to defend and retaliate against foreign-based cyberattacks, but it may lack access to the forensic data necessary to tailor a timely defensive response if such information resides in private computer systems or in foreign jurisdictions. "I can't defend the country until I'm into all the networks," remarked NSA Director Keith Alexander in 2013.[63] Once again, the government's drive to monitor civilian networks is a sign of weakness, for in the absence of threat information therein, it cannot mount a full defensive strategy.

Private actors have few means to carry out a response, particularly of a punitive kind, against an attacker who is located in one or multiple nations. Or else their affected computers and servers may reside in several foreign jurisdictions. In August 2013, culprits in the Syrian Electronic Army, a foreign group sympathetic to President Bashar

Al-Assad, attacked the domain name registrar of *The New York Times*, crashing the newspaper's website for several hours. In another intrusion earlier that year, malware of Chinese origin could have "wreaked havoc" on the company's news coverage during the night of the 2012 U.S. presidential election. Yet in neither instance could the publisher have taken independent action – legally or effectively – against the culprits in Syria, China, or wherever else they may have resided.

Another incident that smashed through multiple borders of the rigid Westphalian system were the cyberattacks in December 2014 against Sony Pictures. Their political master, North Korea's supreme leader Kim Jong-un, was in Pyongyang. The perpetrators reportedly routed the attack via computer infrastructure located in northeastern China. The firm and its affected machines were located in the United States. Its parent company, the technology conglomerate Sony, was based in Japan. Upon which government did responsibility for the reply reside – the United States, Japan, or both? Which nation – North Korea, China, or both – should have been the object of punitive measures? In the midst of the unfolding crisis Michael Lynton, Chief Executive Officer of Sony Pictures, observed: "We are the canary in the coal mine, that's for sure. There's no playbook for this, so you are in essence trying to look at the situation as it unfolds and make decisions without being able to refer to a lot of experiences you've had in the past or other people's experiences. You're on completely new ground."[64] Much the same might have been said of the frequently clueless international relations specialist.

The implementation of automated responses, or "tactical fires," can go far toward restoring strategic depth. Automation is already a common feature in the detection of weaponized code. Conventionally, however, the defeat of sophisticated weapons requires the intervention of engineers, a process that can take months to complete if the code is especially intricate or if the vulnerabilities it exploits are unclear. The retaliatory response, too, requires a human decision-making process that must weigh policy, legal, ethical, and institutional considerations. In 2014, DARPA, the same Pentagon agency that funded the ARPANET, the modern Internet's precursor, launched a program to develop software that could repair itself automatically.[65] A similar program seeks to automate responses to distributed denial-of-service attacks, which work by overwhelming computer services by flooding them with information. Cloud computing infrastructure, for example, currently relies on centralized servers and data centers that make it more difficult to defend against DDoS. The new program seeks to disperse and disguise the cloud facilities and networks during an attack in order to degrade it.[66]

That is not all: the government is also striving to automate some active defense functions. The NSA is reportedly developing a capability – MonsterMind – that can instantaneously and autonomously inflict a retaliatory blow on a foreign attacking machine. Details of the weapon system are shrouded in official secrecy. But former CIA contractor Edward Snowden believes that it will operate by inferring the origins of an attacking machine from patterns of metadata, or data that describe other data (e.g. geotagged coordinates).[67]

The goal of automated defenses is to raise the speed of defense to the speed of machine learning – in short, to improve strategic depth. But by removing the human agent from the response procedure, it introduces unknown risks of inappropriate reaction. Machines may fare no better, and may even be worse, than human decision-makers at calculating correctly the direct and indirect damage that a defensive response causes if it involves action outside the defender's computer terrain.

The limitations inhere in the nature of machine learning on which this determination rests: the decision-making algorithms contain a set of assumptions about goals they must pursue and about the workings of the world in which they pursue these goals. These assumptions are by definition no more accurate or credible than are the thoughts of the designers who programmed them. Moreover, because advanced algorithms often employ thousands of parameters that the machines must consider comprehensively, the designers themselves may not fully comprehend the behavior and consequences of their own inventions.

Escalatory Dangers

Together and individually, the forces of systemic disruption in the cyber domain produce risks of an unwanted or accelerating conflict among contenders who wish to avoid it. The technology's volatility complicates the design of models to contain a conflict within tolerable bounds. Players in a cyber conflict may never command good knowledge of the consequences of their tactical moves, as American decision-makers discovered when considering cyberattacks against Saddam Hussein's financial infrastructure or against Muammar Gaddafi's communications systems. The superiority of offensive arms creates pressures for their acquisition and use – whether preemptively if the adversary has them, preventively if he is acquiring them, or opportunistically if he possesses them to seize a one-off advantage. Obfuscation of the signature of power increases the chances of wrongful retaliation and limits the opportunities for iterated learning, which is the main prerequisite for the emergence of stable cooperative mechanisms. Poor strategic depth gives impetus to the automation of conflict – a trend that carries the dangers of machines fighting machines at machine speed.

Traditionally, an international crisis could be averted through confidence-building measures such as established signaling procedures and diplomatic "hotlines." Failing that, common rules and norms could still provide a minimum measure of expectations and moderating behavior. These safety valves disappear when dealing with a cyberattack. Signaling of intentions becomes murky; channels of communication break down or vanish; shared norms are rudimentary or unenforceable; and the identity, motives, or location of an attacker may not be known. Moreover, the tactical and strategic ambiguities of the related technology impede attempts to design escalatory models for the full spectrum of conceivable cyber conflict. Unclear conversion tables to guide the implementation of the equivalence principle or to orient autonomous agents could prompt a spiral of excessive response among attackers and victims. Such a crisis could be set in motion by cyber exploitation if the defender misconstrues it as a step in preparation for attack and instigates a preemptive blow.

What does this situation mean for analysts? Before all it demands a recognition of the stakes at play. That the real dangers of an accelerating crisis have evoked restraint – so far – among some great powers does not mean that theoreticians can dismiss escalatory risks in the new domain as speculative or that they can desist from orienting the design of policies to control them. Instead, they give a special urgency to the harangues of officials who from the gallery of the Congress of Disciplines warn tirelessly of the prospect, never inevitable but also not remote, of a major showdown that even the most prudent participants in the international jungle may find difficult to control.

CHAPTER 5

Second-Order Cyber Revolution
THE PROBLEM OF THE REVOLUTIONARY STATE

Technology and the Revolutionary State

The virtual weapon influences not only the strategic dealings of rational states, which the previous chapter considered, but also the behavior of revolutionary states. Thus we arrive at the problem of how new technology fuels ideological defection, or what the revolutions framework presented in Chapter 3 labeled systemic revision: the presence and activity in the international system of subversive units who, in pursuance of unorthodox ideologies, whether the whims of a single dictator or the extremist ideals of a state or a group of states, behave in a manner that challenges the basic political framework of international society, the fundamental values and institutions of which they repudiate.

Again, as in the preceding analysis, let us begin with a concession to the skeptical viewpoint. New technology is not ordinarily the primary cause of systemic revision. A historically more important cause has been a domestic revolution that acquired an international ambition or following.

Consider the appearance on the world scene of Soviet Russia in 1917. The Bolsheviks repudiated the dignified customs of diplomacy and denounced the bourgeois capitalist state – its bureaucracy, its army, its economy – as an instrument to oppress the toiling masses. Eschewing the niceties of European statecraft and exalting the working class, a true transnational community with a distinct if sluggish consciousness, as a superior basis for organizing international relations, they appealed to foreign laborers over the heads of their own leaders. Yet despite Russian Communists' ideological fervor against established diplomatic conventions, despite their abstract yearning for a stateless society, theirs was not a political revolution of the first order. Unlike the programs of universal conquest of Napoleon or Hitler, Russia's new leaders did not pursue a generalized war aimed at liquidating the nation state within a World (or European) Leviathan.[1] Instead, the Communist creed was for the Russians largely an instrument of the national interest. They recognized the imperative of strengthening their transformed state within a larger and almost universally hostile states system, some of whose basic conventions – trade agreements, bilateral treaties, international organizations, and so on – they grudgingly adopted following the setbacks to world revolution in 1920–21.[2] Soviet Russia (and from 1922, the Soviet Union) were not agents of systems change. They accepted the necessity of a fragmented political system built around the organizing principle of sovereignty. As Lenin observed of Bukharin in a denunciation that later applied generally to the Soviet ruling class, "Scratch a Russian Communist and you will find a Russian chauvinist."[3]

Yet the Soviet entity was revolutionary in other ways: it was an agent of second-order revolution, or systemic revision. Its ideology and autocratic character gave shape to a foreign policy that defied core international principles and institutions. Leon Trotsky, the People's Commissar, displayed a revolutionary zeal in his astounding revelation in 1917 of the secret treaties of the Tsarist and Provisional governments, which exposed their complicity in imperialist dealings and annexationist cravings. This act may not be surprising in today's era of WikiLeaks, but in those times it challenged the integrity of government and the cherished customs of diplomacy.[4] More fundamentally, succeeding generations of Soviet leaders, beginning with Stalin, discarded received principles of international conduct by repeatedly invading nations that they sought to reduce to a Communist servility – Finland in 1939, the Baltic states in 1940 (and again in 1944), Hungary in 1956, Czechoslovakia in 1968, Afghanistan in 1979. In this context, we can stress the importance of Moscow's aspiration to world revolution.[5] Although it took a back seat to the consolidation of the Soviet state in the Westphalian order, it remained a centerpiece of the Soviet worldview and motivated a foreign policy that strived to refashion smaller neighbors in the master's bizarre image of itself. This was not a unit whose vision of itself and of its place in the world theorists today could easily squeeze into the tidy Conventional Model of international relations, no matter how hard they tried.[6]

In this ideological endeavor, new technology – the nuclear bomb – was a secondary but nevertheless crucial enabling factor. The Soviet Union's acquisition of a fission bomb in 1949 cast a tremor over East–West rivalry that enabled Moscow to carve out its sphere of influence by force without fear that Western nations would thwart its military designs. But nuclear technology had also a restraining effect on Soviet expansionism. As David Armstrong explains, "Nuclear weapons made accommodation with the capitalist powers an urgent long-term necessity rather than a short-term dialectical tactic."[7] It was not nuclear or some other technology in the end that drew a curtain on the Communist Revolution and its chief agent. Rather, this came about largely because of internal political forces: notably, the rise to power in 1985 of Mikhail Gorbachev, who embraced the principles of international society, as revealed for example by his celebrated decision not to veto the United Nations resolution that endorsed the American invasion of Iraq – a Cold War ally of Moscow – following its illegal annexation of Kuwait in 1990. In sum, the relationship between the Communist and nuclear revolutions shows that transforming technology can fuel or restrain, but not by itself instigate or overturn, a concerted program of systemic revision.

We can observe a similar pattern of effects in the virtual weapon's impact upon the conduct of North Korea – the quintessential revolutionary state in our times, more so even than the Soviet Union was in the last century, because the cult of Lenin and Stalin never acquired the dynastic character that has perpetuated the House of Kim through generations. North Korean leaders have fanned antagonisms both regionally and globally in order to disturb international stability. They seek to score political points at home by instigating chaos abroad. In this program of foreign subversion, they have benefited from the widening scope of strategic maneuver that the virtual weapon affords: the peculiar methods of unpeace, or what Chapter 2 described as harmful activity that falls legally and conceptually below the threshold of war, though it may inflict more economic and political harm than a single act of war, and whose effects seem less tolerable to ordinary participants in the international jungle than the familiar means of peaceful rivalry.

A caveat is in order: the development and use of an advanced cyber arsenal has not elevated North Korea to the top rank of global powers, nor could it ever do so. It has not allowed the nation to close the capabilities gap among the three powers which surpass it in raw military manpower (China, the United States, and India) or to match the tactical sophistication of the smaller but nimbler conventional forces of its eternal foe, South Korea.

But as the analysis below will argue, the new capability enables North Korea's leaders to pursue their revolutionary goals of regime preservation – and its attendant foreign policy of subversion – within an almost universally hostile international milieu. The destructive attacks against the computer infrastructure of Sony Pictures Entertainment in December 2014, one of the most spectacular cyberattacks to date, and other bold actions by North Korea show that this revolutionary state uses cyberspace for three notable purposes: to seize economic and financial assets in order to offset economic woes; to undermine its foreign foes' confidence in their own superior economic and military institutions; and to suppress foreign ideological influences that may threaten the revolutionary regime's ability to survive. Crucially, because such actions entail the techniques and consequences of unpeace, the regime can pursue its subversive aims without ever resorting to war, thus evading its certain severe penalties. To understand North Korea's audacious and largely unrestrained use of the new weapon we must first review the origins and peculiar features of the revolutionary program that drives it.

The House of Kim: Profile of a Revolutionary State

An assessment of North Korea's unusual place in the international milieu must begin with this assumption: it is a revolutionary state. Its history foreshadows the magnitude of the problem that it has become for regional and international stability. Its repeated incendiary actions illustrate vividly the challenges of restraining a revolutionary state's development and use of a new technology that lends itself easily to ends of political disorder.

Born out of the conflagration of the Second World War and hardened by the brutal Korean War, this small nation recognizes, like all other states, the imperative of state survival – but only its own and, more specifically, the regime's survival. It repudiates in principle the other states' common desire to sustain a minimum measure of stability and peace in their strategic relations. Its aversion to major war with its chief rivals, the United States and South Korea, rests on self-preservation and fear, not adherence to shared values. Political chaos and overt threats of armed attack, not artful diplomacy and commercial dealings, are the primary instruments of North Korea's distinct brand of foreign policy.

A visitor to this peninsular nation would encounter a bizarre world of intense political cultishness and extreme social deprivation. The most autarkic economy on the planet, one where ordinary shoppers must purchase products they have not browsed on shelves,[8] it receives some manufacturing, energy, and food transfers from its main ally, China, and in times of crisis also from the hated enemies. Yet as a matter of official state religion, the regime champions the philosophy of "Juche," or self-reliance, a belief system that, as one observer put it, "is comparable to a theology" in "a society that exhibits many characteristics of a religious community."[9] This official creed prescribes for its forced and hapless believers a near-total severance from the global economy. During the Cold War, North Korea did not deign to join the Soviet-led Council for Mutual Economic Assistance (COMECON), an international grouping that sought to foster economic ties among socialist states as diverse as Cuba and Albania. It never formally aligned itself with the Eastern bloc, despite enjoying its diplomatic protections.[10] North Korea, in short, is the contemporary world's ultimate ideological defector: it not only defies but also resides, insofar as it can, *outside* the anarchical society of states.

Upon close inspection, this peculiar variety of autarkic Communism appears as absolute monarchism covered in a thick coating of revolutionary slogans. The dynastic founder, Kim Il-sung, a god-ruler who still commands terrestrial reverence two decades after ascending to the heavens, was a fervent believer in Marxist dicta. But his two familial successors appear to have earthlier ambitions. The late Kim Jong-il, the founder's heir and another deceased man-deity, and his son and current leader, Kim Jong-un, have shown a greater fondness for the perversions of capitalist riches (stories of excessive alcohol and female "pleasure squads" abound) and militaristic rituals (feverish mass rallies of troops are common) than for Juche's stoic teachings.

Even by the standards of the Communist bloc's historical litany of despotic regimes, the eccentric habits of the Kim house have revealed a great capacity for imagination in the application of cold-blooded repression. In 2015, one high priest of the state, Defense Minister Hyon Yong-chol, met the fate of execution by an anti-aircraft gun for sleeping during military rallies.[11] Often, the techniques of political horror reach beyond the militarized frontier of the 38th Parallel to the south. Pyongyang operates assassination squads targeting political defectors and opponents. Amazingly, one squad liquidated a good number of South Korean cabinet members and officials in Burma in 1983.[12] Agents also detonated a bomb on Korean Air Flight 858 over the Andaman Sea in 1987, an atrocity that a defecting senior official confessed sought to "create chaos and confusion in South Korea" in blind obeisance to the "god-like figure" of Kim Il-sung.[13] In 2012, Kim Jong-un issued a "standing order" to have his estranged older half-brother, Kim Jong-nam, assassinated. Two young women allegedly carried out the order by poisoning him in a Malaysian airport in 2017.[14] Not even dynastic princes are immune to state brutality.

A house that consumes its own children can have no qualms about disturbing the delicate regional and international order. The regime protests trade sanctions by petulantly launching rockets above Japan – for example, its firing in 1998 of the Taepodong–1 medium-range ballistic missile into the Sea of Japan, less than 400 kilometers from the Noto Peninsula.[15] It is a cunning and persistent feeder of the illegal international arms trade, including the illicit provision of uranium-enrichment centrifuge technology to Pakistan, conventional arms to unsavory African regimes, chemical weapons components to Bashar al-Assad's Syria, and military wares to the repressive government of Myanmar.[16]

To protect the revolutionary homeland from foreign designs, North Korea implements a program of militaristic defiance of international order. It has cultivated a large military apparatus that dominates public life and which menaces regional neighbors. By sheer manpower (1,190,000 active soldiers), the Korean People's Army (KPA) is the fourth largest in the world.[17] Over the years, it has developed an impressive ballistic-missile capability, including the Hwasong–10 intermediate-range ballistic missile (ICBM), which can deliver a warhead of up to 1.25 tons as far away as 4,000 kilometers. Yet the conventional army, which despite its large size is technologically inferior to the forces arrayed against it to the south, has a limited range of maneuver. Although the North can flood troops into and rain fire on South Korea and Japan as well as strike regional military bases of the United States, it cannot yet easily reach the despised enemy's frigid shores of Alaska, much less the temperate and strategically more significant urban centers of Seattle or Los Angeles, although its focused quest to assemble long-range ICBMs such as the Taepodong–2 reveals such an intention.[18]

To close this capabilities gap, North Korea has turned to the development of unconventional technology. Of special importance to the Kims' revolutionary program both at home and abroad is the ultimate technology of conflict, nuclear weapons. The country has built between two and three dozen nuclear warheads.[19] Although the evaluation of North Korean nuclear doctrine is notoriously difficult – its conceiver Kim Il-sung left no written records of his motives and his offspring did not air theirs – its basic elements may be inferred from the regime's political purposes of survival.

One possible goal is Korean unification: a reversal by sheer military force of the artificial separation of the brotherly peoples by a menacing imperial power.[20] As Young Ho Park observed, although the main thrust of North Korea's unification strategy is the enlistment of anti-government activists in the South, not war, "it is difficult to say that North Korea has totally given up the idea of unifying Korea by force of arms."[21] Thus it is conceivable that nuclear weapons are a final instrument of unification. But unification of the Koreas by nuclear war or blackmail is no more achievable today than was the forcible fusion of the two Germanys by a nuclear armed Soviet Union during the Cold War.[22] Nuclear status is likelier to prevent forced unification on the South's terms than it is to bring it about as the North desires.

Therein lies a more plausible purpose for the weapons: existential deterrence, or the prevention of a military invasion by the United States and its ally to the south.[23] In this interpretation, the North's nuclear arms are the central component of an interplay between domestic and international politics. They serve as a deterrent shield to preserve the nation's independence and protect the regime's existence against conventionally superior enemies.[24] But the deterrent function will not be complete until the North is able to detonate nuclear weapons on the other side of the Pacific. The country, however, only very recently mastered the technology of miniaturization. Presently it can mount a warhead onto a medium-range Rodong missile, but not onto a long- or full-range intercontinental missile, which at any rate it does not possess.[25] Yet even when the North breaks through the intercontinental missile barrier (the world awaits with trepidation the answer to the question, "What happens when it does?"),[26] its nuclear capability will provide only limited strategic gains. The country already possesses in its vast arsenal of rocket forces the ability – spontaneously – to obliterate South Korea's (and Japan's) industrial heartland and to wipe out a large number of the 28,500 American soldiers stationed on the peninsula. The addition of a few American cities to this list of possible horrors would significantly raise but not fundamentally alter the deterrence calculus on which the United States already seeks to avoid a military showdown. For this same reason, the North will not likely be the first to launch a nuclear strike or unleash its conventional rockets, except in the face of an imminent threat to the survival of the Kim house.

Instead, the rewards of nuclear weapons are perhaps more political than strategic. Scott Sagan has made the important point that states sometimes acquire nuclear arms not only to thwart foreign threats but also to secure domestic political interests.[27] "Nuclear weapons, like other weapons, are more than tools of national security," he explained. "They are political objects of considerable importance in domestic debates and internal bureaucratic struggles and can also serve as international normative symbols of modernity and identity."[28] In addition, as we shall see below, they are also instruments that repressive leaders can use to defy the international consensus for domestic purposes of regime legitimacy – a different manifestation of the domestic proliferation model than the one Sagan supposes. Normally, this model invokes the complexities of internal bureaucratic interests. As Victor Cha explained, in some states – that is, the "rational" units such as India and Pakistan that inhabit the Conventional Model – the drive toward the bomb may be the method by which rising civilian technocrats displace an "old, corrupt, and inefficient military bureaucracy."[29] These factors need not apply, however, to a nation in which power is so highly concentrated in the figure of a single man. To be sure, the North Korean military elites on whose support the regime's continuity relies require appeasement and inducements.[30] Kim Jong-un must, like any despot, satisfy the interests of a cadre of underlings that together constitute a government elite (though they may not be a "ruling" elite).[31] But to invoke the image of nagging lobbyists, overbearing bureaucrats, and cunning legislators who can twist Kim's arm is to miss the unsurpassed despotic nature and ideological fervor of his regime.

The weapons, moreover, enable the leader to launch menacing rhetorical fires against the international community in an effort to extract diplomatic concessions. The North has in the past sought to trade the prospect of further nuclear expansion and tests for a diminution of international sanctions; for example, in 1994 it accepted economic inducements for halting reactor activity at the Yongbyong nuclear facility, an agreement that the country later abrogated. Since its withdrawal from the Treaty on the Non-Proliferation of Nuclear Weapons in 2003 and its detonation of a fission device in October 2006, nuclear saber-rattling has tended to increase, not diminish, the scale of foreign penalties. Pyongyang must have learned to welcome this regressive cycle of defiance and punishment, for the penalties have not significantly affected its proliferating behavior.[32] The sanctions may in fact bolster the internal sense of existential peril that justifies among key constituencies and the famished population the production of the very weapons that the punishment is meant to curtail.

The regime's bracing nuclear program, therefore, represents a fusion of old and new tendencies: the exaltation of a Manchurian warrior ethos and the crude exhibition of a fearsome and morally repulsive weapon. In a perversion of the domestic model of nuclear proliferation, the mighty political symbolism of nuclear tests and missile launches provides Kim with a costly existential deterrent while augmenting his soldiers' pride and invigorating his citizens' revolutionary zeal. Kim's dazzling displays of the ultimate technology of conflict distract the oppressed subjects' attention from the necessary deprivations of Juche that his belligerent actions inevitably worsen. North Korea's nuclear arsenal is the product of a despotically motivated and ideologically tinged interaction of domestic and international considerations.

The Virtual Weapon as a Revolutionary Instrument of North Korea

The virtual weapon is another technology in which North Korea has invested heavily for similar purposes of regime preservation. While not a member of the top level of cyber players, the country is among a small second tier of nations capable of achieving potent offensive effects. In the words of the general in charge of American forces in the Korean Peninsula, "While I would not characterize [North Korea's cyber warriors] as the best in the world, they are among the best in the world, and the best organized."[33] The North's arsenal of code inspires awe as much for its proven destructive capacity as for the revolutionary purposes that drive its use. The record of this behavior illustrates the new scope for strategic maneuver that the technology affords the revolutionary state in its relations with ordinary states whose goals it repudiates and conventions it defies.

The North's cyber arsenal traces its origins to the electronic warfare (EW) capability of the Korean People's Army in the 1970s. EW denotes offensive or defensive activities within the electromagnetic spectrum. Strictly speaking, it is different from cyber operations because it does not involve the use of code to alter machine functions, but it can impair them significantly if an attacker uses electromagnetic energy, such as a concentrated "pulse," to incapacitate the machines' electronics. On these terms, the common label "cyber electronic warfare" is misleading because the activity affects but does not involve the use of cyberspace to inflict harm. Cyberspace is the *object* but not the medium of harm. Nevertheless, because electromagnetic and cyber operations often rely on similar technologies and expertise, it is natural that the latter capability grew out of the former.[34] Following a study of the lessons of the 1990–91 Gulf War,[35] the KPA expanded its EW capability to include assets in information warfare, a broad notion that encompasses weaponized code but also the use of propaganda and disinformation (discussed further in Chapter 8 in the Russian context).

The most important step in North Korea's ascent in the hierarchy of cyber powers was the establishment in 1998 of the famed Bureau 121. The unit operates within the Reconnaissance General Bureau, the military's principal clandestine and intelligence body. As the nation's principal cyber outfit, it is charged with a singular responsibility: offensive activities in foreign cyberspace.[36] To nourish this unit with skills, North Korea has developed a small but highly specialized computer industry. Although it hosts only approximately one thousand IP addresses – much less than the 112 million in South Korea, whose capital city, Seoul, was designated "the world's leading digital city" and which far surpasses the North in technological ability[37] – this native technological base is not primitive. It has developed its own intranet (although state websites are hosted abroad in China); tablet computers, for example, the "Samjiyon," which features applications tailored to it; and a rudimentary social network, the oddly named "Best Korea's Social

Network," a close imitation of Facebook that connects the country's few thousand Internet users.[38] Thus it is misplaced to claim that North Korea has "no economic potential to speak of,"[39] if by such potential one includes the native capacity to excel in producing some forms of information technology. Technological prowess can grow even under the autarkic conditions of Juche.

The army feeds Bureau 121 with a small but fanatically motivated cadre of technical experts, whose high salaries and other emoluments exempt them from the pauperization of Juche.[40] According to South Korean intelligence reports, in 2014 the unit's size doubled to 6,000 men, some of whom serve from remote locations in China, Thailand, and Russia – a mark of personal prestige for the operatives and an indication of inordinate trust by the paranoid dictator back home.[41] North Korean defectors have claimed that training for the unit begins in school, continues in university, and sometimes culminates with instruction in China and Russia.[42] That the training starts at a young age and entails the intense indoctrination of aspirants reveals a pedagogical dictum that recalls Marvin Minsky's fitting metaphor about humans being machines: one must first manipulate *human* computers with ideological dogmas before applying information to the industry of manipulating *artificial* machines with code.

Bureau 121 has developed a proven offensive capacity. Among its most notable actions are the cyberattacks against Sony Pictures, which involved the destruction of three-fourths of the firm's machines and the disclosure of reputationally harmful private records of senior company executives (more about this below). The unit achieved this feat by cultivating domestic talent, specifically within the so-called Lazarus Group, an advanced persistent adversary that has been active since at least 2009 and crafted the "Destover" wiper that disabled company machines.[43] The group did not rely on significant outside support to mount the operation.[44] Few other nations apart from the main advanced persistent adversaries – the United States, Britain, Russia, and China – possess such a sophisticated offensive arsenal.

An interesting question arises: why would an impoverished, isolated dynasty commit its scarce financial resources and limited technological base to develop an offensive capacity that lacks the overtly violent character of the traditional arms it has so craved in the past? Little academic research on this question exists.[45] Few facts are available to researchers who seek to answer it, for the North is no more forth-coming about the aims of its cyber program than it is about the goals of its nuclear program. Nevertheless, the public record of events offers important clues about these goals. Three stand out.

One goal is offensive: North Korea's cyber arsenal provides a piercing but not overtly violent tool to seize foreign economic assets – all the while avoiding the penalties of doing so with traditional military means. For example, the computer security firm Symantec tied North Korean hackers to attempts to penetrate the Tien Phong Bank in Vietnam.[46] More ominously, in February 2016 the hackers used code to penetrate the computers of the Bangladeshi Central Bank. The attackers manipu-lated weaknesses in the SWIFT interbank messaging system, which handles billions of dollars of transactions each day, to seize $81 million from the bank's account in the Federal Reserve Bank of New York.[47] (The size of the heist might have been much larger had the culprits not misspelled the name of an entity receiving the illicit cash.)[48] Such seizures of foreign money enable North Korea to offset the internal pains of Juche and the economic sanctions for its maligned nuclear program.

A second important goal is psychological: the cyber actions dilute the confidence of North Korea's adversaries in their own superior economic and military base. Recall from the discussion in Chapter 4 that the virtual weapon has enormous depth of power; players can use it to penetrate an opponent's essential computer systems remotely and sometimes permanently. In April 2011, nearly half of the machines in the South Korean Nonghyup agricultural bank crashed. For several days, tens of millions of bank customers were unable to access their cash.[49] In December 2014, the agency that operates the South's twenty-three nuclear-power facilities, Korea Hydro and Nuclear Power Co. Ltd., reported an intrusion into its computer systems. Days later, a Twitter user demanded that three reactors shut down, or else the plants would suffer unspecified destruction (the intruders did not disrupt the reactor cores' activity or seize critical systems data).[50] In March 2016, the North reportedly hacked the mobile phones of several key govern-ment and media employees in the South.[51]

These incidents did not produce large-scale physical damage. Yet they serve as a warning to North Korea's enemies that it can utilize cyberspace to penetrate permanently – and, if necessary, disrupt – the computer infrastructures that sustain the essential economic and civilian functions of advanced industrial societies. Here, the cyber curse of technological superiority in our era, which Chapter 2 discussed, is on sharp display: the nations most adept at harnessing cyberspace for economic and industrial gains are also the most susceptible to threats living within it.

A third major goal of North Korea's virtual stockpiles is coercive and political. It concerns the domestic–international interplay that explains the country's nuclear malfeasance: North Korea uses weaponized code as a tool of coercion to extract concessions that serve the regime's interests at home. Cyberattacks are a means to shield the regime from foreign propaganda campaigns, whose aim can only be to confuse the patriotic zealots of Juche with false dreams and mischievous fabrications. The country's leaders have long shown an acute sensitivity to such "counter-revolutionary" activity. Recently they threatened to shell areas of South Korea (mostly the northwestern coast), from which activists have launched balloons carrying anti-regime and religious scripts. Pyongyang has even compared Seoul's toleration of such activity to an "act of war."[52] It has treated the intrusions of foreign digital teachings (again, that human version of pernicious 0's and 1's, or malicious ideas that can manipulate the man-machines) with a special ferocity, perhaps because this material travels a technological medium that the regime holds in especially high regard. The North's concern is not without grounds. Western analysts have proposed information dissemination campaigns, including the encouragement of computer use inside the reclusive nation, as the only viable means of toppling Kim.[53] To stem the waves of dangerous ideals, the North has sought to intimidate foreign actors with blasts of machine code. That is, it has sought to fight the intrusions of political information with the use of information as force.

The Sony Pictures cyberattacks were the most prominent case of this kind. The attacks occurred only weeks before the entertainment company was scheduled to release a film, *The Interview*, that featured a plot to assassinate Kim. The main aim of the attacks was coercive: they sought to force company executives to suspend the film's imminent general release. This maneuver worked for a few weeks. Sony Pictures decided to halt the premier, but later reversed itself under immense pressure from the public and the White House.[54] "The cyber attack against Sony Pictures Entertainment was not just an attack against a company and its employees," announced Obama. "It was also an attack on our freedom of expression and way of life." Having framed the issue as a compromise of the nation's defining values, the president then voiced a jab directly against the company's submission to the attackers' demand: "That's not who we are. That's not what America is about. Yes, I think they made a mistake. We cannot have a society in which some dictator some place can start imposing censorship here in the United States . . . I wish they'd spoken to me first. I would have told them, 'Do not get into a pattern where you're intimidated by these kinds of attacks.'"[55]

At this point the querulous skeptic will again roar in doubt: virtual weapons, even destructive ones, are poor instruments of international coercion. This view misses the point. Although the attacks against Sony Pictures failed to achieve their immediate censorship objective, it would be misguided to conclude that they had no coercive effect at all. Other entertainment companies will have noticed the operation's destructive intensity. More significant still may be the reputational harm that the attacks caused. Not only did the attackers incapacitate hardware, but also, in a variation of the Russian techniques of kompromat, they also released embarrassing private emails written by senior company executives, including the co-chairwoman and theatrical producer who exchanged racially tinged jokes about Obama. The attack's full effects on self-censorship may never be known, but they almost certainly exist. The initial cowed response of Sony Pictures executives strongly suggests that future disparagers of Kim may think twice about airing their views publicly, thereby contributing to a broader and deeper trend of self-censorship that may be difficult to detect. In other words, one must consider not only the direct censoring effects on Sony Pictures but also broader censoring effects on the global entertainment industry. Ira Deutchmann of Emerging Pictures, a theatrical exhibition company, expressed this concern. She compared the aftermath of the Sony incident with the effects of the terrorist attack the following month against the Paris offices of the satirical newspaper *Charlie Hebdo*.[56] "We were already heading in the direction of possible self-censorship in Hollywood because of the Sony hacking, and this might just reinforce those tendencies," she lamented.[57]

All of the above objectives of North Korea's cyber arsenal – economic, psychological, and political – share a unique attraction that separates it from conventional weapons: because cyber activity falls short of a recognizable act of war, it enables the North to pursue its strategic and political aims while avoiding the stiff penalties that accompany war. Obama himself made this point plain in declaring, publicly and unequivocally, that the cyberattacks against Sony Pictures were not an "act of war." Promising to retaliate "proportionally" – in other words, not militarily – he signed an executive order in January 2015 imposing new financial sanctions on the reclusive nation, excoriating the North for its "provocative, destabilizing, and repressive actions and policies, particularly its destructive and coercive cyber attack."[58] The president subsequently signed an Executive Order that authorized sanctions against North Korea in retaliation for its action.[59] The sanctions froze the U.S.-based assets of the regime, government officials and agents, and officials of the Workers' Party of Korea. The country also suffered unspecified blackouts in its Internet service, an exclusive tool of the regime.[60] Overall, these mild penalties could not have bitten deeply into the hardened skin of Juche's princes.

But evasion of severe penalties is not the new weapons' only attraction. Like nuclear arms, offensive code offers an awe-inspiring technological medallion that the regime can brandish, cavalierly and disruptively, to distract and stir the pride of a pauperized people, who, caught in the glare of the cult leader's repeated acts of defiance against the international order, cannot discern their own misery. Insubordination in foreign cyberspace serves the purpose of stiffening submission in the domestic political space.

Restraining the Revolutionary State

Against the backdrop of intensifying cyberattacks – not least by the agitator-in-chief in Pyongyang – some observers have called for a refinement of institutional and legal mechanisms to restrain such conduct. They have asked for a strengthening of the international normative regime. They have emphasized the need to define "red lines" of behavior. They have lauded the recent agreements to this end within the UN Group of Governmental Experts.[61] Will an institutional and normative approach to stabilize cyber interactions curtail the erratic actions of the revolutionary state north of the 38th Parallel?

It may succeed partially. It may convince nations such as China or Russia, which have hosted North Korean agents, to reduce such support. But the institutional approach to conflict stability also faces a severe limitation: it will not work against North Korea itself. The approach reflects a belief that international antagonisms can be overcome by an appeal to the appropriateness of rules. It embodies the Western conception of diplomacy as a legalistic profession in which international differences are resolvable by prudence and compromise, not impudence and coercion. Rules are an embodiment of the legitimacy of the society of states. Yet the definition of a revolutionary power is that it repudiates the system's legitimacy. Thus in North Korea's case, it is hopeless to attempt to constrain its antagonistic actions by resorting to the normal devices of international law. The growing record of attacks reflects this reality. As opposed to nuclear weapons, which sit menacingly but mostly quietly in secret bunkers, North Korea's cyber arsenal exists for active use. About his prized stock of weaponized code, Kim Jong-un recently remarked: "Cyber warfare, along with nuclear weapons and missiles, is an all-purpose sword that guarantees our military's capability to *strike relentlessly* [emphasis mine]."[62]

Rarely has conflict avoidance occurred under such extreme conditions of deviant behavior. But in few other relationships is it more needed. North Korea's disinhibitions about offensive action mean that only penalties and disabling action will constrain it. Credible promises of severe punishment may deter attacks for the same motive that inspires them: regime preservation. Short of deterrence, disabling action may diminish the country's capacity to attack. These measures may involve active defense steps that neutralize weapons before or as they are used. The cyberattacks that reportedly impaired North Korea's ballistic missiles suggest that adversaries can use code to penetrate its defensive terrain deeply.[63] Similar proactive actions against the regime's computer assets could degrade its virtual weapons. Seeking to rectify North Korean misconduct by appeal to rules asks too much of diplomacy. Fear, not common values, will be the bridge between the enemies.

Technological revolution of the second order, in sum, represents a confluence of two challenges: how to grasp the new scope for action of a transforming weapon; and how to check a revolutionary state's use of it to disturb the international order. Technological revolution compounds political revolution. The ideological goals of systemic revision defy conventional security models. When theoreticians dismiss the relevance of ideology by invoking the eternal "realism" of international politics what they really dismiss is reality. Political truths are frequently messier than rational-choice theory allows. Certainly, this is true of a revolutionary state whose empowerment by new technology challenges received notions about foreign policy. The errant conduct of the irrational player appears to traditionalists as an enigma that is easier dismissed (Anarchy shall straighten him out!) than explained. A consideration of North Korea's place in the international system requires that we set aside the tidy postulates of rationalism and enter a realm in which ideas and creeds shape – sometimes decisively – state behavior.

Let us never tire of repeating it: theory serves reality and not vice versa. If established security models cannot explain brazen actions such as the destructive cyberattacks by a fanatical regime against targets located thousands of kilometers away, the correct response of analysts is to reframe theory, not shun reality.

CHAPTER 6

First-Order Cyber Revolution
PRESSURES FROM OUTSIDE THE STATES SYSTEM

The Sovereignty Gap

Were technological revolution disruptive solely of interstate dealings, its study could stop at the external borders of the international system. Having explored the impact of new inventions upon the competition of ordinary states bound by common basic ends or upon the ideological strivings of revolutionary states bent on subverting them, international relations specialists would not need to consider the influence of players alien to the system. And having reached the system's frontier posts, the concept of technological revolution would have safely exhausted its relevance.

This viewpoint is mainly accurate. Historically, the basic goal of national security policy is to preserve the safety of the state and its subjects against threats arising from other states. The traditional organizing principle of international anarchy is that states are the supreme agents in this program of activity: they possess sovereign resources to carry out their own security policies against each other. Previous revolutions in the technologies of conflict have abided by these postulates. Advances in mechanized warfare during the 1940s enabled a fanatical Nazi Germany to disrupt gravely but not demolish the Westphalian order. Nuclear arms during the Cold War also radically altered the system without destroying it; they may even have strengthened it by solidifying the supremacy of its master units.

Yet in our own era of unprecedented change, the viewpoint is severely limited. The central trends of the cyber revolution challenge classical tenets of international relations. Previously the principal question of security policy was: what actions of other independent states threaten vital national interests? This is increasingly supplanted by the concern: how do forces operating outside state confines imperil the nation? The concern also applied to other security issues before the cyber age such as global terrorism. Cyberspace compounds it. The virtual weapon is driving first-order technological revolution, a force of systems change, whereby actors other than the state challenge its traditional supremacy and even primacy in the management of security affairs.

It is important at this point to address the annoyance of skeptics. States largely retain their primacy in the system; otherwise we would be wrong in calling it "international." They possess the intelligence and other costly resources necessary to mount the most potent cyberattacks, such as the Stuxnet operation against the Natanz nuclear facility in Iran in 2009, which impaired almost one thousand uranium-enrichment centrifuges,[1] or the action that damaged three-quarters of the machines and divulged tens of thousands of private records of employees at Sony Pictures Entertainment in 2014. The influence of states is increasingly felt, moreover, in the area of Internet governance. The Internet – a key sub-realm of cyberspace – was designed to operate, in the words of Vint Cerf, one of its originators, in a "post-Westphalian world." This anarchic (in the classical sense of the word) philosophical outlook was "very deliberate in the design of the network."[2] But as Jack Goldsmith and Tim Wu have shown in a cutting analysis, the levers of power over Internet activity conform more to the rules of Westphalia than to the ideal of a borderless utopia.[3] This is because, as Lawrence Lessig put it, "Whenever someone is in cyberspace, she is also here, in real space."[4] Cyberspace has a basic physical existence comprising routers, machines, and – crucially – human users. Thus its activities and its agents are partly subject to the normal controls of the territorial state: legislatures, courts, and police forces.

Cyberspace, then, is not a magical portal through which citizens and private groups can flee their own sovereigns. It may even provide an instrument by which the sovereigns exercise their power, whether to bar nonstate actors from the system's governing institutions and conventions or to suppress them tightly below it.[5]

Thus the dilution of the states' role – where dilution occurs – does not mean that they are becoming irrelevant, as naïve observers have sometimes claimed. Rather, the point is that the technology is partially but notably diminishing states' supremacy and even primacy. It empowers actors residing outside the Conventional Model, even as the alien players assert their influence over the traditional units and threaten their basic purposes. It is in short a *partial* but still notable force of systems change.

This trend is evident in three ways. First, states are not the sole relevant source of threats to national security; nontraditional players such as political activists, criminal syndicates, and religious extremist groups can also cause significant harm against governmental, financial, even military interests. Second, states are not the only, or in some cases even the primary, national-security providers. In some areas of national security, such as the operation of vital computer infrastructures or the collection and encryption or decryption (in forensic investigations, for instance) of personal data, the private sector is more important. Third, the traditional units are no longer able to maintain full control over the dynamics of conflict among them. Civilian culprits can disturb – sometimes gravely – the fragile political framework of interstate affairs. New departures in thinking about security are therefore necessary.

The Prejudice of Theory

We begin with a review of an intellectual preconception that enjoys a high reputation among theoreticians: the notion of state-centrism, a staple feature of thinking about security and conflict that the cyber sovereignty gap challenges.

All theorists accept the existence of actors other than states. The neorealist thinker Kenneth Waltz has noted: "States are not and never have been the only international actors ... The importance of nonstate actors and the extent of transnational activities are obvious."[6] Yet despite such gratuitous concessions, international relations specialists often design their theoretical models as if there were no room for other players in them. Theorists assume that states are so important to the functioning of the international system as to be the central (some would say only) units of analysis. And not only neorealists: neoliberals,[7] English School theorists,[8] and many constructivists,[9] too, hold this view. This simplifying posture represents, in the words of David Lake, a "methodological bet" that "a focus on states will yield parsimonious yet empirically powerful explanations of world politics."[10] Many other thinkers do not place this bet. They question the state's exalted status: for instance, Ronald Rogowski's analysis of how internal institutional interests rend the monolithic state apart;[11] or Arnold Wolfers' denial of the very existence of "the national interest" and his rejection of the deleterious policy consequences that belief in it has produced.[12] Yet at many tables of the theoretical betting house, certainly the most influential ones, state centrism is a frequent and frequently unquestioned gamble.

One of the clearest examples of this mindset is the assumption, on which much of international relations theory operates, that states are unitarily rational. This view lies at the core of the rational-agent perspective. It holds that for the purpose of analyzing interactions among them, states are individuals, for if they are not, how can they properly be considered "agents"? And if states are irreducible units whose will is a sum total of constituent parts that cannot be separated, then those other parts cannot play a prominent role in models of the units' behavior. Game theory illustrates this perspective. Borrowing from axioms of microeconomics, the theory subjects states to the same cutting simplification that the economic perspective applies to corporations. That is, it neglects the psychology of the decision-maker and the bureaucratic peculiarities of the decision-making process in the same way that microeconomic theory omits the psychology of executives and the bureaucracies of firms. In international relations theory, the state is the theoretical surrogate of the individually rational firm, or John Stuart Mill's peculiar creature, *Homo economicus*, who seeks only materially measurable gains and is able perfectly to select means for obtaining them.[13]

This perspective is in a sense correct: if "international" relations means "interstate" relations, then by definition the theoretical models must banish all other actors, unless they are closely integrated into recognizable state structures, such as in the case of reserve militias (e.g. the U.S. National Guard and the Estonian Defense League) or state-owned enterprises (e.g. Rosoboronexport and China National Nuclear Corporation). And when the alluring simplicity of this model fails to capture relevant unaffiliated players and their actions, as it often does, they typically fall off the radar of relevance.

In many contexts, the simplifying optic of state centrism will sharpen analysis. For the purposes of theory construction, transnational crime – to name just one prominent phenomenon transpiring largely outside the system – is justifiably uninteresting, because the scale of drug dealers' and arms traders' actions rarely rises to the level of national security or disrupts core interactions among states. Or when it does so, as in the infamous case of A. Q. Khan, the official father of Pakistan's nuclear weapons program and the unofficial uncle of North Korea's program, the private culprits often enjoyed close ties to their governments or may not have been able to act without their support.[14]

In other instances, however, the optic is a blinder to new trends. Consider how the statist preconception hindered the study of terrorism prior to the September 11, 2001, attacks against Manhattan and the Pentagon. Even after these momentous attacks, analysts sometimes claimed that the threat of terrorism was exaggerated; they appealed to a common preconception of the discipline – the centrality of military rivalry among large powers. "The capacity for small bands of terrorists to do harm," noted one observer, "is far less than was the case for the great countries behind international Communism who possessed a very impressive military (and nuclear) capacity and had, in addition, shown great skill at political subversion."[15] Yet for all its threats against international order, no single event during the Cold War rivalry produced multinational and multiyear invasions of two other nations by one of the superpowers. One sometimes hears analysts who are skeptical of the terrorist threat remark, "Ten 9/11's would not match even a small war in terms of physical destruction," to which the response is simple: "Except for the ensuing destruction caused by ten Afghanistans and ten Iraqs."

Rational-agent theorists cope with the noises of a vastly more complex reality by appealing to the principle of parsimony, or the plea to remove congestion in causal variables. By resorting to such devices, they hold down the lid on the "black box" of the state.[16] Some thinkers have dared to open it, yet even they often arrive at the same conclusion: the state, albeit an actor with multiple competing characters and interests, one whose single essence is difficult to pin down, is the supreme agent in international affairs. Thus the central preoccupation of international security studies is the threat that states present to other states merely by their autonomous existence. The core theoretical themes that flow from this viewpoint are familiar to specialists: the balance of power among states, the use of armed force among them, the resort to intergovernmental organizations to prevent such behavior, the cultivation of shared norms to limit it, and so on.

The cyber domain does not tolerate such theoretical preconceptions. It does not recognize the absolute ascendancy that the core theories, customs, and principles of the international system confer upon its ordinary units. To be sure, the boundaries of cyberspace and of the states system sometimes neatly overlap. Where this holds true, cyber activity will not impinge on the units' supremacy. For example, the intranets operated by some authoritarian nations, such as Iran, reside firmly within the Westphalian box. In that country, three bodies – the Supreme Council for Cyberspace, the Committee for Determining Criminal Web Content, and the Islamic Cyber Army and Police – tightly censure Internet communications by blocking seditious or "un-Islamic" web content, including foreign "cultural invasion," as one senior Iranian official put it.[17] Conservatives directly appointed by Ayatollah Ali Khamenei control these bodies, for which there is no public accountability.[18] Insofar as such government measures achieve a tight control on the flow of information within their national intranets, these compartmentalized quarters of cyberspace will fit neatly into the Westphalian model. They are an affirmation of and not a challenge to sovereignty, although here it is necessary to distinguish between the supremacy of the state as a secular actor on the international scene, which the intranets may preserve if they block foreign subversive content, and the supremacy of any particular government or regime *within* the state, which the intranets may not preserve if domestic citizens develop means to circumvent state controls.

But where pernicious information – whether weaponized code or subversive ideas – is able to penetrate national borders freely and substantially, that is, where there is an open Internet or there are means to infiltrate the cyber archipelago, then technology may create pressures of change from below state structures. These forces of systems change are greatest in areas where the rigid borders of the states system come into contact with the boundless activity of the technological domain. This important point begins with the ease of proliferation of some capabilities to nonstate actors.

Ease of Proliferation: High Walls and Shallow Moats

Except where the most advanced weapons are concerned, entry into the cyber domain's offensive quarter is not prohibitively expensive.[19] Even unsophisticated actors with limited resources can access it with some ease.[20] The virtual weapon, therefore, empowers a variety of nontraditional players such as religious extremist groups, political activists, criminal syndicates, and even lone agents who can cause significant harm. "Just as Russia and China have advanced cyber capabilities and strategies ranging from stealthy network penetration to intellectual property theft, criminal and terrorist networks are also increasing their cyber operations," averred the U.S. Secretary of Defense Ash Carter.[21] Sometimes they act in collusion with governments, but often operate without their direction or even their knowledge or approval. A remark by Admiral Michael Mullen, Chairman of the U.S. Joint Chiefs of Staff, expresses the proliferation anxieties of the system's old masters: "We're going to have a catastrophic [cyber] event. Some of these tools already being built are going to leak or be sold or be given up to a group that wants to change the world order, and we're incredibly vulnerable."[22]

Understanding the opportunities for and barriers to entry into the domain requires a framework of weapons proliferation that distinguishes different varieties of arms acquisition, the means by which acquisition can occur, and its implications for alien players in the current revolutionary system.

Generally, the term "proliferation" denotes the acquisition of a preexisting or similar weapon by an actor other than its creator, such as the Soviet Union's detonation of its first fission bomb in 1949 – a phenomenon that Waltz termed "horizontal" proliferation. But it can also mean the expansion of arsenals by actors that already possess a given class of weapon, such as the United States' and the Soviet Union's assembly of more powerful thermonuclear devices during the 1950s – "vertical" proliferation. In either case, the meaning of proliferation in traditional realms of conflict is usually clear. In the nuclear domain, for example, it means most significantly the production of a warhead that is deliverable to a target. But one can also speak of *partial* proliferation, which denotes the existence, in a non-nuclear nation, of an active nuclear weapons production program or even a latent capacity to assemble a deployable warhead in a short period of time.[23] The process of nuclear weapons proliferation entails a significant investment in the attainment of tacit knowledge of a complex technology – for instance, knowledge about the functioning of gaseous centrifuges that must rotate at the speed of sound to purify uranium isotopes to weapons grade, a technical challenge that in the absence of deep native expertise brought Iraq in the 1980s to a nuclear dead end.[24] Despite the importance of knowledge transfers to nuclear weapons production, the endpoint of the process is distinctly physical: there can be no bomb without a warhead fitted into a missile or other vehicle to deliver it.

That is not the case in the cyber domain. The virtual weapon, as the label implies, is essentially massless. It does not occupy physical space. It is a knowledge-intensive capability. Technical information is not merely a means to acquiring a weapon; it *is* the weapon. What, then, does proliferation mean in relation to this intangible capability?

There is no clear or agreed-upon answer. Few analysts have posed this question conceptually. Remember that we are still grappling with the very meaning of "weapon." The notion of cyber proliferation is subject to varying interpretations. It is useful to begin by returning to the basic distinction between customized and generalized weapons.

Customized code, as we saw in Chapter 1, is the virtual weapon's most advanced form. It has produced dazzling attacks: the operations that impaired tens of thousands of computers belonging to Saudi Aramco, most machines at Sony Pictures, and hundreds of nuclear centrifuges in Iran. In fact, concerns about such proliferation grew acutely following the revelation of the sophisticated Stuxnet operation against the nuclear facility in Natanz. "Now that Stuxnet is in the wild," averred computer security expert Ralph Langner, "you don't need to be a rocket scientist [to reproduce it.] You've got a blueprint of how to do it."[25] Or as RSA security officer Michael Sconzo put it: "The Stuxnet code has been out there for some time. Anyone with decent knowledge of computers could reverse engineer it."[26] Others went further. Melissa Hathaway, the former Senior Director for Cyberspace at the U.S. National Security Council claimed that the weapon's source code was available on the "black market," "has been analyzed around the world," and was already "replicated" by unknown actors.[27] One private security expert boastfully claimed: "With a few million dollars and five to ten technicians, I, too, could mount a Stuxnet-like attack."[28] While not cheap, this cost is within the capacity of many nonstate actors to absorb.

In the hands of nonstate actors such as religious extremist groups or political agitators with a motive to incapacitate essential infrastructures, the capability could radically alter the face of national security and interstate conflict. Thus the question of its acquisition by system aliens is a crucial one for international order. In considering the pathways to such a scenario, we must identify two main forms of proliferation – *line replication* and *design emulation*, each with different implications for aspiring proliferants.

Line replication of customized code involves simple cutting and pasting: the selective reuse of malware – in whole or in part – to prepare an attack on a computer system other than the original target, yet similar enough to it to be affected by the same arrangement of 0's and 1's. In the nuclear realm, it is analogous to the purchase or theft of a functional warhead; this process is costly because it entails the transfer of rare physical objects among players whose transaction violates international law.

Design emulation works differently. It entails the imitation of a weapon's design principles rather than its code. It is analogous to copying the methods of assembling a nuclear device – centrifuge rotation or neutron radiation of uranium isotopes, for instance. This method of reproduction is made possible by weaknesses in the very architecture of computer technology. The weaknesses inhere in the way machines were designed to operate, communicate, and verify the authenticity of commands (e.g. the use of digital certificates, or tokens which indicate that a computer file is trusted not to contain malicious code but which, in fact, criminals may have found ways to compromise).[29] They do not involve the design of machines individually. Whereas software deficiencies are patchable, design vulnerabilities are not. The former are zero-day weaknesses; the latter, *all*-day weaknesses. As Langner explains: "Patching a design flaw requires a fundamental remodeling of the industrial system, in particular the relationship between the controller and machine parts joined to it." Insofar as design weaknesses in computer architecture can be discovered, they provide an opening for the creation of new exploits. "A keen observer of the Stuxnet attack," Langner said to illustrate the problem, "will learn to focus on the 'certification of system boot drivers' and the 'image input process'"[30] – two features of the Natanz PLC environment that the worm's handlers exploited to load the code into the target machines and to mask its presence.[31] Design emulation is also possible with material weapons, but it requires an intermediary step: physical assembly, such as the acquisition of highly purified uranium isotopes to construct a nuclear device, which may be prohibitively costly except for powerful nations.

Both forms of proliferation are essentially knowledge based, but in different ways. Line replication involves the reproduction of a specific arrangement of data stored as electrons. Design emulation entails the adaptation of the data's ordering elements into a wholly new pattern of 0's and 1's. The two methods can be pursued in isolation or, as we shall see below, combined. Alone, they impose different costs on aspiring nonstate proliferants. Line replication is in principle costless. Because the virtual weapon's payload – a series of lines of code – is intangible, its transmission from one player to another and its copying are simple to achieve. Almost any user with access to the source code could easily replicate it. But the method suffers an inherent limitation. Traditional weapons are indiscriminate in their ability to cause harm. Because the payload is tangible, any physical person or object is susceptible to its force. Not so with cyberweapons. The opportunities to strike targets other than the original computer system diminish in proportion to the payload's degree of customization to it. Thus not all customized code is readily usable against other targets.

Take, for instance, the Stuxnet worm.[32] Even if another industrial facility employed the same programmable logic controller (PLC) as Natanz, the machine parts coupled to it would almost certainly differ, rendering the payload useless because it was designed to affect the Natanz plant's wider logical habitat – not merely its PLC. In this respect, the payload was a "one-shot" weapon.[33] By contrast, the worm's "dropper" package, or the code that opened access vectors into Natanz, was more amenable to replication.[34] Repeated manipulation of these weaknesses – four zero-days in Windows software and two stolen security certificates – is possible as long as two conditions obtain: the targeted facility employs the same operating system and root certificates; and the vulnerabilities remain unpatched. Yet while industrial controllers often use the same operating software, vendors and defenders often patch vulnerabilities after the security community discovers them. Line replication, therefore, will likely provide only limited strategic and tactical returns to actors who do not possess state-like intelligence and financial resources to craft a wholly new customized weapon on their own.[35]

Design emulation is costlier but more useful: costlier because it requires redevelopment of the original source code; more useful because it allows for flexibility in the payload's customization, which is crucial for an attacker seeking to hit a machine that is different from the original target. According to security analysts at Kaspersky Lab, low-skilled criminals have imitated Stuxnet's design philosophy in this way. "Stuxnet was the first really serious malware with a stolen certificate," explained Roel Schouwenberg. "It's become more and more common ever since. Nowadays you can see the use of fake certificates in very common malware."[36] Knowledge of design flaws does not remove the need for zero-day craftsmanship in the design of a weapon, but it can significantly narrow the scope of the search for an entry point.

The Stuxnet case is instructive in illustrating the different limits of the replication and emulation of weapons. At least two possible derivations of Stuxnet exist.[37] One is Duqu. A Trojan Horse discovered by Bulgarian researchers in September 2011, it is by some accounts a direct successor of Stuxnet. The computer security firm Symantec described it as a "precursor to the next Stuxnet" and claimed that it was authored with the use of Stuxnet's source code.[38] Popular outlets as notable as *Wired* magazine designated Duqu a "son of Stuxnet."

These claims have some empirical grounding. Similar to Stuxnet's beacon agent, which quietly transmitted data about the Natanz facility back to the worm's handlers, Duqu collected systems information from the computers of select organizations in Europe. Duqu may have succeeded Stuxnet chronologically: its first recorded activity, in April 2011, occurred well after the Stuxnet operation wound down.[39] In addition, the malware agents exhibited extensive programming similarities, raising the possibility of line replication. According to its Bulgarian discoverers, Duqu "massively re-used" Stuxnet's code, such as its modular structure and injection mechanisms, "in targeted attacks."[40] In fact, the coding similarities were so close that, on first contact with Duqu, workers at the antivirus company F-Secure believed they had stumbled upon Stuxnet.[41] But there were also significant differences, most notably in the payload. Whereas Stuxnet clearly had a destructive intent, Duqu – as far as we can tell – was used strictly for intelligence gathering (though possibly in preparation for a Stuxnet-like attack).

On these grounds, some observers have described Duqu as a horizontal proliferation event. To some observers, this raises the interesting prospect that Duqu was Iran's retaliation for Stuxnet, although they do not explain why computer systems in Europe, rather than the United States or Israel, were targeted.[42] Others have challenged this view. They claim that Duqu is a case of vertical proliferation. Technicians at

McAfee Labs surmised that the two artifacts were the work of the same actors. "One thing for sure is that the Stuxnet team is still active," they concluded shortly after Duqu's discovery.[43]

Flame is another possible successor to Stuxnet. It emerged in May 2012, when Iran's computer emergency response team, MAHER, discovered it in computers belonging to the country's main oil facility on Kharg Island.[44] Machines in Lebanon, Egypt, Syria, Sudan, and the Palestinian territories were also infected. According to MAHER, various features of Flame put it in "close relation" to both Stuxnet and Duqu.[45] The prospect of design emulation appeared. Flame featured similar file-naming conventions as its two possible ancestors. More revealing were the similarities in the propagation method. The virus used different exploits to manipulate the same two programming defects in Windows software – namely, a "special trick" to infect USB drives and "privilege-escalation" weaknesses – that Stuxnet used to disperse itself.[46] According to Hathaway, for this reason Flame represents a possible attempt to "replicate" Stuxnet.[47] Yet Flame's code was more complicated than Stuxnet's.[48] And unlike Stuxnet, Flame's payload had no destructive intent. As a data-sweeping agent, it was more similar to Duqu, yet Flame's technical profile was distinct from Duqu in other respects.[49]

Conceivably, Flame represents a case of proliferation of either one or both of its predecessors. Its similarities with Stuxnet and Duqu mean that its creation may have involved some combination of line replication and design emulation. At the same time, it was sufficiently distinct from them to affect third-party systems.

One view holds that Flame was created by a distinct developer team – an instance of horizontal proliferation.[50] Researchers at the Budapest University of Technology and Economics claimed that "sKyWIper [Flame] and Duqu (Stuxnet) have many differences, and it seems plausible that sKyWIper was not made by the same developer team."[51] We may never know the facts. Duqu's and Flame's perpetrators remain unidentified. For this reason, Kaspersky and Symantec have challenged the depiction of these cases as a horizontal proliferation. "Stuxnet and Duqu belonged to a single chain of attacks," remarked Eugene Kaspersky. "The Flame malware looks to be another phase in this war."[52]

Regardless of the connection (or not) between Flame and other malware, the weapon has its own proliferation contender: the Shamoon virus. In August 2012, it struck the computer systems of the oil firm

Saudi Aramco, the world's largest company by market value. The U.S. Secretary of Defense Leon Panetta described the operation as "a significant escalation of the cyber threat."[53] Shamoon was a self-propagating agent. It manipulated infected computers to corrupt other nodes connected to them via the company's internal network, after which the virus wiped the host machine's master boot record. The attack's direct effects were astounding: almost thirty thousand machines were rendered inoperable. The indirect effects may have been greater still. The attack prompted the company to bar external access to its computer networks, further disrupting corporate activities. Aramco's vice-president for corporate planning alleged that "the main target in this attack was to stop the flow of oil and gas to local and international markets."[54] That did not occur. Nevertheless, some analysts refuse to rule out such an eventuality in the future.[55]

Shamoon's crafters may have emulated some design elements of Flame. According to technicians at Kaspersky Lab, the wiper payload of the virus borrowed design principles from a similar component in Flame-infected Iranian computers. Yet there were also notable differences. It used a different wiper pattern that lacked the distinctive service names and driver filenames of Flame. It was also sloppier: "silly" flaws in the code included the use of an erroneous date comparison and the exchange of uppercase letters for lowercase ones in the code's format string, which impeded its execution.[56]

The identity of the perpetrators remains obscure. Surprisingly, Kaspersky experts believe that Shamoon was likely a "copycat" artifact, the work of "script kiddies inspired by the story [of Flame]."[57] An obscure jihadist militant group, the Cutting Sword of Justice, claimed responsibility for the attack in protest against Riyadh's regional foreign policy. The date that is hardcoded into the body of the virus is the same as the date that this group claimed Aramco's computers were hit.[58] Officials have openly wondered whether Shamoon was Tehran's reprisal for Flame.[59] Saudi Arabia is a close regional security partner of the United States and has vehemently advocated military action against Iranian nuclear facilities. As one study of the operation observed, Iran had both the geopolitical motive and the capability to carry it out.[60]

Ambiguities about the attackers' identity complicate the assessment of whether Shamoon qualifies as horizontal proliferation. But if

Kaspersky technicians' claim to this effect is correct, if Shamoon was indeed the ware of private amateurs, it would profoundly affect our understanding of high-end proliferation by alien players. It would mean that Shamoon – a highly disruptive attack against a strategically important Saudi company – was perpetrated by unsophisticated private coders,[61] thereby demonstrating the ease with which low-resource actors could employ emulation techniques to breach the high walls of the advanced quarters of cyberspace. But there is a likelier alternative hypothesis that some U.S. officials have voiced: the virus was the work of Tehran, which, having learned the "demonstration" lessons of the Stuxnet spectacle, has been rapidly stocking its own virtual basements with increasingly potent offensive code.

In sum, insofar as Duqu and Flame represent possibly mixed cases of replication and emulation of the Stuxnet worm, itself a state-crafted tool, and inasmuch as Shamoon's designers adapted the features of Flame, in all cases the proliferants were likely governments – or even the same government[62] – rather than civilian culprits. So far, the alarming cries of some analysts about the imminent replication and reuse of such genial weapons remain unfulfilled. Kaspersky's unproven assertions aside, private actors have not yet broken into the most advanced offensive quarters of the new domain. The high costs of producing and even reproducing weaponized code present them with a wall too high to surmount in the absence of the intelligence and capital resources of states.

But subversive alien players covet advanced code. Take, for instance, Islamic State. The terrorist group's self-styled Hacking Division has reportedly sought to acquire knowledge of zero-days that would enable it to craft malware to disrupt vital infrastructures in distant lands – a means to claim for the Caliphate a plot in virtual paradise.[63] So far, the quest has not succeeded. Yet one should not be complacent about this threat: European intelligence agencies estimate that hundreds of their citizens have returned to the Continent from IS-held territory in Syria and Iraq. Countless others who have not fought under the jihadist banner may secretly sympathize with the extremist cause.[64] This situation raises the prospect of an insider threat, the nightmare of any security planner: the possibility that a radicalized computer operator or coder in Europe will abuse his or her access to a critical computer system in order to design or deliver malware that inflicts economic and other harm on society.

Generalized cyberweapons, by contrast, have a greater proliferation potential. Their costs of acquisition are far lower than is the case with customized code. Thus the opportunities for nonstate actors to acquire them are notably higher. Here, the alien players encounter not an imposing wall but a shallow moat that is all too easy to bridge with moderate resources.

On the other side of this moat one finds, for instance, botnets: networks of remotely controlled and often compromised machines that can blast web servers with concentrated torrents of data requests (i.e. a distributed denial-of-service (DDoS) attack). The term emerged from the Czech word for robot, "robota," which refers to the armies of machines that constitute the botnet's workforce. The first botnets appeared in the Internet Relay Chats (IRCs) of the early 1990s. They did not have pernicious aims. Their purpose, rather, was to support and aid legitimate communications. This benign state did not last long. Criminal groups soon used the technology to conduct DDoS attacks against individual IRC users and even entire servers.[65] Today they are especially popular among such groups, who use this capability for crimes such as stealing online identities and credit card information.

Because of their low costs of creation and purchase, botnets are one of the main offensive instruments in the hands of private actors. For a seasoned programmer, botnets are not difficult to create. They require only moderate skills, such as the ability to design malware that is able to hijack remote machines or that is downloadable via the Internet. A Google employee who recently searched the Internet for information on constructing a botnet discovered a website that offered free botnet builder tools. Such tools "can be found online in minutes."[66]

The most powerful modern botnets are also rentable. Some criminal markets provide subscription packages offering, depending on the tier of service, an unlimited number of attacks, a duration window of thirty seconds to one or two hours, single or concurrent attacks, and so on. The subscription price is cheap, ranging from $10–30, although truly powerful botnets come at a much higher price.[67] But relative to the high price of acquiring zero-days that go into customizing an advanced payload, their cost is low. Consequently, at any one time, a significant number of all machines connected to the Internet are enrolled in some botnet.

The ability of botnets to cause harm relative to customized weapons is low. They will not destroy nuclear turbines or cause irreparable harm to corporate workstations. They will not normally seize the prized sensitive data of senior government officials.[68] Nor will they instruct dams to open, derail trains carrying hazardous materials, or blank out air-traffic-control systems (all in principle achievable by weaponized code).[69] But they can still cause considerable damage, which can be significant even by the high standards of national security. Culprits have used botnets to interrupt essential computer functions at moments of acute international tension. Most famously, they were the prime means of attack used against Estonia's financial and governmental infrastructures in the spring of 2007 after the government removed a Soviet war memorial, the statue of "the Bronze Soldier," which many citizens regarded as an occupation monument, from central Tallinn to a military hospital. In August 2008, botnet commanders orchestrated DDoS attacks that disrupted the operations of Georgia's national bank and government communications systems during the country's military invasion by Russia. More recently, in 2016, they impaired the functions of Dyn, a company that manages domain name services on which important commercial and media services rely. The attacks, which like the others came in waves, prevented millions of people in numerous countries from accessing popular websites such as Reddit, Airbnb, Netflix, CNN, *The New York Times, The Boston Globe, The Financial Times*, and *The Guardian*.

None of these attacks produced loss of life. None caused irreversible damage to computer functions. Yet the attacks against Estonia convulsed this small nation's governmental services and economic affairs such as online banking, a vital activity in a country whose population conducted 98 percent of financial transactions online, intermittently for a period of about three weeks. "An attack against the state" is how Estonian Defense Minister Jaak Aaviksoo described the incident.[70] The attacks against Georgia hindered the government's ability to organize national defenses and procure essential war materiel while it was fending off a Russian land invasion. The attacks against Dyn disrupted the daily lives of millions of individuals around the globe.

In all of these cases the main agents behind the botnets were private actors. There is reason to suspect some degree of Russian government complicity in the Estonian attacks. But it is clear from the available facts that their main perpetrators were private, not governmental.[71] Anonymous private citizens participated in the campaign en masse from multiple national jurisdictions, including from Estonian soil.

The Russian military could have conducted the cyberattacks against Georgia, but such complicity would have been difficult to mask credibly. "The attackers displayed a convincing amount of disorder without being at all random," observed one of the most detailed analyses of the case. Owing to the "verifiable quantity of civilian cyber-attack activity, any direct Russian military involvement was simply unnecessary."[72] The private organizers of these attacks may have enjoyed advance information about Russia's intentions and the timing of its military maneuvers in Georgia; indeed, the signal to attack must have reached the culprits privately, for they acted with greater sudden force than the ability of online media to recruit adherents.[73] Yet the attack capability itself had a civilian origin. Organized criminal syndicates may have aided the botnet's assembly, because some of its assets were simultaneously employed to commit commercial crimes. The principal tool in the recruitment of zombie machines were social networks. These were not esoteric and shady hacker forums within the vast, murky Dark Web. Rather, they were ordinary chat rooms dedicated to the discussion of mundane matters: dating, hobbies, political interests – and now suddenly instantaneous mobilization to the virtual front on the backdrop of a real war.[74]

The evaluation of Russia's complicity in these attacks requires that we specify a spectrum of proximity between private actors and the state. Four degrees of closeness are possible. The first is *coordinated action*, in which state agencies and private players partake in a simultaneous operation (e.g. both share a common botnet infrastructure). Second is *direct support* by state agencies, which entails the provision by the state of deployable attack tools (e.g. knowledge of zero-days vulnerabilities and payloads) or financing to acquire them (e.g. botnet infrastructure rental). Third is *indirect support*, whereby state agents provide citizens tactical information (e.g. target lists and timetables) to organize an attack but not the means to carry it out. Fourth, is *forbearance*, when the state provides neither direct nor indirect support but knows (or can discover) the identity of perpetrators within its district yet decides not to penalize them.

The campaign against Dyn was of similar private provenance. Having sifted through the forensic evidence of the case, U.S. investigators found no indication of government authorship. While recognizing that the investigation was still ongoing, the Director of National

Intelligence, James Clapper, stated that a nonstate actor was behind the attacks.[75] The computer security firm Flashpoint corroborated Clapper's assessment, pointing out that the "Mirai" botnet infrastructure involved in the attacks was popular among the video-gaming community which comprises hackers who are eager to burnish their computational prowess. Not ideology or politics but the vainglorious impulses of anonymous denizens of the Internet's dark quarters paralyzed broad sectors of the Internet.[76]

Overall the picture of cyber arms proliferation to nonstate actors is mixed. Customized weapons of the kind that can cause direct destructive effects to infrastructures are in principle the cheapest – costless, in fact – to replicate precisely. Yet this method of proliferation is unlikely to yield a payload that is reusable against a target other than the original. Possibly the replicated weapon will prove useless later even against the original target if its operators have patched the previously unknown vulnerabilities on which the weapon relies to gain access or execute the payload. Emulation of weaponized code is far more expensive, requiring a significant redevelopment effort – the harvesting of new zero-day weaknesses, the design of a highly customized payload against a new target, the opening of precise access vectors into it, and so on. Yet the impact factor of a successful emulation can be high, as the possible sons of Stuxnet, Flame, and Duqu revealed. By contrast, a generalized weapon such as a botnet DDoS tool imposes only moderate costs on the aspiring proliferant. Many other actors have freely employed the services of botnets. Their direct and indirect effects, however, are demonstrably less significant than what is achievable with weaponized code.

Yet the main reason for preoccupation when considering the growing influence of actors alien to the states system is not their capabilities, which are conclusively lower than the power of the system's masters, but the nature of their aims, which can be more subversive and wilder and which may clash with the purposes of states. "We've had this disparity or contrast between the capability of the most sophisticated cyber actors, nation-state cyber actors, which are clearly Russia and China," remarked Clapper, noting that these familiar opponents have a "more benign intent." But "then you have other countries who have a more nefarious intent," he continued, a possible allusion to revolutionary states such as North Korea. "And then even more nefarious are non-nation-state actors,"[77] such as political hacktivists, criminal syndicates, and extremist groups – those pests to theory who, in their motives and aims, and increasingly in their capabilities, defy the axioms of conventional security models. Private technology firms, too, could easily bridge the moat of generalized weapons production; they may even be adept at scaling the high walls that block off the most advanced offensive quarter in which some states reside (on which more in Chapter 9).

Defense Fragmentation

A second manifestation of systems change involves the provision of national security: governments are not the supreme, and in some cases not even the primary, defenders against cyber threats in the way that they are against conventional threats. Here, we must draw a distinction between two basic forms of defensive activity: active and passive.

The label "active defense" broadly denotes the virtual weapon's use outside the defender's or other friendly terrain to prevent or preempt a hostile cyber action.[78] This does not imply the use of any specific kind of malware: the defending action can be exploitive, disruptive, or both. Rather, it means that the activity transpires outside the home network terrain for strictly defensive purposes.

States are the main players in the conduct of active defense. They possess the legal prerogative to inflict harm on attacking machines residing outside their jurisdiction. By contrast, most domestic penal codes – for example, the U.S. Computer Fraud and Abuse Act – prohibit private actors from carrying out this activity. Even when they are the targets of a major impending offensive strike, it falls on the government, not the victims, to conduct (or not to conduct) active defense. Governments have good reasons to retain absolute rights over active defense. But many voices, including some in government, have called for an expansion of these rights to the private sector. We will deal with these reasons and their countervailing voices in Chapter 9. For now, it suffices to recognize that when it comes to cyber offense-as-defense, the government's role is as the framers of the Conventional Model would expect: supreme.

Passive defense is more important and more common in the cyber realm than active defense. Passive measures such as resiliency and redundancy – the equivalents of underground shelters and target dispersal in nuclear defense – aim to thicken the defensive glacis and absorb damage from offensive hits. Unlike active defense, passive defense occurs solely within the bounds of the defender's computer terrain. It seeks to neutralize threats that have arrived at or penetrated the home network perimeter.

Unquestionably, the private sector holds the greatest capacity for passive defense on its own terrain, and sometimes also in matters that affect government networks or impinge on national security. It does not commonly coordinate its passive defense measures with the government, for this would require the presence of police and military agents inside private networks that hold data, such as proprietary client data, that companies have legitimate (or illicit) reason to withhold from the prying eyes of the state. Such fragmentation of defense responsibilities is a limiting factor for states when formulating a coherent response to a cyberattack.

The problem of fragmentation begins with the authority over the core operations of cyberspace. The majority of critical computer infrastructures are designed, owned, and operated by private industry. Private utilities own plants that supply more than three-quarters of U.S. electrical power. The computer systems that process securities trades at the world's four largest stock exchanges – NYSE, NASDAQ, the London Stock Exchange, and the Tokyo Stock Exchange – and many other exchanges operate under total private ownership.[79] Eight of the ten largest oil-refining complexes – Reliance Jamnagar Refinery (India); Ulsan Refinery, Yeosu Refinery, and Onsan Refinery (South Korea); Port Arthur Refinery, Baytown Refinery, and Garyville Refinery (United States); and ExxonMobil's Singapore Refinery (Singapore) – also function under private control.[80]

Fragmentation among the public and private sectors is also evident in the design of the Internet. The military resources and imperatives of the Pentagon, specifically the desire to create a communications infrastructure that could withstand a social breakdown, motivated the development of the ARPANET, the precursor to the modern Internet. But the writ of government did not influence the design of the protocols that drove the ARPANET out of its primordial state. This was the work of Cerf and the Xerox Palo Alto Research Center. With a mix of persuasion and coercion, including the unilateral suspension of the old protocol – Network Control Program – they forced the universal adoption of the new TCP/IP (Transmission Control Protocol/Internet Protocol), thereby altering the "digital DNA" of modern network computing.[81]

Internet governance is another area of activity that does not fit neatly within Westphalian institutional confines. Here, the picture is mixed. Internet governance is largely, but not entirely, the preserve of private nonprofit organizations. Four bodies stand out: ICANN, which manages the central ledger of Internet addresses, especially the Domain Name System that translates popular domain names into numerical IP addresses; the Internet Society, an international organization that guides the development of Internet standards and education; the Internet Governance Forum, an arena for policy dialogue that includes a mix of governmental and private actors; and the International Telecommunication Union (ITU), a specialized agency of the United Nations that shapes global technical standards. Thus only one of these entities, the ITU, matches the intergovernmental cast of the Conventional Model. It is the least influential of all of the Internet's stewards. "The ITU has little intrinsic power," explains Jack Goldsmith. "The real power over the Internet lies with nations that are fighting for control over the Net in the ITU and other places."[82]

But it would be wrong to assume that because nations increasingly dominate the battle for control over the Internet, they control the Internet itself. As Goldsmith and Wu explain, nations are caught in a "technological version of the Cold War" in which they have to choose between the open model of the Internet in the United States, which is largely free of government interference, and the politically controlled model, in which government meddling is pervasive, as in the case of the Iranian intranet.[83] Thus, on one side of the governance divide, the contesting nations advocate a model in which the state's role in the Internet's regulation is not primary, even if that role is growing elsewhere.

Most important, the problem of fragmentation bedevils the protection of the government's own interests in vital areas of national security. In many Western countries, the government depends on privately owned computer infrastructures for some of its most basic functions. Of government communications, including some military traffic, 90 percent travel via private networks. Technology firms own and control the vast majority of the enormous amounts of data that citizens generate in their private lives. Insofar as cyberspace is an operational domain like the terrestrial realms of sea and land, the main keepers of this virtual Earth are private companies, not the government.

This last point is especially important. It is the definition of a well-ordered society that the state knows information about its citizens' general affairs which is necessary to protect the public from the nefarious activities of criminals among them. At least since the appearance in the early twentieth century of the "administrative state" comprising vast bureaucracies to collect and sort citizen data,[84] this has meant that among all entities with which citizens interacted – state agencies, shopkeepers, insurance providers, educational institutions, and so on – the government held the most extensive troves of information about their private thoughts and habits. The rise of the Internet as a social sensation has altered this situation drastically. Not the government but private firms – Google and Apple, for instance – possess and control access to the greatest collections of private data. Moreover, they own data about areas of private life not previously captured, such as commercial and driving habits. Consequently, the government can frequently only gain access to crucial information about its citizens at the consent of the private data handlers.

Encryption in this context is a notable area of systems change. Normally, the private affairs of citizens are not a legitimate object of government scrutiny. They become a concern when these affairs impinge on public safety – for example, in the aftermath of a terrorist incident such as the mass shooting in December 2015 by two Islamic State affiliates in San Bernardino, California. Apple had the means to write custom code to unlock one of the shooter's cryptographically sealed iPhones, which FBI officers believed held information that was crucial to their investigation, especially regarding possible accomplices. The FBI's concern betrayed a larger problem: encrypted communications enable members of terrorist cells to plan and execute operations in real time and beyond the ability of government to monitor. The company declined to assist investigators in decrypting the device, arguing that doing so would enable the government to create a backdoor into its phones, broadly imperiling privacy rights.[85] Others suspected a financial motive – an attempt to raise Apple's image as a privacy champion in an age of acute public sensitivity to government surveillance. Thus the standoff presented a clash between the FBI's defense of a public good (security against terrorism) and Apple's interpretation of a competing public good (data privacy), one that matched a private good: the company's own revenue stream. The novelty of the case was not that a private firm expressed a concern for the public good involving the use of one of its products, but that the firm was in a position to adjudicate against the government's wishes between two seemingly incommensurable public goods. In the end, the FBI resorted to the services of private hackers to crack the device.[86] The irony of the case's conclusion is no boon to the statist sentiment: the world's most powerful government overcame the resistance of company executives more powerful than itself in dealing with a matter of national security significance only because the state recruited or bought the sympathies of another private player. One way or another, the private sector was supreme over the sovereign.

The influence of the private sector in the functions of cyberspace ranges from relevance to primacy to supremacy. Even in the realm of active defense, where the government's prerogative is unquestionably supreme, the private sector retains some relevance because the government cannot operate fully in those quarters that it does not control or because the government lacks access to private data that it requires to tailor its foreign operations. The Apple-FBI saga shows that in core areas of national security such as in the aftermath of a terrorist atrocity inspired by foreign miscreants, the state cannot operate with full latitude because it lacks access to sensitive private information or other resources in the domestic cyberspace that it requires for its investigation. Private technology behemoths such as Apple can enable or deny this access, often in defiance of law enforcement needs. When opposition in the boardrooms is unbending, the sovereign can lose not merely its customary supremacy but also its primacy; it may remain relevant only at the leniency of other profit seekers who themselves are in a position to arbitrate among clashing public interests.

Collision of Two Worlds

The third and perhaps gravest manifestation of systems change relates to the emergence of a nascent "world system": a system of relations in which states are no longer the supremely powerful players in conflict among the units. As the global chaos of the cyber domain fuses ever more closely with the rigid states system that struggles to regulate it, the traditional units are less able to prevent, restrain, and terminate meaningful conflicts among themselves and among other relevant players. This problem represents an extension of the two preceding themes: not only can private players use cyberspace to harm the interests of nations or to hinder the organization of their own defenses, they can also disturb the interactions among nations.

Cyber conflict can fit four basic frames of agent interaction: *state-to-state*, in which one state targets another state's strategic computer assets, such as in the Stuxnet operation (this category includes the use by government of obedient civilian proxies); *private-to-state*, which includes cyberattacks by militant groups or hacktivists, such as in the Estonian crisis; *private-to-private*, involving an exchange of attacks between nonstate entities such as private companies; and *state-to-private*, in which a state attacks the private computer systems of another nation, possibly for commercial or other economic gain (see Table 1).

Table 1: Agent frames in an international cyber conflict

		Attacker	
		State	**Private Actor**
Defender	**State**	One state targets another state's strategic computer assets (e.g. Stuxnet operation)	Nonstate actors such as militant groups or 'patriotic' hackers target a foreign state's computer assets (e.g. Estonia, Georgia)
	Private Actor	A state attacks the private computer systems of another state for a strategic or commercial purpose (Saudi Aramco, Sony Pictures)	Exchange of blows among nonstate entities (e.g. attacks by Anonymous affiliates against Islamic State)

The dispersion of power away from states shatters basic distinctions in international relations, which traditionally established order and restraint in international contests for security. It means that the interests and purposes of all relevant parties in a conflict may not be known. While nonstate actors do not possess the maximum of capabilities, and thus by themselves cannot inflict the gravest harm, they can bring a preexisting crisis to the boil. An unfolding interstate confrontation will provide incentives and opportunities for private actors to act without their government's direction and possibly against its wishes.

The Estonian crisis is instructive. No one even generally familiar with it can deny that politically motivated individuals can act irresponsibly and disrupt international affairs. Evidence links the hiring of offensive botnets to the Russian security services.[87] Initially, the Estonian authorities linked the attacks to Russia because they involved IP addresses of machines in the Kremlin. It is reasonable to assume that an organized group with deep financial resources was necessary to hire the botnet infrastructure. The Russian state may also have been involved in the target selection. Jaak Aaviksoo, the Estonian Minister of Defense at the time, argued that the sheer scope, duration, and timing of the attacks against his country, which occurred while his government removed a Soviet Second World War memorial from outside the capital's center, mean that the Russian government must have given the order for or coordinated some of its citizens' actions.[88] "You don't expect spontaneous, populist cyber attacks to have a pre-determined list of targets and precise dates and times for coordinated attacks," explained Mihkel Tammet, Director of Communications and Information Technology in the Estonian Ministry of Defense.[89] The public admission of guilt by Konstantin Goloskokov, a "commissar" of the Nashi youth group that enjoys close ties to the Kremlin, adds credence to this view.[90]

The evidence for direct or indirect support by Russia is circumstantial, however. Officials later publicly retracted their accusation. "Of course, at the moment, I cannot state for certain that the cyber attacks were managed by the Kremlin, or other Russian government agencies," stated Aaviksoo in June 2007.[91] To date, the Estonian government has not formally accused the Kremlin of direct complicity in the attacks, although many will privately attest to their belief in this proposition. As Marina Kaljurand, Estonia's ambassador in Moscow at the time, explained: "Attribution of cyber attacks is always difficult, especially in the case of cross-border attacks. Thus in June 2007, officials in Tallinn invoked a bilateral mutual assistance treaty with Russia in a bid to secure Moscow's assistance in the forensic investigation following the attacks. Moscow did not reply. We requested legal cooperation from Russia, but they did not cooperate with Estonian officials investigating the case. So we had to investigate and attribute unilaterally. There was no direct evidence linking the attacks to the Russian state, but there was enough circumstantial evidence to conclude that these attacks were carried out with the knowledge and support of the Russian state."[92] Thus its degree of proximity to the perpetrators was at least one of forbearance: the Kremlin knew or could have discovered their identities but chose to cast a blind eye.[93]

Whatever the degree of Russian state complicity in the attacks, it is not sufficiently understood that the botnet infrastructure itself was operated by criminal syndicates; that attack tools and target information were readily obtainable online; and that the vast majority of attackers acted without the Kremlin's direction or consent.[94]

Private culprits, mostly inside Russia but also worldwide, participated in the attacks. The attack sequence itself crossed more than one hundred national jurisdictions – including the Vatican City. "One of the reasons why these attacks were a gamechanger," stated Christian-Marc Liflända, the Director of Policy Planning at the Estonian Ministry of Defense, "was their geographic magnitude: they involved the use of computers from around the globe."[95] The attackers' presence in foreign jurisdictions severely impeded the ability of Estonian authorities to punish private culprits for their participation in the attacks. Officials weighed specific "countermeasures" against suspected attackers residing abroad, such as "blacklisting the individuals from travel into the [European Union's visa-free] Schengen zone."[96] Yet none of these measures yielded meaningful penalties. For participation in the botnet campaign, the Estonian courts convicted only one person: Dmitri Galushkevich, a nineteen-year-old ethnic Russian hapless enough to access the online instructions on how to participate in the botnet from inside Estonia, thus rendering him accessible to the local police.[97]

The diplomatic consequences of the uncoordinated intrusions of private citizens were potentially severe. Many people know that the September 11, 2001, terrorist attacks on the United States was the only time that NATO ever invoked its collective defense clause, Article 5, which stipulates that an armed attack on one alliance member is an attack on all of them. Another important clause, Article 4, which provides for formal consultations in situations where a member's "territorial integrity, political independence or security" is threatened, is less well known, but it has also been invoked rarely – only five times in almost seventy years. An invocation of one or both of these articles would represent a major diplomatic and even military development.[98] Few people understand that the Estonian crisis is the only situation other than the 9/11 attacks that immediately prompted a discussion within or among NATO member states regarding the invocation of the two articles. Hostilities in Estonian cyberspace quickly raised the matter of the articles' applicability to this case. In the midst of the crisis, Harri Tiido, at the time Estonia's ambassador to NATO, recalls the alliance's Secretary General, Jaap de Hoop Scheffer, grabbing him by the arm while alliance officials drafted a press release and asking whether it was his government's intention to invoke Article 4.

The answer from Tallinn was no: officials would not invoke either clause. They concluded – wisely – that neither the intensity of the attacks, which, though potent, did not involve physical destruction or loss of life, nor their duration met the high bar for an armed attack. The desire of decision-makers to shape the narrative of the attacks also factored into the decision not to escalate internationally. "The events were interpreted largely as a domestic disturbance – not an international incident," said Liflander. "The Estonian government wanted this perception to prevail: this was nothing but hooligans to be dealt with by law enforcement. International escalation would have broken this narrative."[99]

Yet escalation was in the air. According to Liflander, who was on the scene in Estonia, and Kaljurand, who was stationed in Moscow, the matter of collective defense implications was considered within national decision-making circles. Tiido reported that in the month following the attacks, the Estonian government brought the matter to the attention of the alliance "first and foremost as a political issue," that is, " to make the point that cyberattacks can be as damaging as conventional weapons."[100]

In short order, then, a crisis that unknown private actors outside of NATO territory intensified, if not also precipitated, placed the question and the prospect of the ultimate diplomatic showdown – an activation of the alliance's collective defense provisions – firmly on the regional security agenda. As NATO's Assistant Secretary General for Emerging Security Challenges Sorin Ducaru explained, several years later, at the Wales summit in 2014, the alliance formally drew a "strategic link between cyber defense and collective defense." Two years later, at the Warsaw summit, the alliance designated cyberspace an official "domain," thereby taking the lessons of the Estonian crisis to "the operational front."[101] The Russian leadership could hardly have imagined or desired that these mostly unsophisticated cyberattacks by their own citizens would prompt first a discussion, and eventually an operationalization, of such a momentous shift – "a change of paradigm," in the words of Ducaru – on the other side of the European security divide.

The important observation about the Estonian crisis is not that the cyberattacks fell below the threshold for armed attack, but that officials in Tallinn and later across the NATO alliance closely weighed such an interpretation.[102] The pitfalls of interstate instability meet the dangers of global chaos from below the system. "The political level of decision-making had never dealt with such cyber issues before – ever," avers Lifländer. This is an astonishing admission about the leadership of a nation whose role on the frontiers of the cyber revolution had already earned it the moniker of "E-stonia." He remembers distinctly that "policymakers around the table differed in their interpretations of the severity of the attacks … Some equated it to a nuclear event."[103] The problem was essentially one of correctly interpreting unprecedented events in the absence of clear benchmarks for doing so. Lifländer recounts the pitfalls: "In essence, what you had in this crisis situation was first a perception of the problem and second your projection of your own norms, values, beliefs into what you think is happening." The Speaker of the Estonian Parliament Ene Ergma's analogy of "a nuclear explosion"[104] was, according to Lifländer, "merely her flawed attempt to apply an analogy from previous experience to characterize the events."

Forces of chaos from outside the states system also emerged on the Estonian side. Only barely did the Estonian government succeed in restraining its own patriots from striking back against machines inside Russia.[105] "What was happening to Estonia could happen in reverse among Estonians: patriotic hackers could act as vigilantes," recalls Lifländer. "But we did not see evidence of significant counterattacks happening."[106] As the national drama unfolded, authorities issued public statements asking for calm and abstinence from retaliating against foreign provocations by striking machines inside Russia or elsewhere. At any rate, the technically skilled citizenry was largely absorbed with the immediate task of defending the home networks against an attack sequence that constantly adapted itself to strike new targets. "Part of the restraint is easily explained by the fact that Estonian citizens who had relevant skills were not organized to act."[107] The experience of the crisis revealed the necessity for a coherent scheme to organize national civilian defenses. It played a crucial role in the establishment of the Estonian Cyber Defense League in 2010.[108]

In addition to the threat of feverish masses attacking with little or no state direction, there is the problem of state proxies. States, notably China and Russia, are equipping their civilian sectors with a capacity to hit hard with the new technology. In particular, Russia's relationship with proxy militias – quasi-state agents who receive direction and support from the government but do not belong to it – seems to have grown closer since the Estonian crisis. Dimitri Alperovitch, co-founder of the security firm CrowdStrike, expressed the point: "When someone is identified as being technically proficient in the Russian underground," their pending criminal prosecution "suddenly disappears and those people are never heard from again." That is, they have been informally absorbed into the intelligence apparatus.[109]

China presents a similar picture of the cooptation of civilian talent into the service of state ends. The People's Liberation Army fields an impressive and growing capacity for offensive action. Its outfits include the blandly dubbed Unit 61398 and Unit 61486 but bland their actions are not. In 2014, Washington indicted three of the former unit's servicemen (one indecorously named "UglyGorilla") for seizing prized trade secrets and intellectual property of American firms such as United States Steel Corporation to aid the interests of Chinese state-owned competitors.[110] But Beijing also regularly resorts to hirelings and moonlighters in mounting its operations. Civilian outsourcing often implicates the academy – even esteemed institutions such as Shanghai Jiao Tong University, whose researchers have developed, jointly with Unit 61398, "attack graphs" and "intrusion monitoring" technology."[111] The motives for absorption of civilian talent are evident: irregular militias furnish governments with the option of plausible deniability in a cyberattack (on which more in Chapter 9).

But here, again, pressures of instability appear. There is no guarantee that during a heated interstate conflict, the proxies will heed the instructions of their parent states. For example, cyber militias in several countries have threatened to use cyberweapons against Russia to defend their home nations[112] – a prospect that recalls the concerns of prudent Estonian officials who in 2007 faced similar pressures. What was conceived as a means for states to avoid retribution may in fact become its justification. In sum, the factors of convergence between the world of states and the world of citizens that provide governments with political advantages in a cyber conflict are also the factors that can produce a dangerous and unmanageable collision of these two universes.

A Cyber Breakdown?

There is something remarkable about Ene Ergma's nuclear analogy above: it betrays the belief that a major cyberattack could produce a breakdown of modern society. She is not the only public official to conjure images of a technologically induced cataclysm; one often hears senior officials utter the slogans "Cyber 9/11" and "Cyber Pearl Harbor." Probably these are nothing more than rhetorical devices to raise public awareness about a growing cyber threat that some quarters of society still dismiss as uninteresting or unimportant. But could the virtual weapon's unrestrained power produce so catastrophic a disintegration of modern society that the states system itself collapses?

Security planners at the Pentagon have explored the plausibility of such a scenario. Possibilities have included a coordinated and rolling attack on power grids; the malfunction of oil-refining facilities in Texas; the disabling of hydraulic systems in Californian ports; and the blinding of the air-defense radar systems that monitor U.S. air traffic.[113] Others have warned about the possible collapse of the computer infrastructure that sustains the Internet. Some of the firms that operate this infrastructure, such as Dyn and Verisign, which register top-level domains (for example,. com,. net,. co.uk.), have experienced a growing number of DDoS attacks. Bruce Schneier warns that the attacks appear to be probing operations: sophisticated state actors are calibrating their weapons in ways that would enable concurrent attacks across multiple vectors.[114]

Whatever the plausibility of these scenarios, even their simultaneous occurrence would not result in the wholesale destruction of state structures. At most, they might produce a disintegration of local and provincial authority, possibly resulting in some internal migration and, in borderless regions such as the European Union, international exodus. But generally national border controls and local policing would remain intact. The disruption of transportation networks, moreover, would drastically reduce the means of travel. The situation, in fact, would be doubly paradoxical because nations such as Sudan or Niger, with porous borders and minimal reliance on computer infrastructures to sustain internal sovereign functions, would be least affected by the breakdown.

Thus, in advanced societies where the effects of technological failure are most severe, the political reverberations might at most be localized. In less developed societies where the effects are mildest, the political impact might be negligible. There will be no cyber Armageddon.

The Sovereignty Gap: Convergence and Collision

States are no longer the unquestioned masters of the international system. The gradual flight of power to other players via cyberspace has produced a *sovereignty gap* – if sovereignty means not just an interstate condition, in other words, the state is subject to no other state in the ordering of its internal affairs, as international law and some political theorists commonly define the notion, but also one involving freedom from the interference of unaffiliated actors.[115] Based on the preceding discussion, the problem has three main manifestations.

First, states are no longer the sole or even the main objects of concern of other states in the protection of national security. The ease of proliferation of some – if not the most potent – cyber arms to private players means that national security planning must now consider threats emanating from outside the system. Second, states can no longer take for granted their ability to protect national security against all relevant threats. What in previous eras governments would have deemed an unacceptable renunciation of national security to actors other than themselves has come to pass in the new era. The compulsive quest by some nations to occupy all quarters of cyberspace is a sign of vulnerability and not strength. Third, states are not the sole masters, even of interactions among themselves. All future cyber conflicts will face the dangers that private culprits will intervene in ways that accelerate the crisis or that move it in a direction that the system's old stewards do not want to go.

Security policy, in short, now has to be conducted against and by not only states but also a growing universe of other players of unclear origin and identity. States can no longer conduct their foreign and defense policies as if forces of discord emanating from beyond the states system were suppressible merely by their own will. Ambassador Ducaru, who works at the frontlines of policy planning against unconventional threats to NATO, a cherished organ of the Westphalian order whose forms reflect the finest prejudices of theorists, regards the growing ability of the alien players to wield the virtual weapon against both states and each other as "a fundamental change in the international threat landscape" – even if they are not as mighty as nations, even if policy-makers must preserve the official doctrine that the largest among the ordinary units pose the gravest peril to national and regional security.

The partial forces of systems change – the most important of which is what a senior official in the British Cabinet Office described as "the democratization of threat actors"[116] – produce opportunities for convergence between the world of states and the chaotic global universe that also includes nontraditional players. It enables new opportunities for cooperation between states and nonstate actors who share certain goals and adversaries. Convergence can take a defensive or offensive form. Defensively, the aim may be to enhance cooperation between the government and the private sector in the protection of either party's computer terrain. Offensively, the goal may be to collude in the design of sophisticated attack tools targeting foreign machines.

The main distinguishing feature of the cyber revolution is that it may be the first technological revolution of the first order in the international system. That technology is also at least partly a primary rather than just a secondary cause of change gives it a special uniqueness. These developments have profound implications for the understanding and practice of international order and security. Vanished is the secure belief in the state as both the supreme source of threats to national security and the supreme protector against them. A central feature of the present technological revolution is that the state has become a lesser agent in the management of its own security affairs, regardless of the continued indispensability of governments in the organization of domestic order and in the avoidance of international conflict. Deniers of the revolution are troubled by these incomplete but notable trends of systems change. They are more adept at devising new formulas to mask weaknesses in old concepts than they are proficient at closing the gap between the statist ideal of international order and the fluid reality of global chaos.

PART III

PROBLEMS OF STRATEGY AND POLICY

CHAPTER 7

The Deterrence Puzzle
DOCTRINAL PROBLEMS AND REMEDIES

Doctrinal Problems

The ordinary goal of deterrence policy is to prevent an attack. Thus it is futile to speak of "degrees" of success in deterrence: it either succeeds or it fails. Failure is absolute. There is no reverting to a situation in which the attack did not happen. Consider the nuclear realm of conflict from which deterrence theory emerged. Initial attempts to enshrine strategies of "limited war" in policy did not go far.[1] Aversion to the loss of a single American or Soviet city and its entire population convinced the superpowers that an exchange of nuclear blows must be avoided at all costs. With a quotient of horror measured in millions of lives, the idea of limited losses is repugnant. All tactical amputations seem like a strategic fatality. Thus the temptation of deterrence policy has been to prevent all attacks unconditionally: to pursue deterrence for its own sake.

This policy dogma remains entrenched in contemporary strategy in other realms of conflict. Policymakers repeatedly emphasize the need, as a senior official in the British Cabinet Office put it, "to increase deterrence across the board in the cyber domain."[2] They stress the goal of shoring up defenses to deny adversaries opportunities to compromise networks – "all the way from protecting ordinary computer users to protecting nuclear command codes."[3]

Yet the strategy of total deterrence that has succeeded in the nuclear realm fails in the cyber domain. Denial is notoriously difficult to achieve. As we discussed in Chapter 2, sophisticated cyber operations are hard to foil. Therefore, the emphasis of deterrence policy is on retribution: preventing attacks by expressing a readiness to punish them with maximum available force. The "equivalence principle" that features prominently in American and British national cyber strategies stipulates that a major attack may invoke a military reprisal – a pledge that even a proportionate response will be intense. As Britain's Chancellor of the Exchequer George Osborne defiantly stated in November 2015, "We reserve the right to respond to a cyber attack in any way that we choose."[4]

The prevailing deterrence posture in the cyber domain suffers from two major deficiencies. One involves the dangers of conflict escalation. So far, the equivalence principle has worked – at least in deterring acts of cyberwar.[5] At the time of writing, there has been no cyberwar. But the warning of severe retaliation creates pressures for an accelerating crisis if an exchange of blows occurs. If the logic of penalties fails, the price of a successful cyberattack is the risk of a spiraling war in the conventional domain. In the high spectrum of action encompassing destructive activity, therefore, the logics of deterrence and escalation control are at odds. The logic of penalties in the cyber domain aggravates the difficulties of conflict control in other domains. The new technology gives a new twist to the remark by Raymond Aron: "Everything that increases the likelihood of escalation in advance contributes to deterrence but also makes it, by definition, more difficult to limit war if it breaks out after all."[6] Second, the posture fails in the middle range of action: it has not succeeded in preventing acts of unpeace, the nonviolent but highly damaging activity described in Chapter 2. This activity continues unabated; in fact, it has grown in scope and severity as nations find new ways to employ virtual weapons to harm the national interests and disrupt the internal political affairs of adversaries without ever firing a shot – for instance, Russia's reported hacking and publication of the defamatory email contents of American politicians during the presidential election in 2016. It would be misguided to dismiss such activity – drawing from Clausewitzian prejudices – as tolerable because it falls short of traditional war or interstate coercion. Recall a chief feature of the virtual weapon: it enables new forms of strategic effect that do not involve violence.

This chapter explores problems of total deterrence in the new domain and the possibility of alternative approaches to conflict prevention in order to make readers aware of the limitations of prevailing doctrine and to sketch out a different approach. Neither of the two problems identified above can be easily repaired. Inevitably, the solutions will bring forth new problems. Yet it is important to comprehend where the situation stands and to weigh the option of different and potentially superior policy dogmas. To this end, the analysis develops the outlines of *punctuated deterrence*, an approach that accepts the possibly insurmountable limitations of denial while rejecting policymakers' pervasive obsession with absolute prevention. Instead, it calls for a more flexible logic of punishment that addresses not single actions and particular effects, but *series* of actions and *cumulative* effects.

The High Spectrum of Action: Deterrence and Conflict Escalation

We begin with the first strategic knot: how to reconcile the desire to prevent a major cyberattack with the need to control a crisis if deterrence fails. Modern deterrence theory emerged out of the nuclear revolution, to which the current cyber revolution is, rightly or wrongly, often compared.[7] Traditional deterrence strategy seeks to prevent attack by two techniques: denial and punishment.[8] The virtual weapon spoils the logic of each in important respects.

Deterrence by denial works by reducing the effectiveness of the adversary's weapons. There are at least two ways of achieving this goal in the nuclear realm, to illustrate. One is the development of a defensive glacis (for example, an anti-ballistic missile defense system) capable of nullifying enemy missiles in transit. Another is the mutual reduction of strategic forces (for example, U.S.-Russian arms control treaties) to such a low level that the contenders can defend even against missiles that hit their targets.[9] In both instances, the defender's aim is to reduce the harm of attack upon himself and to raise the costs of mounting the attack on the assailant.

Neither technique of denial is easily attainable against cyberattack.[10] A number of factors complicate the defeat of weaponized code before it reaches the target, as discussed in Chapter 2. The abundance of possible access vectors to computer systems means that an attacker can employ any number of them individually or simultaneously. This holds true even if an air gap envelops the target system. In 2009, the Stuxnet worm reportedly bridged the wall of air at the Natanz nuclear facility in Iran by infecting the personal machine of an unsuspecting plant operator.[11] The sheer speed of malware means that it can travel the globe via the Internet almost instantaneously. Then there are the problems of permanent residency of malware in the defender's system. Because the payload is an intangible with almost no physical signatures, and because it exploits zero-day coding vulnerabilities that the defender does not know about or has not patched, the presence of advanced malware may be impossible to detect. This last factor is an especially worrisome feature of cyberspace, for sophisticated intrusion provides the attacker with the means to predict and thwart the defender's defensive measures. Likelier than the defender denying the attacker in transit is the attacker denying the defender in situ.

Another problem is the difficulty of anticipating attack effects. Direct effects are in principle reproducible and measurable. Technicians can model them in a controlled laboratory setting if they possess relevant data about the target system. For example, the U.S. National Security Agency simulated the Stuxnet worm's payload in a replicated system in order to customize it to the exact specifications of the Natanz plant's industrial control system and to understand the direct effects that the worm would unleash.[12] The indirect effects, however, can vary. Modern society relies on complex computer systems to support core governmental and economic activities. A high degree of interconnectedness exists both between these systems and between the external functions they support. Consequently, a major cyberattack against one system can cause cascading harm that impairs vital activities across a broad range of industries and jurisdictions. These indirect effects are largely unknowable before the attack occurs; it is likely they are impossible to model afterward as well. Furthermore, the fragmentation of responsibility to secure vital infrastructures within and across the public and private sectors will limit the recuperative powers of society during an emergency. The impossibility of understanding and thus preparing for the full indirect effects of cyberattack complicates the ability to deny entry by means of redundancy and resilience. Their attainment will be more difficult than heretofore.

Deterrence by punishment – preventing a major cyberattack by the pledge of severe penalties – is more promising.[13] The equivalence principle represents the quintessence of this preference because it affirms the right of the victim to retaliate with conventional or even nuclear arms. Recall the cavalier statement of one U.S. defense official who threatened to meet a cyberattack with a missile down the enemy's "smokestacks."[14] The notion also appears in a NATO report stating that a major action that meets the threshold of an armed attack could bring about a collective defense response by member states against the attacker.[15] In this way, the doctrine of equivalence ports to the cyber domain the classical and familiar logic of "cross-domain" deterrence: the strategy to prevent a threat in one domain of conflict by the promise of reprisal in another. As NATO Assistant Secretary General Sorin Ducaru explains, "NATO does not see deterrence segmented across different domains – we speak about integrated deterrence."[16]

Whatever the means, the deterring logic of penalties is a psychological mechanism.[17] It works by creating a credible expectation of intolerable losses that induces the opponent to believe that it is in his interest not to initiate an attack. "Reducing vulnerability requires an understanding of people's behaviors as much as it does network topology," explained one British official.[18]

Here, problems abound. The difficulty of attributing the attacker's identity and location degrades the psychological basis of punishment.[19] As we saw in Chapter 4, this difficulty inheres in the opaqueness of the signature of power in cyberspace. It also concerns the international system's state-centric procedures. Weaponized code does not ordinarily respect state sovereignty, which is the organizing principle of international relations. Cyberattacks almost always cross multiple jurisdictions – more than one hundred in the case of the Estonian DDoS attacks of 2007. Thus multilateral devices to facilitate forensic investigation following an attack are crucial. Yet few exist or have proven useful. And as Estonian authorities learned, bilateral diplomatic tools, such as mutual assistance treaties, are cumbersome in dealing with a scenario implicating a sovereign that does not wish to assist. Recalling the attacks against his nation's computer infrastructure, the Estonian ambassador to NATO Harri Tiido explained that "we had an understanding of where they came from, but it was hard at the time to show it – and this is generally true of cyberattacks." This was a major impediment to the invocation of NATO's collective defense mechanisms. Had Estonia invoked them, "the first question around the table among our allies would be, Against whom?" Despite private assertions of complicity by the Russian government, "there was no one to point the finger at."[20]

Another complication concerns the first-order problems of the cyber revolution: it is difficult to adjust the logic of penalties to the motives and aims of private actors. These may vary enormously and be difficult to identify or interpret. Calculations of material loss are unlikely to sway agents of religious extremist groups such as Islamic State. They may not sway a patriotic hacker either, if he is a fervent supporter of the motherland. More than difficult to deter, such actors may be undeterrable. Therefore, even if the defender can overcome attribution problems, he may not know the precise cost structures to defend against all relevant opponents or possess viable means to penalize them. These problems present difficulties for deterrence that transcend the complications of second-order technological revolution (the empowerment of revolutionary states that seek to subvert the international order) and third-order technological revolution (miscalculation and misinterpretation by rational state contenders).

In short, the success of punishment techniques relies on a differentiation of adversaries and an appraisal of tactics appropriate for depriving each of his objectives. The ease of proliferation of some offensive tools multiplies the universe of possible attackers, which multiplies the complexity of the deterrer's task.

There is, however, a caveat to the attribution problem. The greater the sophistication of a cyberattack – for example, the higher the number of expensive zero-day weaknesses it exploits – the lesser the difficulty of authenticating its source. The most advanced offensive operations, especially those with direct destructive effects, would require lengthy planning and enormous resources to mount. This reduces the number of possible instigators of a major cyberattack. Yet the identification of the perpetrator in such a scenario will rest largely on uncertain inference, which reduces the degree of certainty of the attribution and diminishes the legitimacy of the reprisal.

Resolution of the challenges of denial and punishment is not likely. The complications of cyber defense are not diminishing; they may even grow larger. The more computer systems gain in complexity and connectivity, the greater the defender's burden in protecting them. And while the fear of reprisal may induce the most capable contenders – the United States, Russia, China, and Britain – not to exploit the defensive gap for maximum destructive effect, the resulting instability generates conditions for less intrusive offensive action (more on this below).

Another force of restraint among the large powers may be what some thinkers call "self-deterrence," whereby the attacker decides not to attack because he believes that the negative consequences will affect him as well.[21] The unknown risk of blowback has two sources. One involves direct effects: it is possible that the malware agent will inadvertently spread between machines and damage computer systems in the attacker's own terrain or to friendly actors. The danger of direct blowback grows in inverse proportion to the weapon's degree of customization. Thus it is less of a problem with the most advanced attacks, because they are typically highly customized to damage only a single target. The Stuxnet worm was tailored to affect the Siemens-built industrial controller in Natanz, Iran. It infected thousands of machines in numerous other countries. Yet even industrial controllers built by Siemens elsewhere were unaffected by the worm. But imagine that it had been designed to disrupt not the uranium enrichment centrifuges at Natanz, but the Windows-run engineering stations that are commonly used to manage programmable logic controllers (PLCs) (rather than using these stations, as was the case, merely to influence the PLC). Such a poorly customized weapon could have achieved a wide arc of indiscriminate direct effects. Consider, also, the U.S. military's plan to attack Iraq's financial infrastructure in the lead-up to the 2003 invasion. The aim of the operation was to interrupt Saddam Hussein's cash supply. But the Iraqi banking network was connected to a financial communications link located in France. The attack could therefore have incapacitated banks and ATM machines in Europe. (For this reason the attack did not proceed.)[22]

A second source of blowback concerns the indirect effects of cyberattack. Typically, these are greater than the direct effects – hence the potential for problems is higher. As we saw, the issue inheres in the sheer interconnectedness of computer systems in modern society. American officials suspected that in 2004, Russian-built malware infiltrated the NASDAQ stock market. Reportedly the malware could have interrupted equity trading. But it is not only the U.S. financial system that would have suffered; certainly also the public's confidence in stock exchanges in London, Frankfurt, and even Moscow would have dropped. A major cyberattack on a specific financial institution could be construed by analysts and the public as an attack on the integrity of the entire global financial system.

In brief, the logic of self-deterrence rests on the existence of inter-dependence of two different sorts: technological in relation to direct effects that cascade through cyberspace; economic and social in terms of indirect effects that percolate the broad realm of human activity.

The logic of self-deterrence, however, has notable limits. First, it will not factor into the calculus of a highly capable adversary who can craft finely customized weapons. The danger of direct blowback in this case may be severely limited. Second, even the possibility of indirect effects may be small if the target machine affects areas of government or commercial activity that do not impinge on the general economy – for example, the Sony Pictures attack, which inflicted harm only on that firm and its executives. The risk of blowback is not likely to deter major attacks whose evident potential to produce blowback is not high. What is more, insofar as an adversary – for instance, Islamic State – seeks to maximize the arc of harm, the prospect of cascading effects may be an inducement to attack.

We return thus to the logic of penalties. This, too, has limits. For one, the doctrine of equivalence will not restrain an adversary bent on a showdown. For another, it may tempt a rational opportunistic opponent to explore the upper reaches of equivalence – which are not presently specified – in a way that precipitates an unwanted crisis on the basis of miscalculation or misinterpretation of the defender's threshold of toler-ance. This would present a new problem: how to manage a cyber exchange following a failure to deter.

Absorption with the logic of penalties complicates the resolution of this puzzle. It creates forces for an accelerating crisis if a showdown actually occurs. The failure to prevent attack may induce the victim to over-deliver on the promise of reprisal to restore the credibility of the deterrent. This establishes conditions for an intensifying spiral of response and counter-response because clear or proven mechanisms of de-escalation do not exist.

The problem is in part one of procedures. Scholars and public offi-cials have called for the application of core principles of *jus in bello*, such as proportionality, to cyber conflict.[23] Yet what is a "proportional" response to a major disruption of computer systems and networks? What, in cyberspace, is comparable to a conventional strike? If it is the loss of life or the destruction of material property, the traditional criteria of interstate violence supply a clear answer. The virtual weapon, however, challenges this cherished benchmark of security-studies scholars. What price should be paid for a severe yet intangible (at least on military terms) loss? The quest for a satisfactory answer raises particular dangers. If the United States, the equivalence doctrine's chief exponent, has devised such equations, it has not revealed them. In the absence of known or agreed-upon conversion tables to guide the application of equivalence, it is possible that the punished party will perceive the conventional reprisal – whatever its form – as excessive.[24] The resulting grievance may induce a further unreasonable counter-response, possibly in kind. What began as a contest in cyberspace could intensify into a familiar clash of militaries.

Let us nonetheless assume that it will be possible to define a spectrum of intensification that prescribes precise graduated steps in a conflict – a rational scheme of escalation control for the cyber domain, one similar to the framework Herman Kahn expounded for the management of nuclear war.[25] Procedures to implement it may not exist. In a cyber conflict, the decision to restrain, scale down, or terminate the exchange will be ineffective unless the contenders understand the meaning of it. Thus even if the parties share the elemental imperative for the sustenance of order in their strategic dealings – especially during a situation of armed tension – mechanisms to convey their intentions may not exist. There are no proven or established procedures to signal the desire to limit the intensity of a cyber showdown.

One problem is that the placement of code inside an adversary's network cannot easily signal escalatory intent in the way that the diversion of naval ships or bombers to a theatre of contention can. Overt moves of conventional forces display a recognizable intent. They set a measurable period of time (e.g. the time of travel of ships) to avoid a showdown. The insertion of code offers no such signaling potential, because the weapon is already *inside* the adversary's terrain. The defenses are breached; the aggression has begun.

There are other, related dangers of misinterpretation of the new technology. As discussed in Chapter 4, under conditions of dire emergency, even non-offensive behavior can appear menacing. By definition, exploitative cyberweapons do not seek to degrade the operations of the target computer system; instead, their purpose is to seize privileged information. But from the defender's perspective, this fine tactical distinction may not be apparent. If the data are relevant to the understanding of the system from which they were seized, the opponent can use this information either for purposes of industrial espionage or to design weaponized code. Consider the PLA's massive hacking operation of American computer systems that security analysts uncovered in 2013. "We know foreign countries and companies swipe our corporate secrets," remarked U.S. President Barack Obama at the time. "Now our enemies are also seeking the ability to sabotage our power grid, our financial institutions, our air-traffic controllers."[26] The discovery of exploitative malware in vital infrastructures raises the question: is its purpose intelligence gathering, destruction, or both? Valid as the distinction between attack and exploitation may be from a conceptual and legal perspective, doubts about the ultimate aim of exploitation and its potential for misunderstanding by the defender as the initial phase of attack may lead to unnecessary preemptive action.

Two steps can go a long way to reducing these escalatory dangers. One is to specify clearer thresholds of attack beyond which the equivalence principle applies. To be sure, the current posture of declaratory ambiguity has advantages. As Thomas Schelling, a maven of nuclear conflict studies, argued, an uncertain promise of retaliation is more effective than a certain one.[27] A reasonable adversary with access to capable analytical resources may correctly infer from public statements and previous experience where those lines exist – most of the time. For example, the absence of a punitive response from NATO in the aftermath of the 2007 attacks on Estonia showed Moscow that its allies drew the equivalence line well above even a large, politically motivated DDoS attack that paralyzes a nation's economic and financial activities. This does not, however, reveal where the line actually lies. Alliance and member state officials have persistently refused to draw it any more clearly. At a recent summit, NATO Secretary General Jens Stoltenberg stated: "A severe cyber attack may be classified as a case for the alliance. Then NATO can and must react." But he then added ambiguity to this declaration: "How, that will depend on the severity of the attack," he said, without specifying degrees of severity.[28] And if loss of life is a necessary criterion of equivalence, what number of deaths signifies an armed attack has occurred? Western adversaries will be forgiven if they are left guessing whether a destructive attack on a civilian power grid or transportation system is a cause to activate the alliance's collective defense clause.

In the nuclear realm, ambiguity works because the threshold of tolerance for conflict is so low. Leaving to chance the survival of a metropolis or indeed of humanity is a bet that rational players will want to avoid. But with a capability that can cause devastating harm even if it does not produce loss of life, the acceptance of risk is higher. Clearer conversion tables than those that currently exist in official statements would reduce the possibility that an adversary will launch a high-impact cyberattack that inadvertently triggers equivalence or a collective defense response.[29]

A second measure involves the upper limits of equivalence. These, too, are not clearly specified. Some analysts have taken the logic of penalties to the extreme limits of modern technology: nuclear retaliation. In January 2013, for instance, the U.S. Defense Science Board advised the government to include "existential cyber attacks" within the scope of nuclear deterrence policy.[30] Again, escalatory dangers appear. Because the United States has not adopted a No First Use nuclear posture, it is conceivable that the country may even launch a nuclear attack to preempt an adversary which it believes will imminently carry out an existential cyberattack. Thus a nuclear first strike – and counterstrike – may occur even outside the bounds of a strictly nuclear conflict. This problem is easily resolvable only if one dissociates cyberattack from nuclear attack. In other words, the solution to the escalation risks of cross-domain deterrence requires imposing an *upper* limit on the equivalence response itself.[31]

The Middle Spectrum of Action: The Accretional Principle and Punctuated Deterrence

Prevailing deterrence policy does not cease at the border of high-end cyberattacks: it also seeks to prevent action below it. In the words of Ducaru, "Deterrence applies also to sub-threshold action – not just scenarios that unambiguously meet the criteria of Article 5," meaning that it also applies to actions of unpeace.[32] Deterrence at the middle of the spectrum, however, faces its own problems.

The difficulties begin with the first of the remedial steps described above, the specification of thresholds of equivalence. Although it will diminish the risks of unwanted escalation following a high-spectrum cyberattack, it will also increase the chances of attack up to the line at which equivalence applies. The clear promise of severe retaliation reduces the chances of a catastrophic attack, but in the absence of options to punish mid-spectrum action, the promise erodes the expectation of reprisal for such an attack. Adversaries know that so long as their actions do not breach the equivalence thresholds, the victim's response will not be severe. Yet as we saw in Chapter 2, just because an action falls below the established thresholds of war does not mean that it fails to cause grave harm. In fact, acts of unpeace might damage economic interests or disrupt political processes more than even single acts of war.

In short, the doctrine of equivalence creates – to purloin a term from nuclear strategy – a *stability–instability* paradox: the risk of a high-impact cyber event diminishes even while that of lesser aggression rises.[33] The absence of cyberwar alongside rampant mid-spectrum action gives proof to the existence of this paradox.[34] U.S. Director of National Intelligence James Clapper enunciated the problem: "Until such time as we do create both the substance and the mindset of deterrence, this sort of thing is going to continue" because the current regime of punishment has created a "permissive environment" for hostile activity.[35] Despite repeated assertions by President Barack Obama that cyber actions threaten "core national security," despite repeated pledges to retaliate, the record of punishment for actions falling short of war is thin. Jack Goldsmith explains: "[T]he government thinks the nation would lose more – economically, politically, diplomatically, militarily, and/or in intelligence – if it fights back hard."[36] Adversaries grasp this point; each failure to punish increases the willingness to strike again. Inaction therefore creates pressures of conflict.

The paradox comes at a high price, for the costs of mid-spectrum cyber activity are already enormous and growing. The Chinese notion of *lingchi* – death by a thousand cuts – could not be more apt in describing them. Any single or series of "cuts" by themselves may be bearable, including the most significant heists of government data, so long as they do not repeat. But how should one deter the 999th cut, or the point at which the cumulative costs of hostile action are no longer bearable? Even if every deterrence failure produces an outcome that is not itself strategic, the aggregate costs of failure over time may produce such an outcome.

This question has not been answered satisfactorily. Adversaries have been adept at operating within the ambiguous bounds of harm between war and peace. Some of the most damaging hostile actions – say, the cyberattacks against Sony Pictures or the paralysis of Estonia's essential infrastructures – fell below the equivalence criterion. At the same time, they inflicted damage that the victims considered unacceptable and which future potential victims have stated they will seek to deter or punish. "If the intent is to disrupt or destroy our infrastructure," remarked Chief of U.S. Cyber Command General Keith Alexander, referring to high-impact cyberattack, "[then] I think you've crossed a line."[37] Yet he also described cyber espionage by large nations such as China as "the greatest transfer of wealth in history," adding: "That's our future disappearing in front of us . . . The theft of intellectual property is astounding and we've got to stop that."[38]

The range of mid-spectrum hostile action is also expanding. Take, for instance, cyber exploitation. It no longer involves merely the theft of governmental, military, and industrial secrets. It increasingly also entails kompromat operations that involve the seizure of sensitive data about a public official or organization that are divulged in a time and manner that influences and possibly alters the shape of a nation's domestic and foreign policy. The divulgence of seized data represents a significant departure from traditional espionage operations, in which the perpetrator has an interest not to reveal the seized assets, because the revelation diminishes the value of the assets to the perpetrator (the adversary will take actions to remedy his loss), or because it gives the adversary clues about how and where the perpetrator has penetrated the information space.

Attempts to create through public statements an expectation of penalties for mid-spectrum actions have not worked. Western officials have repeatedly asserted a willingness to punish hostile activity short of war – or "cyber misbehavior," as U.S. Secretary of Defense Ashton Carter put it. Here, again, one can observe officials grasping for labels to describe a phenomenon that is neither recognizably war nor recognizably peace.

The principal problem with current doctrine is that it is designed to punish *individual* acts of unpeace. Remember that modern deterrence theory originated in the nuclear arena, in which the focus of strategy is to thwart the direct effects of single attacks. Few thinkers entertained scenarios even of limited war; even fewer considered acceptable a scenario in which the nuclear exchange was prolonged. The very destructive power of nuclear weapons ensured that the upper limit of total destruction was never far away – hence the lower limit of acceptable action was effectively zero.

When applied to the current context, adversaries understand that so long as no single cyber action unambiguously crosses the bar of war, they will escape its certain penalties. Consequently, intelligence officials expect that sub-threshold attacks will only intensify.[39] Policies that were adequate to prevent armed attack become obstacles to the prevention of lesser actions. Consider the following logic derived from the unprecedented events during the 2016 U.S. presidential election. Let us assume for a moment that Russia seeks to disrupt the national elections of a Western country. It employs advanced malware to manipulate voting or vote-counting machines, engages in a kompromat operation that tarnishes the reputation of the candidates whom the Kremlin does not wish to see win, or disseminates false information extolling (or fabricating) the virtues of the preferred candidate and amplifying (or inventing) the flaws of other contenders. The government of the Western nation will want to deter Russia by promising a stern response to such an intrusion; this merely increases Russia's desire to unseat that government. Russia thus increases its subversive activities against that nation – all the while knowing that so long as Russian agents do not fire a single shot or cause fatalities, the adversary may well not carry out his promise of severe retaliation, for the promise has credence only at the high spectrum of action.

Nothing less than a reevaluation of the psychological substance of deterrence is required to address the threats of unpeace.[40] As Obama wisely noted, deterrence against them requires a "creative response,"[41] or what Ducaru described as a "mindshift in approach."[42] We can no longer afford to pursue a policy that seeks to deter individual actions that will never meet punishment thresholds. This problem cannot be settled by adjusting the thresholds themselves in accordance with specific conditions, for if the downward shift in penalties goes too far they will reach a point where the adversary will accept their costs. Moreover, the hostile actions are too frequent and their consequences too diverse to expect that policymakers – already heavily absorbed with thwarting them – can define appropriate penalties in each case. Indeed, the burden of this bureaucratic activity alone may be a sufficient harm to induce the attackers into action – a sort of denial-of-service operation against a civil service that is already consumed with the laborious task of responding to cease-less real incidents before it can even begin to conceive of imagined ones.

What is needed instead is an accretional principle of mid-spectrum deterrence. Such an approach would aim to deter not individual actions but a *series* of actions; not one-off effects but *cumulative* effects. Factors to consider in determining the accumulation of damage are the intensity of harm (physical versus intangible effects), the timescale of harm (prolonged accumulation or acute accumulation), and the range of harm inflicted upon friendly interests (damage to national interests only versus damage to allies or an alliance). Uri Tor has proposed a similar notion, "restrictive cumulative deterrence," which accepts the inevitability of cyber aggression. This view, however, does not stray far from the received paradigm, for it entails "attacking the rival repeatedly in response to specific behaviors, over a long period of time."[43] By contrast, the approach developed below prescribes a *punctuated* regime of punishment: not continuous reprisals for persistent and sometimes simultaneous actions – an approach that saps the political will and disables the bureaucratic ability to respond – but a graduated scheme in which penalties are meted out over time and at a moment of the defender's choosing.

Drawing from the example above, punctuated deterrence would consider not merely Russia's action in the given electoral context, but also its preceding sub-threshold actions, possibly including actions against allied parties – for instance, the attempt to subvert the electoral process of friendly nations or allies. The aim of this approach is to increase the attacker's expectation of the costs that the victim imposes on him following the attack (Ha), as expressed in the classical deterrence formula in Table 2 below. (It is also possible, of course, to diminish the attacker's expected benefits (Ba) and the harm that he expects to inflict (Hv) by way of a counter-information warfare strategy that seeks to dispel falsities.)

The accretional principle of punctuated deterrence faces a major psychological barrier: the adversary may not perceive that his actions constitute a coherent series of moves, even if their damaging consequences accumulate coherently in the eyes of the victim. The possibility of misperception will be especially pronounced if different elements of the adversary's decision-making apparatus pursue disparate actions and if it lacks a single policy framework to tie them together. In this case, the burden of supplying a framework of cumulative penalties falls on the defender. Diplomatic and signaling procedures will be required to demonstrate to adversaries that for the purposes of punishment, individual hostile actions are regarded as a comprehensive package of offensive activity rather than being disparate actions that merit isolated responses.

Table 2: Deterrence formula

$(Ba + Hv) / (Ca + Ha) = Net\ Benefit\ or\ Cost$
Ba = Benefits that accrue to the attacker **Hv** = Harm that the attacker imposes on the victim (i.e. a relative gain to the attacker) **Ca** = Cost paid by the attacker in mounting the action **Ha** = Harm that the attacker expects the victim to inflict on him in retaliation (Source: This rendition of the deterrence formula is based on the equation presented in Michael Warner and Michael Good, "Notes on Deterrence in Cyberspace," *Georgetown Journal of International Affairs* (December 2013), p. 73).

Provided it can overcome signaling and other challenges, the new doctrine offers at least three strategic gains at the middle of the spectrum. First, it can alter the adversary's calculus in a way that strengthens the punishment regime. An adversary may be willing to absorb the retaliatory costs of single actions if the costs (economic and financial penalties, for instance) are meted out over time. A long timescale of attacks invokes a long timescale of punishment, which renders the costs of retaliation easier to manage. This calculation is less likely to hold if the costs are administered in a single blow that concentrates and compounds the punishment.

Second, the new approach transfers spontaneity and initiative from the attacker back to the victim. The traditional impulse to treat single incidents on their own merits creates a psychological pressure to pass judgment on each case soon after it becomes known. This pressure gives the attacker the ability to influence the time and context of the penalties the victim imposes upon him – and whether he imposes them at all. Punctuated deterrence would widen the victim's margin of maneuver: he can shape the moment of punishment to his own advantage, whether in response to a single action because it is severe enough to warrant an isolated response, or to a series of actions because each one does not meet the threshold of severity on its own.

A third benefit concerns the scope of reaction: it provides a community of allied nations with greater options to work together in penalizing common adversaries for similar harmful actions directed against them separately. The focus on responding to single actions ensures that threats affecting different members of an alliance become a means for the attacker to shift the points of tension from one member to another, thereby increasing his chances of avoiding a collective punishment – or even individual punishment, if he rotates attacks among the members in a way that lengthens the timescale of activity for any one of them. By contrast, the emphasis on a series of actions means that every action against any member state could immediately invoke a collective consideration of accumulating effects distributed among them. Punctuated deterrence of a collective form would make it more difficult for the adversary to spread out the retaliation costs of his hostile actions across allied victims who know not how to respond individually.

Some analysts have proclaimed the obsolescence of the deterrence paradigm. They prescribe new categories of thinking to replace it.[44] These postmortems are premature: the patient can still be rescued if only the disease is recognized. The solution to the malaise of deterrence may lie within the doctrine rather than outside of it. The implication of the accretional principle of punishment is that the classical goal, "let us prevent all attacks," is contrary to the purposes of deterrence in the new domain. The prevention of all attacks can no longer supply the definition of "successful" deterrence in the cyber domain as it does in the nuclear and other realms of conflict. Success depends instead on a reduction of the tempo of mid-range hostilities to a tolerable level. This threshold of tolerance has not only a *static* dimension involving the damage from isolated incidents, which the defender can preserve for especially harmful blows, but also an *additive* dimension that weighs the damage of hits over time – even if the adversary does not seek to impose them in their totality. Punctuated deterrence will have achieved its aim if it causes the pace of unpeaceful activity to slow such that even its aggregate effects do not warrant confused and flustered pledges of punishment.

CHAPTER 8

Russia and Cyberspace
MANIFESTATIONS OF THE REVOLUTION

A Virtual Demonstration Shot

For all their confidence in the universal triumph of liberal ideals, for all their pretensions about the political backwardness of the historic adversary Russia, Western powers have confronted the resurgence of the colossal Russian threat on their Eastern periphery. At a time when the West's economic and military architectures absorbed formerly captive nations of the Soviet empire, just as the prophecies of the End of History seemed on the verge of realization,[1] a new weapon came into view. The unsophisticated but intense cyberattacks against Estonia's vital computer infrastructures in the spring of 2007 were a virtual demonstration shot that rang around the world. Here was a technology that could convulse – from multiple remote locations – the economic and governmental affairs of a small nation without requiring the firing of a single gun. It far surpassed in potency previous weapons whose disruptive effects on domestic order fell short of war; it also surpassed some wartime acts.

To be sure, previous cyber actions, including by Russia, had harmed important interests. In 1988, the Morris worm prompted the partitioning of the entire Internet, which then comprised tens of thousands of nodes. In 2005, unidentified foreign culprits seized the designs of NASA's space-launch vehicle from a supposedly secure facility at the Kennedy Space Center in Orlando, Florida.[2] In 2006, suspected Chinese hackers sought to compromise machines at the U.S. Naval War College, leading to the closure of the institution's networks for two weeks.[3] Yet none of these incidents was of such a magnitude as to disturb interstate dealings, even if they affected core national security interests. Oracles of strategy had warned of these dangers with the dire slogan: "Cyberwar is coming!"[4] Few heeded the call until the Estonian crisis – a demonstration of new technological potential as significant for the cyber age as the explosions over Hiroshima and Nagasaki were for the nuclear era.[5] Against this backdrop, the Estonian spectacle had an inaugural significance: it launched an era of unpeace – a state of incessant, intolerable, but so far largely unpunished activity into which we have since been dragged only further.[6]

Security planners and foreign policy specialists began at last to awaken to the gravity of the cyber threat. Before the events in Estonia, no country had published a dedicated cybersecurity strategy; today dozens of countries have done so. No Western intelligence agency had rated the cyber threat as a central concern of national security; presently they regard it as one of the most pressing issues, if not the foremost menace. In 2007, basic questions of security doctrine converged upon the world of diplomacy. How can nations deter major foreign attacks on essential infrastructures? What techniques can reduce the intensity of a cyber conflict following a failure to prevent it? Do the laws of war apply to the restraint of such conduct? How can governments stem the acquisition of weapons whose transmission is nearly costless and instantaneous because the payload is an intangible?

Yet for the nation whose citizens fired this virtual weapon, the move was no leap into unknown doctrine. Like the waves of cyberattacks that ensued against Georgia, Ukraine, and other nations that Moscow perceived as adversaries, the campaign against Estonia in 2007 represented a refinement of Russia's century-old doctrine of information warfare,[7] whose central purpose is to disorient the enemy's leadership, to diminish his capacity for cohesive action, to undermine his confidence in the integrity of his political institutions – in short, to weaken the enemy in his own perception. The doctrine's expansion to account for the new possibilities of cyberspace, including the disruption of foreign elections, as the world witnessed during the American presidential contest in 2016, represents a fusion of two elements: the classical techniques of disinformation in the battle over human minds; and the use of information as force in the battle over machine functions. And because cyberspace smashes geopolitical constraints on human action, the technology enables Russia to practice political subversion not just in the "near" but also in the "far" abroad. It extends the reach of information warfare into the core of Western societies.

Russian Information Warfare: History Meets the Present

Russian information warfare is old even if its refinement in cyberspace is new. From 1917 to 1991, the Soviet leadership guilefully harnessed the methods of information warfare – if we can apply a contemporary label to historical actions that fit its meaning – to aid their revolutionary strivings at home and abroad. During the Soviet state's genesis in the early twentieth century, the Bolsheviks applied the methods with special assiduity. For the radicals in Petrograd, this was a period of great peril. The White Army, loyal to the deposed Tsar and fighting to defend against "Western capitalist bandits," ravaged the regime's centers of power, especially in the south. Although it was losing the First World War in the West, Germany had effectively vanquished the Russians in the East. Riven by internal divisions, the shaky Bolshevik regime faced an existential threat from their direct political competitors, the Mensheviks. Peasant insurrections stirred the ports and countryside. And so on.

What better way to stanch the internal oppositions than by inundating the confused masses with self-assuring falsities? In January 1918, Lenin arranged for the broadcasting of "fake news" about proletarian stirrings in Germany, surely the next capitalist domino to fall, even as Trotsky, the Commissar for Foreign Affairs, prepared to sign a disgraceful peace treaty with the hated Kaiser.[8] Following Lenin's death in 1924, Stalin, regarded by his peers as an uncolorful mediocrity who lacked his predecessor's intellectual depth and oratorical flare, yet possessed a sharp tactical mind and brutal will, produced fictitious evidence of Lenin's support of him when in fact the eminent leader had privately warned against Stalin's succession.[9] To cement his grip on power, the dictator ordered the state security organs to feed murderous show trials in Moscow with fabricated plots that implicated his real or imagined competitors; in the organization of these sweeping purges, the order to "discover" non-existing evidence was as good as a command to produce it.[10] One notorious case was the trial of Grigory Zinoviev and Lev

Kamenev in 1936, which featured the discovery by the police of a "terrorist" plot to assassinate not only Stalin but also the Communist Party luminaries Klim Voroshilov, Andrei Zhdanov, Lazar Kaganovich, Stanislav Kosior, Sergo Orjonikidze, and Pavel Postyshev – fantastical allegations even by the bizarre standards of political deception of the period. The feigned realism of the proceedings was outstanding. Befitting the political theater of the occasion, after which the two former Politburo grandees were to be liquidated, the prosecutors produced minute details of the alleged plot, such as the manner of the assassination (shooting) and its location (at the meeting of the Seventh Comintern Congress).[11]

Information warfare extended far beyond the Soviet Union's borders. Its arena was the world at large. On this stage, the goals of the politics of deception varied from the goals at home, although the techniques were similar. Information warfare was a central activity in Soviet efforts to shape the internal political constitutions or to alter the foreign-policy courses of other nations – friendly, neutral, or antagonistic. Such KGB operations generally employed three sorts of "active measures": *black propaganda*, or the fanning of false rumors, the circulation of forged papers, and covert media insertions; *white propaganda*, or the publication of defamatory falsities in the official Soviet press; and *grey propaganda*, or the clandestine dissemination of radio broadcasts, the resort to front organizations, and the courting of prominent and receptive Westerners – Lenin's *polezniye duraki*, or "useful idiots"[12] who fail to grasp their unwitting role in Moscow's propagandist maneuvers.[13] Examples of these techniques are plentiful. Perhaps the subjugated peoples of Africa would rise up and sever their political and cultural links to the West if an offensive government document materialized "proving" that U.S. President Jimmy Carter supported the oppressive Apartheid regime in South Africa.[14] Maybe the amicable nation of India would abandon once and for all its receptiveness to Western influences if stories made the rounds about an invasion of HIV (then a still mysterious agent about which public knowledge was thin) emanating from American scientific laboratories. This story appeared in 1985 in the obscure Indian newspaper *The Patriot* and later in the better-known Soviet newspaper *Literaturnaya Gazeta* – fabrications that former Russian spymaster Yevgeny Primakov admitted, years later, were the work of KGB agents in the aptly named operation "INFEKTION."[15]

Whatever their specific objective, no matter their geographic setting, the main appeal of information warfare was evident to its Soviet practitioners: the activity enabled the subverters to score political and strategic goals against adversaries while avoiding the high risks and certain penalties that overt methods of war would elicit. The purpose of information warfare was to achieve strategic effects, often remotely, sometimes in situ, but always non-violently, by influencing the minds of unwieldy masses abroad. To apply once again Marvin Minsky's apt metaphor of man-machines, the falsities circulating in forged documents and fabricated news items were analogous to malicious code seeking to alter the functions of human hardware within a global cyberspace – the vast arena of social interactions and the neurological complex of mental processes.

The doctrine of information warfare outlived its Soviet originators. The regime of Russian President Vladimir Putin, himself a former spymaster trained in the KGB's school of subversion, has adapted the technique to the twenty-first century. Central to this redevelopment effort is the "Gerasimov doctrine," named after General Valery Vasilevich Gerasimov who, having served as a divisional commander in the Soviet Union's Baltic Military District, now heads the General Staff of Russia's armed forces. In 2013, he enunciated a dictum which builds on Soviet precepts and that prevails in Russian security policy: the "methods of conflict" now involve "the broad use of political, economic, informational, humanitarian and other non-military measures," or "non-linear war" and "next-generation war."[16] In other words, the lines between war and peace have become blurred.

This new genus of warfare primarily involves not a clash of armies on the battlefield but a clash of competing perceptions of reality. The Gerasimov doctrine imputes to the West Russian intentions and tactics of unpeace. It emerged in reaction to the perceived existence of an antecedent information war waged by the West against Russia and its interests.[17] As Keir Giles explained: "Instead of a statement of Russian intention, what Gerasimov in fact described was the Russian perception of how the US-led West intervenes in the internal affairs of states, exacerbating instability by engendering 'colour revolutions' in those that resist US hegemony, and financing and supplying weapons to rebel groups and mercenaries."[18]

Giving credence to this viewpoint is the fact that Western nations have also long practiced the techniques of disinformation to score geopolitical points. In 1953, as the United States and Britain sought to preserve their control over Iran's oil assets against nationalization, the CIA orchestrated a coup that removed the hostile prime minister, Mohammad Mosaddegh, from power in 1953. But the scheme faced a major impediment: the Shah would not sign orders of deposition whose unpopularity and dubious legality risked his own crown. The CIA circled around the immovable figure of the Shah by falsely reporting to *The New York Times*, the Associated Press, and Tehrani newspapers that he had in fact signed the decrees. They orchestrated the publication of defamatory news reports and cartoons about Mosaddegh in a failed effort to stir popular unrest against him.[19] Decades later, following the Soviet army's invasion of Afghanistan, the CIA planned to publish in newspapers of Muslim countries false stories of "invasion day celebrations" at Soviet embassies.[20]

Wary of such tactics being used against their own population, the Soviet government operated a state censorship organ, the General Directorate for the Protection of State Secrets in the Press – or Glavlit which routinely censored publishers and artistic performers. In 1961, the organization's mandate expanded to include regulation of the private communications of foreign news correspondents.[21] Today, a vast apparatus of Internet surveillance called SORM monitors all online activity inside Russia. Occasionally, botnets blast torrents of data against the websites of independent news media, bloggers, and election monitors. Such attacks serve the interests of the regime, which ordinarily denies authorship of the actions.[22]

The philosophical underpinnings of modern information warfare reveal an essential truth about the Russian worldview. It is a truth that exponents of Samuel Huntington's "clash of civilizations" thesis will recognize: the doctrine's adherents presume the existence of a grand contest of conceptions about the nature of international and domestic order between Russia and the West, a battle for political and social domination within defined cultural and regional areas. States such as Estonia, Georgia, and Ukraine lying at the rift between civilizations are central arenas of contention among the core nations.[23] This viewpoint does not refute the existence of a society of states; it merely supposes that the social element of the system is primitively developed even if its mechanical aspects are mature.[24] Despite the existence of a civilizational clash that occasionally erupts in violence in places such as Ukraine, the ripples in the international order result not in a millenarian or generalized war, but in a limited and manageable conflict. The civilizational prism does not paint all units outside the Russian-led universe like revolutionary actors. Obama or Trump are not to Putin what Napoleon was to Alexander I or Hitler to Stalin. But it means that the central dramas of international politics are – contra rationalist mantra – primarily cultural and ideological rather than material and interest based, even if Putin and the *siloviki* who shape Russian security policy regard military power as a crucial element of international status and influence in the grand clash of ideals.

The Russian political scientist Alexandr Dugin is a poignant and influential exponent of this philosophy. Despite his fervent visions of inevitable European war and his public strivings to instigate it, Dugin has enjoyed some proximity to establishment figures such as the late Primakov and even Putin himself. Some speculators, probably more creative than accurate, described Dugin as the intellectual author of the seizure of Crimea in February 2014.[25] Dugin's acerbic nationalist commentary strives to marshal religious conservative forces against the liberal influences of foreign meddlers. He defends the nation's disorienting maneuvers abroad as a legitimate response to perceived U.S.-led information warfare targeting it – a concerted campaign to weaken the current Russian regime by the manipulation of the media and the use of propaganda directed at the masses of citizens. In this worldview, Russia and the West are locked into a global struggle over the control of information spaces. There is a consensus among Russian conservative thinkers that information operations were a key factor in the Soviet Union's downfall – an event that Putin has deplored as "the greatest geopolitical catastrophe" of the twentieth century.[26] In response, Dugin calls for the creation of a countervailing Eurasian information network that feeds the state apparatus with the nation's rich cultural and linguistic resources.

How does the doctrine of information warfare play out in pursuance of this worldview? Gerasimov and his followers speak of war; the very term "information warfare" alludes to it. Here, again, is a conflation of notions. Even if its guiding political motives are warlike, even if its practitioners are colonels and generals, the conduct they describe is not war but rather aggression lying below the criteria for interstate violence. The doctrine appears to recognize the West's superior military forces; it accepts the folly of a direct military clash. "No matter what forces the enemy has, no matter how well developed his forces and means of armed conflict may be," declared Gerasimov, "forms and methods for overcoming them can be found."[27] Thus the doctrine's main purpose is not to augment war, though this may be so in limited instances, but to *circumvent* it by opposing the adversary where his vulnerability is greatest and his doctrinal understanding retarded: in the disruption of the open and sometimes fragile information spaces of liberal democracies. The very openness that Western nations perceive makes their political system superior to all others is, in the Russian perception, a source of weakness.

The Russian notion of "reflexive control" follows this thinking.[28] Timothy Thomas defined the notion as "a means of conveying to a partner or an opponent specially prepared information to incline him to voluntarily make the predetermined decision,"[29] one that is advantageous to Russia. The program has two faces. One involves influencing the minds of elites and publics abroad in order to lure the adversary into a limited confrontation that Russia desires but it does not wish to initiate or be seen to initiate. This approach was on display in the Russo-Georgian War of 2008. As James Sherr related, "Putin primed the mechanism for war" by preparing belligerent action but "was assiduous in ensuring that [Georgian President] Saakashvili started it."[30] Surreptitious acts of aggression by Russia or its local proxies combined with false news reports and statements to needle Georgia into invading the disputed territory of South Ossetia, which in turn prompted Russia's larger invasion of Georgia. Moscow maneuvered within Georgia's information space to manufacture a conflict that sapped NATO's political will to welcome the country into the alliance.

A second face of reflexive control works in the opposite direction: it employs information warfare to shift the adversary's foreign and security policy toward a less confrontational, even amicable relationship with Russia. The goal is to draw the other side into a course of action that is not in his interests, but rather than needling, the method is wheedling. This approach was on display in the struggle over the control of Ukraine's eastern region from 2014 to the present. Perhaps a torrent of social media and news postings favorable to Russia and its magnificent leader would erode the adversaries' will to penalize it for its aggressions. To this effect, Russia has employed "troll armies" comprising countless anonymous hirelings who countered remarks critical of it.[31] One former recruit recounts a long line of people filing into a nondescript building on 55 Savushkina Street in St Petersburg after 9 p.m. to replace the shift of toilers inside. Trolls worked two dozen to a room. Superior orcs – one in each room – oversaw the content of their posts, imposing fines for ideological deviance. The posts mixed levity and salaciousness ("signs you are dating the wrong girl") with falsehood ("The majority of experts agree that the US is deliberately trying to weaken Russia [in Ukraine]").[32] For their efforts, the laborers received fixed sums for a quota of activity – fifty posts per day, for instance.[33]

The essence of Russia's modern information warfare doctrine, therefore, is the belief – Bolshevik in its historical origins, civilizational in its political implications – that modern conflict centers on the domination of informational rather than geographic spaces. To avoid geopolitical disasters in this grand clash of conceptions, to avert a repeat of a Russian downfall, the doctrine prescribes the penetration and disruption of foreign information spaces. It routinely beseeches patriotic Russians to organize and execute social media activism in the service of the state.[34] The doctrine conveys a recognition that in the twenty-first century, power no longer resides merely in physical space: it is also a feature of cyberspace. Informational assets can augment national power just as much as physical assets. If manipulated, disrupted, or destroyed, cyberspace can weaken, disorient, and even turn the adversary nearer (if not very near) to one's conception. Cyberspace offers new pathways for great-power competition. If one can manipulate social media in a way that alters the aggregate of social views, then a foreign population can be convinced to believe – falsely but usefully – that certain political views are popular when in fact they are the product of trolls and bots. And if the aggregated views favor one's interests while constraining the opponent's arc of maneuver, then one has attained an important strategic effect. That is, if one can manipulate the opponent's information spaces to undermine the legitimacy of his political institutions to the point that coherent policy is not possible, then one can alter strategic behavior without ever having to enter into the realm of Clausewitzian war. Actions in cyberspace can impact national behavior more substantially than geographic movements. The disruption of acts of unpeace can be more potent than the destruction of acts of war.

The Estonian crisis presaged and illustrated this confluence of methods. Social disturbances in the streets of Tallinn (fueled partly by media falsities) combined with machine disturbances in the national cyberspace. The interruption of commerce in the streets and shops was compounded by the paralysis of banks and governmental activities online. But for all its dazzling effects, the episode was mostly demonstrative: it announced the new possibilities of information warfare that cyberspace affords without revealing its full potential. A more faithful representation of this expanding potential occurred in 2016 during the presidential election that delivered Donald Trump to the White House.

Subversion of the Democratic Process

It is in the nature of a presidential system of government that the contenders for the top job appear as centers of public drama and controversy, because the position to which they aspire is the star around which all influential but lesser objects orbit. Meteors and asteroids shape policy and travel the sky, often shining brightly, but ultimately it is back toward the center that the gravitational force of executive responsibility and authority draws public attention. Every four years in the United States the celestial objects align on opposing sides of the firmament in a contest to preserve or replace the star in its central position. In this astronomical clash of personalities and parties, the displacement of a single rock can disturb the entire constellation.

A disturbance of this sort occurred in July 2016 during the heat of the presidential race between Donald Trump and Hillary Clinton, respectively the Republican Party and Democratic Party contenders. The news-leaking organization WikiLeaks placed on the public web almost twenty thousand email records belonging to the Democratic National Committee (DNC), the governing body of the Democratic Party. The vast depot of data contained emails from seven DNC officials, including remarks by the body's chairwoman, Debbie Wasserman Schultz, that denigrated staff members of the losing candidate in the Democratic primary race, Senator Bernie Sanders.[35] American intelligence officials later concluded with a "very high" degree of certainty that APT-28, or Fancy Bear, a known Russian hacking group linked to GRU, a Russian military intelligence organ, had seized the material from private computer servers. They stated that Russia sought to erode public faith in their country's democratic process, impair Clinton's electability, and aid Trump's,[36] who during the campaign had declared the NATO alliance "obsolete" while praising Putin as a strong leader of his nation.[37]

This cyber operation combined two techniques: a classic exploitation action involving the seizure of private records of secret conversations among politicians; and kompromat, or the public divulgence of exfiltrated data that is timed to inflict reputational harm on a political or strategic target. The first technique was an intelligence-gathering activity which large nations routinely carry out against each other and that no international treaty prohibits. The second move was stunning and more controversial, for it marked the first time in history that a state applied exploitative methods to cause reputational harm against foreign politicians in order to disrupt and possibly subvert their country's electoral process. Drawing from the technical concepts described in Chapter 1, the operation was not a cyberattack because it produced no notable direct effects upon the compromised machines. But we can regard whatever effects the kompromat action exerted on the election outcome and on the political system generally as indirect results. These effects are conceivably more important. Recall a general claim of this book: more important than the direct effects that code exerts upon machines are the indirect effects it generates within the political and social world.

What were the indirect effects in this case? Schultz's remarks caused a fury within large quarters of her party's base. Particularly incensed were Sanders' supporters, many of whose allegiance to the candidate surpassed their commitment to the party. Party officials were meant to observe a strict neutrality in their posture toward the candidates for nomination. Never mind that the perception of prejudice against Sanders already existed; the emails proved that the insistent rumors were fact. Sanders pleaded for forgiveness of the party whose chairwoman had privately betrayed him. But the Democratic National Convention, which began only days after the hacking fiasco, was at times a scene of disorder. Insurrectionists within the Sanders faction met his earnest supplications for support of Clinton with boos. An untold number of them proclaimed that they would not vote for the designated party candidate, Clinton, in the election. A larger number of other party adherents who had only warily supported her until then may not have materialized at the booths on election day.[38] Four months later Clinton lost the election, one of the closest on record. Winning the popular vote by almost three million votes, she succumbed to Trump in the contest for the Electoral College by small margins (tens of thousands of votes) in crucial states that sophisticated but unreliable electoral models had projected were hers to take. Clinton and some commentators claimed that the DNC twist, combined with the controversy over FBI Director James Comey's ongoing investigation of her use of a private email server at home while serving as Secretary of State,[39] denied Clinton an otherwise safe victory against her highly controversial Republican opponent.

Every honest historian knows that it is impossible to prove counterfactual arguments. The causes of Clinton's loss are multifactorial; the evidence that the WikiLeaks embarrassment drained her of supporters circumstantial.[40] The skeptic will carp that the Russian maneuvers did not conclusively derail Clinton's path to the White House. Nor did it directly damage the United States' military or other significant material interests. This thinking is misguided. Even if the information operations did not deliver the presidency to Trump, their effects on the West's relations with Russia and on debates about the integrity and survivability of democratic electoral processes are larger than even some armed conflicts have produced. Anyone who witnessed the tense drama of the election will recall the fierce controversy that erupted in the aftermath of the hacking relevations. Reince Priebus, then Wasserman's counterpart at the Republican National Committee, offered the taunting statement: "Today's events show really what an uphill climb the Democrats are facing this week in unifying their party. Starting out the week by losing your party chairman over longstanding bitterness between factions is no way to keep something together."[41] True, the bitterness had existed, but not the scintillating personal controversies and the large insurrection against the party leaders. The explosion of a single meteor in cyberspace combined with events outside of it to shake the celestial arrangement of American politics.

The truth is that we shall never know the answer to this political mystery. But we must examine it further, for in it lie four clues to Russia's integration of cyberspace into modern information warfare and to revolutionary trends in contemporary security affairs.

The first clue concerns complications of defense: the intruders penetrated the DNC's email systems with apparent ease. Already in July 2015, Russian intelligence organs had reportedly gained access to their target; the intruders remained undiscovered for at least eleven months.[42]

A further testament to the skillful hackers' irrepressibility was their successful penetration of other sensitive targets, such as the machines of the Democratic Congressional Campaign Committee and the Gmail account of John Podesta, who may have succumbed to a phishing technique. According to forensic reports, someone, possibly Podesta himself, clicked the link in the malicious message to him twice. If he or another user entered his login credentials into the linked website, the hackers would have gained access to his email account.[43] These successful intrusions give proof – once again – to the dictum purloined from Stanley Baldwin in Chapter 2: malware will always get through.

A second clue for our times emerges out of the kompromat operation's obscure signature of power. The heated debates about the operation's authorship show that in the aftermath of a major cyber event, the mere question of its source can become a moment of political convulsion. To repeat: we cannot know with full certainty that Russian state agents were behind the email theft. Both Trump and the Russian government denied Russian authorship. The FBI's summary report about the hacking incident included few new facts; it listed malware that non-Russian hacking groups had used elsewhere.[44] Subsequent false stories about a Russian cyberattack against the American power grid did not aid those who saw Russia's hand in the DNC hacking.[45] This erroneous implication of Russia in an attack that did not occur both illustrated the difficulties of authenticating the source and even the nature of a cyber action. It showed that the possibility of false positives may pose just as much of a risk to political discussions about the attribution of major incidents as false negatives.

Yet some denials of Russian authorship were clearly specious. The most ingenious speculators claimed that the operation was a false-flag event orchestrated by American intelligence operators seeking to tarnish Russia's image. Julian Assange, founder of WikiLeaks, publicly sided with the doubters. He affirmed that Russian agents did not give his organization the illicit DNC data. He questioned whether Moscow was behind the intrusion of Clinton campaign chairman John Podesta's email account. His fantastical remark that "a 14-year-old could have hacked Podesta"[46] bespeaks the confusion that disingenuous players can cause in the midst of a foreign disinformation campaign. The forensic evidence paints a compelling picture of Russian authorship of the operation. Guccifer 2.0, a boastful crank who is widely reviled within the hacker

community, claimed to have singlehandedly obtained and delivered the
email records to WikiLeaks and other outlets.[47] But as Thomas Rid laid
out in a careful analysis, Guccifer 2.0 was a fictitious persona in a deception operation mounted by GRU.[48] Seventeen U.S. intelligence agencies
and their director also reached this conclusion. "We assess that only
Russia's senior-most officials could have authorized the recent election-
focused data thefts and disclosures, based on the scope and sensitivity of
the targets," said the Director of National Intelligence, James Clapper.[49]

Yet to stress the near certainty of Russian complicity is to miss an
important point: difficulties of attribution enable new forms of disruptive
political opportunism. They give subversive operators room to maneuver
when, for reasons of self-interest, they wish to undermine claims of
authorship of a hostile action even when the case for authorship is notably
strong. No sooner did U.S. investigators implicate Moscow than Trump
played the attribution card to sow public doubts about their findings. "I
know a lot about hacking," declared the new president in late January
2017. "And hacking is a very hard thing to prove,"[50] he said, echoing his
earlier assertion during the presidential debates: "I mean, it could be
Russia, but it could also be China. It could also be lots of other people. It
also could be somebody sitting on their bed that weighs 400 pounds,
OK? You don't know who broke in to (the) DNC."[51] He also rejected the
intelligence agencies' account of the motives of the operation.[52] Thus
with a few colorful remarks, a master of political dissimulation threw into
the public perception more variables and correlations than it could
reasonably assimilate on a technically complex question which, though
its answer is unknown and possibly unknowable, the intelligence experts
had for their part solved conclusively.

A third clue for our times involves the confluence of the world of
states and other actors. Moscow's influence campaign comprised overt
efforts by not only Russian government agencies, but also proxy and
private actors: state-funded media companies, social media users,
and third-party intermediaries.[53] Like the kompromat operation, their
aim was to undermine the integrity of the American election process
and to erode – preemptively – the legitimacy of a Clinton victory, which
the political masters in Moscow may reasonably have anticipated.[54]

During the election season, Russian-backed news outlets with channels across the United States worked assiduously at weakening Clinton's
respectability. The RT television network, a state-backed company,

aired a defamatory video in English about Clinton and the Clinton Foundation (a charity organization) that attracted millions of views on social media. Its most accessed and coddling video about Trump (which also featured Assange) also obtained millions of views.[55]

Armies of trolls – both human and machine – were also at work. In December 2015, social media accounts that had previously supported Russia's activity in Ukraine began to support Trump.[56] On election night, pro-Kremlin bloggers organized a Twitter campaign dubbed #DemocracyRIP, which they had to scrap – possibly unexpectedly – the next day following Trump's victory.[57] Among the disparagers of Clinton were networks of machines, those inanimate thinking objects that at the command of code will serve their masters' political purpose unquestioningly and tirelessly. A study by Philip Howard and Oxford researchers found that during the second presidential debate, automated Twitter users produced four times as many favorable tweets about Trump than about Clinton.[58] Here is another lesson to note: where the political affiliations or interests of states and private players converge, governments can recruit citizens and machines to augment state-driven information operations.

The most important lesson of the episode is the fourth: the unpeaceful methods of kompromat raise political and doctrinal quandaries for victims who wish to punish the opponent but cannot figure out how. Regardless of the hacking operation's final effects on the election, the action was an unprecedented intrusion into the American electoral process by a foreign power. Of this much the grain of official American opinion seems certain. Intelligence officials described it as "the most recent expression of Moscow's longstanding desire to undermine the US-led liberal democratic order."[59] The operation illustrated how Russia seeks to employ cyberspace to undermine the confidence of liberal democracies in their own institutional substance and to weaken the economic, ideological, and military bonds among them.

Yet this subversion of internal politics went largely unpunished. For all his assertiveness in ascribing Russian motives and authorship to the hacking events, for his claim that the United States should "be alarmed by Russia's action,"[60] President Barack Obama's response was tepid. His administration expelled thirty-five Russian diplomats from American soil and applied financial sanctions to two Russian state agencies, four individual officers, and three private organizations that it believed supported the operation – notable inconveniences for the persons involved, but a gentle punishment by the sometimes harsh standards of diplomacy. Obama promised a sterner response to come. "These actions are not the sum total of our response to Russia's aggressive activities," he announced. "We will continue to take a variety of actions at a time and place of our choosing, some of which will not be publicized."[61] Publicly, the response never materialized. Three weeks before assuming the presidency, and thus the mantle of leadership in Western relations with Russia, Trump contemptuously nullified Obama's response by praising Putin's decision not to retaliate to these actions in kind – the opposite of what diplomatic custom dictated.

After all this, the international relations specialist may ask: why should this hacking episode matter to observers concerned primarily with problems of international rather than domestic order? The main reason is that the two levels of order are in this case (as in many others) closely intertwined. The possible effects of Trump's stance extend far beyond the domestic political arena. Obama's muted response and Trump's questioning of Russia's complicity will support the expectation of some autocratic governments that they can use the virtual weapon to establish congenial regimes in foreign capitals as the basis for influencing the international order. The episode will teach aspiring disrupters an important lesson: the virtual weapon is a powerful and possibly unpunishable tool of foreign political subversion and influence.

In sum, Russia's century-old theory of information warfare refutes the idea of a decisive military clash that is so central to Western security thinking. Its core tenet is that the psychological element of conflict is as important as the physical one. On the backdrop of a contest of perceptions of international order, Russian strategists exhort actions that seek to deny adversaries the internal political cohesion necessary to act purposefully abroad. Cyberspace offers a rich plane onto which practitioners can extend this activity. The vast information skin comprising interconnected machines magnifies the possibilities for political disruption within the adversary's core terrain. The doctrine finds in the peculiar features of cyberspace something to exploit: an instrument to disable the opponent by interrupting vital infrastructure, to fan seditious ideas and sow discord in distant lands, to lure antagonists and court unwitting sympathizers toward one's cause – all remotely, instantaneously, and often with plausible grounds to deny the intrusion into domestic life. The doctrine's universal element is pernicious information, whether information as force to alter machine behavior or disinformation to sway people's minds. It realizes in short a total fusion in strategy and tactics of Turing's thinking machines and Minsky's machine thinkers.

CHAPTER 9

Private Sector Active Defense
AN ADEQUATE RESPONSE TO THE SOVEREIGNTY GAP?

The Sovereignty Gap Revisited

The technological forces of systems change and the resulting sovereignty gap in cyberspace have far-reaching implications for the private sector: it can no longer take for granted the ability of the government to protect it against all relevant threats. Thus the challenge of cybersecurity is essentially one of *civil defense*: how to equip the private sector to protect its own computer terrain in the absence of decisive government involvement.

Ordinarily, civil defense in the new domain has involved passive measures, such as resilience and redundancy, which aim to harden defenses and deflect offensive hits. But foiling a sophisticated offensive operation that is already in train is very difficult, particularly if deep exploitation of the target networks preceded the attack.[1] Denial of the adversary's arms has a higher chance of success if it occurs before they reach the defending line. Passive measures, therefore, will not redress the defensive gap unless they are complemented by a proactive approach – especially the techniques of "active defense," or offense-as-defense, which attempt to counter ongoing external threats and neutralize them before they are carried out. As a senior official in the British Cabinet Office put it: "Successful defense requires making life harder for the enemy." It demands a posture of aggressiveness: "We're not going to just sit there and let you get us – we will go after you in cyberspace and make your life more difficult. This is why one sees offensive actions."[2] Yet presently in the United States, Britain, and many other domestic jurisdictions, the authority to implement active defense belongs exclusively to the government. Top American officials have called for changes in law and policy that would bolster the private sector's use of active defense techniques such as "strikeback" or "hackback" technology: in effect, arming of the civilian quarters of cyberspace.[3] The main body of government opinion has successfully resisted these calls – so far.

This chapter asks: what are the possible strategic and other consequences of enabling the private sector to arm itself with active defenses? Little or no systematic analysis of this question exists. The chapter argues that while the potential defensive and other benefits of private sector arms are significant, the risks to defenders, innocent parties, and international conflict stability are notably greater.

But first, a clarification of key terms is in order. The label "private sector" in this analysis denotes the entirety of nonstate groups and individuals who comprise the economy and society and who are not under direct state control but are possibly under its informal direction. Conceptually, the difference between formal state "control" and informal "direction" is subtle but crucial: the former implies membership of the state; the latter, exclusion. On this basis, the private sector encompasses some forms of proxy actors such as criminal syndicates or privately owned firms (for example, Kaspersky Lab)[4] that have established informal working relationships with the government, but it excludes state-affiliated civilian actors such as paramilitary militias (for example, Estonian Cyber Defense League) or publicly controlled firms (Huawei).[5] Consistent with the framework of concepts introduced in Chapter 1, the term "cyberweapon" or "arm" signifies the software and hardware instruments necessary to carry out cyber exploitation or attack. The term "active defense" – a contested and ambiguous notion – is broadly construed to denote the use of such instruments outside the defender's or other friendly terrain to prevent or preempt attack. This interpretation of active defense does not imply the use of any specific kind of cyberweapon; merely that the activity transpires in extra-defensive terrains (more on this below).

The chapter has three sections: first, it defines the concept of active defense; second, it reviews the current state of private sector active defense; and, finally, it analyzes potential strategic benefits and risks associated with the development of private sector arms.

The Meaning of Active Defense

The first step in analyzing private sector active defense is to define active defense. The notion features prominently in national strategy papers and public debates about cybersecurity, yet it has never been satisfactorily defined. Within official policy circles, there is no clear or precise definition; or if there is such a definition, it is veiled by government secrecy: the research community does not know its full contents. Official U.S. strategy papers supply only ambiguous meanings. The Department of Defense describes "active cyber defense" as "[the] synchronized, real-time capability to deter, detect, analyze, and mitigate threats and vulnerabilities" – but reveals very little about the types of action involved.[6] Other nations have publicly claimed possession of a capability but fail to define it even vaguely.[7] This section attempts to define active defense so that it may serve as a useful tool of analysis.

Three defining characteristics of active defense stand out: defensive purpose, out-of-perimeter location, and tactical flexibility. These characteristics may apply to the concept of active defense in any domain of conflict; the focus here will be on the cyber context.

Defensive Purpose

As the label implies, the aim of active defense is to enhance the security of the defender's assets: to deny proactively but not to penalize the attacker. The attacker, by definition, is affected only if he engages or prepares to engage or is perceived to engage the target. Thus the essence of active defense lies in the eye of the defender. It entails the reasonable *perception* – not necessarily the fact – of an adversary's intention and capability to attack. For this reason, retaliation to deter future attack does not qualify as active defense unless it seeks to degrade the attack sequence itself and transpires while the threat is still active.

Offensive activity that extends beyond the minimum threshold of action necessary to neutralize an imminent threat or endures after the threat has subsided also does not constitute active defense. Here the criterion of imminence is debatable: does it include only tactical or also broader strategic threats? History provides a clue. As early as 1936, Japan presented a strategic threat to the United States by virtue of its intrinsic military potential and imperial designs in the Pacific, but it had few means to affect American interests directly. The Japanese threat did not become imminent until the Combined Imperial Fleet devised, in 1941, a viable tactical plan to attack Pearl Harbor. Thus the criterion of imminence demands the presence or the perception of a deployable, or nearly deployable, tactical capability to attack the defender.

What does imminence mean in the cyber domain? Two possibilities occur almost at once. The first and clearest scenario concerns the discovery within the defender's systems of sleeper malware – code customized to impair the target's functions but which has not yet struck. Of course, it may be difficult to ascertain the precise nature of the payload: is it exploitative or destructive? But forensic testing may provide credible clues. A second scenario involves the detection of exploitative code whose aim the defender believes is to open a vector of access to attack or to harvest systems data that are relevant to the preparation of an attack. Whether the defender can infer from the activity an actual capability to disrupt the compromised system may depend on the activity's duration. The longer the length of action, the higher the chances the intruder will have harvested enough information to customize an attack payload. Here it may be difficult to ascertain the true intent of intelligence collection: is it a case of stand-alone exploitation or a step in preparation for attack? The defender cannot penetrate the mind of the intruder; he may not even know the intruder's identity or location. Thus the perception of imminence will rest – inevitably – on the reliability of the defender's forensic knowledge of the intrusion and on the soundness of the reasoning upon which he construes the intruder's intent, both of which will remain open to interpretation.

Out-of-Perimeter Location

The "active" quality of the concept refers not to offensive activity, as some thinkers suppose (see below), but to the activity's out-of-perimeter location. Passive measures are those the defender conducts within his own terrain; active measures are those he conducts *outside* it – that is, within adversarial or neutral terrain, including the terrain of innocent parties whose computer identity or functions the attacker has usurped.

This characteristic of active defense features more prominently in British than in U.S. strategy papers, which do not clearly recognize it. For example, a report by the Joint Intelligence and Security Committee of Britain's House of Commons defines active defense as "interfering with the systems of those trying to hack into UK networks."[8]

The definition, it is important to realize, differs from the view of some information security professionals. One technical report described active defense as "the process of analysts monitoring for, responding to, learning from, and applying their knowledge to threats *internal to the network*." This definition, therefore, expressly excludes hacking back: "It is important to add the ending piece of 'internal to the network' to further discourage misrepresentation of the definition into the idea of a hack-back strategy. Analysts that can fall into this category include incident responders, malware reverse engineers, threat analysts, network security monitoring analysts, and other security personnel who utilize their environment to hunt for the adversary and respond to them."[9]

Any proactive measures such as honeypots or sinkholes that exist entirely within servers that the defender legitimately controls do not qualify as active defense.[10] For if they did, why the controversy over expanding private sector arms? Law and custom broadly recognize the right of a computer operator to take whatever measures within his own terrain are necessary to defend it.

Tactical Flexibility

There is one sense in which common ambiguities in the meaning of active defense are warranted: the concept implies nothing about the scale, type, or intensity of the defender's action. Tactically, active defense may involve a variety of actions – intelligence collection, disruption (including destruction), or some combination of the two. On this basis, it is possible to conceive of three broad sorts of active defense: *nondisruptive*, *disruptive*, or *mixed* (in other words similar to a "multistage" cyberattack that involves both preliminary exploitation and subsequent disruption).[11] It is therefore imprecise to define active defense simply as offensive action to defeat an ongoing attack, although some observers suggest this interpretation,[12] because the concept could, in fact, involve entirely nondisruptive measures, such as the insertion of exploitative beacons in enemy networks to capture threat data.

Table 3: Passive vs. active defense in the cyber domain

	Within Perimeter	**Out of Perimeter**
Undisruptive Defense	Passive Resilience, redundancy, organizational reform, information sharing	Active Standalone defensive exploitation (e.g. to gain knowledge of the adversary's capabilities)
Disruptive Defense	Passive Honeypots, sinkholes, beacon neutralization	Active Disruption of the adversary's command and control systems (may require preliminary exploitation)

In sum, the chief distinguishing features of active defense are not the scale, intensity, or form of activity but rather *defensive* measures of threat neutralization – whether nondisruptive or disruptive or both – that a defender implements *outside* his own or other friendly terrain. Table 3 summarizes and illustrates the differences between passive and active defense.

The Current State of Affairs

The current state of private sector active defense may be assessed from four viewpoints: law, policy, practice, and capability. First is the legal viewpoint. In the U.S. federal context, the most important law is the Computer Fraud and Abuse Act (CFAA). Of the CFAA's seven sections, two are directly relevant to the regulation of active defense: section (a)(2)(C), which forbids unauthorized access to a computer to obtain data in it;

and section (a)(5), which forbids the intentional use of computer code to impair the operations of a protected computer system.[13] Moreover, the Federal Wiretap Act's section 2511(2)(a)(i) forbids the unauthorized interception or recording of electronic communication transiting between machines. The fines for infringement of these rules can be severe.

The legal consequences of the recently passed Cybersecurity Information Sharing Act for private sector active defense in the United States are unclear. Possibly the bill will broaden the monitoring powers of private actors, but only if they work in conjunction with government authorities: in other words, as an informal arm of the state. Probably the changes will not be drastic. Although the bill allows the deployment of "countermeasures" that legitimately target threats and which damage data or machines on other networks, legally such countermeasures must be deployed within the defender's own network. Any resulting damage to external parties must therefore be unintentional.[14] Thus CISA's provision for countermeasures does not satisfy the out-of-perimeter criterion of active defense; it is beyond the scope of the present analysis.

There is little case law that elucidates the legal ramifications associated with the use of private sector arms.[15] Yet the prevailing legal viewpoint is clear: the practice of active defense is unlawful – if only because of the activity's second defining characteristic, that is, the intentional intrusion into or disruption of computers to which the defender lacks authorized access. Some officials have vocally pressed for changes in U.S. federal law that would allow the greater use of private active defense.[16] For now, however, the legal environment remains unequivocally proscriptive.

A second viewpoint concerns policy: official opinion reflects and supports the prevailing legal condition. The U.S. Department of Justice strongly discourages exploitative active defense. One of its guidebooks states:

A victimized organization should not attempt to access, damage, or impair another system that may appear to be involved in the intrusion or attack. Regardless of motive, doing so is likely illegal under U.S. and some foreign laws, and could result in civil and/or criminal liability. Furthermore, many intrusions and attacks are launched from compromised systems. Consequently, "hacking back" can damage or impair another innocent victim's system rather than the intruder's.[17]

Similarly, in a speech in 2015 the Assistant Attorney General, Leslie R. Caldwell, publicly denounced the use of strikeback techniques of any kind by firms and other private actors.

Other officials have occupied a more ambiguous position on the borderline between passive dissuasion and tacit acceptance. A recent comment by Admiral Mike Rogers, Director of the National Security Agency (NSA), embodies such ambiguity: "I'm not a big fan of the corporate world taking on this idea," he stated, but added, "It's not without precedence. If you go back to a time where nation states lacked capacity on their own, oftentimes they have turned to the corporate sector."[18] More revealingly, John Lynch, the head of the Justice Department's Computer Crime and Intellectual Property Section, drew a distinction between different types of active defense and their varying tolerability. He endorsed the nondisruptive use of beacon technology as lawful but condemned disruptive instruments, for example, artifacts that gain root access to modify other machines.[19] Moreover, the FBI has shown selective toleration of some uses of strikeback when it appeared urgent and proportionate to the security needs of the victim. Insofar as U.S. authorities are lenient toward private actors who employ defensive arms, they allow it not by changing the law but by evading it.

Third is practice: the question of what is actually happening regardless of the legal and policy conditions. The question is not easy to answer. Companies are no more translucent than governments when it comes to disclosing information about maneuvers within networks that they do not own or operate. The legal and reputational ramifications of disclosure are potentially high; they are not conducive to a culture of transparency on hacking and striking back. The near total absence of relevant case law reflects the prevailing culture of secrecy.

But if officials with knowledge of undisclosed cases are correct, the practice of active defense by the private sector far exceeds the record of it. As Tom Kellermann, chief cybersecurity officer and a former member of Obama's Commission on Cybersecurity, attested: "[Private] active defense is happening. It's not mainstream. It's very selective."[20] Of respondents to a 2012 poll at the Black Hat USA security conference, 36 percent claimed to have conducted "retaliatory" hacking at least once (the poll was based on a sample of 181 conference attendees). Some American firms have recruited companies abroad to attack hackers on their behalf. At least a few times the freelancers provided strikeback as a courtesy to the victim. In brief, active defense activity by the private sector is increasingly common, if restrained, because of the moderate leniency of policymakers toward it.

Fourth, there is the question of capability: what is currently possible in the realm of private sector active defense and what future developments await? Again, a wall of secrecy conceals many facts. Like governments, firms and other private actors rarely disclose information about their capacity to operate antagonistically in external networks. Nonetheless, observable cases of strikeback reveal that private sector arsenals are significant and growing.

Some technology firms conduct advanced research on and guardedly deploy active defense capabilities. For example, some have deployed "spam-back" software (albeit without much success).[21] Microsoft possesses sophisticated measures to take down botnet command-and-control servers throughout the globe. In 2010, the company collaborated with the FBI to design and direct a remote "kill signal" to incapacitate machines infected with the Coreflood Trojan.[22] In 2014, Dell SecureWorks and Crowdstrike provided essential technical assistance to the FBI in an operation to take down the "GameOver Zeus" botnet.[23] Juniper Networks has begun to integrate elements of strikeback into its products.

Whatever the state of the private sector's active defense capability, actors, particularly large technology firms, are caught in an inconsistency between the legal and policy conditions – which are broadly but not entirely prohibitive – and the state of practice – which seems far more indulgent. A remark by Juniper Network's chief technology officer captures the discrepancy: "The dirty little secret is if there were no worries ethically and legally, everyone [would want] a 'nuke from orbit' button."[24]

Arming of the Private Sector: Strategic Benefits and Risks

Would private sector active defense impact national and international security positively or negatively? In examining these consequences, the discussion will consider effects on the defending players, their parent governments, innocent third parties, and international conflict stability.

Possible Benefits

The development of private sector arms may yield at least four positive consequences: improvement of strategic depth; closer civil–military integration; new options for plausible deniability by states; and a reduced defensive burden.[25]

One advantage involves *strategic depth*. Ordinarily, strategic depth in the cyber domain in the absence of active defense is very poor. The defender must wait until the attacker has made his move, after which the time to mount an effective defense is extremely short because the threat travels between machines at the speed of electrons and can achieve tactical results within a matter of seconds or even milliseconds. By contrast, the defensive response, unless it is automated, may require cumbersome procedures such as information-sharing and coordination with law-enforcement agencies, which in turn must take time to evaluate the legal, ethical, and tactical appropriateness of different policy options. For instance, it took the U.S. government several weeks simply to identify North Korea as the source of the attack against Sony Pictures in December 2014.[26] Moreover, detection itself may be very difficult to achieve. The civilian sector owns or operates approximately 80–90 percent of critical computer systems and networks. Of U.S. government communications, including classified information, 98 percent travel over these networks.[27] It is therefore reasonable to assume that at all times some form of attack code resides undiscovered within much of the civilian sector's essential computer infrastructures.

One possible solution to the problem of strategic depth is greater information-sharing between the private and public sectors. The Cybersecurity Information Sharing Act (CISA) aims to foster such sharing.[28] So far, however, firms have been reluctant to share, on a regular basis, their incident and threat data with the government; much less are they willing to allow governments to monitor their networks directly owing to concerns about the privacy of proprietary information, the disclosure of which may harm corporate and client interests.

Private sector active defense could improve civilian strategic depth in a way that circumvents these concerns. It enables firms to identify and neutralize threats outside their networks without placing proprietary data at risk of government scrutiny. The insertion of beacons or "web bugs" – a form of exploitative active defense that some companies already use to track down stolen data – into adversary networks could enable these firms to design *disruptive* techniques that they can then use to neutralize threats at the point of origin, or, if the threat is in transit, in neutral systems. Here neutralization could be tactical, in other words a specific attack sequence is defeated but the attacker retains the ability to redeploy, or it could be strategic, in other words the attacker is dissuaded from or deprived of the ability to attack the target again. Exploitative tools could also support the government's *own* threat-monitoring and neutralization effort without themselves engaging in disruptive action. For example, third-party threat-intelligence companies may sell their services to the government, thereby serving as intermediaries between the victim and the government – an arrangement that could help to preserve the victim's anonymity.

A second advantage is enhanced *civil–military integration*. Western societies face an acute shortage of workers trained in technical disciplines relevant to cybersecurity, such as computer science and software engineering. The relevant skills base resides primarily in the private sector. Large technology firms (for example, Google, Apple, Microsoft) are able to offer salaries many times larger than military and security agencies (USCYBERCOM, NSA, GCHQ) can offer. "We are competing in a tough marketplace against a private sector that is in a position to offer a lot more money," lamented the U.S. Secretary of Homeland Security, Jeh Johnson. "We need more cybertalent without a doubt in D.H.S., in the federal government, and we are not where we should be right now, that is without a doubt."[29] Similarly, in Britain, the government skills gap is so severe that former GCHQ Director Iain Lobban said that his agency might have to employ non-nationals for a brief period – that is, before they, too, are inevitably absorbed by the private sector.[30] Another drain on skills occurs when defense contractors hire the manpower of government agencies, only later to sell their services back to the government.

Governments have reacted to asymmetry in the technological skills base in two ways: first, by attempting to assimilate civilian talent into loose state structures such as military reserves; and second, by cooperating with private technology providers to develop joint capabilities.

In the first approach, the government assumes a direct role in equipping the private sector. It drafts, trains, arms, and retrains elements of the civilian population in the methods of cyber operations. This may be achieved by establishing a voluntary paramilitary defense force, such as Estonia's Cyber Defense League (*Küberkaitseliit*), a civilian defense organization that supports the military and Ministry of Defense;[31] or by way of conscription, as in Israel's Unit 8200, whose ranks include drafted servicemen who after an initial term of service enter the army reserves.[32] This approach has achieved moderate success in small nations such as Estonia and Israel, which have vibrant technological innovation hubs and a popular tradition of mass conscription. But it has paid only limited returns in large countries such as the United States and Britain where the National Guard or Reserves and the Territorial Army often fail to attract high-skilled elements of the civilian workforce.[33]

The second approach entails an extension of the concept of "private military companies" (PMCs) into the new domains. PMCs provide military and security services – even armed force – to the state or to other private entities.[34] This approach may be better suited to large nations with sizeable private technology industries but poorly developed traditions of military service. It would, however, require a greater commitment on behalf of participating companies to develop the sorts of strategic and tactical technologies that governments need to achieve national security goals. Some firms already provide the U.S. and other governments with sophisticated surveillance tools such as tracking and eavesdropping software.[35] Few companies, however, have invested in the other side of active defense – advanced disruptive tools – because of the legal and policy prohibitions or because the business case for doing so is not clear. Yet the private sector is well poised to develop them. Cisco's dominance of the router market, Google's near monopoly of online searches, and Microsoft's preponderance in the sale of desktop operating systems afford these firms tremendous (and legal) access to a significant proportion of Internet traffic and global hardware components. Some of this access is directly relevant to the harvesting of zero-day vulnerabilities and to the design of access vectors and payloads that governments require to mount sophisticated cyber operations.[36] CISA's relaxation of prohibitions against private sector exploitation performed under government sanction may foster more cooperation of this sort, although at present the structural incentives for such cooperation are not clear.

In brief, some elements of the technological sector possess merely by their existence a latent capacity to acquire sophisticated cyberweapons. The development of private sector cyber arms under informal government direction could enable governments to harness the civilian sector's technological prowess while avoiding the cumbersome organizational costs of traditional military formations.

Many firms, especially those with global commercial enterprises, may find the reputational costs of collusion with government unacceptable, especially in a post-Edward Snowden world. Indeed, Google, Facebook, and other U.S. technology companies have sought to distance themselves from the perception that they work with the government to develop joint surveillance capabilities. But the alleged cooperation of RSA and Microsoft with the government proves that at least some level of complicity is acceptable even to large multinational firms with significant commercial interests abroad.[37] Most likely to succeed is the Israeli model of integrating the private sector into the national cyber establishment, which relies on the cultivation of ties with small start-ups that operate mostly in domestic markets – for example, NSO Group and Kaymera, which develop exploitative tools that allow the remote manipulation of smartphones.[38]

A third advantage is *plausible deniability*. Credible attribution of the source of a cyberattack is important because it enables the defender to inflict penalties on the attacker; without it the attacker can avoid them. States that develop offensive capabilities, therefore, have an incentive to devise means to complicate attribution (unless they desire positive attribution because they want to achieve a deterrent or demonstration effect). The more sophisticated the offensive operation, the smaller the universe of possible assailants – hence the higher the chances, *a priori*, that the defender will credibly attribute the attack so long as he detects it. This is a problem for the small number of states that possess the most advanced offensive weapons. After the Stuxnet attack became known, few people in Tehran asked: did Jordan or Turkey do it? Similarly, no one asked: was it Siemens (which built the Natanz nuclear facility's industrial control system) or Microsoft (the engineering stations)? Rather, the suspicion fell immediately upon the United States and Israel. Allowing the private sector to arm itself with sophisticated exploitative and disruptive tools would widen the field of theoretical attackers, thus complicating – in principle – the defender's attribution of the real attacker (a positive outcome for the attacker).

But the effect on attribution will be limited unless the firms in question are known to have offensive motives that seem credible to the adversary. Moreover, the development of PMCs may weaken the perception in the minds of adversaries of a neat separation between the public and private sectors. There is also the problem of "state responsibility," the principle of international law which stipulates that governments are responsible for harmful actions emanating from inside their jurisdictions. Thus the victim may attribute blame to the attacker's parent government even in the absence of direct government complicity.

Fourth, is the reduction of the *defender's burden*. When a multi-national firm is attacked, its possession of active defense capabilities could release the countries that host its headquarters or subsidiary branches from the burden of conducting defensive or retaliatory action against the offender. The transnational quality of modern production chains and commercial activity means that in contemporary society no large firm can enjoy the protection of a single state in all sectors of the global market within which it operates.[39] Firms may face attacks against interests and servers located in any one or in a variety of foreign jurisdictions. For example, considering the cyberattacks against Sony Pictures, a U.S.-based entertainment subsidiary of Sony, the Japanese technology conglomerate, the question is: in the absence of private sector arms, who strikes back – Washington or Tokyo? By enabling the company to respond itself, private sector arms would release the governments involved in the defensive response, assuming they desire one, from the burden of taking direct action.

The prospect of armed multinational enterprises acting under informal single-state direction recalls the partial successes of pirate merchants during the sixteenth and seventeenth centuries. Formally, pirates were unaffiliated (and thus differed from privateers, who operated under official government sanction). Yet occasionally they performed tasks at the direction of states, often changing flags in the process.[40] The use of pirates provided states with a means of waging undeclared and plausibly deniable war against other states.[41] Yet now, as then, the main obstacle to the success of the "piracy" model of public–private collusion is the difficulty of aligning the goals of the state, which are generally political, with those of private firms, which are mainly economic.

Possible Risks

The use of cyber arms by the private sector entails at least three risks: foreign government penalties; innocent third-party harm; and inadvertent or accelerating international conflict. The last directly involves state interests and is potentially the gravest.

First is the danger of *foreign government penalties*. Even if CISA or other U.S. legislation permitted the private sector to deploy active defense tools, foreign domestic law will most likely continue to prohibit them; as explained above, almost all domestic penal codes presently criminalize active defense measures. Thus in such a world, the activity would be legal only in cases where the attack sequence originated in servers located exclusively within the defender's own jurisdiction and which did not cross any national boundaries – that is, in a negligibly small number of conceivable cyberattack scenarios.

It is possible that some other countries could amend their laws to allow the private sector the use of weapons in select cases. Or else governments may cast a blind eye when a player based in a friendly foreign country conducts active defense within its own jurisdiction under controlled conditions for demonstrably defensive aims. Two considerations would nevertheless diminish the appeal of private sector active defense. First, because they are on friendly diplomatic terms with the defender's parent country, the nations likeliest to permit or tolerate the use of private sector arms in their virtual terrain are also the likeliest to offer legal and police assistance during an attack implicating their jurisdiction – thus diminishing the need for private action in the first place. Second, and conversely, nations that have adversarial diplomatic relations with the defender's parent country are the least likely to permit or tolerate the use of private sector active defense against machines located within their jurisdiction. Even if they permitted the activity in some limited cases (for example, if the attacker is a common enemy), foreign nations would almost certainly penalize it in cases where they or their proxy agents were complicit in the attack. The difficulties of attaining certain attribution of the attack's sponsorship would mean that even if the defender believes the foreign government is not complicit, he may never be certain that this is in fact the case.[42] The possibility of punishment would remain agonizingly real – especially if the inhibition to punish a firm by imposing financial penalties is lower than the inhibition to penalize another government with weightier measures such as economic sanctions.

A second risk is the potential for *innocent third-party harm*. Recall one of the main distinguishing aspects of active defense: it transpires outside the defender's terrain – including, possibly, in neutral terrain. Now note two important features of offensive cyber operations: they can be very difficult to attribute; and they often use multiple neutral machines and networks to access the target. Almost inevitably, therefore, active defense measures will impair to some degree the operations or data of third-party computer users, either because the defender misattributes the source of the attack to a machine that is in fact not involved because the attacker employs spoofing software that alters the compromise indicators (for example, the IP address); or because the defender correctly attributes the source or transit point of the attack but the identified machine is in fact innocent because the attacker has hijacked it. And as the number of injured parties multiplies, the potential for the conflict to accelerate and broaden grows.

The third type of danger is the gravest of all: *inadvertent and escalating conflict*, or the possibility of unwanted international crises. Some international relations thinkers have questioned the ability of private actors to destabilize the dynamics of interstate security competitions.[43] A world not far from the one in which we live challenges this view. Extending the private sector's ability to carry out active defense may produce instability in the following ways, *inter alia*:

(a) A private actor based in country A executes a disruptive active defense action on an attacking machine in country B. The government of country B interprets the action as an offensive strike by the government of country A. It retaliates against the defender and the government of country A.

(b) A private actor based in country A executes a disruptive active defense action on an innocent machine in country C whose identity an attacker in country B has in fact spoofed. The government of country C retaliates against both the defender and the government of country A.

(c) A private actor based in country A executes exploitative active defense activities against a machine in country B because he suspects that the machine may be preparing an attack. The machine in country B misinterprets the defender's move as a prelude to attack and launches its own preemptive strike against the defender in country A.

(d) The governments of countries A and B are engaged in an international exchange of cyber blows that both sides seek to de-escalate and terminate. Armed private technology firms recruited into the conflict by the two countries misinterpret or choose to ignore their government's instructions. The firms continue to launch strikes against targets located in the other side's territory. The governments of countries A and B misinterpret the strikes as actions conducted or condoned by the opposing country. Rather than de-escalate, the conflict rapidly and uncontrollably intensifies.

(e) An ideologically motivated and technically savvy employee of a private firm in country A illegitimately employs (in other words, for offensive purposes) disruptive active defense tools against multiple innocent machines in country B while spoofing his identity to resemble a government player in country C (a hated country of the rogue employee). The government of country B misattributes the location of the attacker as country C. It attacks targets in country C. The government of country C retaliates in kind against targets in country B. The rogue employee repeats the deceptive maneuver but instead of attacking machines in country B targets those in country D. The cycle repeats.

Convergence at the Cost of Collision

Equipment of the private sector with cyberweapons would intensify a broader trend in the contemporary era: the partial fusion of the world of states and the world of citizens and other groups – that is, systems change. Many thinkers traditionally treat these two worlds as separate behavioral universes; they customarily ban private agents from theoretical models of the states system. Legal scholars point to the prevailing positivist doctrine by which the consent of states, whether formal or customary, is the only true source of international law.[44] Political scientists normally emphasize the state's supreme political authority in the ordering of both domestic and international affairs. Yet the growing influence of a variety of nonstate actors in the twenty-first century challenges these rigid models of political order. Multinational firms influence, sometimes decisively, the fiscal and developmental agendas of states. Religious militant groups export pernicious ideologies and fighters to distant societies. Private military corporations affect the outcomes of foreign military occupations. Pirates scour the high seas and penetrate foreign coastlines. And so on.

The expansion of active defense activities to the private sector would intensify this trend of systems change. It would further challenge

prevailing patterns of security competition and order in the international system. This disruptive trend could positively affect national
security in the following ways: by improving strategic depth in a framework of interaction where private players are especially disadvantaged
in defense; by fostering civil–military integration in a domain where
technological prowess is indispensable but scarce; by offering governments new options to deny responsibility for offensive actions; and by
lessening the sovereign burden of governments in a domain where the
protection of the private sector – their traditional duty – is increasingly
difficult to guarantee. That is, it may generate new opportunities for
convergence, or what Chapter 6 described as cooperation between states
and nonstate actors who share objectives and enemies.

The trend also invites new perils, however. A world in which private
firms and citizen groups are free to carry out the prerogatives of national
security policy against each other and against states is a world in which
the risks of harm to innocent parties and accelerating conflict are potentially grave. The international system is the product of centuries of
evolution in the design of mechanisms to regulate and restrain conflict
among the main units: states. Continued erosion of that model through
the empowerment of players that are alien to the system and that may
not share the goal or even comprehend the intricate requirements of
international order invites not only the benefits of deeper convergence
but also the dangers of collision between the states system and the
global system. Cyber civil defense should remain a reactive enterprise.

CHAPTER 10

Cyber Futures

A revolution can be mastered only if it is recognized. This task imposes different demands on analysts than it does on practitioners. Analysts must develop conceptual models that make unprecedented chaos seem ordinary. Practitioners must apply these models to craft regulatory devices that render it orderly. The two efforts are closely related, because policy succeeds or fails based on the correctness of the theory that underlies it. It is only when statesmen grasp the relevance or irrelevance of old axioms and adapt their habits to new realities that the revolutionary condition ends.

In our times the challenge of adaptation to revolution is greatest because the source of disruption is technological. Analysts must resolve not only social and political but also technical complexities and their interrelations. Ultimately, however, the revolutionary potential of new technology resides not in the technology itself but in its effects upon the political and social world. Thus not all technological revolutions require conceptual revolutions in the study of security affairs. Some fit within the conventional models; others demand new departures in thinking.

The dislocations of the cyber age are so complex that the interaction of many communities of knowledge is necessary for a full appraisal of its problems. Yet several quarters of the Congress of Disciplines that is cyber studies remain unfilled. We saw in Chapter 1 that the section reserved for students of international relations and security studies is especially, though not entirely, silent. Tensions arise on this thinly occupied bench from the residue of concepts – largely centered on Clausewitz's traditional framework of interstate violence – that the participants inherited from a previous era but which are not fully appropriate to the evaluation of unprecedented events. Among the thinkers present, few warn about the gravity of cyber threat. Fewer still merge them into theory. The very few who do both are a small and beleaguered party. As they rise to the rostrum to utter a message of alarm and change, skeptics hurl old concepts at them; toleration of dissent from received notions of interstate war and conquest is not a distinguishing trait of the Clausewitzian faction. Occasionally, delegates on the technical benches join this internecine fracas, often in defense of those voicing alarm.

The argument throughout this book is that the international relations delegation could be more vocal and daring, less wary or apathetic, about joining the grand chamber of learning and debate. Other non-technical benches reflect a bolder attitude toward the study of cyber issues than the attitude of retreat that prevails among international relations specialists, some of whom lurk outside the entrance of the congress wondering whether they need a token of technical expertise to join the proceedings. Witness the superb ability of some legal scholars to adapt, or at least apply, their concepts and reorient their agendas to ongoing technological changes. Twenty years have passed since Lawrence Lessig and others began shaping the "small and quirky field of cyberlaw."[1] More than thirty if we begin from the analysis of data privacy and data protection in the pre-commercial Internet.[2] These founding intellectual investments – intrepid at a time when the Internet was still an infant technology of limited social and political scope – have prevented the dilatoriness that arose in our discipline to beset theirs.

After a time, indifference to the implications of new technology brings forth a sense of separation from present realities. It is a distinguishing mark of an international relations profession trained to read history – even ancient history – as a prologue to the future that it subsumes new trends in political action within familiar deductive theories. Traditionalists in the discipline deny revolution more than experience it.

This situation was not always so, the intellectual record reveals. Before it became an organized scholarly profession, before enthusiasm for abstract models overcame attention to raw history, the study of politics and international affairs did not display indifference to transforming inventions. Previous analysts of technological revolution – Kissinger,

Niebuhr, Osgood, and others – arrived at the congress of nuclear studies almost no sooner than physicists created the underlying technology. Among the very first to arrive in that chamber, they entered with a sense of mental impoverishment: they were not so sure of the relevance of even recent historical experience to want to extend its universal lessons to the new technological domain. Skepticism manifested itself against established views, not against the evidence of new patterns of behavior. Some makers of policy in the gallery, for example, Eisenhower and Dulles, who clung to the old doctrine of "general retaliation," looked down upon the somber gathering of thinkers below them a bit foolishly. A recognition of change and an impatience with the follies of old policy habits gave rise, slowly and sometimes acrimoniously, to a field of intellectual endeavor on the unfamiliar challenges of a new invention.

In our own context, by contrast, most of the intellectual achievements await in the future. The partial vacancy of the international relations delegation, particularly the security studies bench, reflects not only some scholars' disdain for technical intricacy, but also ingrained theoretical views about the workings of the international system – the tendency to privilege the problems of order among rational states and to prioritize their historical concern for military security and physical survival. At every stage of interpretation of new threats, the tendency appears and often prevails to assimilate them into conventional theories of statecraft.

The impact of this rigid viewpoint on the resolution of contemporary security problems is pernicious. It is possible to conclude from the a nalysis in Chapter 2 that the distinguishing feature of the cyber revolution is the priority it gives to the virtual over the physical world, to nonmilitary over military threats. The cyber danger will not disappear merely because theorists peering through the Clausewitzian prism of war fail to perceive its true and novel essence: that the virtual weapon is enabling new forms of antagonism and expanding the range of possible harm between the binary notions of peace and war. The most damaging cyber actions are not war – so far – but nor are they peace. Commentators often conflate these two terms under meaningless statements such as "War in Peacetime." What they really want is a distinct label that is neither term. This book suggested such a label: *unpeace*, a new form of mid-spectrum harm and international rivalry that is neither fatal or physically destructive like traditional war, nor desirable or even tolerable like conventional forms of peaceful rivalry.

That adversaries who engage in such unpeaceful activity permanently reside – as a starting axiom of theory – inside vital computer infrastructures gives problems of security in our times a special uniqueness that spoils core tenets of security strategy. The main concern of policy in a geographical conception of security is to deny the opponent access to the home terrain; the central concern in a virtual conception is to deny him the ability to harm you from *within* your own soil.

The limitations of prevailing theory do not end with Clausewitzian notions of security. They also implicate the very meaning of revolution. Theorists' ability to recognize the cyber revolution depends on their criteria of what counts as a "revolution" in the first place. All too often, international relations specialists reduce the security problems of international anarchy to a theory in which states' rational interest in material gains supersedes moral purpose and ideology. This viewpoint, so central to the Clausewitzian security paradigm, does not imply the inevitable development toward an orderly harmony among nations; much less does it mean eventual perpetual peace. Rather, it conveys the belief of theoreticians that the interstate contests for security are rooted in the incessant uncertainty of anarchy and, therefore, that the severity of the rivalry is reducible by balances of military power, institutional contrivances, or appeals to the reasonableness of law. It means that rivalry among states is both unnecessary and inevitable: unnecessary, because if only the units could overcome their anxieties over each other's intentions then conflict would not occur; inevitable, because in the absence of a central authority to punish hostile acts, those anxieties are permanent. Again, the obstacles to understanding arising from old theory are enormous. The established security paradigm leads to a common neglect of two central truths: the possibility that occasionally one or a group of states may, for reasons of extreme ideology, regard the conflict as necessary and desirable; and the prospect that actors alien to the states system may subvert the political order within it.

If we are to ask the right questions – and avoid giving the wrong answers – about contemporary security affairs, then we require broader benchmarks of revolutionary change in the international system than conventional theory supplies. The study of technological revolution in international affairs cannot be examined solely on the basis of rational interstate dealings. A major shortcoming of specialists who write about the impact of new inventions is the neglect of a topic that clashes with their commitment – sometimes explicit, often unintentional – to inhabit a simplified theoretical realm that ends at the bounds of the Conventional Model of the international system: the question of how actors other than states can influence security affairs. This failing is even more unfortunate in the analysis of cyberspace than in discussion of other technologies, such as nuclear arms, that so far have tended to reinforce the preconception that in the global system states reign supreme.

The most important effect of technological revolution on international order concerns not the balance of power but the balance of players. Certainly a change in the balance of power among states – a chief concern of some international relations specialists – can have important destabilizing effects. It may increase the risk of war or make its costs seem unbearable to rational contenders. Yet none of these effects is as profound as an alteration of the international system's organizing principle: the supremacy of states over all other units. Not even the appearance of a revolutionary giant, such as Republican France in 1789 or Soviet Russia in 1917, matches the degree of change implied by the ascent of a new class of actors – the earlier establishment of nation states as the dominant units, for instance. Domestic revolution may produce an ideological conflagration of epic proportions among nations whose basic ends are incompatible. Yet except in the most extreme cases, such as Nazi Germany's quest for universal empire, in which there could be but one truly dominant state, it does not imperil the system's building blocks. The difference between, on the one hand, a rebalancing of power or a change in the political identity of states and, on the other, a change in the balance of players, is the difference between a revolution *within* the existing system and a revolution *among* distinct systems.

Thus there are degrees of revolution that new technology can help to bring about either as a primary cause, in which case the technology is a necessary driver of deep political change, or a secondary cause, whereby technology accelerates but does not give rise to change. On the basis of this understanding, the analysis of Chapter 3 developed a revolutions framework to orient the study of change in the international system. The framework distinguished three orders of transformation that cyberspace can produce or accelerate even if it does not fulfill all of their criteria. One is third-order revolution, or systemic disruption. This concept denotes a disturbance to the regularized interactions of rational state contenders that share the basic purposes of survival and the preservation of a minimum measure of stability and peace in their relations. Another form of change is second-order revolution, or what this book has labeled systemic revision. It signifies a more fundamental disturbance of the states system arising from the empowerment of a state or a group of states that repudiates the common basic goals of the units and rejects the accepted methods of achieving them, in particular restraints on the ends and means of war. Last is the problem of first-order revolution, or systems change. This is the most extreme form of conceivable revolution: it occurs when players alien to the system challenge the supremacy of the dominant units, whose purposes the new entrants may reject or may not even understand, but whose affairs they nevertheless significantly affect.

Based on the historical analysis of this book, we can conclude that the virtual weapon meets – fully or partly – some of the test principles of revolutionary change in international relations. The first four principles relate to systemic disruption. The discussion in Chapter 4 showed that while the new capability is not significantly redrawing the balance of power among states – a chief concern of some analysts – it nevertheless disturbs their strategic relations in four important ways. First, the new technology is so novel and the vulnerabilities it exploits are so inscrutable that understanding its behavior is difficult. This situation of technological uncertainty increases the chances of inadvertent damage in a conflict. Second, the signature of power in cyberspace is often very difficult to discern. This problem weakens deterrence logics and impedes the development of interstate cooperative models over time. Third, the position of dominance enjoyed by some offensive forces increases the chances that those in possession of weaponized code will use it to seize strategic gains. Fourth, the depth of power in the cyber domain – the awesome speed and range of code – means that organizing a coherent response to a major attack will strain the bureaucratic resources of the defender. The current tendency to narrow the reactive time by implementing automated defenses raises new dangers of machine-driven escalation. Together, these features of the new domain mean that the risks of inadvertent conflict are high even among rational state adversaries.

The virtual weapon is also a force of systemic revision. It empowers revolutionary states, or states that repudiate the basic goals and principles of the established international order. Chapter 5 explored this problem in the context of North Korea – the quintessential revolutionary state in our times. Cyberweapons, to be sure, are not a primary cause of this form of revolution, but they nevertheless catalyze it. The discussion of North Korea's cyberattacks against Sony Pictures and the country's pervasive penetration and occasional disruption of its adversaries' essential infrastructures demonstrate how a revolutionary state can carry out spectacular moves in cyberspace in order to seize financial gains to offset the effects of economic sanctions, to erode the confidence of adversaries in their own economic and social institutions, and to suppress the production or dissemination of foreign ideas that criticize the perverse rule of the House of Kim. Technologically enabled insubordination abroad supports the revolutionary regime's interests at home. The disruptive and sometimes unrestrainable actions of this revolutionary state illustrate an important point: equally significant as the properties of a new technology are the ends that its possessors seek to achieve with it. What marks the difference between systemic disruption and systemic revision, then, is not the nature of the technology but the nature of its owner.

The virtual weapon's effects on international order also partially satisfy the criteria of systems change – the most important change of all. Chapter 6 considered how the technology gives impetus to the emergence of a partial "world system," or a system in which states are no longer absolutely in control even of their own internal affairs but nevertheless retain much of their primacy over all other actors – hence why the emergent world system is not nearly complete. This trend is evident in three ways. First is the ease of proliferation of some capabilities, especially generalized weapons such as botnets. Alien players can enter the new domain's offensive quarter with some ease, even if they lack (for now) the intelligence and other resources to scale the high walls that deprive them of the most advanced weaponized code such as the Stuxnet worm. Consequently, other states are no longer the only relevant source of threats to national security and domestic order. In some cases, they may not even be the primary cause of concern. Other players, such as the political activists who crashed computer systems in Estonia in 2007, may be more important. Concerning threat agency, then, the cyber revolution is at a middle point of the spectrum of systems change: while states enjoy supremacy in high-end weapons, lesser private actors pose highly relevant threats. Second, states are not the sole or supreme national security providers. In crucial areas involving the workings and regulation of cyberspace such as data ownership, data encryption, and Internet governance, the private sector is more important. Here the revolution is at a higher point in the spectrum: players other than states – such as the large technology firms Apple and Google – are not only primary, but may even be supreme. Third, the traditional units can no longer wholly steer the dynamics of conflict among them. Private culprits can use cyberspace to disturb the fragile political framework of international anarchy, as in the Estonian crisis, which launched an abrupt quest within NATO for a new collective defense identity. Good diplomacy to be sure managed to prevent the crisis from boiling over into an armed confrontation among states, but that is less a source of reassurance than a cause for concern. The main lesson of the crisis is not that the system's state masters in the end suppressed it, but that it was even possible. The remote actions of innumerable, unnamed culprits raised quandaries of international law and defense strategy that decision-makers verged closely on answering immoderately and that – ten years later – remain largely unresolved even by seasoned statesmen within the world's preeminent military alliance.

Therefrom stems the sovereignty gap of cyberspace: the functions of national security provision and international crisis control no longer belong to the state alone or in some areas even primarily. Among security planners there is an air of consternation about the virtual weapon's meaning for political order, especially the dangers of collision between the world of states and the chaotic universe of unrecognized players. Officials no less influential than the Chairman of the U.S. Joint Chiefs of Staff have warned that the offensive code their governments are crafting may fall into the hands of unaffiliated actors who not only fail to grasp the conditions of a stable international order, but also wish to subvert it.

The forces of systems change mean that theoreticians and strategists must consider not only familiar problems of the international state of nature but also new problems of global chaos. It is insufficient to examine only the disturbances within the states system; one must also consider the destabilizing pressures emanating from below it. The traditional masters of the system are not the sole agents of this technological revolution. Alien players whose aims and motives may be subversive of national and international order and who repudiate the political framework of international society are also relevant. Political anarchy in other words is no longer a state of nature among like units. Famously, Thomas Hobbes identified two distinct states of nature in human society: the one among men and the one among states. Crucially, in his conception these were separate ideal types. One entered into the one state only by exiting the other. The different units of the two universes did not clash, for they did not meet. Hobbes treated the state as an analogue of man; the question did not occur to him: what is a state without the individuals?

The cyber revolution welds these two universes together. At times, there will be a convergence of interests and activities among the different players. Consider the Russian government's benefit from the disruption by political activists of Georgia's vital computer systems during the Russo-Georgian War of 2008, or the FBI's resort to Microsoft to incapacitate botnet infrastructures in 2010. At others, a collision will occur that produces destabilization. It is along these major points of encounter that old theory will most fail to explain and conventional policy will least succeed in mitigating new security problems.

This book also considered three major issues of contemporary statecraft. Chapter 7 explored the relationship between the desire to deter major cyberattacks with the threat of severe penalties and the interest in controlling a crisis when deterrence fails. It also reviewed the necessity for a new approach – *punctuated deterrence* – to prevent acts of unpeace. This approach calls for reevaluation of the purpose of deterrence: the goal is not to prevent all attacks, the classical goal of deterrence, but to reduce their cumulative effects to a tolerable level. A graduated scheme of punishment in which the defender metes out penalties for attacks over time and at a moment of his own choosing offers the defender greater initiative and scope of maneuver than the traditional approach of total deterrence, which in the face of relentless aggression produces a tendency to paralysis and inaction.

Chapter 8 reviewed Russia's refinement of the doctrine of information warfare. Remarkably displayed in the kompromat operation during the U.S. presidential election in 2016, the revised doctrine reveals an important truth about the contemporary world: strategic power resides not merely in physical space but also in cyberspace. The technological domain offers new avenues to achieve foreign-policy preferences. Manipulation of information spaces enables actors to alter an opponent's strategic behavior without ever having to resort to Clausewitzian war. The subtle methods of unpeace can be a more potent source of national power and influence than the overt violence of war. Russian doctrinal thinkers present their information warfare as a refinement of the art of war; in fact, it is a *departure* from the means of war – and that is its main appeal: although acts of unpeace can be more potent than acts of war, they are less easily punishable.

Chapter 9 explored the implications of a current policy debate concerning the wisdom of improving cyber civil defense by allowing the private sector to arm itself. While this move could positively affect national security, its potential risks to innocent third parties, private companies, and international conflict stability are far greater. Cyber civil defense should remain as law, policy, and prudence – if not always practice – dictate: strictly reactive, if only to arrest systems change.

What lies in store for the future? We can begin to understand the answer to this question only if we recognize the inversion of the relationship between technological prowess and security that the cyber revolution has wrought. In previous eras, technological superiority elevated the military security of nations. Supremacy in naval arms enabled Britain to expand and conserve its empire in the nineteenth century. In the mid-twentieth century, advances in mechanized warfare allowed Germany to seize vast territories in Europe and northern Africa. Mastery of the atom conferred upon the United States and the Soviet Union the ability to annihilate all possible military contenders. New technology was traditionally a source of relative security for its possessor.

Against this backdrop, the cyber age presents an irony: it awards technological virtuosity with peril. Every advantage borne of the new technology also invites its dangers. Online banking enables cybercrime; digital communications bring forth surveillance; computerized industrial systems allow infrastructural damage; and so on. The security and utility of cyberspace exist in fundamental tension. This is the root paradox of security in our times: those nations that are most adept at harnessing cyberspace to achieve economic, social, even military gains are also the ones most vulnerable to threats propagating through it.

Current technological trends do not portend a correction of this paradox. No one today can accurately divine the full security implications of the Internet of Things – the rapid and uneven expansion of the networks into everyday objects in the home, the office, and public spaces.

While this next phase of technological development will bring tangible economic and other benefits, it also heralds new dangers. One study describes the Internet of Things as a "prime mechanism" for government surveillance.[3] The multiplication of connections will also furnish opportunistic attackers with countless new vectors of entry and assault.

Another major technological disruption in the offing lies in the field of quantum computing. Most Internet services today rely for their security on what is known as asymmetric or public-key cryptography. The strength of this encryption system is its ease of use. The system allows any person to encrypt a message by using the receiver's public key, but only a holder of his private key can decipher the contents. This is the underlying technology that secures email communications, online banking and commerce, digital identification systems – almost all services that rely on Internet transmissions. Universal quantum computers promise to render public-key encryption instantly obsolete. By relying on the peculiar ability of "qubits," or information stored as photons that can be superimposed in two states at once, these supermachines will be able to smash the mathematical barriers of asymmetric ciphers.[4] Estimates of the timescale of this breakthrough vary between five and thirty years. Whatever the actual date of achievement, it is likely that the configuration of cyberspace will undergo a drastic redesign within the current or next generation of policymakers and analysts.

These emerging inventions in computing ability and society's changing reliance on it suggest that the shifting technological currents will never subside. Some aspects of cyberspace evolve so quickly that it may permanently be a technology-in-the-making. Humans will be able to define many of its chief properties but without controlling or even grasping the security implications of its applications in society. Thus the distinguishing feature of security affairs in the current epoch is not the existence of a revolutionary condition but the prospect that it may never end. Against this backdrop, the international relations specialist has a duty to supply concepts that can close the gap between theory and new technology to the narrowest degree possible before the forces of change unleash new rounds of disturbance in the known order.

Notes

Introduction

1. The words are those of Nick Harvey, the United Kingdom's Armed Forces Minister. Nick Hopkins, "UK Developing Cyber-Weapons Programme to Counter Cyber War Threat," *The Guardian*, May 30, 2011.
2. Within international security studies, examples of skeptical thinking include the following works: Erik Gartzke, "The Myth of Cyberwar: Bringing War in Cyberspace Back Down to Earth," *International Security*, Vol. 38, No. 2 (Fall 2013), pp. 41–73; Jon R. Lindsay, "Stuxnet and the Limits of Cyber Warfare," *Security Studies*, Vol. 22, No. 3 (2013), pp. 365–404; and Brandon Valeriano and Ryan C. Maness, *Cyber War Versus Cyber Realities: Cyber Conflict in the International System* (Oxford: Oxford University Press, 2015).
3. For the sake of simplicity, this work refers to cyberspace as a single technology – much as observers often refer to nuclear enrichment facilities, warheads, delivery vehicles, and so on as nuclear technology. But readers should note that cyberspace is, in fact, a *series* of technologies – each complex in its own right – that encompasses servers, routers, machine nodes, and various forms and layers of applications and software architecture.
4. See Cliff Stoll, *The Cuckoo's Egg: Tracking a Spy through the Maze of Computer Espionage* (New York: Doubleday, 1989), Epilogue.
5. See John Arquilla and David Ronfeldt, *Cyber War Is Coming!* (Santa Monica, CA: RAND, 1993).
6. See Arnaud de Borchgrave, Frank J. Cilluffo, Sharon L. Cardash, and Michele M. Ledgerwood, *Cyber Threats and Information Security Meeting the 21st Century Challenge* (Washington, D.C.: U.S. Department of Justice, Office of Justice Programs, 2001).
7. The cyberattacks against Estonian computer systems in the spring of 2007 thrust this question upon national security planners.
8. See Marvin Minsky, *The Society of Mind* (New York: Simon and Schuster, 1988). The notion of the comparability of the human and machine minds is rooted in the earliest attempts to create artificial intelligence. In the 1960s, for instance, Frank Rosenblatt sought to design a mechanical brain, Perceptron, which he described as "a machine which senses, recognizes, remembers, and responds like the human mind." Minsky and his colleague Seymour Papert achieved fame by criticizing this design – ambitious for its times – as severely limited because it could not solve even simple logical problems. See Marvin Minsky and Seymour Papert, *Perceptrons: An Introduction to Computational*

Geometry (Cambridge, MA: The MIT Press, 1969); and Gary Marcus, "Is 'Deep Learning' a Revolution in Artificial Intelligence?," *The New Yorker* (November 25, 2012).

9. On the distinction between direct and indirect cyberattack effects, see Lucas Kello, "The Meaning of the Cyber Revolution," *International Security*, Vol. 38, No. 2 (Fall 2013), p. 19.

10. See Lucas Kello, "The Virtual Weapon: Dilemmas and Future Scenarios," *Politique étrangère*, Vol. 79, No. 4 (Winter 2014–15), p. 6.

11. See Lawrence Lessig, *Code* (New York: Basic Books, 1999).

12. See Gregory J. Rattray, *Strategic Warfare in Cyberspace* (Cambridge, MA: MIT Press, 2001).

13. See Jack Goldsmith and Tim Wu, *Who Controls the Internet? Illusions of a Borderless World* (New York: Oxford University Press, 2006).

14. See Martin C. Libicki, *Conquest in Cyberspace: National Security and Information Warfare* (New York: Cambridge University Press, 2007); and Martin C. Libicki, *Cyberdeterrence and Cyberwar* (Santa Monica, CA: RAND Corporation, 2009).

15. See Jason Healey, *A Fierce Domain: Conflict in Cyberspace, 1986 to 2012* (Arlington, VA: Cyber Conflict Studies Association, 2012).

16. See Michael N. Schmitt, ed., *Tallinn Manual on the International Law Applicable to Cyber Warfare* (Cambridge: Cambridge University Press, 2013).

17. See Adam Segal, *The Hacked World Order: How Nations Fight, Trade, Maneuver, and Manipulate in the Digital Age* (New York: PublicAffairs, 2015). Other important book-length studies of cyber issues include Chris C. Demchak, *Wars of Disruption and Resilience: Cybered Conflict, Power, and National Security* (Athens, GA: University of Georgia Press, 2011); Derek S. Reveron, ed., *Cyberspace and National Security: Threats, Opportunities, and Power in a Virtual World* (Washington, D.C.: Georgetown University Press, 2012); and Martin C. Libicki, *Crisis and Escalation in Cyberspace* (Santa Monica, CA: RAND Corporation, 2012).

18. See Valeriano and Maness, *Cyber War Versus Cyber Realities*, p. 61.

19. See Joseph S. Nye, *The Future of Power* (New York: PublicAffairs, 2011), Chapter 5; and Nazli Choucri, *Cyber Politics in International Relations* (Cambridge, MA: MIT Press, 2012). Other works focus less on developing theoretical frameworks and more on explaining and predicting empirical trends. See, for instance, Valeriano and Maness, *Cyber War Versus Cyber Realities*.

20. See, for instance, Friedrich Kratochwil, "The Embarrassment of Change: Neo-Realism as the Science of Realpolitik without Politics," *Review of International Studies*, Vol. 19, No. 1 (January 1993), pp. 63–80.

21. A notable work in this regard is P. W. Singer and Allan Friedman, *Cybersecurity and Cyberwar: What Everyone Needs to Know* (Oxford: Oxford University Press, 2014).

22. In this book, the label "international security studies," or plainly security studies, denotes the subfield of the discipline of international relations. Thus the label automatically captures the theories, concepts, concerns, and aims of international relations. Where the arguments of the book relate more generally to the discipline rather than the subfield, the book uses the label "international relations."

23. On the value of single case studies, see Alexander L. George and Andrew Bennett, *Case Studies and Theory Development in the Social Sciences* (Cambridge, MA: MIT Press, 2005), pp. 81–82. See also Chapter 1 of this book.

24. See, for example, *Défense et Sécurité nationale: Le Livre blanc* (Paris: La Documentation française, June 2008); *A Strong Britain in an Age of Uncertainty: The UK National Security Strategy* (London: Cabinet Office, 2010); and James R. Clapper to the U.S. Senate Intelligence Committee (Washington, D.C.: U.S. Government Printing Office, March 12, 2013).

25. See Donna Miles, "Stavridis Spotlights Top National Security Issues," American Force Press Service, U.S. Department of Defense, March 15, 2012. See also comments by Keith B. Alexander to the U.S. Senate Committee on Armed Services (Washington, D.C.: U.S. Government Printing Office, April 15, 2010), p. 219; Joseph S. Nye, Jr.,

"Nuclear Lessons for Cyber Security?" *Strategic Studies Quarterly*, Vol. 5, No. 4 (Winter 2011), pp. 18–38; and Kello, "The Meaning of the Cyber Revolution."

26. See, for instance, Kenneth A. Oye, ed., *Cooperation Under Anarchy* (Princeton, N.J.: Princeton University Press, 1986).

27. Among American officials, the operation was known by the code name "Olympic Games."

1 The Quest for Cyber Theory

1. See Matt Bishop, "What is Computer Security?" *IEEE Security & Privacy* (January/February 2003), p. 67.

2. See below the discussion of the distinction between "cyberspace" and "cyber domain."

3. See Dawn Youngblood, "Interdisciplinary Studies and the Bridging Disciplines: A Matter of Process," *Journal of Research Practice*, Vol. 3, No. 2 (2007), p. 2. On the problems of scientific interdisciplinarity, see David Alvargonzález, "Multidisciplinarity, Interdisciplinarity, Transdisciplinarity, and the Sciences," *International Studies in the Philosophy of Science*, Vol. 25, No. 4 (2011), pp. 387–403.

4. The notion of a "discipline of cybersecurity" has already crept up in some quarters. It appears in the scholarly literature; see, for instance, Dan Shoemaker, Anne Kohnke, and Ken Sigler, *A Guide to the National Initiative for Cybersecurity Education (NICE) Cybersecurity Workforce Framework (2.0)* (London: CRC Press, 2016), pp. xvii, 16, 130. Others use the label to denote a comprehensive field of study within only one discipline, such as computer science; see Daniel P. Shoemaker, "The Colloquium for Information Security Education (CISSE) – The Adventure Continues," *ACM Inroads*, Vol. 5, No. 2 (June 2014), p. 51. Furthermore, some academic degree programs – for example, the University of Oxford's doctoral program in Cyber Security – refer to cybersecurity explicitly, but are in fact properly interdisciplinary in the sense described here because they integrate "a range of academic disciplines." See "CDT Programme," Centre for Doctoral Training in Cyber Security, University of Oxford, https://www.cybersecurity. ox.ac.uk/education/cdt/cdt-programme.

5. See Lucas Kello, "Correspondence: A Cyber Disagreement," *International Security*, Vol. 39, No. 2 (Fall 2014).

6. For a technical definition of information security, see H. S. Vinter and J. H. P. Eloff, "A Taxonomy of Information Security Technologies," *Computers and Security*, Vol. 22, No. 4 (May 2003), p. 299. The nontechnical usage prevails among political scientists and in international policy circles. See, for instance, "Agreement between the Governments of the Member States of the Shanghai Cooperation Organization on Cooperation in the Field of International Information Security," Dushanbe Summit, Dushanbe, Tajikistan, September 11–12, 2014. For a more complete treatment of concepts, see section below, "Conceptual and Technical Rudiments for Cyber Studies."

7. See Alan M. Turing, "On Computable Numbers, with an Application to the *Entscheidungsproblem*," *Proceedings of the London Mathematical Society*, Vol. 2, No. 42 (1937 [delivered to the Society in 1936]), pp. 230–65.

8. Not all mathematical problems can be solved by Turing machines, however. For example, it is impossible to design an algorithm that will always produce a correct Yes or No answer to the Halting Problem, which asks a computer to execute or cease executing an arbitrary program on the basis of a finite input. I am grateful to Dave Aitel for this insight.

9. Kenneth Thompson, "Reflections on Trusting Trust," *Communication of the ACM*, Vol. 27, No. 8 (August 1984), pp. 761–63.

10. See Jack L. Goldsmith, "Against Cyberanarchy," *Chicago Law Review*, Vol. 1199 (Fall 1998); and Vivek Mohan and John Villasenor, "Decrypting the Fifth Amendment: The Limits of Self-Incrimination in the Digital Era," *University of Pennsylvania Journal of Constitutional Law Heightened Scrutiny*, Vol. 15 (October 2012), pp. 11–28.

11. See David S. Wall, *Cybercrime: The Transformation of Crime in the Information Age* (Cambridge: Polity Press, 2007).

12. See Tyler Moore, Richard Clayton, and Ross Anderson, "The Economics of Online Crime," *Journal of Economic Perspectives*, Vol. 23, No. 3 (Summer 2009), pp. 3–20.
13. See Sharon S. Dawes, "The Continuing Challenges of E-Governance," *Public Administration Review*, Vol. 68, No. 1 [Special Issue] (December 2008), pp. 586–602.
14. The number of scholarly publications that focus on international security aspects of the cyber question is small. These works include Ronald J. Deibert, "Black Code: Censorship, Surveillance, and Militarization of Cyberspace," *Millennium*, Vol. 32, No. 2 (December 2003), pp. 501–30; Johan Eriksson and Giampiero Giacomello, "The Information Revolution, Security, and International Relations: The (IR)relevant Theory?" *International Political Science Review*, Vol. 27, No. 3 (July 2006), pp. 221–44; Lene Hansen and Helen Nissenbaum, "Digital Disaster, Cyber Security, and the Copenhagen School," *International Studies Quarterly*, Vol. 53, No. 4 (December 2009), pp. 1,155–75; and Mary M. Manjikian, "From Global Village to Virtual Battlespace: The Colonizing of the Internet and the Extension of Realpolitik," *International Studies Quarterly*, Vol. 54, No. 2 (June 2010), pp. 381–401; Lucas Kello, "The Meaning of the Cyber Revolution: Perils to Theory and Statecraft," *International Security*, Vol. 38, No. 2 (Fall 2013), pp. 7–40; Eric Gartzke, "The Myth of Cyberwar: Bringing War in Cyberspace Back Down to Earth," *International Security*, Vol. 38, No. 2 (Fall 2013), pp. 41–73; and Jon R. Lindsay, "The Impact of China on Cybersecurity: Fiction and Friction," *International Security*, Vol. 39, No. 3 (Winter 2014/15), pp. 7–47. See Introduction, p. 9.
15. See David E. Sanger, *Confront and Conceal: Obama's Secret Wars and Surprising Use of American Power* (New York: Crown, 2012), p. 291.
16. In the official statement, the last point came first. See Ben Gummer, "Government Departments: Cybercrime: Written question – 55021," UK Cabinet Office (December 5, 2016), http://www.parliament.uk/business/publications/written-questions-answers-statements/written-question/Commons/2016-11-28/55021/.
17. One poll in Britain found that three-fourths of firms did not report computer breaches to the police, let alone the public. See Kate Palmer, "Businesses Keep Quiet over Cyber Attacks, as EU Cracks Down on Underreporting," *The Telegraph* (March 3, 2016), http://www.telegraph.co.uk/business/2016/03/02/businesses-keep-quiet-over-cyber-attacks-as-eu-cracks-down-on-un/.
18. Stephen M. Walt, "Is the Cyber Threat Overblown?" *Stephen M. Walt* blog, *Foreign Policy* (March 30, 2010), http://walt.foreignpolicy.com/posts/2010/03/30/is_the_cyber_threat_overblown. Elsewhere, Walt calls for systematic study of the cyber issue by a "panel of experts." See Stephen M. Walt, "What Does Stuxnet Tell Us about the Future of Cyber-Warfare?" *Stephen M. Walt* blog, *Foreign Policy* (October 7, 2010), http://walt.foreignpolicy.com/posts/2010/10/07/what_does_stuxnet_tell_us_about_the_future_of_cyber_warfare.
19. See Thomas G. Mahnken, "Cyber War and Cyber Warfare," in Kristin M. Lord and Travis Sharp, eds., *America's Cyber Future: Security and Prosperity in the Information Age* (Washington, D.C.: Center for a New American Security, 2011); and Thomas Rid, "Cyber War Will Not Take Place," *Journal of Strategic Studies*, Vol. 35, No. 1 (February 2012), pp. 5–32.
20. See Thomas Rid, "Think Again: Cyberwar," *Foreign Policy*, Vol. 192 (March/April 2012), pp. 80–84.
21. Joseph S. Nye, Jr., "Cyber War and Peace," *Project Syndicate* (April 10, 2012).
22. Rid, "Think Again, p. 84. Rid does not explain why sophisticated cyberattack should not therefore concern lesser powers.
23. See Michael Howard, *Clausewitz: A Very Short Introduction* (Oxford: Oxford University Press, 2002), p. 22.
24. Bruce Schneier, "Threat of 'Cyberwar' Has Been Hugely Hyped," *CNN* (July 7, 2010). Similarly, Schneier also warned about the dangerous implications of the "militarization" of cyberspace for the civilian control of the Internet and for the protection of user privacy. See Schneier, "Militarizing Cyberspace Will Do More Harm Than Good," *The Irish Times* (November 29, 2012).

25. See Barry Buzan and Lene Hansen, *The Evolution of International Security Studies* (Cambridge: Cambridge University Press, 2009), p. 12.

26. See Stephen M. Walt, "The Enduring Relevance of the Realist Tradition," in Ira Katznelson and Helen V. Milner, eds., *Political Science: State of the Discipline* (New York: W. W. Norton, 2002), p. 220.

27. See Stanley Hoffmann, *The State of War: Essays on the Theory and Practice of International Politics* (New York: Praeger, 1965), pp. 7–8.

28. The quote appears in Niall Ferguson, *Kissinger, 1923–1968: The Idealist* (London: Penguin, 2015), p. 336 (emphasis mine). It is from a letter by Kissinger to Arthur Schlesinger dated February 16, 1955. Shortly after, Kissinger developed his argument in a book-length study, *Nuclear Weapons and Foreign Policy* (New York: Council on Foreign Relations, 1957).

29. Holsti wrote: "power may be viewed from several aspects: it is a means, it is based on capabilities, it is a relationship, and a process, and it can also be a quantity." Kalevi J. Holsti, "The Concept of Power in the Study of International Relations," *Background*, Vol. 7, No. 4 (February 1964), p. 182.

30. *Nuclear Tipping Point*, documentary film (2010).

31. See, for instance, Friedrich Kratochwil, "The Embarrassment of Change: Neo-Realism as the Science of Realpolitik without Politics," *Review of International Studies*, Vol. 19, No. 1 (January 1993), pp. 63–80.

32. Stephen M. Walt, "The Relationship between Theory and Policy in International Relations," *Annual Review of Political Science*, Vol. 8 (2005), pp. 41–42.

33. For a historical elaboration of the problem of technological revolution and strategic adaptation, see Chapter 3.

34. Joseph S. Nye, Jr., "Nuclear Lessons for Cyber Security?" *Strategic Studies Quarterly*, Vol. 5, No. 4 (Winter 2011), p. 19.

35. For an excellent account of the Stuxnet deliberations, see Sanger, *Confront and Conceal*, Chapter 8.

36. This was "a huge amount of code" compared to other known malware. See Sharon Weinberger, "Is this the Start of Cyberwarfare?" *Nature*, Vol. 474, pp. 142–43.

37. Despite the attack code's sophistication, analysts have found "basic errors" in its design and in the code itself. For example, Tom Parker observed that "the command-and-control mechanism is poorly done and sends its traffic in the clear and the worm ended up propagating on the Internet, which was likely not the intent." Dennis Fisher, "Stuxnet Authors Made Several Basic Errors," *Threatpost* (January 18, 2011), https://threatpost.com/stuxnet-authors-made-several-basic-errors–011811/74856/. See also Nat Lawson, "Stuxnet is Embarrassing, Not Amazing," *rdist* (January 17, 2011), https://rdist.root.org/2011/01/17/stuxnet-is-embarrassing-not-amazing/#comment–6451. Despite these criticisms, computer security specialists broadly regard Stuxnet as a genial weapon.

38. David Newsom, "Foreign Policy and Academia," *Foreign Policy*, Vol. 101 (Winter 1995), p. 66.

39. Although Stuxnet's custodians sought to contain the worm within the Natanz facility, thousands of external machines were infected (more than 40 percent of them outside Iran).

40. An example of such new legislation is the Cyber Security Information Sharing Act (CISA) that was signed into law in December 2015.

41. James Blitz, "UK Becomes First State to Admit to Offensive Cyber Attack Capability," *Financial Times* (September 29, 2013).

42. Mark Pomerlau, "Carter Looking to Drop 'Cyber Bombs' on ISIS," *Defence Systems* (February 29, 2016).

43. See, for instance, Louis Klarevas, "Political Realism: A Culprit for the 9/11 Attacks," *Harvard International Review*, Vol. 26, No. 3 (Fall 2004), pp. 18–21.

44. Valeriano and Maness, *Cyber War versus Cyber Realities*. Similarly, the authors state: "Evidence and facts are needed in order to counter hype and bluster" about the cyber threat (p. 209).

45. Sam Jones, "Ministry of Defence Fends Off 'Thousands' of Daily Cyber Attacks," *The Financial Times* (June 25, 2015), http://www.ft.com/intl/cms/s/0/2f6de47e–1a9a–11e5–8201-cbdb03d71480.html.

46. Shaun Walker, "Kremlin Pours Cold Water on MI5 Chief's Claims of Russian Threat," *The Guardian* (November 1, 2016).

47. See Michael S. Schmidt, "New Interest in Hacking as Threat to Security," *The New York Times* (March 13, 2012).

48. See Jack Kim, "North Korea Mounts Long-Running Hack of South Korea Computers, Says Seoul," *Reuters* (June 13, 2016), http://www.reuters.com/article/us-northkorea-southkorea-cyber-idUSKCN0YZ0BE.

49. See "Military Investigators Raid Cyber Command in Hacking Probe," *Yonhap News Agency* (December 13, 2016), http://english.yonhapnews.co.kr/northkorea/2016/12/13/0401000000AEN20161213006500315.html.

50. François Clemenceau and Antoine Malo, "Le Drian sur le cyberespionnage: La France n'est pas à l'abri, il ne faut pas être naïf," *Le Journal du Dimanche* (January 7, 2017), http://www.lejdd.fr/International/Le-Drian-sur-le-cyberespionnage-La-France-n-est-pas-a-l-abri-il-ne-faut-pas-etre-naif-837985#xtor=CS1–4.

51. See Amy Chozick, "Hillary Clinton Blames F.B.I. Director for Election Losses," *The New York Times* (November 12, 2016); and Jason Blakely, "Is Political Science this Year's Election Casualty?" *The Atlantic* (November 14, 2016).

52. The journal *International Security*, published by MIT Press, features primarily works of international relations.

53. The quote is by the journalist Peter Passell. Joseph B. Treaster, "Herman Kahn Dies; Futurist and Thinker on Nuclear Strategy," *The New York Times* (July 8, 1983).

54. The comment is by political scientist Roman Kolkowicz. Michael Intriligator, Roman Kolkowicz, and Andrzej Korbonski, "Bernard Brodie, Political Science: Los Angeles," *Calisphere*, University of California (September 1979).

55. PhD in International Relations, University of Chicago.

56. Masters in Mathematical Logic, Columbia University. Some observers regard mathematics as a natural science; indeed, many university departments group it with physics, chemistry, biology, etc. But the "Queen of the Sciences," as German thinker Carl Friedrich Gauss called mathematics, is also the basis for much non-scientific inquiry – ranging from logic to aesthetics. At any rate, it is certainly not an engineering or technical science.

57. AB and PhD in Government, Harvard University.

58. AB and PhD in Government, Harvard University.

59. BA in Economics, University of California, Berkeley; PhD in Economics, Harvard University.

60. This trend is reflected in the overtly technical tone of important works of military tactics, such as Martin C. Libicki, *Conquest in Cyberspace: National Security and Information Warfare* (New York: Cambridge University Press, 2007).

61. The proposed framework draws from, but also adapts, concepts introduced in William A. Owens, Kenneth W. Dam, and Herbert S. Lin, eds., *Technology, Policy, Law, and Ethics Regarding U.S. Acquisition and Use of Cyberattack Capabilities* (Washington, D.C.: National Academies Press, 2009).

62. See Richard A. Clarke and Robert K. Knake, *Cyber War: The Next Threat to National Security and What to Do About It* (New York: HarperCollins, 2010), p. 69. For an instructive, more technical review of some of these concepts, see Matthew Monte, *Network Attacks and Exploitation: A Framework* (Indianapolis, IN: John Wiley and Sons, 2015).

63. See German Federal Ministry of the Interior, *Cyber Security Strategy for Germany* (Berlin: German Federal Ministry of the Interior, February 2011), p. 14.

64. See Andrew Greenberg, "Hacker Lexicon: What is the Dark Web?," *Wired* (November 19, 2014). The Dark Web is also not to be confused with the Deep Web, of which it is a small part and which denotes the vast swathes of the Internet that search engines such

as Google do not index. See "Going Dark: The Internet Behind the Internet," *NPR* (May 25, 2014).

65. See, for instance, Jon R. Lindsay and Lucas Kello, "Correspondence: A Cyber Disagreement," *International Security*, Vol. 39, No. 2 (Fall 2014), p. 187.

66. Some working concepts omit social agents. See, for example, Nazli Choucri and David Clark, "Cyberspace and International Relations: Towards an Integrated System," paper presented at the Massachusetts Institute of Technology, Cambridge, Massachusetts, August 2011, p. 8.

67. See Lindsay and Kello, "Correspondence: A Cyber Disagreement," pp. 188–92.

68. The logical layer comprises the service platforms on which computer systems and networks function (e.g. software applications). The information layer includes the data that flow between interconnected nodes. The physical layer comprises physical machines. On the "layers" model, see Choucri and Clark, "Cyberspace and International Relations."

69. An information security operation of this kind occurred in November 2015 in the aftermath of the Paris massacre perpetrated by Islamic State operatives. See Paul Mozur, "China Cuts Mobile Service of Xinjiang Residents Evading Internet Filters," *The New York Times* (November 23, 2015).

70. Gary King, Jennifer Pan, and Margaret E. Roberts, "How Censorship in China Allows Government Criticism but Silences Collective Expression," *American Political Science Review*, Vol. 2 (May 2013), pp. 1–18.

71. For a gripping account of Russian Internet censorship generally and of this case particularly, see Andrei Soldatov and Irina Borogan, *The Red Web: The Struggle between Russia's Digital Dictators and the New Online Revolutionaries* (New York: PublicAffairs, 2015). See also Hal Roberts and Bruce Etling, "Coordinated DDoS Attack during Russian Duma Elections," *Internet and Democracy Blog*, Berkman Center for Internet and Society, Harvard University (December 8, 2011).

72. For an excellent discussion of freedom of speech over the Internet, see Timothy Garton Ash, *Free Speech: Ten Principles for a Connected World* (New Haven, CT: Yale University Press, 2016).

73. See Steven M. Bellovin, Susan Landau, and Herbert S. Lin, "Limiting the Undesired Impact of Cyber Weapons: Technical Requirements and Policy Implications," unpublished paper, p. 3.

74. See Luke Harding, "Top Democrat's Emails Hacked by Russia after Aide Made Typo, Investigation Finds," *The Guardian* (December 14, 2016).

75. See Mohammad Tehranipoor and Farinaz Koushanfar, "A Survey of Hardware Trojan Taxonomy and Detection," *IEEE Design and Test of Computers*, Vol. 27, No. 1 (2010), pp. 10–25; and Masoud Roustami, Farinaz Koushanfar, Jeyavijayan Rajendran, and Ramesh Karri, "Hardware Security: Threat Models and Metrics," *ICCAD '13 Proceedings of the International Conference on Computer-Aided Design, IEEE* (November 18–21, 2013), pp. 819–23.

76. Therefore, in instances where the sole medium of entry to a target is the Internet or some physical device, the weapon lacks a penetration element all its own.

77. See Cecilia Kang, "A Tweet to Kurt Eichenwald, a Strobe and a Seizure. Now, an Arrest," *The New York Times* (March 17, 2017).

78. On problems of global governance in the cyber domain, see, for example, Laura DeNardis, *Protocol Politics: The Globalization of Internet Governance* (Cambridge, MA: MIT Press, 2009); Joseph S. Nye, Jr., "The Regime Complex for Managing Global Cyber Activities," *Global Commission on Internet Governance*, Issue Paper Series, No. 1 (May 2014); and Lucas Kello, "Cyber Security: Gridlock and Innovation," *Beyond Gridlock* (Cambridge: Polity, 2017). Cyber governance, which deals with the management of cybersecurity issues, especially cyberattacks and cyber espionage, should not be confused with Internet governance, an older field that involves the management of the globe's computer network infrastructure.

79. See Thomas C. Reed, *At the Abyss: An Insider's History of the Cold War* (New York: Random House, 2005), Chapter 17.

80. The term "industrial controller" signifies computer systems that govern processes of industrial production. It includes supervisory control and data acquisition (SCADA) systems and programmable logic controllers (PLCs).
81. See Owens, Dam, and Lin, *Technology, Policy, Law, and Ethics*, pp. 1–2.
82. For technical details on Stuxnet's destructive procedure, see Nicholas Falliere, Liam O. Murchu, and Eric Chien, "W32.Stuxnet Dossier," ver. 1.4 (Cupertino, CA: Symantec, February 2011).
83. The standard usage can be relabeled as follows: "first-order" direct effects exerted on an industrial controller; and "second-order" direct effects influencing machine parts governed by it.
84. For a similar definition, see Nye, "Nuclear Lessons for Cyber Security?" p. 21.
85. On hacktivism as a modern form of political activism, see François Paget, *Cybercrime and Hacktivism* (Santa Clara, CA: McAfee, 2010), pp. 10–12.
86. Bellovin, Landau, and Lin, "Limiting the Undesired Impact of Cyber Weapons," pp. 4–5.
87. See David D. Clark and Susan Landau, "Untangling Attribution," in *Proceedings of a Workshop on Deterring Cyberattacks: Informing Strategies and Developing Options for U.S. Policy* (Washington, D.C.: National Academies Press, 2010), pp. 25–40.
88. See, for example, Alexander Klimburg and Heli Tirmaa-Klaar, *Cybersecurity and Cyberpower: Concepts, Conditions, and Capabilities for Cooperation for Action within the EU* (Brussels: European Parliament Directorate General for External Policies of the Union, Policy Department, April 2011), p. 5.
89. Bruce Schneier, "When Does Cyber Spying Become a Cyber Attack," *Defense One* (March 10, 2014), http://www.defenseone.com/technology/2014/03/when-does-cyber-spying-become-cyber-attack/80206/.
90. The common term is "advanced persistent threat," or APT, which refers to an actor (such as a large state) able to penetrate an adversary's computer systems persistently and successfully. I prefer the term advanced persistent *adversary* because the meaning of APT focuses on the *threat* posed by the agent, rather than the more important *agent* posing the threat.
91. Stephen M. Walt, "The Renaissance of Security Studies," *International Studies Quarterly*, Vol. 35, No. 2 (1991), p. 212.
92. See Adam P. Liff, "Cyberwar: A New 'Absolute Weapon'? The Proliferation of Cyberwarfare Capabilities and Interstate War," *Journal of Strategic Studies*, Vol. 35, No. 3 (June 2012), pp. 401–28; Thomas Rid, *Cyber War Will Not Take Place* (London: Hurst, 2013); and Erik Gartzke, "The Myth of Cyberwar: Bringing War in Cyberspace Back Down to Earth," *International Security*, Vol. 38, No. 2 (Fall 2013), pp. 41–73.
93. For a discussion of the shape of the cyber danger, see Chapter 2.
94. Brandon Valeriano and Ryan C. Maness, "The Dynamics of Cyber Conflict between Rival Antagonists, 2001–11," *Journal of Peace Research*, Vol. 51, No. 3 (2014), p. 355. This analysis ignores nonstate actors unless "they are considered part of a state's national security apparatus, or if the initiators are clearly acting on behalf of their home government" (p. 355). Thus it excludes a vast number of unaffiliated or subversive players. The authors' book-length study repeats this omission. See Valeriano and Maness, *Cyber War Versus Cyber Realities*.

2 The Cyber Curse: Complications of Defense

1. As one academic study concluded, "[C]yber disputes are rare. When they do happen, the impact tends to be minimal." Brandon Valeriano and Ryan C. Maness, "The Dynamics of Cyber Conflict between Rival Antagonists, 2001–11," *Journal of Peace Research*, Vol. 51, No. 3 (2014), p. 359. See also the comments by Bruce Schneier in "Threat of 'Cyberwar' Has Been Hugely Hyped," CNN (July 7, 2010).
2. Barack H. Obama, "Remarks by the President on Securing Our Nation's Cyber Infrastructure," White House Press Office (May 29, 2009).

3. "War in the Fifth Domain," *The Economist* (July 1, 2010).
4. See "James R. Clapper to the U.S. Senate Intelligence Committee" (Washington, D.C.: U.S. Government Printing Office, March 12, 2013). This was only the second time after the September 11, 2001 terrorist attacks in New York and Washington, D.C., that terrorism does not top the list of U.S. security concerns. See also Aaron Boyd, "DNI Clapper: Cyber Bigger than Terrorism," *Federal Times* (February 4, 2016). By contrast, in 2007, when the DNI published the first threat ranking, the cyber threat did not even figure among the top ten.
5. See *Le Livre blanc: Défense et sécurité nationale* (Paris: La Documentation française, June 2013).
6. See *Public Uncertain, Divided over America's Place in the World* (Washington, D.C.: Pew Research Center, April, 2016), p. 23.
7. Government officials and media representatives have varyingly used these terms. See, for example, Republican National Committee, *Republican Platform 2016* (July 2016), p. 53; and Joseph Marks, "Officials Worry about 'cyber Fort Hood'," *Politico* (September 9, 2014). "Fort Hood" refers to the shooting, in 2009, by U.S. Army Major Nidal Hassan, a radicalized Muslim who killed thirteen people and injured another thirty. Not all media outlets, of course, exhibit this inflammatory rhetorical tendency; some in fact resist it. See, for example, Henry Farrell, "Cyber-Pearl Harbor Is a Myth," The Monkey Cage (blog), *Washington Post* (November 11, 2011).
8. See *A Strong Britain in an Age of Uncertainty: The UK National Security Strategy* (London: Cabinet Office, 2010).
9. See William J. Lynn, III, "Defending a New Domain," *Foreign Affairs*, Vol. 89, No. 5 (September/October 2009), pp. 97–108.
10. This view sometimes leads to cynical interpretations of threat inflation: for example, the view that governments hype the threat in order to raise public awareness about the reality of the danger; or that they exaggerate the threat scale to seize institutional advantages in a "power struggle" among the public and private sectors about the legitimacy of the government's control of private networks – and by sounding the alarm of war, the government wins the power struggle. (Schneier, "Threat of 'Cyberwar' Has Been Hugely Hyped.")
11. Innumerable because the victims of attack often withhold knowledge of it to avoid reputational and other harm and because even within the observable universe, the number of incidents and the diversity of targets are enormous. Possibly, a fatal cyberattack has occurred that officials have been able to conceal from the public. But the number of such incidents is likely to be low – low enough, at least, that they meet under the criterion of homicide, not acts of war.
12. Perhaps no other hypothesis – indeed prediction – in the study of international relations has proven so resistant to empirical falsification as this one. See, for example, Bruce Russett, *Grasping the Democratic Peace: Principles for a Post-Cold War World* (Princeton, N.J.: Princeton University Press, 1993); and Michael E. Brown, Sean M. Lynn-Jones, and Steven E. Miller, *Debating the Democratic Peace* (Cambridge, MA: MIT Press, 1996).
13. For instance, some thinkers set the minimum number of deaths at 200, others at 1,000. See Spencer R. Weart, *Never at War: Why Democracies Will Not Fight Each Other* (New Haven, CT: Yale University Press, 1998); and the *Correlates of War Project*, "Data Sets," http://www.correlatesofwar.org/data-sets/COW-war.
14. TCP/IP signifies the suite of communications protocols that governs data transmission via the Internet.
15. "Has the Cyberwar Threat Been Exaggerated?," Intelligence Squared U.S., Washington, D.C. (June 16, 2010), http://intelligencesquaredus.org/debates/past-debates/item/576-the-cyberwar-threat-has-been-grossly-exaggerated.
16. Letter from General Martin E. Dempsey to John D. Rockefeller IV, chairman, U.S. Senate Committee on Commerce, Science, and Transportation (August 1, 2012) (Washington, D.C.: U.S. Government Printing Office).
17. Donna Miles, "U.S. European Command, NATO Boost Cyber Defenses," American

Force Press Service, U.S. Department of Defense (May 18, 2012), http://www.defense.gov/news/newsarticle.aspx?id_116394.

18. See President of Estonia Toomas H. Ilves, address given at the European Union Ministerial Conference on Critical Infrastructure Protection, Tallinn, Estonia (April 27, 2009).

19. Thomas Rid, "Cyber War Will Not Take Place," *Journal of Strategic Studies*, Vol. 35, No. 1 (February 2012), p. 12.

20. See U.S. Cyber Consequences Unit (US-CCU), *Overview by the US-CCU of the Cyber Campaign against Georgia in August 2008*, Special Report, US-CCU (August 2009), http://www.registan.net/wp-content/uploads/2009/08/US-CCU-Georgia-Cyber-Campaign-Overview.pdf.

21. See "The Shamoon Attacks," Symantic Official Blog (August 16, 2012); and Christopher Bronk and Eneken Tikk-Ringas, "The Cyber Attack on Saudi Aramco," *Survival: Global Politics and Strategy*, Vol. 55, No. 2 (2013), pp. 81–96.

22. See David E. Sanger, "Obama Order Sped Up Wave of Cyberattacks against Iran," *The New York Times* (June 1, 2012).

23. See Gabi Siboni and Zvi Magen, "The Cyber Attack on the Ukrainian Electrical Infrastructure: Another Warning," *INSS Insights*, No. 798 (February 17, 2016).

24. See Eneken Tikk-Ringas quoted in "Could Cyber Skirmish Lead to War?," NBC News (June 11, 2010), http://www.nbcnews.com/technology/could-cyber-skirmish-lead-u-s-war–6C10406234.

25. Kim Chipman, "Cruz Says Russia, China Have Committed Acts of 'Cyber War,'" *Bloomberg* (August 7, 2015).

26. Oliver Laughland and Dominic Rushe, "Sony Pulling the Interview Was 'a Mistake' Says Obama," *The Guardian* (December 20, 2014).

27. Richard Waters, "US Struggles to Find Response to Hack Attack on Sony," *The Financial Times* (December 21, 2014).

28. See Rid, "Cyber War Will Not Take Place."

29. On calculated ambiguity in other domains of conflict, see Scott D. Sagan, "The Commitment Trap: Why the United States Should Not Use Nuclear Weapons to Deter Biological and Chemical Weapons Attacks," *International Security*, Vol. 24, No. 4 (Spring 2000), pp. 85–115.

30. Siobhan Gorman and Julian E. Barnes, "Cyber Combat: Act of War," *Wall Street Journal* (May 30, 2011).

31. See Chapter 7.

32. See *Congressional Record, U.S. Senate, Proceedings and Debates of the 114th Congress, First Session*, Vol. 161, No. 126 (August 5, 2015), p. S6338.

33. Aaron Boyd, "SecDef Nominee: Cyber Threats Require Holistic Defense Strategy," *Federal Times* (February 4, 2015).

34. National Research Council of the National Academies, *Terrorism and the Electric Power Delivery System* (Washington, D.C.: National Academies Press, 2012), p. 16.

35. See Barack H. Obama, "Taking the Cyberattack Threat Seriously," op-ed, *Wall Street Journal* (July 19, 2012).

36. Some officials speculate that Iran retaliated for Stuxnet with DDoS attacks against U.S. financial institutions. See Senator Joseph Lieberman, interview on *Newsmakers*, C-SPAN (September 23, 2012).

37. See Adam P. Liff, "Cyberwar: A New 'Absolute Weapon?' The Proliferation of Cyberwarfare Capabilities and Interstate War," *Journal of Strategic Studies*, Vol. 35, No. 3 (June 2012), p. 401.

38. See William J. Lynn III, "Defending a New Domain," *Foreign Affairs*, Vol. 89, No. 5 (September 2010), pp. 97–108.

39. The term "PLC environment" denotes the PLC computers and the engineering stations used to program them.

40. For a discussion of potential reproduction, in whole or in part, of the Stuxnet worm, see Chapter 6.

41. See Thomas Rid, "Think Again: Cyberwar," *Foreign Policy*, Vol. 192 (March/April 2012). A more nuanced argument about offense superiority in limited scenarios involving specific organizational abilities and technologies appears in Rebecca Slayton, "What Is the Cyber Offense-Defense Balance? Conceptions, Causes, and Assessment," *International Security*, Vol. 41, No. 3 (Winter 2016–17), pp. 72–109.

42. On the difficulties of cyber defense, see Stewart Baker, Natalia Filipiak, and Katrina Timlin, *In the Dark: Crucial Industries Confront Cyberattacks* (Santa Clara, CA: Center for International and Strategic Studies and McAfee, 2011); and John Arquilla, "Cyberwar Is Already Upon Us," *Foreign Policy* (February 27, 2012), www.foreignpolicy. com/articles/2012/02/27/cyberwar_is_already_upon_us.

43. Paul Roberts, "Update – Stuxnet Expert: Analysis Shows Design Flaw, Not Vulnerability Sunk Siemens," *Threatpost* (January 19, 2012).

44. According to one report, the average detection time of zero-day attacks is approximately ten months. The median is eight months. See Leyla Bilge and Tudor Dumitras, "Before We Knew It: An Empirical Study of Zero-Day Attacks in the Real World," *Proceedings of the 2012 ACM Conference on Computer and Communications Security, October 16–18, 2012*, p. 834.

45. The problem of undetectable malware is reflected in the technical community's common fixation with the search for viable means of identifying APTs.

46. This figure is a simplification. The lag time between compromise and detection depends on the class and effects of the hostile action. A higher figure applies to cyber exploitation rather than cyberattacks. Indeed, some attacks – such as ransomware, which incapacitates the target machine – may be discovered immediately. See *2016 Data Breach Investigations Report*, Verizon (April 24, 2016), pp. 10–11. The policy process from the time that investigators identified North Korea as the culprit to publicly outing it took longer than the time between when investigators first learned of the breach and when they identified North Korea.

47. *Edward W. Krippendorf vs. United States of America, Office of Personnel Management; and Keypoint Government Solutions*, Case 1:15 cv 01321 (August 14, 2015), p. 25.

48. See Jessica Silver-Greenberg, Matthew Goldstein, and Nicole Perlroth, "Hackers' Attack on JPMorgan Chase Affects Millions," *The New York Times* (October 2, 2014).

49. See Danny Yardon, "Three Months Later, State Department Hasn't Rooted Out Hackers," *Wall Street Journal* (February 19, 2015).

50. Andrea Shalal, "Nearly Every U.S. Arms Program Found Vulnerable to Cyber Attacks," *Reuters* (January 21, 2015).

51. Lorenzo Franceschi-Bicchierai, "FBI Says a Mysterious Hacking Group Has Had Access to US Government Files for Years," *Motherboard* (April 4, 2016).

52. In one case, the detection lag may have been about one year. See Kim Zetter, "Kaspersky Finds New Nation-State Attack – In its Own Network," *Wired* (October 6, 2015).

53. Franceschi-Bicchierai, "FBI Says a Mysterious Hacking Group Has Had Access to US Government Files for Years."

54. See Luke Harding, "Top Democrat's Emails Hacked by Russia after Aide Made Typo, Investigation Finds," *The Guardian* (December 14, 2016).

55. See Sam Thielman, "Yahoo Hack: 1bn Accounts Compromised by Biggest Data Breach in History," *The Guardian* (December 15, 2016).

56. Robert S. Mueller, III, "Remarks at RSA Cyber Security Conference, San Francisco, CA" (March 21, 2012), https://archives.fbi.gov/archives/news/speeches/combating-threats-in-the-cyber-world-outsmarting-terrorists-hackers-and-spies.

57. Baldwin's original dictum was: "The bomber will always get through." Yet the inventive acuity of British scientists proved his dire prediction wrong, as the Royal Air Force's victory against the Luftwaffe during the Battle of Britain in 1940 showed. See Chapter 3 in this volume.

58. See Matthew Monte, *Network Attacks and Exploitation* (Indianapolis, IN: Wiley, 2015), p. 150.

59. See Thomas C. Schelling, *Arms and Influence* (New Haven, CT: Yale University Press, 1966).

60. According to sources, the data breach, which involved the exfiltration of several terabytes of information, occurred in 2007 and 2008. See Daniel Nasaw, "Hackers Breach Defences of Joint Strike Fighter Jet Programme," *The Guardian*, April 21, 2009.

61. The diplomatic dispute over the control of the Spratly and Paracel Islands and other island archipelagos in the South China Sea has a long and complex history. The islands underwent military occupations by various powers, the most recent of which was China's stationing of an advanced surface-to-air missile system (HQ–9) on Woody Island in February 2016 – a move that the United States and regional countries have denounced. The Philippines government has taken its dispute with China over the Spratlys to the Permanent Court of Arbitration in The Hague, which in July 2016 ruled against China's historic claims to the islands' resources.

62. John J. Mearsheimer, *Conventional Deterrence* (Ithaca, N.Y.: Cornell University Press, 1983), p. 26.

63. See Amir Efrati and Steve Nellis, "Inside Apple's Cloud Infrastructure Troubles," *Business Insider* (March 23, 2016).

64. See "Chinese Government Bans Windows 8 from its Computers," *The Guardian* (May 20, 2014).

65. An example of this effort is the proposal for a new legislative bill (H.R.5793 – Cyber Supply Chain Management and Transparency Act of 2014 113th Congress, 2013–14) requiring all private contractors that supply software or hardware to the U.S. government to provide "a bill of materials of all third party and open source components used," demonstrate that those component do not have known vulnerabilities, provide "secure update mechanisms" when a new vulnerability is detected, and supply remediation "within a reasonable specified time."

66. In 2010, Google announced that sophisticated Chinese agents had breached its systems, and in 2011, unknown parties compromised RSA's authentication products. This was followed by attempts to penetrate computers at Lockheed Martin, an RSA client.

67. See Sean M. Lynn-Jones, "Offense-Defense Theory and its Critics," *Security Studies*, Vol. 4, No. 4 (Summer 1995), p. 665.

68. Brian Groom, "Ministers Warn on Threat from Cyber Attacks," *The Financial Times* (September 4, 2012).

69. Robert O'Harrow, Jr., "Understanding Cyberspace Is Key to Defending against Digital Attacks," *Washington Post* (June 2, 2012).

70. See Lucas Kello, "The Meaning of the Cyber Revolution: Perils to Theory and Statecraft," *International Security*, Vol. 38, No. 2 (Fall 2013), p. 22.

71. Brandon Valeriano and Ryan C. Maness, "The Coming Cyberpeace: The Normative Argument against Cyberwarfare," *Foreign Affairs* (May 13, 2015).

72. See Michael Riley, "How Russian Hackers Stole the Nasdaq," *Bloomberg* (July 17, 2014).

73. See Dave Majumdar, "America's F–35 Stealth Fighter vs. China's New J–31: Who Wins?" *National Interest* (September 25, 2015).

74. Josh Rogin, "NSA Chief: Cybercrime Constitutes the 'Greatest Transfer of Wealth in History'," *Foreign Policy* (July 9, 2012).

75. James Lewis, "Significant Cyber Incidents Since 2006," Center for Strategic and International Studies (August 2016), file:///C:/Users/LK/Downloads/160824_Significant_Cyber_Events_List.pdf.

76 John Barrasso (chairman), Mary Fallin, and Virginia Foxx, *Republican Platform 2016* (Cleveland, OH: Consolidated Solutions, 2016), p. 53.

77. James R. Van de Velde, "War in Peace," *American Interest* (September 6, 2016).

78. Fergus Hanson, "Waging War in Peacetime: Cyber Attacks and International Norms," *The Interpreter* (October 20, 2015).

3 Technological Revolution and International Order

1. Exceptions to this trend include William Ogburn, ed., *Technology and International Relations* (Chicago, IL: Chicago University Press, 1949); Eugene B. Skolnikoff, *The*

Elusive Transformation: Science, Technology, and the Evolution of Technological Politics (Princeton, N.J.: Princeton University Press, 1993); Geoffrey L. Herrera, *Technology and International Transformation: The Railroad, the Atom Bomb, and the Politics of International Change* (New York: State University of New York Press, 2006); Stefan Fritsch, "Technology and Global Affairs," *International Studies Perspectives*, Vol. 12, No. 1 (2011), pp. 27–45; and Fritsch, "Conceptualizing the Ambivalent Role of Technology in International Relations: Between Systemic Change and Continuity," in Maximilian Mayer, Mariana Carpes, and Ruth Knoblich, eds., *The Global Politics of Science and Technology. Vol. 1: Concepts from International Relations and Other Disciplines* (Berlin, Heidelberg: Springer, 2014).

2. Two classic studies are John H. Herz, *International Politics in the Atomic Age* (New York: Columbia University Press, 1959); and Robert Jervis, *The Meaning of the Nuclear Revolution: Statecraft and the Prospect of Armageddon* (Ithaca, N.Y.: Cornell University Press, 1989).

3. See Francis Hoeber, *Slow to Take Offense: Bombers, Cruise Missiles and Prudent Deterrence* (Washington, D.C.: Georgetown University Center for Strategic and International Studies, 1977); and Elmo R. Zumwalt, "Correspondence: An Assessment of the Bomber-Cruise Missile Controversy," *International Security*, Vol. 2, No. 1 (Summer 1977), pp. 47–58.

4. See, for example, Peter W. Singer, *Wired for War: The Robotics Revolution and Conflict in the 21st Century* (New York: Penguin, 2009).

5. By "modern" history I mean international relations since the consecration of the nation state as the dominant political unit in the system beginning in the mid-seventeenth century.

6. See, for example, Robert Gilpin, *War and Change in World Politics* (Cambridge: Cambridge University Press, 1989).

7. Rational-choice theorists hold that the evolution of international affairs occurs only at the level of material facts. A state that pursues alternate ends, such as moral purposes not linked to the achievement of objective ends, does so at peril of its own survival. See Kenneth N. Waltz, *Theory of International Politics* (New York: McGraw-Hill, 1979). On the problem of change in international relations, see for instance Friedrich Kratochwil, "The Embarrassment of Change: Neo-Realism as the Science of Realpolitik without Politics," *Review of International Studies*, Vol. 19, No. 1 (January 1993), pp. 63–80.

8. See Waltz, *Theory of International Politics*. For Waltz, the ordering principle of international politics is anarchy, or the absence of centralized government, which denotes the same condition suggested here: i.e. sovereign states are the supreme units.

9. See Hedley Bull, *The Anarchical Society: A Study of Order in World Politics*, second edition (London: Macmillan, 1995), pp. 67–68.

10. For a discussion of non-traditional international systems, see ibid., Chapter 10.

11. Structure is not, however, the mere agglomeration of unit-level attributes. The features of structure are also attributes of units: navies, capital reserves, commercial goods, norms, and political purposes are all commanded, owned, manufactured, or held by states. But it is the essence of systemic theory that unit-specific factors are *relational*: they matter most in terms of whether and how other units possess them. It is this quality that provides for the notion of structure.

12. Mill expounds his image of "economic man" in the treatise "On the Definition of Political Economy; and on the Method of Investigation Proper to It," *Essays on Some Unsettled Questions of Political Economy* (London: Longmans, Green, Reader, and Dyer, 1874).

13. Edward H. Carr, *The Twenty Years' Crisis, 1919–1939: An Introduction to the Study of International Relations* (New York: Harper and Row, 1964), p. 41. On the affinity of Carr's work and English School thinking, see Timothy Dunne, "The Social Construction of International Society," *European Journal of International Relations*, Vol. 1, No. 3 (September 1995), pp. 367–89.

14. In the context of debates about European integration, for instance, the school of "geopolitical intergovernmentalism" represents the former view, "liberal intergovernmentalism" the latter. See Inis L. Claude, Jr., *Swords into Ploughshares: The Problems and*

Progress of International Organization, fourth edition (London: Random House, 1988); and Andrew Moravcsik, *The Choice for Europe: Social Purpose and State Power from Messina to Maastricht* (Ithaca, NY: Cornell University Press, 1998).

15. For a discussion of the self-reliant pursuit of autonomy in international relations, see Richard J. Harknett and Hasan B. Yalcin, "The Struggle for Autonomy: A Realist Structural Theory of International Relations," *International Studies Review,* Vol. 14 (2012), pp. 499–521.

16. This treatment of power transition as a revolution is consistent with Stanley Hoffmann's discussion of "revolutionary systems." See Stanley Hoffmann, *Gulliver's Travels, Or the Setting of American Foreign Policy* (New York: McGraw-Hill, 1968), p. 14.

17. See Moravcsik, *The Choice for Europe.*

18. Stephen Krasner, "Globalization and Sovereignty," in David A. Smith, Dorothy J. Solinger, and Steven C. Topik, eds., *States and Sovereignty in the Global Economy* (London: Routledge, 1999).

19. Gilpin, *War and Change in World Politics,* p. 50.

20. Ibid., p. 52.

21. Ibid., p. 52.

22. Ibid., p. 9.

23. For John Ruggie the sources of ontological objectivism lie in methodology – i.e. in what this book calls scientism, or the fixation in some quarters of political science with explanatory and especially quantitative analysis. See John G. Ruggie, "Continuity and Transformation in the World Polity: Toward a Neorealist Synthesis," *World Politics,* Vol. 35, No. 2 (January 1983), p. 285; and Chapter 1 of this work.

24. This is not to mean, however, that state preferences are symmetrical – only that under-lying conceptions of interests (such as territorial security or welfare gains), which underpin specific preferences, are uniform. Indeed, rationalist theories of preference formation abound.

25. Arnold Wolfers, *Discord and Collaboration* (Baltimore, MD: Johns Hopkins Press, 1962).

26. Mainstream constructivist theorists do not challenge the assumption of actor rationality; rather, they claim that self-interested behavior is influenced by identities and normative understandings – thus some thinkers refer to the complementarity of rationalist and constructivist scholarship. On constructivism, see for instance Alexander Wendt, *Social Theory of International Politics* (Cambridge: Cambridge University Press, 1999); and Audie Klotz and Cecelia M. Lynch, *Strategies for Research in Constructivist International Relations* (London: M. E. Sharpe, 2007). On the complementarity between rationalism and constructivism, see for example Joseph Jupille, James A. Caporaso, and Jeffrey T. Checkel, "Integrating Institutions: Rationalism, Constructivism, and the Study of the European Union," *Comparative Political Studies,* Vol. 36, No. 7 (February–March 2003), pp. 7–40; and James Fearon and Alexander Wendt, "Rationalism versus Constructivism: A Skeptical View," in Walter Carlsnaes, Thomas Risse, and Beth A. Simmons, *Handbook of International Relations* (London: Sage, 2002). Some liberal thinkers, such as Democratic Peace theorists, also ascribe an important role to ideas. See Ido Oren, "The Subjectivity of the 'Democratic' Peace: Changing U.S. Perceptions of Imperial Germany," in Michael E. Brown, Sean M. Lynn-Jones, and Steven E. Miller, *Debating the Democratic Peace: An International Security Reader* (Cambridge, MA: The MIT Press, 1996), pp. 263–300.

27. On the limits of humanitarian intervention, a classical account is Stanley Hoffmann, *Duties Beyond Borders: On the Limits and Possibilities of Ethical International Politics* (Syracuse, N.Y.: Syracuse University Press, 1981).

28. On the development of the responsibility to protect, see Jennifer M. Welsh, "Implementing the 'Responsibility to Protect': Where Expectations Meet Reality," *Ethics and International Affairs,* Vol. 24, No. 4 (Winter 2010), pp. 415–30; and Alex J. Bellamy, *Global Politics and the Responsibility to Protect: From Words to Deeds* (London: Routledge, 2011).

29. See Thomas Berger, "Changing Norms of Defense and Security in Japan and Germany," in Peter J. Katzenstein, ed., *The Culture of National Security: Norms and Identity in World Politics* (New York: Columbia University Press, 1996), pp. 317–56.

30. See Stephen M. Walt, *Revolution and War* (Ithaca, N.Y.: Cornell University Press, 1996). Nevertheless, advances in communications technology – not least the Internet and social media – may create conditions in which political winds of domestic revolution blow rapidly and unexpectedly across national borders. For a discussion of this phenomenon in the context of the Arab Spring, see Philip N. Howard, Aiden Duffy, Deen Freelon, Muzammil M. Hussain, Will Mari, and Marwa Maziad. "Opening Closed Regimes: What Was the Role of Social Media during the Arab Spring?" (2011), available at SSRN: https://ssrn.com/abstract=2595096 or http://dx.doi.org/10.2139/ssrn.2595096.

31. See Walt, *Revolution and War*.

32. Bull, *The Anarchical Society*, p. 25.

33. For an elaboration of this point, see John Vincent, *Human Rights and International Relations: Issues and Reponses* (Cambridge: Cambridge University Press, 1996).

34. Bull, *The Anarchical Society*, p. 22. See also Hedley Bull, *Justice in International Relations: Hagey Lectures* (Waterloo: University of Waterloo, 1983), p. 13. This understanding of the connection between world and international society is similar to Locke's social-contract theory, in which the legitimacy of sovereignty is thought to derive from the ability of the state to protect its citizens' natural rights. Other thinkers, such as Martin Wight and Andrew Linklater, view the relationship between state sovereignty and individual moral claims as oppositional. See Martin Wight, *International Theory: The Three Traditions* (London: Leicester University Press, 1991); and Andrew Linklater, "Citizenship and Sovereignty in the Post-Westphalian State," *European Journal of International Relations*, Vol. 2, No. 1 (March 1996), pp. 77–103.

35. Gilpin, *War and Change in World Politics*, p. 211. Thucydides himself claimed to have written for posterity. See also Barry Buzan and Richard Little, *International Systems in World History: Remaking the Study of International Relations* (Oxford: Oxford University Press, 2000), p. 2. For other theories of international change that conform to rational-choice assumptions, see Paul Kennedy, *The Rise and Fall of the Great Powers: Economic Change and Military Conflict from 1500 to 2000* (New York: Vintage Books, 1987); and Charles Kindleberger, *The World in Depression, 1929–1939* (Berkeley, CA: University of California Press, 1996).

36. The analysis of this section combined procedural reforms, or what Gilpin termed "interaction changes," with larger changes in the international system's material structure. Together, these two elements, which Gilpin treats separately, are the main features of systemic disruption.

37. Bull, *Anarchical Society*, p. 311.

38. Marx's theory of the state is rooted in his understanding of the state as a guarantor of private property and, therefore, his expectation that a classless society would also be stateless. In pursuing this vision, Lenin in fact violated it: he emphasized the necessity of an intermediary stage, "the dictatorship of the proletariat," in which the state's influence on economic and personal life was supreme. See Friedrich Engels and Karl Marx, *The German Ideology*, second edition (London: Laurence and Wishart, 1974); and Vladimir Lenin, *The State and Revolution: The Marxist Theory of the State and the Tasks of the Proletariat in the Revolution* (London: Union Books, 2013).

39. See Chapter 5.

40. See Andrew Hurrell, *On Global Order: Power, Values and the Constitution of International Society* (Oxford: Oxford University Press, 2007), p. 69. For an intellectual history of war and peace in European thought, see Michael Howard, *War in Modern History* (Oxford: Oxford University Press, 1976); and Justine Lacroix and Kalypso A. Nicolaïdis, eds., *European Stories: Intellectual Debates on Europe in National Contexts* (Oxford: Oxford University Press, 2011). On modern peace theories and proposals, see F. H. Hinsley, *Power and the Pursuit of Peace: Theory and Practice in the History of Relations between States* (Cambridge: Cambridge University Press, 1967).

41. See Immanuel Kant, *Perpetual Peace and Other Essays on Politics, History and Morals*, trans. T. Humphrey (Indianapolis, IN: Hackett, 1983).
42. See Hurrell, *On Global Order*, p. 69.
43. This form of moderate federalism differed from the vision of radical federalists such as Altiero Spinelli, Carlo Sforza, and Helmuth von Moltke, whose central concern was the wholesale eradication of the nation state within a single European entity. See Walter Lipgens, *A History of European Integration* (Oxford: Oxford University Press, 1982); and Walter Lipgens and Wilfried Loth, eds., *Documents on the History of European Integration: The Struggle for European Union by Political Parties and Pressure Groups in Western European Countries, 1945–1950* (New York: De Gruyter, 1988).
44. The evaluation of systemic revision confronts an analytical challenge: analysts must determine whether observed changes in states' shared goals and principles signal the emergence of new political ideals or represent, instead, a mere adaptation of previously existing values. Or more succinctly: At what point does normative change become systemic revision? See Barry Buzan, *From International to World Society? English School Theory and the Social Structure of Globalisation* (Cambridge: Cambridge University Press, 2004), p. 182.
45. This concept is different from Geoffrey Herrera's "system change," a label he employs interchangeably with the more common "systemic change." See Herrera, *Technology and International Transformation*.
46. See Richard Rosecrance, *The Resurgence of the West: How a Transatlantic Union Can Prevent War and Restore the United States and Europe* (New Haven, CT: Yale University Press, 2013).
47. See Margaret E. Keck and Kathryn Sikkink, *Activists Beyond Borders: Advocacy Networks in International Politics* (Ithaca, N.Y.: Cornell University Press, 1998).
48. See Herrera, *Technology and International Transformation*, p. 22.
49. Bull's original term was "world political system."
50. Bull, *Anarchical Society*, p. 266.
51. Ibid., p. 268. Critical theories of international relations also supply a range of concepts with which to build a model of the system that does not privilege the state. This perspective emphasizes the importance not only of structures of power but also the very *nature* of power, especially shifting hierarchical relationships among state and nonstate players; it focuses not just on the actions of observers and practitioners but also their *minds*, especially normative choices in favor of or against a particular social conception of hierarchical agents; in brief, it draws attention to the question of how a new system comes about rather than how established systems adapt and endure. The critical approach, however, has its limits. Not least of these is the essential duality in which deep change occurs. Forces of change in the contemporary world exist within, and are thus shaped and constrained by, the very social arrangement that they strive to supplant. This limits, as Robert Cox acknowledged, "the range of choice to alternative orders which are feasible transformations of the existing world." (Robert W. Cox, "Social Forces, States, and World Orders," *Millennium: Journal of International Studies*, Vol. 10, No. 2 [1981], p. 130.) The basic theoretical challenge, then, is to provide conceptual benchmarks of revolutionary change that separate changes *within* the international system and more exceptional changes *of* the system itself – the central aim of this chapter.
52. David Armstrong, *Revolution and World Order: The Revolutionary State in International Society* (Oxford: Clarendon Press, 1993), p. 33. There were, in fact, two treaties – of Osnabrück and Münster.
53. See Robert Jackson, *Sovereignty: The Evolution of an Idea* (Cambridge: Polity, 2007), p. 38. Andrew Hurrell disputes the Westphalia-based story of the states system's genesis, noting that the legal and moral practices of modern international society developed between 1750 and 1914. See Hurrell, *On Global Order*, p. 54; and Andreas Osiander, "Sovereignty, International Relations and the Westphalian Myth," *International Organization*, Vol. 55, No. 2 (April 2001), pp. 251–87.

54. Wight, *International Theory*, p. 41. Wight cites Christian Wolff as a principal exponent of this dogma.

55. See J. D. Cockcroft and E. T. S. Walton, "Experiments with High Velocity Positive Ions. II. The Disintegration of Elements by High Velocity Protons," *Proceedings of the Royal Society of London* (July 1932).

56. In 1934, American physicist Leo Szilard observed that neutrons could sustain a nuclear chain reaction that could generate an enormous amount of energy. See Leo Szilard and T. H. Chalmers, "Detection of Neutrons Liberated from Beryllium by Gamma Rays: A New Technique for Inducing Radioactivity," *Nature*, Vol. 134 (September 1934), pp. 494–95.

57. Oak Ridge housed one of the first centers of nuclear medicine in the United States. Doctors used cesium–137 to kill cancerous tissue. See Alan Taylor, "The Secret City," *The Atlantic* (June 25, 2012).

58. On technological determinism, see John G. Ruggie, "International Responses to Technology: Concepts and Trends", *International Organization* (Summer 1975), pp. 558–83; Merritt R. Smith and Leo Marx, eds., *Does Technology Drive History? The Dilemma of Technological Determinism* (Cambridge, MA: MIT Press, 1994); and Herrera, *Technology and International Transformation*, pp. 29–39.

59. According to one interesting study, globalization can reduce states' reliance on the use of military force to pursue national interests. That is, integration provides "an additional mechanism for competition beyond cheap talk, but short of military violence." Erik Gartzke and Quan Li, "War, Peace, and the Invisible Hand: Positive Political Externalities of Economic Globalization," *International Studies Quarterly*, Vol. 47 (November 2003), pp. 561–86.

60. Skolnikoff, *The Elusive Transformation*, p. 11.

61. For an example of such a view, see Keir A. Lieber, *War and the Engineers: The Primacy of Politics over Technology* (Ithaca, N.Y.: Cornell University Press, 2005).

62. See William Potter, ed., *International Nuclear Trade and Nonproliferation: The Challenge of Emerging Suppliers* (Lexington, MA: Lexington Books, 1990); Chaim Braun and Christopher F. Chyba, "Proliferation Rings: New Challenges to the Nuclear Nonproliferation Regime," *International Security*, Vol. 29, No. 2 (Fall 2004), pp. 5–49; Olav Njølstad, *Nuclear Proliferation and International Order: Challenges to the Non-Proliferation Regime* (New York, NY: Routledge, 2011).

63. See Vinton G. Cerf and Robert E. Kahn, "A Protocol for Packet Network Interconnection," *IEEE Transactions on Communications, COM–22*, Vol. 5 (1974); and John Naughton, *A Brief History of the Future: Origins of the Internet* (London: Weidenfeld and Nicolson, 1999).

64. David D. Clark, "The Design Philosophy of the DARPA Internet Protocols," *Proceedings of the SIGCOMM '88, Computer Communication Review*, Vol. 18, No. 4 (1988), pp. 106–14. See also Clark, "Designs for an Internet," Draft version 2.0 ed. s.l., unpublished manuscript (2016), p. 22.

65. Clark, "Designs for an Internet," p. 22.

66. On the history of ARPANET, see Clark, "The Design Philosophy of the DARPA Internet Protocols"; Barry M. Leiner, "Brief History of the Internet" (The Internet Society, http://www.internetsociety.org/internet/internet–51/history-internet/brief-history-internet); Janet Abbate, *Inventing the Internet* (Cambridge, MA: MIT Press, 1999), Chapters 1–4; and Naughton, *A Brief History of the Future*.

67. This trend may reverse if countries such as Russia and China succeed in efforts to impose sovereign control over the Internet. See Chapter 1 of this book.

68. See Ruggie, "International Responses to Technology," p. 558.

69. The notion of "sociotechnical" systems captures the interaction of technology and politics. See Herrera, *Technology and International Transformation*.

70. In fact, this is the essence of Gilpin's definition of systemic change. See Gilpin, *War and Change in World Politics*, p. 9.

71. Thucydides, *History of the Peloponnesian War*, trans. Steven Lattimore (Indianapolis, IN: Hackett, 1998).

72. The disturbance of the balance resulted largely from the growth of Athens' navy and from its construction of a defensive wall around the port of Piraeus, the completion of which would have complicated Sparta's ability to check Athenian expansion in the Aegean region. See Thucydides, *History of the Peloponnesian War*, pp. 33 and 67–70.

73. See Paul M. Kennedy, *The Rise and Fall of the Great Powers: Economic Change and Military Conflict from 1500 to 2000* (New York: Random House, 1987), pp. 148–52; and Paul Bairoch, "International Industrialization Levels from 1750 to 1980," *Journal of European Economic History*, Vol. 11 (1982). Notably, Kennedy's work contains only passing references to the important role of technological innovation in the historical rise and fall of great powers. He notes, for example, that "The advanced technology of steam engines and machine-made tools gave Europe decisive economic and military advantages [over non-European societies during the eighteenth and nineteenth centuries]. The improvements in the muzzle-loading gun (percussion caps, rifling, etc.) were ominous enough; the coming of the breechloader, vastly increasing the rate of fire, was an even greater advance; and the Gatling guns, Maxims and light field artillery put the final touches to a new 'firepower revolution' which quite eradicated the chances of a successful resistance by indigenous peoples reliant upon older weaponry" (p. 150). Yet this work does not develop a theory of technological revolution and great power transition.

74. For the purposes of illustrating the effects of nuclear arms on the international balance of power, this discussion does not consider the revolutionary nature of Soviet foreign policy (for a discussion, see Chapter 5). Insofar as these aims were revolutionary, the nuclear revolution in this instance produced second-order, not third-order effects.

75. See William Easterly and Stanley Fischer, "The Soviet Economic Decline: Historical and Republican Data," *NBER Working Paper No. 4735* (May 1994), p. 1.

76. See William H. Cooper, *Russia's Economic Performance and Policies and Their Implications for the United States* (Washington, D.C.: Congressional Research Service, June 29, 2009), p. 5.

77. Ukraine's fate after 1991 demonstrates the expansionist dangers that non-nuclear states face against nuclear powers. Although some Ukrainian leaders have strived to steer their country towards NATO and the European Union, a Russian military incursion that began in 2014 has stalled both accessions. Had Ukraine retained the nuclear deterrent that it inherited from the Soviet Union, its Western-oriented leaders' may have realized their political ambitions. See John J. Mearsheimer, "The Case for a Ukrainian Nuclear Deterrent," *Foreign Affairs* (Summer 1993).

78. The words are from Admiral Sir Arthur Wilson. Quoted in Stephen W. Roskill, *Naval Policy between the Wars* (London: Walker, 1968), p. 231.

79. The Royal Navy Submarine Service was founded in 1901. By August 1914, it numbered 71 vessels, many of which, however, were training vessels. This number is larger than the number of vessels (61) that the Germany Navy fielded at any one time during the war. The largest fleet belonged to the French, who possessed 123 vessels, of which few were fit for battle.

80. The most reliable form of submarine detection – the sighting of a periscope – almost always came too late to deflect a fatal blow. Defensive measures – such as minefields, net barrages, and depth charges – were only partly effective; the first sinking of a German submarine (U–68) by depth charges did not occur until March 1916. See Richard Compton-Hall, *Submarines and the War at Sea* (London: Macmillan, 1991); and Robert K. Massie, *Castles of Steel: Britain, Germany and the Winning of the Great War at Sea* (New York: Random House, 2003).

81. As developments in antisubmarine warfare (e.g. sonar) later showed, there was nothing about the nature of the new technology that intrinsically favored the offense over the defense.

82. Henry A. Kissinger, *Nuclear Weapons and Foreign Policy* (New York: Council on Foreign Relations, 1957), p. 73.

83. Some observers question whether the "Joe 4" test was a true thermonuclear detonation, because its yield (400 kilotons of TNT) was less than what was normal for a hydrogen

bomb (in comparison, the American test, "Ivy Mike," yielded 10.4 megatons). See Michael Kort, *The Columbia Guide to the Cold War* (New York: Columbia University Press, 1998), p. 187.

84. See "Statement by Lewis L. Strauss, Chairman, United States Atomic Energy Commission," USAEC Release (March 31, 1954); A. H. Sturtevant, "Social Implications of the Genetics of Man," *Science*, Vol. 120 (September 10, 1954), pp. 405–07; Ralph E. Lapp, "Radioactive Fall-out," *Bulletin of the Atomic Scientists*, Vol. 11 (February 1955), pp. 206–09; and Carolyn Kopp, "The Origins of the American Scientific Debate over Fallout Hazards," *Social Studies of Science*, Vol. 9 (1979), pp. 404–6.

85. See U.S. Senate, *Study of Airpower: Hearings before the Subcommittee on the Air Force of the Committee on Armed Services* (Washington, D.C.: Government Publication Office, 1956), p. 165.

86. See *National Intelligence Estimate: Soviet Capabilities for Clandestine Attack against the U.S. with Weapons of Mass Destruction and the Vulnerability of the U.S.* (Langley, VA: Central Intelligence Agency, 1951).

87. See Donald P. Steury, *Intentions and Capabilities: Estimates on Soviet Strategic Forces, 1950–1983* (Langley, VA: Center for the Study of Intelligence, Central Intelligence Agency, 1996), p. 18; and *Report of the Defense Science Board Task Force on Preventing and Defending Against Clandestine Nuclear Attack* (Washington, D.C.: Office of the Under Secretary of Defense For Acquisition, Technology, and Logistics, June 2004). For a discussion of this problem in the context of nuclear terrorism, see Benjamin E. Schwartz, *Right of Boom: What Follows an Untraceable Nuclear Attack?* (New York: Overlook Press, 2015).

88. Charles L. Glaser and Chaim Kauffman, "What is the Offense-Defense Balance and Can We Measure It?" *International Security*, Vol. 22, No. 4 (Spring 1998), pp. 44–82.

89. See Stephen Van Evera, "The Cult of the Offensive and the Origins of the First World War," *International Security*, Vol. 9, No. 1 (Summer 1984), p. 59.

90. See Marshall Joffre, *Mémoires du Maréchal Joffre* (Paris: Librarie Plon, 1932), p. 33; and Van Evera, "The Cult of the Offensive and the Origins of the First World War," p. 61.

91. The German plan for a Swiss invasion, "Operation Tannenbaum," envisaged a concentrated thrust from Lake Geneva to Lake Constance. Its bold authors warned about the perilous Jura Mountains and the steep banks of the Aare River. On Germany's war plans in Switzerland, see Werner Roesch, *Bedrohte Schweiz: Die Deutsche Operationsplanungen gegen die Schweiz im Sommer/Herbst 1940 und die Abwehr-Bereitschaft der Armee in Oktober 1940* (Frauenfeld: Huber, 1986).

92. See Lieber, *War and the Engineers*, p. 115.

93. Lindemann himself sought to prioritize other inventions, such as aerial mines, over the radar's development. The Germans had not invested in the development of radar technology because Hitler did not regard it as necessary for the attainment of crushing offensive victories. See William Manchester and Paul Reid, *The Last Lion: Winston Spencer Churchill, Defender of the Realm, 1940–1965* (New York: Little, Brown, and Company, 2012), Chapter 1.

94. See Lucas Kello, "Security," in Joel Krieger, ed., *The Oxford Companion to International Relations*, third edition (Oxford: Oxford University Press, 2014).

95. Thucydides' tragic tale of Athens and Sparta was later translated and elaborated on by the seventeenth-century English philosopher Thomas Hobbes. See Thomas Hobbes, *Leviathan*, edited with an introduction by C. B. Macpherson (New York: Penguin, 1968). In modern times, the logic of the security dilemma has induced nations to adopt strategic postures that also resulted in war: Germany's bellicose reaction in 1914 to perceived encirclement by France and Russia; Japan's attack on the United States in 1941 in anticipation of a military contest in the Pacific; or the U.S.-led invasion of Iraq in 2003 to dismantle suspected weapons-of-mass-destruction sites. In all of these cases, the despotic and militaristic regimes of Germany, Japan, and Iraq aggravated the security dilemma, showing that domestic-level factors can combine with systemic factors to increase the chances of conflict.

96. Robert O. Keohane and Joseph S. Nye, Jr., *Power and Interdependence* (New York: Longman, 1979), p. 40.

97. Or in the academic language of international relations, the former occurs at the second "level of analysis," the latter at the third. On the levels of analysis in international relations – or "images," as Waltz called them – see Kenneth N. Waltz, *Man, the State, and War: A Theoretical Analysis* (New York: Columbia University Press, 1959).

98. On Napoleon's mastery of the weapons of war, see Martin Van Creveld, *Technology and War: From 2000 B.C. to the Present* (New York: Macmillan, 1989), Chapter 3.

99. This rearming process began in earnest following the Nazi seizure of power in 1933. Often, the process advanced by subterfuge because of the Versailles Treaty's restrictions on German military capacity – for example, the use of the German Air Transport School (*Deutsche Verkehrsfliegerschule*), an outwardly civilian organization, to train Luftwaffe pilots. The key development was Hitler's remilitarization of the Rhineland in 1936, which made the security relationship with France dangerous. See P. Laurent, "The Reversal of Belgian Foreign Policy, 1936–37," *Review of Politics*, Vol. 31, No. 3 (July 1969), p. 372.

100. One man who correctly divined the shifting tides of strategy during the interwar period was Colonel Charles de Gaulle, who urged the creation of a French *armée de métier* comprising shock mechanized units. Believing that war had not changed in its essence since 1918, his superiors quashed the proposal. See Charles de Gaulle, *Vers l'armée de métier* (Paris: Plon, 1981).

101. Quoted in Steven Waugh, *Essential Modern World History* (Cheltenham: Thomas Nelson, 2001), p. 52.

102. See A. G. Armstrong, "The Army Today," *RUSI Journal*, Vol. 81, No. 523 (1936); "The Army's New Weapons and Equipment," *RUSI Journal*, Vol. 84, No. 534 (1939); and Damian P. O'Connor, *Between Peace and War: British Defence and the Royal United Services Institute, 1931–2010* (London: Royal United Services Institute, 2011), pp. 176–77.

103. In 1940, France had about 2,900 deployable tanks in the country's northeast. This number was higher than Germany's, even if one counts the tanks that Germany seized from Czechoslovakia. French tanks, moreover, were qualitatively superior; they included the SOMUA S35, which packed more firepower than its German equivalent, the Panzer III. See Julian Jackson, *The Fall of France: The Nazi Invasion of 1940* (Oxford: Oxford University Press, 2003), pp. 12–13.

104. Interaction capacity signifies "the level of transportation, communication, and organization capability in the unit/system that determines what types and levels of interaction are possible." Buzan and Little, *International Systems in World History*, p. 441.

105. See Benedict Anderson, *Under Three Flags: Anarchism and the Anti-Colonial Imagination* (London: Verso, 2005).

106. See William M. Ramsay, *The Imperial Peace: An Ideal in European History* (Oxford: The Clarendon Press, 1913).

107. On Roman military technology, see Simon James, *Rome and the Sword: How Warriors and Weapons Shaped Roman History* (London: Thames and Hudson, 2011).

108. See Thomas Powers, *Heisenberg's War: The Secret History of the German Bomb* (New York: De Capo Press, 2000).

109. See Robert Farley, "What if Hitler Developed Nuclear Weapons during World War II?" *The National Interest* (October 8, 2016).

110. A German atomic victory, which likely would have involved the incineration of at least London and Moscow, would have looked very different from a conventional German victory, in which big Allied population centres may have survived the war largely intact, much as Paris did following France's defeat in the spring of 1940. In either scenario, it is probable that the post-war order would have resembled a combination of World Leviathan within the European pan-Germanic Empire, or *Großgermanisches Reich*, colonial dominion in parts of Africa, and hegemony elsewhere, possibly in conjunction with the Japanese Empire. As Geoffrey Stoakes has argued, Hitler sought to assert direct control only over certain parts of the globe while exercising leadership

elsewhere. See Geoffrey Stoakes, *Hitler and the Quest for World Dominion* (Leamington Spa: Berg, 1986), p. 235.

111. A world system is in Bull's terms different from a world society, which as we saw conveys a concern for the interests of actors other than states even as it retains the assumption that states are the supreme agents of international life. See Hedley Bull, *The Anarchical Society: A Study of Order in World Politics*, second edition (London: Macmillan, 1995).

112. See Graham Allison, *Nuclear Terrorism: The Greatest Preventable Catastrophe* (New York: Henry Holt, 2005), Chapter 1.

113. This would equate to approximately one or two deployed warheads. By "deployed" I mean devices that are usable because they are mounted on missiles or other delivery systems. If one includes total nuclear warheads, the figure rises to seven. See Shannon N. Kile and Hans M. Kristensen, *Trends in Nuclear Forces, 2016: SIPRI FACT Sheet* (Solna, Sweden: Stockholm International Peace Research Institute, June 2016), p. 2. The nuclear devices such as "dirty bombs" that terrorists could plausibly deploy may differ significantly both in the manner of deployment and explosive yield. Even allowing for a greatly reduced range of delivery and power, the effect on international security of a dirty nuclear attack by terrorists could be profound. On nuclear terrorism, see Allison, *Nuclear Terrorism*.

114. Allison, *Nuclear Terrorism*, p. 227.

115. Michael J. Mills, Owen B. Toon, Julia Lee-Taylor, and Alan Robock, "Multidecadal Global Cooling and Unprecedented Ozone Loss Following a Regional Nuclear Conflict," *Earth's Future*, Vol. 2, No. 4 (April 2014), pp. 161–76.

116. See Ryan Rasteger, "How Many Nukes Would It Take to Render Earth Uninhabitable," *Global Zero: A World Without Nuclear Weapons* (July 9, 2015), http://www.globalzero. org/blog/how-many-nukes-would-it-take-render-earth-uninhabitable.

117. Thomas S. Kuhn, *The Structure of Scientific Revolutions*, third edition (Chicago, IL: University of Chicago Press, 1996), p. 151. Kuhn observed that intellectual resistance to paradigmatic adjustment can last a lifetime, particularly in the case of individuals "whose careers have committed them to an older tradition of normal science" (p. 151).

4 Third-Order Cyber Revolution: Problems of Inadvertent Conflict

1. Nazi Germany's mastery of tank warfare was one among several important factors in the country's rise to the top of the European hierarchy of power. The acquisition of nuclear weapons, by contrast, was singularly important in the emergence of the United States and the Soviet Union as superpowers. But as we saw, the disruption of the balance of power was in the case of Nazi Germany and the Soviet Union an instance of systemic revision rather than systemic disruption owing to the revolutionary character of the two countries' political leadership.

2. For a contrasting, if simplistic but interesting account, see Christopher Whyte, "Power and Predation in Cyberspace," *Strategic Studies Quarterly* (Spring 2015), pp. 100–18.

3. Some analysts disagree with this assessment. Ivanka Barzashka argued that the operation's effect on Iranian enrichment activity "in the medium-to-long term was limited at best" and that the ensuing "misrepresentation of Stuxnet's effects may have hindered diplomatic solutions at a time when they could have had real threat-reduction and confidence-building benefits." Ivanka Barzashka, "Are Cyber-Weapons Effective?" *RUSI Journal*, Vol. 158, No. 2 (2013), pp. 48–49. What is certain is that the U.S. government, one of Stuxnet's reported authors, devised a plan ("Nitro Zeus") for further cyberattacks if the diplomatic effort failed and war erupted. See David E. Sanger and Mark Mazzetti, "U.S. Had Cyberattack Plan if Iran Nuclear Dispute Led to Conflict," *The New York Times* (February 16, 2016).

4. Sony Pictures' initial reaction was to suspend the film's theatrical release – thus setting the stage for the first successful coercive cyber action across international lines. But following intense public criticism, the company distributed the film freely (for a limited time) over

the Internet. See Peter Bradshaw, "The Interview: Sony's Retreat Signals an Unprecedented Defeat on American Turf," *The Guardian* (December 18, 2014); and Chapter 5.

5. B. Valeriano and C. Maness, *Cyber War Versus Cyber Realities: Cyber Conflict in the International System* (Oxford: Oxford University Press, 2015), p. 6 (emphasis mine).

6. Ibid., p. 21 (emphasis mine).

7. See Lucas Kello, "The Meaning of the Cyber Revolution: Perils to Theory and Statecraft," *International Security*, Vol. 38, No. 2 (Fall 2013), pp. 7–40.

8. See Austin Wright, "Cybersecurity Tests Delayed over Vulnerability Concerns," *Politico*, (November 2015), https://www.politicopro.com/defense/story/2015/11/cybersecurity-tests-delayed-over-vulnerability-concerns-0752266.

9. See Nicholas Watt, "Trident Could Be Vulnerable to Cyber-Attack, Says Former Defence Secretary," *The Guardian* (November 23, 2015). The quoted words belong to Franklin Miller, a former White House defense policy official under President George W. Bush. As the Stuxnet operation showed, air gaps are not impervious to malware. All computer systems, including those residing within the cyber archipelago, are susceptible to cyber intrusion. Thus Miller's statement would be correct only in the impossible case that nuclear command and control functions, and the weapons themselves, were entirely manually operated.

10. For a fine elaboration of this line of argumentation, see Erik Gartzke, "The Myth of Cyberwar: Bringing War in Cyberspace Back Down to Earth," *International Security*, Vol. 38, No. 2 (Fall 2013), pp. 41–73.

11. This core feature of the Conventional Model of the international system is reflected in the common tendency of some theorists to integrate into the study of international politics assumptions from microeconomic theory. As Kenneth Waltz put it: "Just as economists define markets in terms of firms, so I define international political structures in terms of states." Kenneth N. Waltz, *Theory of International Politics* (New York: McGraw-Hill, 1979), p. 94.

12. Donna Miles, "Stavridis Spotlights Top National Security Issues," American Force Press Service, U.S. Department of Defense (March 15, 2012).

13. On the notion of "bounded rationality" in human decision-making, see Herbert A. Simon, *Administrative Behavior: A Study of Human Decision-Making Processes in Administrative Organization* (New York: Macmillan, 1947); and Daniel Kahneman, "A Perspective on Judgment and Choice: Mapping Bounded Rationality," *American Psychologist*, Vol. 58, No. 9 (September 2003), pp. 697–720.

14. For a discussion of systemic disruption in the nuclear context, see Graham T. Allison, Albert Carnesale, and Joseph S. Nye, eds., *Hawks, Doves, and Owls: An Agenda for Avoiding Nuclear War* (New York: W. W. Norton, 1985), Chapter 1.

15. See Ralph Lander, *To Kill a Centrifuge: A Technical Analysis of What Stuxnet's Creators Tried to Achieve* (Arlington, VT: The Langner Group, November 2013), p. 34.

16. See Vivian Yeo, "Stuxnet Infections Spread to 115 Countries," *ZDNet Asia* (August 9, 2010).

17. This is because the worm exploited a shortcut facility in Windows software. See Sharon Weinberger, "Computer Security: Is This the Start of Cyberwarfare?" *Nature*, Vol. 474 (2011), pp. 142–45.

18. The algorithm failed to specify either a price or a time for the execution of the order, producing an enormous sell pressure. See *Findings Regarding the Market Events of May 6, 2010: Report of the Staffs of the CFTC and SEC to the Joint Advisory Committee on Emerging Regulatory Issues* (Washington, D.C.: U.S. Commodity Futures Trading Commission and U.S. Securities & Exchange Commission, September 30, 2010).

19. See Nathaniel Popper, "The Stock Market Bell Rings, Computers Fail, Wall Street Cringes," *The New York Times* (July 8, 2015).

20. See Bradley Hope and Saumya Vaishampayan, "Glitch Freezes NYSE Trading for Hours," *Wall Street Journal* (July 8, 2015).

21. See William A. Owens, Kenneth W. Dam, and Herbert S. Lin, eds., *Technology, Policy,*

Law, and Ethics Regarding U.S. Acquisition and Use of Cyberattack Capabilities (Washington, D.C.: National Academies Press, 2009), pp. 2–32.

22. See "Cyberwar Against Iraq," *News Max* (March 12, 2003). A further problem arose when U.S. tacticians explored options to insert code into Iraq's military command networks. The country's military and civilian telecommunications networks were closely linked, thus raising risks of collateral damage if the former was attacked.

23. "Cyberwar Against Iraq," *News Max*.

24. On the problem of adaptive malware and responses to it, see Sean Price, "Adaptive Threats and Defenses," in Harold F. Tipton and Micki Krause, eds., *Information Security Management Handbook*, sixth edition, Vol. 4 (New York: Auerbach Publications, 2010).

25. See *McAfee Labs Threats Report* (Santa Clara, CA: McAfee Labs, June 2016).

26. See Peter W. Singer and Allan Friedman, *Cybersecurity and Cyberwar: What Everyone Needs to Know* (Oxford: Oxford University Press, 2014), p. 31.

27. For example, Russia. See Jonathan Medalia, *Comprehensive Nuclear Test-Ban Treaty: Updated Safeguards and Net Assessments* (Washington, D.C.: Congressional Research Service, June 3, 2009).

28. Other treaties that ensued in the first ten years after the PTBT include the Outer Space Treaty and Treaty of Tlatelolco (1967), the Seabed Arms Control Treaty (1972), and the Anti-Ballistic Missile Treaty (1972). A Comprehensive Test-Ban Treaty was signed in 1996 but still awaits ratification.

29. Matthew Evangelista, *Unarmed Forces: The Transnational Movement to End the Cold War* (Ithaca, N.Y.: Cornell University Press, 1999).

30. See *Impact of a Threshold Test Ban Treaty on Soviet Military Programs: National Intelligence Estimate Number 11–11–66*, United States Intelligence Board (May 25, 1966).

31. See *Nuclear Weapons Life Cycle* (Washington, D.C.: National Nuclear Security Administration), https://nnsa.energy.gov/ourmission/managingthestockpile/nwlifecycle.

32. See William J. Broad and David E. Sanger, "As U.S. Modernizes Nuclear Weapons, 'Smaller' Leaves Some Uneasy," *The New York Times* (January 11, 2016).

33. See "Treaty Banning Nuclear Weapon Tests in the Atmosphere, in Outer Space and Under Water," U.S. Department of State, http://www.state.gov/t/isn/4797.htm.

34. On the backdrop of the recent controversy over Hillary Clinton's use of private email servers in official State Department communications, Graham gleefully stated: "I haven't worried about an email being hacked, since I've never sent one. I'm, like, ahead of my time." Yet pictures exist of the senator using a mobile phone – hence, some of his communications are susceptible to hacking. See "Quotation of the Day," *The New York Times* (September 15, 2016).

35. On the attribution problem, see for instance, Clark and Landau, "Untangling Attribution"; and Thomas Rid and Ben Buchanan, "Attributing Cyber Attacks," *Journal of Strategic Studies*, Vol. 38, No. 1 (2014), pp. 4–37.

36. Herbert S. Lin, "Some Interesting Aspects of Cyberconflict for Discussion," presentation at the Harvard Kennedy School, Cambridge, Massachusetts (February 8, 2012).

37. Dmitri Galushkevich, an ethnic Russian from Tallinn, was convicted of disrupting the website of the Reform Party of Estonian Prime Minister Andrus Ansip. He was fined 17,500 Estonian kroons (about $1,600). For more on the Estonian attacks, see Chapter 6.

38. On cyber deterrence, see Patrick M. Morgan, "Applicability of Traditional Deterrence Concepts and Theory to the Cyber Realm," in *Proceedings of a Workshop on Deterring Cyberattacks: Informing Strategies and Developing Options for U.S. Policy* (Washington, D.C.: National Academies Press, 2010), pp. 55–76.

39. See Jordan Carney, "Wasserman Schultz Called Top Sanders Aide a 'Damn Liar' in Leaked Email," *The Hill* (July 22, 2016).

40. As Chapter 8 discusses, a declassified U.S. intelligence report stated: "Russia's goals were to undermine public faith in the US democratic process, denigrate Secretary Clinton, and harm her electability and potential presidency. We further assess Putin and the

Russian government developed a clear preference for President-elect Trump. We have *high confidence* in these judgments." *Background to "Assessing Russian Activities and Intentions in Recent US Elections": The Analytic Process and Cyber Incident Attribution* (Washington, D.C.: Office of the Director of National Intelligence, January 6, 2017) (emphasis mine). In October, the Obama administration officially accused Russia of hacking DNC email accounts. Overall, the available evidence is not entirely conclusive; it does not prove beyond doubt Russia's involvement and motives in the political hacking operation. Some of the forensic indicators in the U.S. government's public report are crude. They merit skeptical treatment. Yet the burden of skeptics to disprove Russian involvement is greater than that of the believers. Certainly, it is a fact that the DNC's email servers were compromised by a highly capable player using sophisticated intrusion techniques. Disbelievers must present a more convincing alternative account of the hacking: If not Russia, then who?

41. See "Trump Questions Claims of Russian Hacking: 'I Know Things Others Don't'," *The Guardian* (January 1, 2017).

42. See Elizabeth Weise, "Tech Crowd Goes Wild for Trump's '400-Pound Hacker'," *USA Today* (September 27, 2016). Some security analysts and journalists also questioned Russia's authorship of the DNC hack. See, for example, Matt Taibbi, "Something About This Russia Story Stinks," *Rolling Stone* (December 30, 2016).

43. Confronted by the allegation that the Kremlin sought to help him win the elections, the president-elect replied: "I think it's [the allegation] ridiculous ... No, I don't believe it at all." Elise Viebeck, "Trump Denies CIA Report that Russia Intervened to Help Him Win Election," *Washington Post* (December 11, 2016).

44. Axelrod is especially concerned with the resolution of problems of collective action, in which individually rational behavior produces collectively irrational outcomes. See Robert Axelrod, *The Evolution of Cooperation* (New York: Basic Books, 1984).

45. Ibid., p. 174.

46. See Thomas C. Schelling and Morton H. Halperin, *Strategy and Arms Control* (Washington, D.C.: Twentieth Century Fund, 1961).

47. See Romney B. Duffey and John Saull, *Managing Risk: The Human Element* (Chichester: Wiley, 2008), p. 124, fn. 3. Against some Iraqi missiles, such as the Tactical Ballistic Missile (TBM), the advantage was 100 percent – i.e. a clear position of dominance – although the sample size of interceptions (nine) is small. See "Operation Iraqi Freedom – Patriot," *GlobalSecurity.Org* (July 21, 2011), http://www.globalsecurity.org/space/ops/oif-patriot.htm.

48. The difference between superiority and dominance in offensive weapons is reflected in official doctrine – for instance, in NATO's distinction between "air supremacy" and "air superiority." See *AAP–06 Edition 2013: NATO Glossary of Terms and Definitions* (Brussels: NATO, 2013).

49. See Gregory H. Canavan, *Missile Defense for the 21st Century* (Washington, D.C.: The Heritage Foundation, 2003), p. 3.

50. By definition, strategic advantages also entail tactical advantages. The reverse is not necessarily true.

51. See Daniel Ford, "B-36 Bomber at the Crossroads," *Air and Space Magazine* (April 1996).

52. Comptroller and Auditor General, *The UK Cyber Security Strategy: Landscape Report* (London: National Audit Office, February 12, 2013), p. 4. The report notes that the three most popular account passwords in 2012 were "password," "123456," and "12345678." Even a simple brute force attack could crack such phrases. See also Leyla Bilge and Tudor Dumitras, "Before We Knew It: An Empirical Study of Zero-Day Attacks in the Real World," *Proceedings of the 2012 ACM Conference on Computer and Communications Security, October 16–18, 2012*, pp. 833–44.

53. See David E. Sanger, "Obama Order Sped Up Wave of Cyberattacks against Iran," *The New York Times* (June 1, 2012).

54. See Jon R. Lindsay, "Stuxnet and the Limits of Cyber Warfare," *Security Studies*, Vol. 22, No. 3 (2013), pp. 365–404.

55. See Martin C. Libicki, *Conquest in Cyberspace* (Cambridge: Cambridge University Press, 2007), p. 87; and Max Smeets, "A Matter of Time: On the Transitory Nature of Cyberweapons," *Journal of Strategic Studies* (February 2017), pp. 1–28. For a game-theoretic analysis of this problem, see Robert Axelrod and Rumen Iliev, "Timing of Cyber Conflict," *Proceedings of the National Academy of Sciences of the United States of America*, Vol. 11, No. 4 (October 2013), pp. 1,298–1,303.

56. A classic analysis of the problem is Robert Jervis, "Cooperation under the Security Dilemma," *World Politics*, Vol. 30, No. 2 (January 1978), pp. 167–214. For a discussion of the problem in the cyber context, see Ben Buchanan, *The Cybersecurity Dilemma: Hacking, Trust and Fear Between Nations* (Oxford: Oxford University Press, 2017).

57. See Editorial Board, "A New Kind of Warfare," *The New York Times* (September 9, 2012).

58. At the time of writing, the U.S. government denies its widely suspected involvement (along with Israel) in the Stuxnet operation.

59. See Senator Joseph Lieberman, interview on Newsmakers, C-SPAN (September 23, 2012).

60. On active defense, see U.S. Department of Defense, *Department of Defense Strategy for Operating in Cyberspace* (Washington, D.C.: U.S. Department of Defense, July 2011), p. 7.

61. Fergus Hanson, "Waging War in Peacetime: Cyber Attacks and International Norms," *The Interpreter* (October 20, 2015).

62. David E. Sanger, "U.S. Tries Candor to Assure China on Cyberattacks," *The New York Times* (April 6, 2014).

63. David E. Sanger, "N.S.A. Leaks Make Plan for Cyberdefense Unlikely," *The New York Times* (August 12, 2013).

64. Tami Abdollaha, "Sony Pictures Had to Draft New Playbook on the Fly," *The Japan Times* (January 11, 2015).

65. See Anjana Ahuja, "Cyber Security Will Soon Be the Work of Machines," *The Financial Times* (July 10, 2016).

66. See Aliya Sternstein, "The Pentagon Wants to Wage War on Denial-of-Service Cyber Attacks," *Defense One* (August 18, 2015).

67. See Kim Zetter, "Meet MonsterMind, the NSA Bot that Could Wage Cyberwar Autonomously," *Wired* (August 13, 2014). As this article notes, it is not clear that MonsterMind exists. Knowledge of its existence rests on the authority of Edward Snowden. See James Bamford, "The Most Wanted Man in the World," *Wired* (August 2014).

5 Second-Order Cyber Revolution: The Problem of the Revolutionary State

1. On the repudiation by the Soviets of "Hitler-style military aggression," see John Mueller, "Think Again: Nuclear Weapons," *Foreign Policy* (December 18, 2009).

2. A classic account of Soviet Russia's partial normalization within international society is Edward H. Carr, *The Bolshevik Revolution, 1917–23*, Vol. 3 (New York: Penguin, 1977).

3. Adam B. Ulam, *Stalin: The Man and His Era* (London: Tauris, 1989), p. 182.

4. See Leon Trostsky, "Publication of the Secret Treaties," *Izvestiia*, No. 221 (November 22, 1917).

5. For a discussion of Soviet Russia as a revolutionary state, see David Armstrong, *Revolution and World Order: The Revolutionary State in International Society* (Oxford: Oxford University Press, 1993), Chapter 4.

6. For a discussion of the Soviet Union as a rational actor in the context of the Cuban Missile Crisis, see Graham Allison and Philip D. Zelikow, *The Essence of Decision: Explaining the Cuban Missile Crisis*, second edition. (New York, NY: Longman, 1999).

7. Armstrong, *Revolution and World Order*, p. 147.

8. The Soviet-like experience of shopping in North Korea has gradually begun to change following the recent introduction of experimental Western-style supermarkets. Only

the rich can buy there, though. Your ordinary comrade will have to brave the whims of the shopkeeper who retrieves the desired merchandise from a shelf behind the counter. See "North Koreans Experience the Marvels of a Supermarket Firsthand," *Business Insider* (February 25, 2012).

9. Han S. Park, *North Korea: The Politics of Unconventional Wisdom* (Boulder, CO: Lynne Rienner, 2002).

10. A leading position in the Non-Aligned Movement distinguished North Korea from the Soviet Union and China. See Bernd Schaefer, "North Korean 'Adventurism' and China's Long Shadow, 1966–1972," *Cold War International History Project Working Paper*, Woodrow Wilson International Center for Scholars (2004).

11. See "North Korea Defence Chief Yong-Chol 'Executed'," BBC (May 13, 2015).

12. See Clyde Haberman, "Bomb Kills 19, Including 6 Key Koreans," *The New York Times* (October 10, 1983).

13. Rupert Wingfield-Hayes, "The North Korean Spy Who Blew Up a Plane," *BBC News* (April 22, 2013).

14. See Anna Fifield, "Malaysian Airport Assassination Focuses New Attention on North Korean Leader," *Washington Post* (February 15, 2017).

15. North Korea performed a similar act of defiance by firing a medium-range rocket into the Sea of Japan in February 2017. See Bryan Harris and Kana Inagaki, "North Korea Tests Trump with Missile Launch," *The Financial Times* (February 12, 2017).

16. North Korea received uranium-enrichment technology and equipment from Pakistan in exchange for its ballistic-missile technology. In the mid-2000s, North Korea began building a nuclear reactor in Syria, which the Israelis destroyed in September 2007 with a surgical air strike. See Sharon A. Squassoni, *Weapons of Mass Destruction: Trade between North Korea and Pakistan* (Washington, D.C.: Congressional Research Service, 2006); and Scott Snyder, "North Korea's Illicit Arms Trade Unmasked," *Forbes* (March 19, 2014).

17. See *The Military Balance*, Vol. 117, No. 1 (2017), International Institute for Strategic Studies, p. 304.

18. To reach Alaska, North Korea requires missiles with a minimum range of 7,000 km. The Taepodong–2, a variant of which is a full-range ICBM, has a theoretical reach of up to 12,000 km. See "Missles," *WMD Around the World*, Federation of American Scientists, https://fas.org/nuke/guide/dprk/missile/ (last updated on October 21, 2016).

19. See *NTI Nuclear Materials Index Security Index: Building a Framework for Assurance, Accountability, and Action*, second edition (Washington, D.C.: Nuclear Threat Initiative, January 2014), p. 19.

20. See Park Young Ho, "South and North Korea's Views on the Unification of the Korean Peninsula and Inter-Korean Relations," paper presented at the Second KRIS-Brookings Joint Conference on Security and Diplomatic Cooperation between ROK and US for the Unification of the Korean Peninsula (January 21, 2014), p. 5.

21. Ibid., p. 7.

22. See the record of the discussions between the North Korean defector Hwang Jang-Yop and Selig Harrison in Don Oberdorfer, *The Two Koreas* (New York: Addison-Wesley, 1998), p. 401; and Hwang's remarks in Robert Myers, *Korea in the Cross Currents* (New York: M. E. Sharpe, 2000). For a general analysis of North Korea's nuclear strategy, see Victor D. Cha, "North Korea's Weapons of Mass Destruction: Badges, Shields, or Swords?" *Political Science Quarterly*, Vol. 117, No. 2 (2002), pp. 209–30.

23. See, for instance, John S. Park and Dong Sun Lee, "North Korea: Existential Deterrence and Diplomatic Leverage," in Muthiah Alagappa, ed., *The Long Shadow: Nuclear Weapons and Security in 21st Century Asia* (Stanford, CA: Stanford University Press, 2008).

24. For an exposition of this argument, see Samuel S. Kim, "North Korea's Nuclear Strategy and the Interface between International and Domestic Politics," *Asian Perspectives*, Vol. 34, No. 1 (2010), pp. 49–85.

25. See Richard Lloyd Parry, "North Korea 'Succeeds in Miniaturising Nuclear Warhead'," *The Times* (April 7, 2016).

26. The failed launch of an Earth observation satellite in February 2016 betrays the obstacles to Pyongyang's missile ambition.

27. See Scott D. Sagan, "Why Do States Build Nuclear Weapons? Three Models in Search of a Bomb," *International Security*, Vol. 21, No. 3 (Winter 1996–97).

28. Ibid., p. 55.

29. Cha, "North Korea's Weapons of Mass Destruction," p. 227.

30. As Daniel Byman explained, the regime has used economic and other inducements (conveyed in the "military-first" or *songun* principle) to co-opt the country's military elites. See Daniel Byman, "Pyongyang's Survival Strategy: Tools of Authoritarian Control in North Korea," *International Security*, Vol. 35, No. 1 (Summer 2010), pp. 44–74.

31. As John Park has shown, the Kim house sustains the loyalty of elites by operating a web of state-trading companies that generate income for special interest budgets. See John S. Park, "North Korea, Inc.: Gaining Insights into North Korean Regime Stability from Recent Commercial Activities," United States Institute of Peace Working Paper, Washington, D.C. (May 2009).

32. For a discussion of the limited effects of economic sanctions on North Korea's nuclear ambitions, see Stephen Haggard and Marcus Noland, "Engaging North Korea: The Efficacy of Sanctions and Inducements," in Etel Solingen, ed., *Sanctions, Statecraft, and Nuclear Proliferation* (Cambridge: Cambridge University Press, 2012).

33. "Hearings to Examine the Nomination of General Vincent K. Brooks, USA, for Reappointment to the Grade of General and to be Commander, United Nations Command/Combined Forces Command/United States Forces Korea," U.S. Congressional Committee Hearing, C-SPAN (April 19, 2016), https://www.c-span.org/video/?408108–1/nomination-brooks/.

34. The closeness between the two domains is reflected in their operational integration within the U.S. Marine Corps: for example, the creation of a Cyber Electronic Warfare Coordination Center. See Matthew E. Poole and Jason C. Schuette, "Cyber Electronic Warfare. Closing the Operational Seams," *Marine Corps Gazette*, Vol. 99, No. 8 (August 2015), pp. 60–62.

35. Some analysts regard Desert Storm as the first "information war." See Edward Mann, "Desert Storm: The First Information War?" *Airpower Journal* (Winter 2014).

36. See "Chapter Six: Asia," *The Military Balance*, Vol. 117, No. 1 (2017), p. 306.

37. See "Seoul Ranked World's Top Digital City," *Chosun Ilbo* (June 20, 2007). The city has gained plaudits for its integration of information technologies into urban planning and services. See Anthony M. Townsend, "Seoul: Birth of a Broadband Metropolis," *Environment and Planning B: Urban Analytics and City Science*, Vol. 34, No. 3 (2007), pp. 396–413.

38. The North Korean government severely restricts the public's access to Internet services. Jean H. Lee, the Associated Press bureau chief in the country, explained that ordinary citizens have "access to the state media, information sources that are vetted by the government, and picked and pulled from the Internet and posted to their intranet site." Clyde Stanhope, "How Bad Is the North Korean Cyber Threat?" *HackRead* (July 2016).

39. See Andrei Lankov, "Changing North Korea: An Information Campaign Can Beat the Regime," *Foreign Affairs*, Vol. 88, No. 6 (November/December 2009), p. 95.

40. See Ju-min Park and James Pearson, "In North Korea, Hackers Are a Handpicked, Pampered Elite," *Reuters* (December 5, 2014).

41. See "North Korea Boosted 'Cyber Forces' to 6,000 Troops, South Says," *Reuters* (January 6, 2015).

42. See Youkyung Lee, "A Look at North Korea's Cyberwar Capabilities," *Washington Times* (December 18, 2004).

43. For technical details about the Lazarus Group's malicious activities, see Costin Raiu, Global Research and Analysis Team, Juan Andrés Guerrero-Saade, "Operation Blockbuster Revealed," *Securelist* (February 24, 2016), https://securelist.com/blog/incidents/73914/operation-blockbuster-revealed/.

44. Unconfirmed sources, however, suggest that a Sony Pictures employee or Russian

nationalists abroad may have assisted the attackers. See Bruce Schneier, "We Still Don't Know Who Hacked Sony," *Schneier on Security* (January 5, 2015).

45. But see, for instance, Christopher Whyte, "Ending Cyber Coercion: Computer Network Attack, Exploitation and the Case of North Korea," *Comparative Strategy*, Vol. 35, No. 2 (July 2016), pp. 93–102.

46. See Symantec Security Response, "SWIFT Attackers' Malware Linked to More Financial Attacks," *Symantec Official Blog* (May 26, 2016).

47. See Nicole Perlroth and Michael Corkery, "North Korea Linked to Digital Attacks on Global Banks," *The New York Times* (May 26, 2016).

48. See Kim Zetter, "That Insane, $81m Bangladesh Bank Heist? Here's What We Know," *Wired* (May 17, 2016).

49. See Chico Harlan and Ellen Nakashima, "Suspected North Korean Cyberattack on a Bank Raises Fears for S. Korea, Allies," *Washington Post* (August 29, 2011).

50. See "Cyber-Attacks on South Korean Nuclear Power Operator Continue," *The Guardian* (December 28, 2014).

51. See "N. K. Hacked Government Bigwigs," *Korea Herald* (March 7, 2016).

52. See Ju-min Park, "South Korea Group Launches Anti-North Leaflets amid Threats from Pyongyang," *Reuters* (October 25, 2014).

53. See Lankov, "Changing North Korea"; and Jieun Baek, *North Korea's Hidden Revolution: How the Information Underground Is Transforming a Closed Society* (New Haven, CT: Yale University Press, 2015).

54. Following the cyberattacks, suspected North Korean agents also delivered emails which vaguely threatened physical attacks against theaters that screened the film. See Tatiana Siegel, "Sony Hack: New Leaked Docs Reveal Michael Lynton's Email Inbox," *Hollywood Reporter* (December 16, 2016).

55. Chang Jae soon, "Obama Vows to 'Respond Proportionally' to Sony Hack Blamed on N. Korea," *Yonhap News Agency* (December 20, 2014).

56. The newspaper had published satirical images of the prophet Muhammad that offended some religious sensibilities.

57. Brent Lang and Ted Johnson, "Fear and Censorship: Paris, Sony Attacks Put Creative Freedoms under Fire," *Variety* (January 7, 2015).

58. Barack Obama, "Executive Order 13687 – Imposing Additional Sanctions With Respect to North Korea" (January 2, 2015), published online by Gerhard Peters and John T. Woolley, *The American Presidency Project*, http://www.presidency.ucsb.edu/ws/?pid=108103.

59. See Michael Daniel, "Our Latest Tool to Combat Cyber Attacks: What You Need to Know," *The White House* (April 1, 2015), https://obamawhitehouse.archives.gov/blog/2015/04/01/our-latest-tool-combat-cyber-attacks-what-you-need-know.

60. Some American officials denied that their country caused the interruption of North Korea's Internet. Others, however, affirmed this. See Chris Strohm, "North Korea Web Outage Response to Sony Hack, Lawmaker Says," *Bloomberg* (March 17, 2015).

61. See Roger Hurwitz, "Keeping Cool: Steps for Avoiding Conflict and Escalation in Cyberspace," *Georgetown Journal of International Affairs* (July 2015), pp. 17–23.

62. Quoted in Stanhope, "How Bad is the North Korean Cyber Threat?" The original source language is available here: http://nk.joins.com/news/view.asp?aid=12640100.

63. See David E. Sanger and William J. Broad, "Trump Inherits a Secret Cyberwar Against North Korean Missiles," *The New York Times* (March 4, 2017). On active defense, see Chapter 9.

6 First-Order Cyber Revolution: Pressures from Outside the States System

1. On the costs of mounting the Stuxnet operation, see Rebecca Slayton, "What Is the Cyber Offense-Defense Balance? Conceptions, Causes, and Assessment," *International Security*, Vol. 41, No. 3 (Winter 2016/2017), pp. 72–109.

2. Benjamin Fox, "Who Governs the Online World?" *EU Observer* (December 26, 2014).

3. See Jack Goldsmith and Tim Wu, *Who Controls the Internet? Illusions of a Borderless World* (New York: Oxford University Press, 2006).
4. Lawrence Lessig, *Code* (New York: Basic Books, 1999), p. 298.
5. See for instance Ronald Deibert, John Palfrey, Rafal Rohozinski, and Jonathan Zittrain, *Contested: Security, Identity, and Resistance in Asian Cyberspace* (Cambridge, MA: MIT Press, 2011).
6. Kenneth N. Waltz, *Theory of International Politics* (New York: McGraw-Hill, 1979), pp. 93–94.
7. See Robert O. Keohane, *After Hegemony: Cooperation and Discord in the World Political Economy* (Princeton, N.J.: Princeton University Press, 1984); and Lisa L. Martin, "Neoliberalism," in Tim Dunne, Milya Kurki, and Steve Smith, eds., *International Relations Theories: Discipline and Diversity* (Oxford: Oxford University Press, 2007).
8. See Hedley Bull, *The Anarchical Society: A Study of Order in World Politics*, second edition (London: Macmillan, 1995).
9. See Alexander Wendt, *Social Theory of International Politics* (Cambridge: Cambridge University Press, 1999); and Christian Reus-Smit, *The Moral Purpose of the State: Culture, Social Identity, and Institutional Rationality in International Relations* (Princeton, N.J.: Princeton University Press, 1999).
10. David A. Lake, "The State and International Relations," in Christian Reus-Smit and Duncan Snidal, eds., *The Oxford Handbook of International Relations* (Oxford: Oxford University Press, 2015), p. 2.
11. Ronald Rogowski, "Institutions as Constraints on Strategic Choice," in David A. Lake and Richard Powell, eds., *Strategic Choice and International Relations* (Princeton, N.J.: Princeton University Press, 1999).
12. See Arnold Wolfers, "'National Security' as an Ambiguous Symbol," *Political Science Quarterly*, Vol. 67 (December 1952), pp. 481–502. A countervailing view is found in Steven D. Krasner, *Defending the National Interest: Raw Materials Investments and US Foreign Policy* (Princeton, N.J.: Princeton University Press, 1978).
13. Mill himself never used this term, although it appeared in reaction to his writings. See John Stuart Mill, *Essays on Some Unsettled Questions of Political Economy*, second edition (London: Longmans, 1874), Essay 5; and Joseph Persky, "The Ethology of *Homo Economicus*," *Journal of Economic Perspectives*, Vol. 9, No. 2 (Spring 1995), p. 222.
14. Khan has claimed in his defense that Pakistan's Prime Minister, Benazir Bhutto, instructed him to exchange technological secrets with North Korea. See Mark Fitzpatrick, "Dr. A. Q. Khan and the Rise and Fall of Proliferation Networks," *Nuclear Black Markets* (London: International Institute for Strategic Studies, 2007).
15. John Mueller, "Simplicity and the Spook: Terrorism and the Dynamics of Threat Exaggeration," *International Studies Perspectives* (2005), p. 220.
16. Even some prominent social theorists are content with keeping the lid closed. Alexander Wendt, for instance, regards "the constitution of states as 'unitary actors,' which is the starting point for theorizing about the international system." Alexander Wendt, *Social Theory of International Politics* (Cambridge: Cambridge University Press, 1999), p. 195.
17. Christopher Rhoads and Farnaz Fassihi, "Iran Vows to Unplug the Internet," *Wall Street Journal* (May 28, 2011).
18. See Saeed Kamali Dehghan, "Iran Clamps Down on Internet Use," *The Guardian* (January 5, 2012).
19. On the high costs of mounting a sophisticated cyberattack such as the Stuxnet operation, see for example Jon Lindsay, "Stuxnet and the Limits of Cyber Warfare," *Security Studies*, Vol. 22, No. 3 (2013), pp. 365–404.
20. For a discussion of this topic, see Joseph S. Nye, Jr., *The Future of Power* (New York: PublicAffairs, 2011), Chapter 5.
21. Ash Carter, "Drell Lecture: 'Rewiring the Pentagon: Charting a New Path on Innovation and Cybersecurity,'" Stanford University (April 23, 2015), http://archive.defense.gov/speeches/speech.aspx?SpeechID=1935.

22. Alexander Fitzpatrick, "Cybersecurity Experts Needed to Meet Growing Demand," *Washington Post* (May 29, 2012).

23. For a discussion of nuclear weapons' programs and the possession of nuclear weapons, see Dong-Joon Jo and Erik Gartzke, "Determinants of Nuclear Weapons Proliferation," *Journal of Conflict Resolution*, Vol. 51, No. 1 (February 2007), pp. 167–94.

24. See Matthew Kroenig, "Importing the Bomb: Sensitive Nuclear Assistance and Nuclear Proliferation," *Journal of Conflict Resolution*, Vol. 53, No. 2 (April 2009), p. 164; and Donald MacKenzie and Graham Spinardi, "Tacit Knowledge, Weapons Design, and the Uninvention of Nuclear Weapons," *American Journal of Sociology*, Vol. 100 (1995), pp. 44–99.

25. David E. Sanger, *Confront and Conceal: Obama's Secret Wars and Surprising Use of American Power* (New York: Crown, 2012), p. 235.

26. "Stuxnet Clone 'Duqu': The Hydrogen Bomb of Cyberwarfare?" *Fox News* (October 19, 2011),http://www.foxnews.com/tech/2011/10/19/stuxnet-clone-duqu-hydrogen-bomb-cyberwarfare.

27. Melissa E. Hathaway, "Leadership and Responsibility for Cybersecurity," *Georgetown Journal of International Affairs* (2012), p. 77. Similarly, a recent NATO report expressed alarm at the extent of proliferation of destructive cyber artifacts such as Stuxnet. See Melissa E Hathaway and Alexander Klimburg, "Preliminary Considerations: On National Cyber Security," in Alexander Klimburg, ed., *National Cyber Security Framework Manual* (Tallinn: NATO CCD-COE, 2012), p. 7.

28. Author interview with a senior computer security expert (anonymous).

29. The use of compromised digital certificates is a prized technique of malicious actors because some antivirus programs automatically consider files signed by the certificates to be secure. See Andrey Ladikov, "Why You Shouldn't Completely Trust Files Signed with Digital Certificates," *Securelist* (January 29, 2015), https://securelist.com/blog/security-policies/68593/why-you-shouldnt-completely-trust-files-signed-with-digital-certificates/.

30. Author interview with Ralph Langner (March 20, 2013).

31. See Nicholas Falliere, Liam O. Murchu, and Eric Chien, "W32.Stuxnet Dossier," ver. 1.4 (Cupertino, CA: Symantec, February 2011).

32. This discussion refers to the second variant of Stuxnet; that is, not the variant that appeared in 2007, but the more sophisticated one that struck the Natanz plant in 2009. See Ralph Langner, "Stuxnet's Secret Twin," *Foreign Policy* (November 19, 2013).

33. Ralph Langner, *Stuxnet Logbook* (September 17, 2010), http://www.langner.com/en/2010/09/16/stuxnet-logbook-sep–16–2010–1200-hours-mesz/.

34. See Ralph Langner, "Stuxnet and the Hacker Nonsense," Langner.com (blog) (February 14, 2011), http://www.langner.com/en/2011/02/14/stuxnet-and-the-hacker-nonsense.

35. On the life cycle of customized code, see Max Smeets, "A Matter of Time: On the Transitory Nature of Cyberweapons," *Journal of Strategic Studies* (February 2017), pp. 1–28.

36. Quoted in Tom Simonite, "Stuxnet Tricks Copied by Computer Criminals," *Technology Review* (September 19, 2012).

37. The ensuing discussion of cyber incidents is not definitive – nor could it be, because much of the empirical record about the cases remains inaccessible to researchers. Rather, the purpose of the analysis is to illustrate conceptual distinctions and broad trends.

38. Symantec, *W32.Duqu: The Precursor to the Next Stuxnet*, ver. 1.4 (November 23, 2011), p. 1. See also Kim Zetter, "Son of Stuxnet Found in the Wild on Systems in Europe," *Wired* (October 18, 2011).

39. An updated and more advanced version, dubbed "Duqu 2.0," appeared in 2015. See Kaspersky Lab's Global Research and Analysis Team, "The Mystery of Duqu 2.0: A Sophisticated Cyberespionage Actor Returns," *Securelist* (June 10, 2015), https://securelist.com/blog/research/70504/the-mystery-of-duqu–2–0-a-sophisticated-cyberespionage-actorreturns/.

40. Laboratory of Cryptography and Systems Security, *Duqu: A Stuxnet-Like Malware Found in the Wild* (Budapest: Budapest University of Technology and Economics, October 14, 2011), p. 2.

41. Lee Ferran, "Son of Stuxnet? Researchers Warn of Coming Cyber Attack," *ABC News* (October 18, 2011), http://abcnews.go.com/Blotter/stuxnet-returns-duqu-researchers-warn-similar-cyber-attack/story?id=14763854.

42. See "Stuxnet Clone 'Duqu'," *Fox News*.

43. Guillherme Venere and Peter Szor, "The Day of the Golden Jackal – The Next Tale in the Stuxnet Files: Duqu Updated" (McAfee Labs, October 18, 2011), http://blogs.mcafee.com/mcafee-labs/the-day-of-the-golden-jackal-%E2%80%93-further-tales-of-the-stuxnet-files.

44. See Darren Pauli, "Iran CERT Fingers Flame for Oil Refinery Attacks," *SC Magazine* (May 30, 2012), http://www.scmagazine.com.au/Tools/Print.aspx?CIID=302718.

45. "Identification of a New Targeted Cyber-Attack," *MAHER* (May 28, 2012), http://www.webcitation.org/682bfkhaU.

46. Dan Goodin, "Discovery of New 'Zero-Day' Exploit Links Developers of Stuxnet, Flame," *Ars Technica* (June 11, 2012).

47. See Hathaway, "Leadership and Responsibility for Cybersecurity," p. 77.

48. According to some analysts, Flame's code was twenty times more complicated than Stuxnet's. See Kim Zetter, "Meet 'Flame,' The Massive Spy Malware Infiltrating Iranian Computers," *Wired* (May 28, 2012), http://www.wired.com/threatlevel/2012/05/flame/.

49. For a comparison of Flame with Stuxnet and Duqu, see *sKyWIper (a.k.a. Flame a.k.a. Flamer: A Complex Malware for Targeted Attacks* (Budapest: Laboratory of Cryptography and System Security, Budapest University of Technology and Economics, May 2012), http://www.crysys.hu/skywiper/skywiper.pdf.

50. Ibid., p. 7.

51. Ibid.

52. Ibid. Some Kaspersky researchers have even described Flame as a *predecessor* of Stuxnet. See Dan Goodin, "Discovery of New 'Zero-Day' Exploit Links Developers of Stuxnet, Flame." Some analysts suspect that three other operations feature the same command-and-control functionality as Flame. Little is known about these separate programs. The full scope of Flame's proliferation is therefore unclear. The research community has only scratched the surface of this case.

53. Nicole Perlroth, "In Cyberattack on Saudi Firm, U.S. Sees Iran Firing Back," *The New York Times* (October 23, 2012).

54. "Aramco Says Cyberattack Was Aimed at Production," *The New York Times* (December 9, 2012). Computer operations at the Qatari oil firm RasGas were also infected.

55. For technical details on Shamoon, see "The Shamoon Attacks," *Symantec Official Blog* (August 16, 2012), http://www.symantec.com/connect/blogs/shamoon-attacks.

56. See Charlie Osborne, "Kasperksy: Shamoon Malware Nothing More than 'Quick and Dirty'," *ZDNet* (September 14, 2012); see Dmitry Tarakanov, "Shamoon the Wiper: Further Details (Part II)," *Securelist* (September 11, 2012), https://securelist.com/blog/incidents/57784/shamoon-the-wiper-further-details-part-ii/.

57. Kaspersky Lab's Global Research and Analysis Team, "Shamoon the Wiper – Copycats at Work," *Securelist* (August 16, 2012), http://www.securelist.com/en/blog/208193786/Shamoon_the_Wiper_Copycats_at_Work. Wiper strains were also discovered in two other malware agents: "Disstrack" and "Narilam."

58. See Tarakanov, "Shamoon the Wiper."

59. See ibid.

60. See Christopher Bronk and Eneken Tikk-Ringas, "The Cyber Attack on Saudi Aramco," *Survival*, Vol. 33 (2013), pp. 81–96.

61. In the technical community, "script kiddies" is a colloquial, sometimes derogatory term for unsophisticated coders.

62. It is also possible that the Stuxnet worm itself was based on earlier code, the USB worm

"Fanny," which security researchers have also tied to Duqu and Flame. See Boldizsár Bencsáth, "Duqu, Flame, Gauss: Followers of Stuxnet," *RSA Conference Europe 2012*, http://www.rsaconference.com/writable/presentations/file_upload/br–208_bencsath. pdf. In this scenario, Stuxnet, Duqu, and Flame may have been "stepbrothers."

63. See Jamie Dettmer, "Digital Jihad: ISIS, Al Qaeda Seek a Cyber Caliphate to Launch Attacks on US," *Fox News* (September 14, 2014).

64. See Daniel Byman and Jeremy Shapiro, "Be Afraid. Be a Little Afraid: The Threat of Terrorism from Western Fighters in Syria and Iraq," Foreign Policy and Brookings, Policy Paper No. 34 (Washington, D.C.: Brookings, November 2014).

65. See Giles Hogben, ed., *Botnets: Detection, Measurement, Disinfection, and Defence* (Heraklion: European Network and Information Security Agency, 2011), p. 13.

66. Brian Proffitt, "How to Build a Botnet in 15 Minutes," *Readwrite* (July 31, 2013).

67. See Brian Krebs, "Stress-Testing the Booter Services, Financially," *KrebsonSecurity.com* (August 15, 2016).

68. Some botnets, however, have been used to conduct governmental espionage – for example, GOZ, a botnet that issued detailed queries to computers in Georgia and Turkey in search of classified documents. See Michael Sandee, *GameOver Zeus: Background on the Badguys and the Backends* (Delft: Fox-IT, July 2015), p. 9.

69. Some forms of sophisticated espionage code, though, began their life as botnet components – for instance, BlackEnergy, a malware package that targeted Ukrainian government institutions in 2014. See *BlackEnergy and Quedagh: The Convergence of Crimeware and APT Attacks*, White Paper (Helsinki: F-Secure, 2014).

70. "US Warns Cyber-Attacks Will Increase," *Financial Times* (May 18, 2007).

71. See Noah Shachtman, "Kremlin Kids: We Launched the Estonian Cyber War," *Wired* (March 11, 2009).

72. U.S. Cyber Consequences Unit (US-CCU), *Overview by the US-CCU of the Cyber Campaign against Georgia in August 2008*, Special Report, US-CCU (August 2009), www. registan.net/wp-content/uploads/2009/08/US-CCU-Georgia-Cyber-Campaign-Overview.pdf, p. 3.

73. Ibid.

74. According to the U.S. Cyber Consequences Unit, the criminal groups participating in the DDoS attacks "wanted to claim credit" for them. See ibid.

75. James R. Clapper and Charlie Rose, "A Conversation with James Clapper," *Council on Foreign Relations* (October 25, 2016), http://www.cfr.org/intelligence/conversation-james-clapper/p38426.

76. Flashpoint investigators dismissed with moderate confidence the claims of authorship by self-styled Russian state actor "Jester" and by supporters of Wikileaks. See Allison Nixon, John Costello, and Zach Wikholm, "An After-Action Analysis of the Mirai Botnet Attacks on Dyn," *Flashpoint* (October 25, 2016), https://www.flashpoint-intel. com/action-analysis-mirai-botnet-attacks-dyn/.

77. Clapper and Rose, "A Conversation with James Clapper."

78. The meaning of the notion is, in fact, ambiguous and contested. For a more detailed discussion, see Chapter 9.

79. The fifth largest market, the Shanghai Stock Exchange, is a non-profit organization under the direct supervision of the China Securities Regulatory Commission, which is an institution of the State Council – hence it is not privately operated.

80. The two exceptions are Paraguana Refining Centre, which belongs to the Venezuelan state oil firm PDVSA; and the Ras Tanura Refinery, which is the property of the publicly owned firm Saudi Aramco. See "Top 10 Large Oil Refineries," *HydrocarbonsTechnology.com* (September 30, 2013).

81. The Pentagon's Defense Advanced Research Projects Agency (DARPA) supported but did not drive the protocol transition. See John Naughton, *A Brief History of the Future: The Origins of the Internet* (London: Weidenfeld and Nicolson, 1999), pp. 166–67; and Vint Cerf, "How the Internet Came to Be," in Bernard Adoba, ed., *The Online User's Encyclopedia* (Boston, MA: Addison-Wesley, 1993).

82. Jack Goldsmith, "WCIT–12: An Opinionated Primer and Hysteria-Debunker," *Lawfare (blog)* (November 30, 2012).

83. Jack Goldsmith and Tim Wu, *Who Controls the Internet? Illusions of a Borderless World* (Oxford: Oxford University Press, 2006).

84. An early example of this trend is the establishment, in 1935, of the U.S. Social Security Administration under President Franklin D. Roosevelt's "New Deal." The SSA collected large volumes of citizen data to support innovative social programs. See Martha Derthick, *Agency under Duress: The Social Security Administration in American Government* (Washington, D.C.: The Brookings Institution, 1990).

85. See Tim Cook, "A Message to Our Customers," *Apple.com* (February 16, 2016).

86. Some reports stated that the Israeli company Cellebrite provided this service. See Ellen Nakashima, "FBI Paid Professional Hackers One-Time Fee to Crack San Bernardino iPhone," *Washington Post* (April 12, 2016).

87. See Iain Thomson, "Russia 'Hired Botnets' for Estonia Cyber-War," *IT News* (June 1, 2007).

88. Author interview with Jaak Aaviksoo (February 17, 2017). Or as the editor of the nation's largest daily newspaper put it at the time, "The cyber-attacks are from Russia. There is no question. It's political." Ian Traynor, "Russia Accused of Unleashing Cyberwar to Disable Estonia," *The Guardian* (May 17, 2007). The head of Estonia's CERT unit, however, publicly questioned claims that the Russian government launched the attacks. See Bill Brenner, "Experts Doubt Russian Government Launched DDoS Attacks," *Tech Target* (May 2007).

89. See "Estonia's Cyber Attacks: World's First Virtual Attack Against Nation State," Wikileaks Cable No. 07TALLINN366_a. This view was corroborated by Aaviksoo in an author interview (February 17, 2017).

90. A classified report by the U.S. National Security Agency concluded that Nashi activists participated in the attacks. See Nicole Perlroth, "Online Security Experts Link More Breaches to Russian Government," *The New York Times* (October 28, 2014).

91. "Estonia Has Evidence of Kremlin Involvement in Cyber Attacks," *RIA Novosti* (June 9, 2007).

92. Author interview with Marina Kaljurand (January 19, 2017).

93. Kaljurand also raised the possibility of direct or indirect support by Moscow. "We think that there were hacktivists involved in the attacks who wanted to express discontent" with the removal of the "Bronze soldier." "But they were not the only ones. Russia is not a country where people feel free to massively protest or express their views. So this was not a people's movement. It was an organized movement. The attacks had to be financed and orchestrated by the Kremlin."

94. Russian computer security expert Eugene Kaspersky faulted "angry Russian spammers" for the attacks. See "Kasperski: Spammers, not the Kremlin behind Anti-Estonian Cyber-Attacks," BBN (June 28, 2011). See also Noah Shachtman, "Kremlin Kids: We Launched the Estonian Cyber War," *Wired* (March 11, 2009).

95. Author interview with Christian-Marc Liflländer (August 28, 2016).

96. Author interview with Kaljurand.

97. See Cyrus Farivar, "A Brief Examination of Media Coverage of Cyberattacks (2007–Present)," in Christian Czosseck and Kenneth Geers, *The Virtual Battlefield: Perspectives on Cyber Warfare* (Amsterdam: IOS Press, 2009), p. 189.

98. UK House of Commons Parliament Defence Committee, *Third Report Towards the next Defence and Security Review: Part Two-NATO*, 4, The UK and NATO's Capacity to Respond (July 22, 2014).

99. Author interview with Liflländer. The absence of clear attribution of the attacks was another reason not to invoke the clauses: there was no one to invoke the clauses against. See the discussion of deterrence in Chapter 7.

100. Author interview with Harri Tiido (February 21, 2017).

101. Author interview with Sorin Ducaru (January 20, 2017).

102. According to Tiido, the 2007 crisis prompted the production of the so-called Tallinn

Manual, an extensive study of the applicability of international law in the cyber domain. See Michael N. Schmitt, ed., *Tallinn Manual on the International Law Applicable to Cyber Warfare* (Cambridge: Cambridge University Press, 2013).

103. Author interview with Lifländer.
104. See Kevin Poulsen, "'Cyberwar' and Estonia's Panic Attack," *Wired* (August 22, 2007).
105. Author interview with Lifländer.
106. Ibid.
107. Ibid.
108. Ibid.
109. Cory Bennett, "Kremlin's Ties to Russian Cyber Gangs Sow US Concerns," *The Hill* (October 11, 2015). On Russia's use of proxies, see Chapter 8.
110. Eric Holder, "Attorney General Eric Holder Speaks at the Press Conference Announcing U.S. Charges Against Five Chinese Military Hackers for Cyber Espionage," Washington, D.C. (May 19, 2014).
111. "Papers Link Top China University to Army 'Hacking' Unit," *Phys.org* (March 24, 2013). See also Melanie Lee, "Top China College in Focus with Ties to Army's Cyber-Spying Unit," *Reuters* (March 24, 2013). On China's use of private agents in cyber exploitation operations, see Robert Sheldon and Joe McReynolds, "Civil-Military Integration and Cybersecurity: A Study of Chinese Information Warfare Militias," in Jon R. Lindsay, Tai Ming Cheung, and Derek S. Reveron, eds., *China and Cybersecurity: Espionage, Strategy, and Politics in the Digital Domain* (New York: Oxford University Press, 2015).
112. See Richard B. Andres, "Cyber-Gang Warfare: State-Sponsored Militias Are Coming to a Server Near You," *Foreign Policy* (February 11, 2013).
113. One recent simulation of this kind, "Cyber Guard," gathered about 1,000 military and civilian representatives. See Andrew Tilghman, *Military Times* (June 21, 2016).
114. See Bruce Schneier, "Someone Is Learning How to Take Down the Internet," *Lawfare* (September 13, 2016).
115. See "Wimbledon Case," Permanent Court of International Justice, A1 (1923).
116. Author interview with a senior official in the British Cabinet Office (February 17, 2017).

7 The Deterrence Puzzle: Doctrinal Problems and Remedies

1. A preeminent case in support of the notion of limited nuclear war – a bold idea for its times – appeared in Henry A. Kissinger, *Nuclear Weapons and Foreign Policy* (New York: Council on Foreign Relations, 1957). Apart from the unknown and possibly uncontrollable risks of escalation from limited to general nuclear war, critics of limited war have also pointed out that even a small number of nuclear explosions could devastate the Earth's climate, producing as many fatalities as the Second World War. The focus of the study was on smoke emissions of incinerated buildings. See Rutgers, the State University of New Jersey, "Regional Nuclear War Could Devastate Global Climate," *Science Daily* (December 11, 2016), www.sciencedaily.com/releases/2006/12/061211090729.htm. The concept of limited nuclear war never disappeared entirely from military planning, however. It featured, for example, in the 1983 war game titled "Proud Prophet," which enacted a scenario of "limited de-escalatory" nuclear strikes. See Geoff Wilson and Will Saetren, "Quite Possibly the Dumbest Military Concept Ever: A 'Limited' Nuclear War," *The National Interest* (May 27, 2016), http://nationalinterest.org/blog/the-buzz/quite-possibly-the-dumbest-military-concept-ever-limited–16394?page=show.
2. Author interview with a senior official in the British Cabinet Office (February 17, 2017).
3. Ibid.
4. George Osborne, "Chancellor's Speech to GCHQ on Cyber Security," *HM Treasury*

(November 17, 2015), https://www.gov.uk/government/speeches/chancellors-speech-to-gchq-on-cyber-security.

5. An alternative explanation for the absence of cyberwar is the belief that it will not advance the attacker's interests even in the absence of retaliation.

6. Raymond Aron, *Penser la guerre, Clausewitz*, Vol. 2, *L'âge planétaire* (Paris: Gallimard, 1976), pp. 162–63, translated in Stanley Hoffmann, *Janus and Minerva: Essays in the Theory and Practice of International Politics* (London: Westview Press, 1987), p. 60.

7. See, for instance, Joseph S. Nye, Jr., "Nuclear Lessons for Cyber Security?" *Strategic Studies Quarterly* (Winter 2011), pp. 18–38.

8. See Bernard Brodie, "The Anatomy of Deterrence," in Bernard Brodie, ed., *Strategy in the Missile Age* (Princeton, N.J.: Princeton University Press, 1958); Bruce M. Russett, "The Calculus of Deterrence," *Journal of Conflict Resolution*, Vol. 7, No. 2 (June 1963), pp. 97–109; Albert Wohlstetter, "The Delicate Balance of Terror," in Henry A. Kissinger, ed., *Problems of National Strategy: A Book of Readings* (New York: Praeger, 1965); and Patrick M. Morgan, *Deterrence* (Beverly Hills, CA: Sage, 1977).

9. For a discussion of these techniques, see Glenn H. Snyder, *Deterrence and Defense* (Princeton, N.J.: Princeton University Press, 1961); Robert Jervis, *The Meaning of the Nuclear Revolution: Statecraft and the Prospect of Armageddon* (Ithaca, N.Y.: Cornell University Press, 1989), p. 10; and Richard J. Harknett, "The Logic of Conventional Deterrence and the End of the Cold War," *Security Studies*, Vol. 4, No. 1 (1994), pp. 86–114.

10. For a discussion of some of these problems, see, for example, Kenneth Geers, "The Challenge of Cyber Attack Deterrence," *Computer Law and Security Review*, Vol. 26, No. 3 (May 2010), pp. 298–303; Lucas Kello, "The Virtual Weapon: Dilemmas and Future Scenarios," *Politique étrangere*, Vol. 79, No. 4 (Winter 2014/2015), pp, 139–150; and Joseph S. Nye, Jr., "Deterrence and Dissuasion in Cyberspace," *International Security*, Vol. 41, No. 3 (Winter 2016/2017), pp. 44–71.

11. Some new forms of malware emit acoustic signals that can manipulate data in air-gapped devices. So far, however, the practical applications of this intrusion method are limited by the requirement that the targeted system be previously infected by malware. See Mordechai Guri, Yosef Solewicz, Andrey Daidakulov, and Yuval Elovici, "DiskFiltration: Data Exfiltration from Speakerless Air-Gapped Computers via Covert Hard Drive Noise," *arXiv.org* (August 11, 2016).

12. See David E. Sanger, *Confront and Conceal: Obama's Secret Wars and Surprising Use of American Power* (New York: Crown, 2012), Chapter 8.

13. The early nuclear era witnessed a similar tendency in strategic thinking toward punishment. See Bernard Brodie, *The Absolute Weapon* (New York: Harcourt, 1946); and Robert Powell, *Nuclear Deterrence Theory: The Search for Credibility* (Cambridge: Cambridge University Press, 1990).

14. See Chapter 4 in this volume; and the Defense Science Board of the Department of Defense, *Resilient Military Systems and the Advanced Cyber Threat* (Washington, D.C., January 2013).

15. See Madeleine Albright (chairwoman), *NATO 2020: Assured Security; Dynamic Engagement* (Brussels: NATO Public Diplomacy Division, May 17, 2010). NATO's formal designation of cyberspace as an "operational domain" of the alliance in 2016 gives credence to this interpretation.

16. Author interview with Sorin Ducaru (January 20, 2017).

17. See Patrick M. Morgan, "Applicability of Traditional Deterrence Concepts and Theory to the Cyber Realm," in *Proceedings of a Workshop on Deterring Cyberattacks: Informing Strategies and Developing Options for U.S. Policy* (Washington, D.C.: National Academies Press, 2010), p. 56.

18. Nick Harvey (MP), "Meeting the Cyber Challenge," speech delivered at Chatham House (November 9, 2010).

19. On the problem of attribution, see David D. Clark and Susan Landau, "Untangling Attribution," in *Proceedings of a Workshop on Deterring Cyberattacks*, pp. 25–40.

20. Author interview with Harri Tiido (February 17, 2017).
21. Nye labels this logic deterrence by entanglement. See Nye, "Deterrence and Dissuasion in Cyberspace," p. 59.
22. See Charles Smith, "Cyber War against Iraq," *Newsmax* (March 12, 2003).
23. See James A. Lewis, *A Note on the Laws of War in Cyberspace* (Washington, D.C.: Center for Strategic and International Studies, April 2010).
24. On problems of escalatory ambiguity, see Martin C. Libicki, *Crisis and Escalation in Cyberspace* (Santa Monica, CA: RAND, 2012), Chapter 4.
25. See Herman Kahn, *On Escalation: Metaphors and Scenarios* (London: Pall Mall Press, 1965).
26. David E. Sanger, David Barboza, and Nicole Perlroth, "Chinese Army Unit Is Seen as Tied to Hacking Against U.S.," *The New York Times* (February 18, 2013).
27. See Thomas C. Schelling, *The Strategy of Conflict* (Cambridge, MA: Harvard University Press, 1960).
28. See François Lenoir, "Massive Cyber Attack Could Trigger NATO Response: Stoltenberg," *Reuters* (June 16, 2016).
29. Unofficial reports have specified Article 5 scenarios, but these are not official policy statements.
30. See *Task Force Report: Resilient Military Systems and the Advanced Cyber Threat* (Washington, D.C.: Department of Defense Science Board, January 2013).
31. Some former officials have called for such a limit. See comments by Richard A. Clarke and Steven Andreasen, "Cyberwar's Threat Does Not Justify a New Policy of Nuclear Deterrence," *Washington Post* (June 14, 2013).
32. Author interview with Ducaru.
33. See Lucas Kello, "The Virtual Weapon: Dilemmas and Future Scenarios," *Politique étrangère*, Vol. 79, No. 4 (Winter 2014/2015), p. 146; and Jon R. Lindsay, "Tipping the Scales: The Attribution Problem and the Feasibility of Deterrence against Cyberattack," *Journal of Cybersecurity*, Vol. 1, No. 1 (2015), p. 59.
34. See Michael S. Schmidt, "New Interest in Hacking as Threat to Security," *The New York Times* (March 13, 2012).
35. Ken Dilanian, "Intelligence Chief Sees 'Permissive Environment' for Cyberattacks against US Interests," *US News* (September 10, 2015).
36. Jack Goldsmith, "Disconcerting U.S. Cyber Deterrence Troubles Continue," *Lawfare* (September 15, 2015).
37. Jim Michaels, "Pentagon Seeking 'Rules of Engagement' for Cyber-War," *USA Today* (April 4, 2013).
38. Josh Rogin, "NSA Chief: Cybercrime Constitutes the 'Greatest Transfer of Wealth in History'," *Foreign Policy* (July 9, 2012).
39. See "Intelligence Chief: Little Penalty for Cyberattacks," *Associated Press* (September 10, 2015).
40. Another approach to resolving deterrence failures at the middle of the spectrum is by neutralizing threats *before* the opponent realizes them – that is, active defense. For a discussion of the meaning of active defense, see Chapter 9.
41. Specifically, Obama was weighing in on Chinese espionage. See Natash Bertrand, "China Caught the US 'With Our Pants Down' – and the Obama Administration is Struggling to Respond," *Business Insider* (August 4, 2015).
42. Interview with Ducaru.
43. Uri Tor, "'Cumulative Deterrence' as a New Paradigm for Cyber Deterrence," *Journal of Strategic Studies*, Vol. 40, No. 1 (2017), pp. 92–117.
44. Richard Harknett, for instance, has claimed that "deterrence is the wrong framework for explaining cyber aggression and for formulating policy." Instead, he advocates a logic of "offense persistence" that comprises better defense – both passive and active – in an environment of constant contact among adversaries. See Richard J. Harknett, "Toward a Logic of Offensive Persistence," *International Security* (2017).

8 Russia and Cyberspace: Manifestations of the Revolution

1. The thesis of the "end of history" stipulated the lasting and universal triumph of liberal democratic ideals following the collapse of Communism in 1989. See Francis Fukuyama, *The End of History and the Last Man* (New York: The Free Press, 1992).
2. See Benjamin Elgin, "Network Security Breaches Plague NASA," *Bloomberg* (November 20, 2008).
3. Western academic institutions are a common target of Chinese state hackers searching for intellectual and commercial prizes. According to former NSA security contractor Edward Snowden, the NSA hacks Chinese universities for unspecified purposes. See Adam Segal, "The Code Not Taken: China, the United States, and the Future of Cyber Espionage," *Bulletin of the Atomic Scientists*, Vol. 69, No. 5 (2013), pp. 38–45; and Jon R. Lindsay, "The Impact of China on Cybersecurity: Fiction and Friction," *International Security*, Vol. 39, No. 3 (Winter 2014–15), pp. 7–47.
4. John Arquilla and David Ronfeldt, *Cyberwar is Coming!* (Santa Monica, CA: RAND, 1993). Others, too, saw the signs. A critique praising another book by the same authors remarked: "Arquilla and Ronfeldt are a rare breed: strategic thinkers of the information age. In *Networks and Netwars* they grasp an emerging reality still lost on those preoccupied with the geostrategic balance of power: War in the future will be waged by leaderless networks that can come together quickly out of cyberspace to 'swarm' an opponent. Like few others, they recognize that the flipside of the celebrated global civil society born of the Internet is the 'uncivil society' of terrorists and criminals who will use the same means to spread havoc and instability." Comments by Nathan Gardels in John Arquilla and David Ronfeldt, *Networks and Netwars: The Future of Terror, Crime, and Militancy* (Santa Monica, CA: RAND, 2001).
5. This comparison, it is important to note, implies no equivalence in destructive power between cyber and nuclear weapons; it merely suggests that the two episodes had a similarly profound effect in their respective eras in launching searching discussions about the implications of a new technology for conflict prevention, crisis stability, and the defense against offensively superior arms.
6. Adam Segal identifies the period from June 2012 to June 2013 as "Year Zero" in the "battle over cyberspace." He referred to the reassertion of state control over Internet data flows (i.e. information security) in various nations. The year 2007 is a more relevant starting point for a book about the analysis of international cyber issues because it marked the beginning of the era of conflict *through* cyberspace and its associated strategy and policy debates. See Adam Segal, *The Hacked World Order: How Nations Fight, Trade, and Manipulate in the Digital Age* (New York: Council on Foreign Relations, 2016), p. 1.
7. Although this work generally eschews the use of the words "war" and "warfare" in labeling offensive activity that falls short of their traditional criteria (e.g. significant physical violence and loss of life), the label "information warfare" is appropriate because it has a long history in discussions about Russian security doctrine.
8. See Adam B. Ulam, *Bolsheviks: The Intellectual, Personal and Political History of the Triumph of Communism in Russia* (New York: Macmillan, 1968), p. 392.
9. See Adam B. Ulam, *Stalin: The Man and His Era* (Boston, MA: Beacon, 1989), p. 234.
10. See ibid., pp. 414–15; and Aleksandr Orlov, *The Secret History of Stalin's Crimes* (New York: Jarrolds, 1953), p. 35.
11. See Ulam, *Stalin*, pp. 417–18, fn. 70. Among the other members of the first Politburo established in 1917 were Lenin, Stalin, Trotsky, Sokolnikov, and Bubnov. The latter three also succumbed to Stalin's Great Purge.
12. A more accurate and less offensive translation of this popular term is "useful fool." Often attributed to Lenin after his time, the term may in fact not be his. See William Safire, "On Language," *The New York Times* (April 12, 1987).
13. Black propaganda was overseen by the KGB's Service A; white and grey propaganda by the Ideology Department of the Soviet Communist Party. See Fletcher Schoen and Christopher J. Lamb, *Deception, Disinformation, and Strategic Communications:*

How One Interagency Group Made a Major Difference (Washington, D.C.: National Defense University Press, June 2012); and Steve Abrams, "Beyond Propaganda: Soviet Active Measures in Putin's Russia," *Connections: The Quarterly Journal*, Vol. 15, No. 1 (2016), p. 12.

14. KGB agents at Soviet embassies around the globe disseminated the U.S. National Security Council document, titled "Carter's Secret Plan to Keep Black Africans and Black Americans at Odds." See Schoen and Lamb, *Deception, Disinformation, and Strategic Communications*, p. 24; and J. Michael Waller, *Strategic Influence: Public Diplomacy, Counterpropaganda, and Political Warfare* (Washington, D.C.: Institute of World Politics Press, 2009), pp. 159–61.

15. See Tony Barber, "Russia's Dark Art of Disinformation," *The Financial Times* (September 16, 2016); and Thomas Boghardt, "Soviet Bloc Intelligence and Its AIDS Disinformation Campaign," *Studies in Intelligence*, Vol. 53, No. 4 (December 2009), pp. 1–24. On KGB disinformation campaigns generally, see Ladislav Bittman, *The KGB and Soviet Disinformation: An Insider's View* (Oxford: Pergamon, 1985); and Ion Mihai Pacepa and Ronald Rychlak, *Disinformation: Former Spy Chief Reveals Secret Strategies for Undermining Freedom, Attacking Religion, and Promoting Terrorism* (Washington, D.C.: WND Books, 2013).

16. Valeriy Gerasimov, "Ценность науки в предвидении" ["The Value of Science is in Foresight"], Военно-промышленный курьер (February 27, 2013), http://vpk-news. ru/sites/default/files/pdf/VPK_08_476.pdf. For an English translation and commentary, see "The 'Gerasimov Doctrine' and Russian Non-Linear Warpage," in https://inmoscowsshadows.wordpress.com/2014/07/06/the-gerasimov-doctrine-and-russian-non-linear-war/. See also Sergey Chekinov and Sergey A. Bogdanov, "The Nature and Content of a New-Generation War," *Military Thought*, No. 4 (2013).

17. See Jolanta Darczewska, *The Anatomy of Russian Information Warfare. The Crimean Operation: A Case Study* (Warsaw: Centre for Eastern Studies, May 2014).

18. Keir Giles, "Russia's 'New' Tools for Confronting the West: Continuity and Innovation in Moscow's Exercise of Power," Research Paper, Russia and Eurasia Programme, Chatham House (March 2016), p. 10. Gerasimov himself has pointed as evidence of this reality to the popular uprisings in the Arab world in 2011 and in Ukraine in 2014. See *A Primer on Modern Russian Unconventional Warfare, Ukraine 2013–14 (Unclassified version)* (Fort Bragg, N.C.: The United States Army Special Operations Command, 2015), p. 16.

19. See James Risen, "The C.I.A. in Iran – A Special Report; How a Plot Convulsed Iran in '53 (and in '79)," *The New York Times* (April 16, 2000).

20. See Adam Taylor, "Before 'Fake News' There Was Soviet 'Disinformation'," *Washington Post* (November 26, 2016).

21. See Andrei Soldatov and Irina Borogan, *The Red Web: The Struggle between Russia's Digital Dictators and the New Online Revolutionaries* (New York: PublicAffairs, 2015), p. 25.

22. One notable incident was the DDoS attack against liberal and independent websites during the 2011 Duma elections. See Hal Roberts and Bruce Etling, "Coordinated DDoS Attack During Russian Duma Elections," *Internet and Democracy Blog* (December 8, 2011), http://blogs.harvard.edu/idblog/2011/12/08/coordinated-ddos-attack-during-russian-duma-elections/.

23. See Samuel P. Huntington, *The Clash of Civilizations and the Remaking of World Order* (New York: Simon and Schuster, 1996).

24. Indeed, Huntington's conception of a thin basis of universal values among countries in different civilizations has affinities with Bull's "pluralist" notion of international society. See ibid., p. 54.

25. See Dina Newman, "Russian Nationalist Thinker Dugin Sees War with Ukraine," *BBC News* (July 10, 2014), http://www.bbc.co.uk/news/world-europe-28229785.

26. "Putin Deplores Collapse of USSR," BBC (April 25, 2005).

27. "The 'Gerasimov Doctrine' and Russian Non-Linear Warpage."

28. See James Sherr, "Ukraine and the Black Sea Region: The Russian Military Perspective," in Stephen Blank, ed., *The Russian Military in Contemporary Perspective* (Carlisle, PA: Strategic Studies Institute, U.S. Army War College, forthcoming).

29. Timothy L. Thomas, "Russia's Reflexive Control Theory and the Military," *Journal of Slavic Military Studies*, Vol. 17, No. 2 (2004), p. 237. See also Maria Snegovaya, "Executive Summary: Putin's Information Warfare in Ukraine: Soviet Origins of Russia's Hybrid Warfare," Institute for the Study of War (September 2015).

30. Sherr, "Ukraine and the Black Sea Region."

31. See Daisy Sindelar, "Inside Russia's Disinformation Campaign," *Defense One* (August 12, 2014); and Patrick Michael Duggan, "Strategic Development of Special Warfare in Cyberspace," *Joint Force Quarterly*, Vol. 79, No. 4 (October 2015).

32. Shaun Walker, "Salutin' Putin: Inside a Russian Troll House," *The Guardian* (April 2, 2015).

33. Sindelar, "Inside Russia's Disinformation Campaign."

34. For a review of Dugin's school of thought on information warfare, see *Little Green Men*, p. 16.

35. Officially, Clinton did not win the party's nomination until the Democratic National Convention selected her four days later, but by the time of the email leaks it was clear that Sanders would likely lose. Trump had obtained the Republican Party's nomination on July 19, 2016.

36. See "Background to 'Assessing Russian Activities and Intentions in Recent US Elections'." See also Adam Meyers, "Danger Close: Fancy Bear Tracking of Ukrainian Field Artillery Units," Crowdstrike Blog (December 22, 2016), https://www.crowdstrike.com/blog/danger-close-fancy-bear-tracking-ukrainian-field-artillery-units/; and Matt Flegenheimer, "Countering Trump, Bipartisan Voices Strongly Affirm Findings on Russian Hacking," *The New York Times* (January 5, 2017).

37. See Krishnadev Calamur, "NATO Shmato?," *The Atlantic* (July 21, 2016).

38. The deep cleavage within the Democratic Party pre-dated the hacking event. According to an *Economist*/YouGov poll conducted four months earlier, 55 percent of Sanders supporters would feel "dissatisfied" or "upset" if Clinton won the Democratic Party's nomination. The party nomination boosted Clinton's support within her party, but the cleavage persisted. In a survey the month after the Convention, about one-third of Sanders sympathizers still rejected her. See "*The Economist*/YouGov Poll," *YouGov UK* (March 10–12, 2016), https://d25d2506sfb94s.cloudfront.net/cumulus_uploads/document/055qdf83nv/econTabReport.pdf; and David Weigel, "Sanders Absolves Clinton on Hacked Emails, but Other Voices on the Left Are Angry," *Washington Post* (October 12, 2016); and Harry Enten, "About a Third of Bernie Sanders' Supporters Still Aren't Backing Hillary Clinton," *FiveThirtyEight* (August 8, 2016), http://fivethirtyeight.com/features/about-a-third-of-bernie-sanders-supporters-still-arent-backing-hillary-clinton/?ex_cid=538twitter.

39. See Sari Horwitz, "FBI Director James B. Comey Under Fire for His Controversial Decision on the Clinton Email Inquiry," *Washington Post* (October 29, 2016).

40. For his part, Trump dismissed this assessment as sore-losing bluster. See Harry Enten, "How Much Did Wikileaks Hurt Hillary Clinton?," *FiveThirtyEight* (December 23, 2016), https://fivethirtyeight.com/features/wikileaks-hillary-clinton/.

41. Sabrina Siddiqui, "Priebus and Manafort Seize on Wasserman Schultz DNC Resignation," *The Guardian* (July 25, 2017).

42. "Background to 'Assessing Russian Activities and Intentions in Recent US Elections': The Analytic Process and Cyber Incident Attribution," Report of the Director of National Intelligence (January 6, 2017).

43. See Lorenzo Franceschi-Bicchierai, "How Hackers Broke Into John Podesta and Colin Powell's Gmail Accounts," *Motherboard* (October 20, 2016), https://motherboard.vicecom/en_us/article/how-hackers-broke-into-john-podesta-and-colin-powells-gmail-accounts.

44. See Jeffrey Carr, "FBI/DHS Joint Analysis Report: A Fatally Flawed Effort," *Medium* (December 30, 2016), https://medium.com/@jeffreycarr/fbi-dhs-joint-analysis-report-a-fatally-flawed-effort-b6a98fafe2fa.

45. The origin of the Vermont power grid story was an anonymous source who spoke to the *Washington Post*. The incident was not an attack, because it did not involve a disruption of computer functions – merely the discovery of malware in a single computer. Nor was it an action directed against the national power grid, because the infected machine was not connected to the grid system of the affected Vermont company, Burlington Electrical Department. See Richard Chirgwin, "Russian 'Grid Attack' Turns Out to Be a Damp Squib," *The Register* (January 3, 2017).

46. Melissa Chan, "Julian Assange Says a '14-Year-Old Kid Could Have Hacked Podesta' Emails," *Time* (January 4, 2017).

47. Guccifer divulged some material on outlets such as Wordpress blog, Gaker, and DCLeaks. The DCLeaks website was established in June 2016 with the purpose of publishing leaks of emails belonging to prominent government and military figures in the United States. See 'Threat Connect Identifies DC Leaks as Another Russian-backed Influence Outlet,' *ThreatConnect* (August 12, 2016).

48. See Thomas Rid, "All Signs Point to Russia Being Behind the DNC Hack," *Motherboard* (July 25, 2017).

49. "Opening Statement by SASC Chairman John McCain at Hearing on Foreign Cyber Threats to the United States," Floor Statements, official webpage of U.S. Senator John McCain (January 5, 2017), https://www.mccain.senate.gov/public/index.cfm/floor-statements?ID=810C2B63–6714–4DF0-A337–5B46D9C6BBD9.

50. "Trump Questions Claims of Russian Hacking: 'I Know Things Others Don't'," *The Guardian* (January 1, 2017).

51. Elizabet Weise, "Tech Crowd Goes Wild for Trump's '400-Pound Hacker'," *USA Today* (September 27, 2016). Some security analysts and journalists also questioned Russia's authorship of the DNC hack. See, for example, Matt Taibbi, "Something About This Russia Story Stinks," *Rolling Stone* (December 30, 2016).

52. Confronted by the allegation that the Kremlin sought to help him win the election, the president-elect replied: "I think it's [the allegation] ridiculous ... No, I don't believe it at all." Elise Viebeck, "Trump Denies CIA Report that Russia Intervened to Help Him Win Election," *Washington Post* (December 11, 2016).

53. Ibid.

54. Polling data pointed to Clinton victory throughout much of the post-convention stage. See Vann R. Newkirk II, "What Went Wrong With the 2016 Polls?" *The Atlantic* (November 9, 2012).

55. The title of the Clinton video was "How 100% of the Clintons' 'Charity' Went to ... Themselves." The title of the Trump video was "Trump Will Not Be Permitted To Win" (that is, by the U.S. political establishment). For details on Russian disinformation activities during the campaign, see "Background to 'Assessing Russian Activities and Intentions in Recent US Elections'," pp. 3–4.

56. See "Background to 'Assessing Russian Activities and Intentions in Recent US Elections'."

57. Ibid.

58. See Evan Osnos, David Remnick, and Joshua Yaffa, "Trump, Putin, and the New Cold War," *The New Yorker* (March 6, 2017).

59. "Background to 'Assessing Russian Activities and Intentions in Recent US Elections'."

60. Lauren Gambino, "Obama Orders Sanctions against Russia in Response to US Election Interference," *The Guardian* (December 29, 2016).

61. Ibid.

9 Private Sector Active Defense: An Adequate Response to the Sovereignty Gap?

1. This is often the case: for example, the handlers of the Stuxnet worm that hit the Natanz nuclear facility in Iran in 2009 may have compromised the industrial controller several years earlier. See David E. Sanger, *Confront and Conceal: Obama's Secret Wars and Surprising Use of American Power* (New York: Crown, 2012), Chapter 8.

2. Author interview with a senior official in the British Cabinet Office (February 17, 2017).

3. "Chairman of the U.S. House Intelligence Committee Mike Rogers in Washington Post Live: Cybersecurity 2014," *Washington Post* (October 2, 2014).

4. See Riley C. Matlack, M. Riley, and J. Robertson, "The Company Securing Your Internet Has Close Ties to Russian Spies," *Bloomberg* (March 15, 2015).

5. Huawei describes itself as an employee-owned "collective," but some commentators have questioned its freedom from Chinese state control. See Richard McGregor, *The Party: The Secret World of China's Communist Rulers* (New York: HarperCollins, 2010); and M. Rogers and C. A. D. Ruppersberger, *Investigative Report on the U.S. National Security Issues Posed by Chinese Telecommunications Companies Huawei and ZTE*, U.S. House of Representatives 112th Congress, Permanent Select Committee on Intelligence (October 8, 2012).

6. See *Department of Defense Strategy for Operating in Cyberspace* (Washington, D.C.: U.S. Department of Defense, July 2011), p. 7.

7. See *Cyber Security Strategy, 2014–2017* (Tallinn: Ministry of Economic Affairs and Communications, 2014).

8. C. Green, "UK Becomes First Country to Disclose Plans for Cyber Attack Capability," *Information Age* (September 30, 2013).

9. Robert M. Lee, *The Sliding Scale of Cyber Security – A SANS Analyst Whitepaper* (Boston, MA: SANS Institute, 2015), pp. 9–11.

10. Honeypots consist of decoy data that the defender uses to lure an attacker to study and disrupt his methods. See Loras R. Even, *Honey Pot Systems Explained* (Boston, MA: SANS Institute, July 12, 2000). Sinkholes refer to a DNS computer server that produces false data to prevent the attacker from using the true domain name. See Guy Bruneau, *DNS Sinkhole* (Boston, MA: SANS Institute, August 7, 2010).

11. See David D. Clark and Susan Landau, "Untangling Attribution," *Harvard National Security Journal* (March 2011).

12. See, for instance, Alexander Klimburg and Jason Healey, "Strategic Goals and Stakeholders," in Alexander Klimburg, ed., *National Cyber Security Framework and Manual* (Tallinn: NATO Cooperative Cyber Defence Centre of Excellence, 2012), pp. 74–5 and 80; Tim Maurer and Robert Morgus, *Compilation of Existing Cybersecurity and Information Security Related Definitions* (New America, October 2012), p. 71; and Jay P. Kesan and Carol M. Hayes, "Mitigative Counterstriking: Self-Defense and Deterrence in Cyberspace," *Harvard Journal of Law and Technology*, Vol. 25, No. 2 (Spring 2012), p. 460.

13. There are debates about the requirements of "authorization." See *Searching and Seizing Computers and Obtaining Electronic Evidence in Criminal Investigations*, third edition (Washington, D.C.: Department of Justice Office of Legal Council, 2009).

14. It is unclear, however, whether *intentional* damage resulting from actions taken entirely *within* one's networks is lawful. See "Cyber-Surveillance Bill to Move Forward, Secretly" (Washington, D.C.: Center for Democracy and Technology, March 4, 2015).

15. One notable case is *Susan Clements Jeffrey vs. Absolute Software* involving a company that used beacon technology to capture explicit data from a computer the operator did not know was stolen. The court ruled against the company. See "Absolute Software Settles Lawsuit Over Nude Photos," *Forbes* (September 6, 2011).

16. See remarks by the Homeland Security Secretary, Janet Napolitano, in Joseph Menn, "Hacked Companies Fight Back with Controversial Steps," *Reuters* (June 18, 2012); and remarks by Chairman of the U.S. House Intelligence Committee Mike Rogers in "Washington Post Live: Cybersecurity 2014," *Washington Post* (October 2, 2014).

17. *Best Practices for Victim Response and Reporting of Cyber Incidents* (Washington, D.C.: Department of Justice, April 2015).

18. Michael S. Rogers, "Cyber Threats and Next-Generation Cyber Operations," Keynote Speech at the Annual Cybersecurity Technology Summit, AFCEA, Washington, D.C. (April 2, 2015).

19. Interview with John Lynch, *Steptoe Cyberlaw Podcast* (January 21, 2016).

20. Hannah Kuchler, "Cyber Insecurity: Hacking Back," *The Financial Times* (July 27, 2015).
21. See Tom Spring, "Spam Slayer: Bringing Spammers to Their Knees," *PCWorld* (July 18, 2008).
22. See Kim Zetter, "FBI vs. Coreflood Botnet: Round 1 Goes to the Feds," *Wired* (April 11, 2011).
23. See Brian Krebs, " 'Operation Tovar' Targets 'Gameover' ZeuS Botnet, CryptoLocker Scourge," *KrebsonSecurity* (June 2, 2014).
24. Kuchler, "Cyber Insecurity."
25. These consequences are positive from the perspective of private defenders and their parent governments; other players may not share this view.
26. The attackers activated the "Wiper" malware on 24 November; the FBI publicly attributed the attack to North Korea on 19 December. See "Update on Sony Investigation," Federal Bureau of Investigation (December 19, 2014), https://www.fbi.gov/news/pressrel/press-releases/update-on-sony-investigation.
27. See Peter W. Singer and Allan Friedman, *Cybersecurity and Cyberwar* (Oxford: Oxford University Press, 2014).
28. To share information derived from classified sources the U.S. government resorts to four selective commercial service providers: AT&T, CenturyLink, Lockheed Martin, and Verizon. See Andy Ozment, *DHS's Enhanced Cybersecurity Services Program Unveils New "Netflow" Service Offering* (Washington, S.C.: U.S. Department of Homeland Security, January 26, 2016), https://www.dhs.gov/blog/2016/01/26/dhs%E2%80%99s-enhanced-cybersecurity-services-program-unveils-new-%E2%80%9Cnetflow%E2%80%9D-service-offering.
29. Ron Nixon, "Homeland Security Dept. Struggles to Hire Staff to Combat Cyberattacks," *International New York Times* (April 6, 2016).
30. See Oliver Wright, "GCHQ's 'Spook First' Programme to Train Britain's Most Talented Tech Entrepreneurs," *The Independent* (January 1, 2015); and Jamie Collier, "Proxy Actors in the Cyber Domain" (unpublished paper).
31. See Christian Czosseck, Rain Ottis, and Anna-Maria Talihärm, "Estonia After the 2007 Cyber Attacks: Legal, Strategic and Organisational Changes in Cyber Security," in M. Warren, ed., *Case Studies in Information Warfare and Security* (Reading: Academic Conferences and Publishing International Limited, 2013).
32. See Lior Tabansky and Itzhak Ben Israel, *Striking with Bits? The IDF and Cyber-Warfare* (Cham: Springer, 2015).
33. See "National Guard to Stand Up 13 New Cyber Units in 23 States," *Army Times* (December 15, 2015).
34. See James Pattison, *The Morality of Private War: The Challenge of Private Military Companies and Security Companies* (Oxford: Oxford University Press, 2014); and A. Alexandra, D.-P. Baker, and M. Caparini, eds., *Private Military Companies: Ethics, Policies and Civil-Military Relations* (London: Routledge, 2008).
35. See Sari Horwitz, Shyamantha Asokan, and Julie Tate, "Trade in Surveillance Technology Raises Worries," *Washington Post* (December 1, 2011).
36. See Lillian Ablon, Martin C. Libicki, and Andrea A. Golay, *Markets for Cybercrime Tools and Stolen Data* (Santa Monica, CA: RAND, March 14, 2014).
37. See James Vincent, "Edward Snowden Claims Microsoft Collaborated with NSA and FBI to Allow Access to User Data," *The Independent* (July 12, 2013).
38. See Gabrielle Coppola, "Israeli Entrepreneurs Play Both Sides of the Cyber Wars," *Bloomberg* (September 29, 2014).
39. See Stephen Krasner, "State Power and the Structure of International Trade," *World Politics*, Vol. 28, No. 3 (April 1976), pp. 317–47; and Richard N. Rosecrance, *The Resurgence of the West: How a Transatlantic Union Can Prevent War and Restore the United States and Europe* (New Haven, CT: Yale University Press, 2013).
40. See Florian Egloff, "Cybersecurity and the Age of Privateering: A Historical Analogy," *Cyber Studies Working Paper No. 1*, University of Oxford (March 2015).

41. See Fernand Braudel, *The Mediterranean and the Mediterranean World in the Age of Philip II* (Berkeley, CA: University of California Press, 1995).
42. Some thinkers question whether attribution is as hard as many observers believe it to be. See Jon R. Lindsay, "Tipping the Scales: The Attribution Problem and the Feasibility of Deterrence against Cyberattack," *Journal of Cybersecurity*, Vol. 1, No. 1 (2015), pp. 53–67; and Thomas Rid, "Attributing Cyber Attacks," *Journal of Strategic Studies* (2015), p. 38.
43. See Brandon Valeriano and Ryan C. Maness, *Cyber War Versus Cyber Realities: Cyber Conflict in the International System* (Oxford: Oxford University Press, 2015).
44. Legal scholars who support the "natural law" tradition developed by Aquinas, Locke, and Vattel have challenged the positivist doctrine's position as the legitimate source of international law. See James L. Brierly, *The Basis of Obligations in International Law* (Oxford: Clarendon Press, 1958); and Hersch Lauterpacht, *International Law and Human Rights* (London: Stevens and Sons, 1950).

10 Cyber Futures

1. See "The Path of Cyberlaw," *Yale Law Journal*, Vol. 104, No. 7 (May 1995), pp. 1,743–55; and "The Zones of Cyberspace Symposium: Surveying Law and Borders," *Stanford Law Review*, Vol. 48 (1995–96), pp. 1,403–11.
2. See, for example, Rein Turn, "Privacy Protection and Security in Transnational Data Processing Systems," *Stanford Journal of International Law*, Vol. 16 (Summer 1980), pp. 67–86.
3. See Elaine McArdle, "The New Age of Surveillance," *Harvard Law Bulletin* (Spring 2016).
4. Parallel developments in the area of quantum cryptography will not neutralize this threat. Computer specialists expect that the technique will reinforce only "symmetric cryptography," a more cumbersome encryption method than asymmetric encryption that is used to secure Top Secret government documents and other highly sensitive data. Workshop on European Cybersecurity: Future Trends and Policy Challenges, January 27–28, 2017, Cyber Studies Programme, University of Oxford.

Bibliography

Abbate, Janet. *Inventing the Internet*. Cambridge, MA: MIT Press, 1999

Ablon, Lillian, Martin C. Libicki, and Andrea A. Golay. *Markets for Cybercrime Tools and Stolen Data*. Santa Monica, CA: RAND, March 14, 2014

Abrams, Steve. "Beyond Propaganda: Soviet Active Measures in Putin's Russia," *Connections: The Quarterly Journal*, Vol. 15, No. 1 (2016)

Allison, Graham. *Nuclear Terrorism: The Greatest Preventable Catastrophe*. New York: Henry Holt, 2005

Allison, Graham, Albert Carnesale, and Joseph S. Nye, eds. *Hawks, Doves, and Owls: An Agenda for Avoiding Nuclear War*. New York: W. W. Norton, 1985

Allison, Graham and Philip D. Zelikow. *The Essence of Decision: Explaining the Cuban Missile Crisis*, second edition. New York: Longman, 1999

Alvargonzález, David. "Multidisciplinarity, Interdisciplinarity, Transdisciplinarity, and the Sciences," *International Studies in the Philosophy of Science*, Vol. 25, No. 4 (2011), pp. 387–403

Anderson, Benedict. *Under Three Flags: Anarchism and the Anti-Colonial Imagination*. London: Verso, 2005

Andres, Richard B. "Cyber-Gang Warfare: State-Sponsored Militias Are Coming to a Server Near You," *Foreign Policy* (February 11, 2013)

Armstrong, A. G. "The Army Today," *RUSI Journal*, Vol. 81, No. 523 (1936)

———. "The Army's New Weapons and Equipment," *RUSI Journal*, Vol. 84, No. 534 (1939)

———. *Revolution and World Order: The Revolutionary State in International Society*. Oxford: Clarendon Press, 1993

Aron, Raymond. *Penser la guerre, Clausewitz*, Vol. 2, *L'âge planétaire*. Paris: Gallimard, 1976

Arquilla, John. "Cyberwar Is Already Upon Us," *Foreign Policy* (February 27, 2012)

Arquilla, John and David Ronfeldt. *Cyber War Is Coming!* Santa Monica, CA: RAND, 1993

———. *Networks and Netwars: The Future of Terror, Crime, and Militancy*. Santa Monica, CA: RAND, 2001

Ash, Timothy Garton. *Free Speech: Ten Principles for a Connected World*. New Haven, CT: Yale University Press, 2016

Axelrod, Robert. *The Evolution of Cooperation*. New York: Basic Books, 1984

Axelrod, Robert and Rumen Iliev. "Timing of Cyber Conflict," *Proceedings of the National Academy of Sciences of the United States of America*, Vol. 11, No. 4 (October 2013), pp. 1,298–1,303

Baek, Jieun. *North Korea's Hidden Revolution: How the Information Underground Is Transforming a Closed Society*. New Haven, CT: Yale University Press, 2015

Bairoch, Paul. "International Industrialization Levels from 1750 to 1980," *Journal of European Economic History*, Vol. 11 (1982)

Baker, Stewart, Natalia Filipiak, and Katrina Timlin. *In the Dark: Crucial Industries Confront Cyberattacks*. Santa Clara, CA: Center for International and Strategic Studies and McAfee, 2011

Barzashka, Ivanka. "Are Cyber-Weapons Effective?" *The RUSI Journal*, Vol. 158, No. 2 (2013)

Bellamy, Alex J. *Global Politics and the Responsibility to Protect: From Words to Deeds*. London: Routledge, 2011

Bellovin, Steven M., Susan Landau, and Herbert S. Lin. "Limiting the Undesired Impact of Cyber Weapons: Technical Requirements and Policy Implications," unpublished paper

Bencsáth, Boldizsár. "Duqu, Flame, Gauss: Followers of Stuxnet," *RSA Conference Europe 2012*

Berger, Thomas. "Changing Norms of Defense and Security in Japan and Germany," in Peter J. Katzenstein, ed., *The Culture of National Security: Norms and Identity in World Politics*. New York: Columbia University Press, 1996

Bilge, Leyla and Tudor Dumitras. "Before We Knew It: An Empirical Study of Zero-Day Attacks in the Real World," *Proceedings of the 2012 ACM Conference on Computer and Communications Security, October 16–18, 2012*

Bishop, Matt. "What is Computer Security?," *IEEE Security & Privacy* (January/February 2003), pp. 67–69

Bittman, Ladislav. *The KGB and Soviet Disinformation: An Insider's View*. Oxford: Pergamon, 1985

Blakely, Jason. "Is Political Science This Year's Election Casualty?" *The Atlantic* (November 14, 2016)

Boghardt, Thomas. "Soviet Bloc Intelligence and Its AIDS Disinformation Campaign," *Studies in Intelligence*, Vol. 53, No. 4 (December 2009), pp. 1–24

Braudel, Fernand. *The Mediterranean and the Mediterranean World in the Age of Philip II*. Berkely, CA: University of California Press, 1995

Braun, Chaim and Christopher F. Chyba. "Proliferation Rings: New Challenges to the Nuclear Nonproliferation Regime," *International Security*, Vol. 29, No. 2 (Fall 2004), pp. 5–49

Brierly, James L. *The Basis of Obligations in International Law*. Oxford: Clarendon Press, 1958

Brodie, Bernard. *The Absolute Weapon*. New York: Harcourt, 1946

——. "The Anatomy of Deterrence," in Bernard Brodie, ed., *Strategy in the Missile Age*. Princeton, N.J.: Princeton University Press, 1958

Bronk, Christopher and Eneken Tikk-Ringas. "The Cyber Attack on Saudi Aramco," *Survival: Global Politics and Strategy*, Vol. 55, No. 2 (2013), pp. 81–96

Brown, Michael E., Sean M. Lynn-Jones, and Steven E. Miller. *Debating the Democratic Peace*. Cambridge, MA: MIT Press, 1996

Bruneau, Guy. *DNS Sinkhole*. Boston, MA: SANS Institute, August 7, 2010

Buchanan, Ben. *The Cybersecurity Dilemma: Hacking, Trust and Fear Between Nations*. Oxford: Oxford University Press, 2017

Bull, Hedley. *Justice in International Relations: Hagey Lectures*. Waterloo: University of Waterloo, 1983

——. *The Anarchical Society: A Study of Order in World Politics*, second edition. London: Macmillan, 1995

Buzan, Barry. *From International to World Society? English School Theory and the Social Structure of Globalisation*. Cambridge: Cambridge University Press, 2004

Buzan, Barry and Lene Hansen. *The Evolution of International Security Studies*. Cambridge: Cambridge University Press, 2009

Buzan, Barry and Richard Little. *International Systems in World History: Remaking the Study of International Relations*. Oxford: Oxford University Press, 2000

Byman, Daniel. "Pyongyang's Survival Strategy: Tools of Authoritarian Control in North Korea," *International Security*, Vol. 35, No. 1 (Summer 2010), pp. 44–74

Byman, Daniel and Jeremy Shapiro. "Be Afraid. Be a Little Afraid: The Threat of Terrorism from Western Fighters in Syria and Iraq," Foreign Policy and Brookings, Policy Paper No. 34, Washington, D.C.: Brookings (November 2014)

Canavan, Gregory H. *Missile Defense for the 21st Century*. Washington, D.C.: The Heritage Foundation, 2003

Carr, Edward H. *The Twenty Years' Crisis, 1919–1939: An Introduction to the Study of International Relations*. New York: Harper and Row, 1964

———. *The Bolshevik Revolution, 1917–23*, Vol. 3. New York: Penguin, 1977

Carter, Ash. "Drell Lecture: 'Rewiring the Pentagon: Charting a New Path on Innovation and Cybersecurity'," Stanford University (April 23, 2015)

Cerf, Vinton G. "How the Internet Came to Be," in Bernard Adoba, ed., *The Online User's Encyclopedia*. Boston, MA: Addison-Wesley, 1993

Cerf, Vinton G. and Robert E. Kahn. "A Protocol for Packet Network Interconnection," *IEEE Transactions on Communications, COM-22*, Vol. 5 (1974)

Cha, Victor D. "North Korea's Weapons of Mass Destruction: Badges, Shields, or Swords?" *Political Science Quarterly*, Vol. 117, No. 2 (2002), pp. 209–30

Chekinov, Sergey and Sergey A. Bogdanov. "The Nature and Content of a New-Generation War," *Military Thought*, No. 4 (2013)

Choucri, Nazli. *Cyber Politics in International Relations*. Cambridge, MA: MIT Press, 2012

Choucri, Nazli and David Clark. "Cyberspace and International Relations: Towards an Integrated System," paper presented at the Massachusetts Institute of Technology, Cambridge, Massachusetts, August 2011

Clark, David D. "The Design Philosophy of the DARPA Internet Protocols," *Proceedings of the SIGCOMM '88, Computer Communication Review*, Vol. 18, No. 4 (1988), pp. 106–14

———. "Designs for an Internet", Draft version 2.0 ed. s.l., unpublished manuscript, 2016

Clark, David D. and Susan Landau. "Untangling Attribution," in *Proceedings of a Workshop on Deterring Cyberattacks: Informing Strategies and Developing Options for U.S. Policy*. Washington, D.C.: National Academies Press, 2010

Clarke, Richard A. and Robert K. Knake. *Cyber War: The Next Threat to National Security and What to Do About It*. New York: HarperCollins, 2010

Claude, Inis L. Claude, Jr. *Swords into Ploughshares: The Problems and Progress of International Organization*, fourth edition. London: Random House, 1988

Cockcroft, J.D. and E. T. S. Walton. "Experiments with High Velocity Positive Ions. II. The Disintegration of Elements by High Velocity Protons," *Proceedings of the Royal Society of London* (July 1932)

Compton-Hall, Richard. *Submarines and the War at Sea*. London: Macmillan, 1991

Cooper, William H. *Russia's Economic Performance and Policies and Their Implications for the United States*. Washington, D.C.: Congressional Research Service, June 29, 2009

Cox, Robert W. "Social Forces, States, and World Orders," *Millennium: Journal of International Studies*, Vol. 10, No. 2 (1981)

Czosseck, Christian, Rain Ottis, and Anna-Maria Talihärm. "Estonia After the 2007 Cyber Attacks: Legal, Strategic and Organisational Changes in Cyber Security," in M. Warren, ed., *Case Studies in Information Warfare and Security*. Reading: Academic Conferences and Publishing International Limited, 2013

Darczewska, Jolanta. *The Anatomy of Russian Information Warfare. The Crimean Operation: A Case Study*. Warsaw: Centre for Eastern Studies, May 2014

Dawes, Sharon S. "The Continuing Challenges of E-Governance," *Public Administration Review*, Vol. 68, No. 1 [Special Issue] (December 2008), pp. 586–602

De Borchgrave, Arnaud, Frank J. Cilluffo, Sharon L. Cardash, and Michele M. Ledgerwood. *Cyber Threats and Information Security: Meeting the 21st Century Challenge*. Washington, D.C.: U.S. Department of Justice, Office of Justice Programs, 2001

De Gaulle, Charles. *Vers l'armée de métier*. Paris: Plon, 1981

Deibert, Ronald J. "Black Code: Censorship, Surveillance, and Militarization of Cyberspace," *Millennium*, Vol. 32, No. 2 (December 2003), pp. 501–30

Deibert, Ronald, John Palfrey, Rafal Rohozinski, and Jonathan Zittrain. *Contested: Security, Identity, and Resistance in Asian Cyberspace*. Cambridge, MA: MIT Press, 2011

Demchak, Chris C. *Wars of Disruption and Resilience: Cybered Conflict, Power, and National Security*. Athens, GA: University of Georgia Press, 2011

DeNardis, Laura. *Protocol Politics: The Globalization of Internet Governance*. Cambridge, MA: MIT Press, 2009

Derthick, Martha. *Agency Under Duress: The Social Security Administration in American Government*. Washington, D.C.: The Brookings Institution, 1990

Duffrey, Romney B. and John Saull. *Managing Risk: The Human Element*. Chichester: Wiley, 2008

Duggan, Patrick Michael. "Strategic Development of Special Warfare in Cyberspace," *Joint Force Quarterly*, Vol. 79, No. 4 (October 2015)

Dunn Cavelty, Myriam. "The Militarization of Cyber Security as a Source of Global Tension," *Strategic Trends 2012: Key Developments in Global Affairs*. Zurich: Center for Strategic Studies, 2012

Dunne, Timothy. "The Social Construction of International Society," *European Journal of International Relations*, Vol. 1, No. 3 (September 1995), pp. 367–89

Easterly, William and Stanley Fischer. "The Soviet Economic Decline: Historical and Republican Data," *NBER Working Paper No. 4735* (May 1994)

Egloff, Florian. "Cybersecurity and the Age of Privateering: A Historical Analogy," *Cyber Studies Working Paper No. 1*, University of Oxford (March 2015)

Engels, Friedrich and Karl Marx. *The German Ideology*, second edition. London: Laurence and Wishart, 1974

Eriksson, Johan and Giampiero Giacomello. "The Information Revolution, Security, and International Relations: The (IR)relevant Theory?" *International Political Science Review*, Vol. 27, No. 3 (July 2006), pp. 221–44

Evangelista, Matthew. *Unarmed Forces: The Transnational Movement to End the Cold War*. Ithaca, NY: Cornell University Press, 1999

Even, Loras R. *Honey Pot Systems Explained*. Boston, MA: SANS Institute, July 12, 2000

Falliere, Nicholas, Liam O. Murchu, and Eric Chien. *W32.Stuxnet Dossier*, ver. 1.4. Cupertino, CA: Symantec, February 2011

Farivar, Cyrus. "A Brief Examination of Media Coverage of Cyberattacks (2007–Present)," in Christian Czosseck and Kenneth Geers. *The Virtual Battlefield: Perspectives on Cyber Warfare*. Amsterdam: IOS Press, 2009

Farley, Robert. "What if Hitler Developed Nuclear Weapons During World War II?" *The National Interest* (October 8, 2016)

Fearon, James and Alexander Wendt. "Rationalism versus Constructivism: A Skeptical View," in Walter Carlsnaes, Thomas Risse, and Beth A. Simmons, *Handbook of International Relations*. London: Sage, 2002

Ferguson, Niall. *Kissinger, 1923–1968: The Idealist*. London: Penguin, 2015

Fitzpatrick, Mark. "Dr. A. Q. Khan and the Rise and Fall of Proliferation Networks," *Nuclear Black Markets*. London: International Institute for Strategic Studies, 2007

Fritsch, Stefan. "Technology and Global Affairs," *International Studies Perspectives*, Vol. 12, No. 1 (2011), pp. 27–45

——. "Conceptualizing the Ambivalent Role of Technology in International Relations: Between Systemic Change and Continuity," in Maximilian Mayer, Mariana Carpes, and Ruth Knoblich, eds., *The Global Politics of Science and Technology. Vol. 1: Concepts from International Relations and Other Disciplines*. Berlin, Heidelberg: Springer, 2014

Fukuyama, Francis. *The End of History and the Last Man*. New York: The Free Press, 1992

Gartzke, Erik. "The Myth of Cyberwar: Bringing War in Cyberspace Back Down to Earth," *International Security*, Vol. 38, No. 2 (Fall 2013), pp. 41–73

Gartzke, Erik and Quan Li. "War, Peace, and the Invisible Hand: Positive Political Externalities of Economic Globalization," *International Studies Quarterly* (November 2003)

Geers, Kenneth. "The Challenge of Cyber Attack Deterrence," *Computer Law and Security Review*, Vol. 26, No. 3 (May 2010), pp. 298–303

George, Alexander L. and Andrew Bennett. *Case Studies and Theory Development in the Social Sciences*. Cambridge, MA: MIT Press, 2005

Gerasimov, Valeriy. "Ценность науки в предвидении (The Value of Science is in Foresight," Военно-промышленный курьер (February 27, 2013)

Giles, Keir. "Russia's 'New' Tools for Confronting the West. Continuity and Innovation in Moscow's Exercise of Power," Research Paper, Russia and Eurasia Programme, Chatham House (March 2016)

Gilpin, Robert. *War and Change in World Politics*. Cambridge: Cambridge University Press, 1989

Glaser, Charles L. and Chaim Kauffman. "What is the Offense-Defense Balance and Can We Measure It?" *International Security*, Vol. 22, No. 4 (Spring 1998), pp. 44–82

Goldsmith, Jack L. "Against Cyberanarchy," *Chicago Law Review*, Vol. 1199 (Fall 1998)

——. "WCIT-12: An Opinionated Primer and Hysteria-Debunker," *Lawfare (blog)* (November 30, 2012)

——. "Disconcerting U.S. Cyber Deterrence Troubles Continue," *Lawfare* (September 15, 2015)

Goldsmith, Jack L. and Tim Wu. *Who Controls the Internet? Illusions of a Borderless World*. New York: Oxford University Press, 2006

Guri, Mordechai, Yosef Solewicz, Andrey Daidakulov, and Yuval Elovici. "DiskFiltration: Data Exfiltration from Speakerless Air-Gapped Computers via Covert Hard Drive Noise," *arXiv.org* (August 11, 2016)

Haggard, Stephen and Marcus Noland. "Engaging North Korea: The Efficacy of Sanctions and Inducements," in Etel Solingen, ed., *Sanctions, Statecraft, and Nuclear Proliferation*. Cambridge: Cambridge University Press, 2012

Hansen, Lene and Helen Nissenbaum. "Digital Disaster, Cyber Security, and the Copenhagen School," *International Studies Quarterly*, Vol. 53, No. 4 (December 2009), pp. 1,155–75

Harknett, Richard J. "The Logic of Conventional Deterrence and the End of the Cold War," *Security Studies*, Vol. 4, No. 1 (1994), pp. 86–114

——. "Toward a Logic of Offensive Persistence," *International Security* (2017)

Harknett, Richard J. and Hasan B. Yalcin. "The Struggle for Autonomy: A Realist Structural Theory of International Relations," *International Studies Review*, Vol. 14 (2012), pp. 499–521

Hathaway, Melissa E. "Leadership and Responsibility for Cybersecurity," *Georgetown Journal of International Affairs* (2012)

Hathaway, Melissa E. and Alexander Klimburg. "Preliminary Considerations: On National Cyber Security," in Alexander Klimburg, ed., *National Cyber Security Framework Manual*. Tallinn: NATO CCD-COE, 2012

Healey, Jason. *A Fierce Domain: Conflict in Cyberspace, 1986 to 2012*. Arlington, VA: Cyber Conflict Studies Association, 2012

Herrera, Geoffrey L. *Technology and International Transformation: The Railroad, the Atom Bomb, and the Politics of Technological Change*. New York: State University of New York Press, 2006

Herz, John H. *International Politics in the Atomic Age*. New York: Columbia University Press, 1959

Hinsley, F. H. *Power and the Pursuit of Peace: Theory and Practice in the History of Relations between States*. Cambridge: Cambridge University Press, 1967

Ho, Park Young, "South and North Korea's Views on the Unification of the Korean Peninsula and Inter-Korean Relations," Paper presented at the Second KRIS-Brookings Joint Conference on Security and Diplomatic Cooperation between ROK and US for the Unification of the Korean Peninsula (January 21, 2014)

Hobbes, Thomas. *Leviathan*, edited with an introduction by C. B. Macpherson. New York: Penguin, 1968

Hoeber, Francis. *Slow to Take Offense: Bombers, Cruise Missiles and Prudent Deterrence.* Washington, D.C.: Georgetown University Center for Strategic and International Studies, 1977

Hoffmann, Stanley. *The State of War: Essays on the Theory and Practice of International Politics.* New York: Praeger, 1965

——. *Gulliver's Travels, Or the Setting of American Foreign Policy.* New York: McGraw-Hill, 1968

——. *Duties Beyond Borders: On the Limits and Possibilities of Ethical International Politics.* Syracuse, N.Y.: Syracuse University Press, 1981

Hogben, Giles, ed. *Botnets: Detection, Measurement, Disinfection, and Defence.* Heraklion: European Network and Information Security Agency, 2011

Holsti, Kalevi J. "The Concept of Power in the Study of International Relations," *Background,* Vol. 7, No. 4 (February 1964)

Howard, Michael. *War in Modern History.* Oxford: Oxford University Press, 1976

——. *Clausewitz: A Very Short Introduction.* Oxford: Oxford University Press, 2002

Howard, Philip N., Aiden Duffy Deen Freelon, Muzammil M. Hussain, Will Mari, and Marwa Maziad. "Opening Closed Regimes: What Was the Role of Social Media During the Arab Spring?," (2011), available at SSRN: https://ssrn.com/abstract=2595096 or http://dx.doi.org/10.2139/ssrn.2595096

Huntingon, Samuel P. *The Clash of Civilizations and the Remaking of World Order.* New York: Simon and Schuster, 1996

Hurrell, Andrew. *On Global Order: Power, Values and the Constitution of International Society.* Oxford: Oxford University Press, 2007

Hurwitz, Roger. "Keeping Cool: Steps for Avoiding Conflict and Escalation in Cyberspace," *Georgetown Journal of International Affairs* (July 2015), pp. 17—23

Jang-Yop, Hwang and Selig Harrison. *The Two Koreas.* New York: Addison-Wesley, 1998

Jackson, Julia. *The Fall of France: The Nazi Invasion of 1940.* Oxford: Oxford University Press, 2003

Jackson, Robert. *Sovereignty: The Evolution of an Idea.* Cambridge: Polity, 2007

James, Simon. *Rome and the Sword: How Warriors and Weapons Shaped Roman History.* London: Thames and Hudson, 2011

Jervis, Robert. "Cooperation under the Security Dilemma," *World Politics,* Vol. 30, No. 2 (January 1978), pp. 167–214

——. *The Meaning of the Nuclear Revolution: Statecraft and the Prospect of Armageddon.* Ithaca, N.Y.: Cornell University Press, 1989

Jo, Dong-Joon and Erik Gartzke. "Determinants of Nuclear Weapons Proliferation," *Journal of Conflict Resolution,* Vol. 51, No. 1 (February 2007), pp. 167–94

Joffre, Marshall. *Mémoires du Maréchal Joffre.* Paris: Librarie Plon, 1932

Jupille, Joseph, James A. Caporaso, and Jeffrey T. Checkel. "Integrating Institutions: Rationalism, Constructivism, and the Study of the European Union," *Comparative Political Studies,* Vol. 36, No. 7 (February–March 2003), pp. 7–40

Kahn, Herman. *On Escalation: Metaphors and Scenarios.* London: Pall Mall Press, 1965

Kahneman, Daniel. "A Perspective on Judgment and Choice: Mapping Bounded Rationality," *American Psychologist,* Vol. 58, No. 9 (September 2003), pp. 697–720

Kant, Immanuel. *Perpetual Peace and Other Essays on Politics, History and Morals,* trans. T. Humphrey. Indianapolis, IN: Hackett, 1983

Keck, Margaret E. and Kathryn Sikkink. *Activists Beyond Borders: Advocacy Networks in International Politics.* Ithaca, N.Y.: Cornell University Press, 1998

Kello, Lucas. "The Meaning of the Cyber Revolution: Perils to Theory and Statecraft," *International Security,* Vol. 38, No. 2 (Fall 2013), pp. 7–40

——. "Security," in Joel Krieger, ed., *The Oxford Companion to International Relations,* third edition. Oxford: Oxford University Press, 2014

——. "The Virtual Weapon: Dilemmas and Future Scenarios," *Politique étrangère,* Vol. 79, No. 4 (Winter 2014–15), pp. 139–50

——. "Cyber Security: Gridlock and Innovation," in *Beyond Gridlock.* Cambridge: Polity, 2017

Kennedy, Paul. *The Rise and Fall of the Great Powers: Economic Change and Military Conflict from 1500 to 2000*. New York: Vintage Books, 1987

Keohane, Robert O. and Joseph S. Nye, Jr. *Power and Interdependence*. New York: Longman, 1979

——. *After Hegemony: Cooperation and Discord in the World Political Economy*. Princeton, N.J.: Princeton University Press, 1984

Kesan, Jay P. and Carol M. Hayes. "Mitigative Counterstriking: Self-Defense and Deterrence in Cyberspace," *Harvard Journal of Law and Technology*, Vol. 25, No. 2 (Spring 2012)

Kile, Shannon N. and Hans M. Kristensen. *Trends in Nuclear Forces, 2016: SIPRI FACT Sheet*. Solna, Sweden: Stockholm International Peace Research Institute, June 2016

Kim, Samuel S. "North Korea's Nuclear Strategy and the Interface between International and Domestic Politics," *Asian Perspectives*, Vol. 34, No. 1 (2010), pp. 49–85

Kindleberger, Charles. *The World in Depression, 1929–1939*. Berkeley, CA: University of California Press, 1996

King, Gary, Jennifer Pan, and Margaret E. Roberts. "How Censorship in China Allows Government Criticism but Silences Collective Expression," *American Political Science Review*, Vol. 2 (May 2013), pp. 1–18

Kissinger, Henry A. *Nuclear Weapons and Foreign Policy*. New York: Council on Foreign Relations, 1957

Klaveras, Louis. "Political Realism: A Culprit for the 9/11 Attacks," *Harvard International Review*, Vol. 26, No. 3 (Fall 2004)

Klimburg, Alexander and Heli Tirmaa-Klaar. *Cybersecurity and Cyberpower: Concepts, Conditions, and Capabilities for Cooperation for Action within the EU*. Brussels: European Parliament Directorate General for External Policies of the Union, Policy Department, April 2011

Klimburg, Alexander and Jason Healey. "Strategic Goals and Stakeholders," in Alexander Klimburg, ed., *National Cyber Security Framework and Manual*. Tallinn: NATO Cooperative Cyber Defence Centre of Excellence, 2012

Klotz, Audie and Cecelia M. Lynch. *Strategies for Research in Constructivist International Relations*. London: M. E. Sharpe, 2007

Kopp, Carolyn. "The Origins of the American Scientific Debate over Fallout Hazards," *Social Studies of Science*, Vol. 9 (1979), pp. 404–06

Kort, Michael. *The Columbia Guide to the Cold War*. New York: Columbia University Press, 1998

Krasner, Stephen. "State Power and the Structure of International Trade," *World Politics*, Vol. 28, No. 3 (April 1976), pp. 317–47

——. *Defending the National Interest: Raw Materials Investments and US Foreign Policy*. Princeton, N.J.: Princeton University Press, 1978

——. "Globalization and Sovereignty," in David A. Smith, Dorothy J. Solinger, and Steven C. Topik, eds., *States and Sovereignty in the Global Economy*. London: Routledge, 1999

Kratochwil, Friedrich. "The Embarrassment of Change: Neo-Realism as the Science of Realpolitik without Politics," *Review of International Studies*, Vol. 19, No. 1 (January 1993), pp. 63–80

Kroenig, Matthew. "Importing the Bomb: Sensitive Nuclear Assistance and Nuclear Proliferation," *Journal of Conflict Resolution*, Vol. 53, No. 2 (April 2009)

Kuhn, Thomas S. *The Structure of Scientific Revolutions*, third edition. Chicago, IL: University of Chicago Press, 1996

Laboratory of Cryptography and Systems Security. *Duqu: A Stuxnet-Like Malware Found in the Wild*. Budapest: Budapest University of Technology and Economics, October 14, 2011

Lacroix, Justine and Kalypso A. Nicolaïdis, eds. *European Stories: Intellectual Debates on Europe in National Contexts*. Oxford: Oxford University Press, 2011

Lake, David A. Lake. "The State and International Relations," in Christian Reus-Smit and Duncan Snidal, eds., *The Oxford Handbook of International Relations*. Oxford: Oxford University Press, 2015

Langner, Ralph. "Stuxnet and the Hacker Nonsense," Langner.com (blog) (February 14, 2011)

——. "Stuxnet's Secret Twin," *Foreign Policy* (November 19, 2013)

——. *To Kill a Centrifuge: A Technical Analysis of What Stuxnet's Creators Tried to Achieve.* Arlington, VT: The Langner Group, November 2013

Lankov, Andrei. "Changing North Korea: An Information Campaign Can Beat the Regime," *Foreign Affairs*, Vol. 88, No. 6 (November/December 2009)

Lapp, Ralph E. "Radioactive Fall-out," *Bulletin of the Atomic Scientists*, Vol. 11 (February 1955), pp. 206–09

Laurent, P. "The Reversal of Belgian Foreign Policy, 1936–37," *Review of Politics*, Vol. 31, No. 3 (July 1969)

Lauterpacht, Hersch. *International Law and Human Rights.* London: Stevens and Sons, 1950

Lee, Robert M. *The Sliding Scale of Cyber Security – A SANS Analyst Whitepaper.* Boston, MA: SANS Institute, 2015

Lenin, Vladimir. *The State and Revolution: The Marxist Theory of the State and the Tasks of the Proletariat in the Revolution.* London: Union Books, 2013

Lessig, Lawrence. "The Path of Cyberlaw," *Yale Law Journal*, Vol. 104, No. 7 (1995)

——. *Code.* New York: Basic Books, 1999

Lewis, James A. *A Note on the Laws of War in Cyberspace.* Washington, D.C.: Center for Strategic and International Studies, April 2010

Libicki, Martin C. *Conquest in Cyberspace: National Security and Information Warfare.* New York: Cambridge University Press, 2007

——. *Cyberdeterrence and Cyberwar.* Santa Monica, CA: RAND Corporation, 2009

——. *Crisis and Escalation in Cyberspace.* Santa Monica, CA: RAND Corporation, 2012

Lieber, Keir A. *War and the Engineers: The Primacy of Politics over Technology.* Ithaca, NY: Cornell University Press, 2005

Liff, Adam P. "Cyberwar: A New 'Absolute Weapon'? The Proliferation of Cyberwarfare Capabilities and Interstate War," *Journal of Strategic Studies*, Vol. 35, No. 3 (June 2012), pp. 401–28

Lin, Herbert S. "Some Interesting Aspects of Cyberconflict for Discussion," presentation at the Harvard Kennedy School, Cambridge, Massachusetts (February 8, 2012)

Lindsay, Jon R. "Stuxnet and the Limits of Cyber Warfare," *Security Studies*, Vol. 22, No. 3 (2013), pp. 365–404

——. "The Impact of China on Cybersecurity: Fiction and Friction," *International Security*, Vol. 39, No. 3 (Winter 2014/2015), pp. 7–47

——. "Tipping the Scales: The Attribution Problem and the Feasibility of Deterrence against Cyberattack," *Journal of Cybersecurity*, Vol. 1, No. 1 (2015)

Lindsay, Jon R. and Lucas Kello. "Correspondence: A Cyber Disagreement," *International Security*, Vol. 39, No. 2 (Fall 2014)

Linklater, Andrew. "Citizenship and Sovereignty in the Post-Westphalian State," *European Journal of International Relations*, Vol. 2, No. 1 (March 1996), pp. 77–103

Lipgens, Walter. *A History of European Integration.* Oxford: Oxford University Press, 1982

Lipgens, Walter and Wilfried Loth, eds. *Documents on the History of European Integration: The Struggle for European Union by Political Parties and Pressure Groups in Western European Countries, 1945–1950.* New York: De Gruyter, 1988

Lynn, III, William J. "Defending a New Domain," *Foreign Affairs*, Vol. 89, No. 5 (September/October 2009), pp. 97–108

Lynn-Jones, Sean M. "Offense-Defense Theory and its Critics, *Security Studies*, Vol. 4, No. 4 (Summer 1995), pp. 660–91

McArdle, Elaine. "The New Age of Surveillance," *Harvard Law Bulletin* (Spring 2016)

McGregor, Richard. *The Party: The Secret World of China's Communist Rulers.* New York: HarperCollins, 2010

MacKenzie, Donald and Graham Spinardi. "Tacit Knowledge, Weapons Design, and the Uninvention of Nuclear Weapons," *American Journal of Sociology*, Vol. 100 (1995), pp. 44–99

Mahnken, Thomas G. "Cyber War and Cyber Warfare," in Kristin M. Lord and Travis Sharp, eds., *America's Cyber Future: Security and Prosperity in the Information Age.* Washington, D.C.: Center for a New American Security, 2011

Majumdar, Dave. "America's F-35 Stealth Fighter vs. China's New J-31: Who Wins?" *The National Interest* (September 25, 2015)

Manchester, William and Paul Reid. *The Last Lion: Winston Spencer Churchill, Defender of the Realm, 1940–1965.* New York: Little, Brown, and Company, 2012

Manjikian, Mary M. "From Global Village to Virtual Battlespace: The Colonizing of the Internet and the Extension of Realpolitik," *International Studies Quarterly*, Vol. 54, No. 2 (June 2010), pp. 381–401

Mann, Edward. "Desert Storm: The First Information War?" *Airpower Journal* (Winter 2014)

Marcus, Gary. "Is 'Deep Learning' a Revolution in Artificial Intelligence?" *The New Yorker* (November 25, 2012)

Martin, Lisa L. "Neoliberalism," in Tim Dunne, Milya Kurki, and Steve Smith, eds., *International Relations Theories: Discipline and Diversity.* Oxford: Oxford University Press, 2007

Maurer, Tim and Robert Morgus. *Compilation of Existing Cybersecurity and Information Security Related Definitions.* New America, October 2012

Massie, Robert K. *Castles of Steel: Britain, Germany and the Winning of the Great War at Sea.* New York: Random House, 2003

Mearsheimer, John J. *Conventional Deterrence.* Ithaca, N.Y.: Cornell University Press, 1983

——. "The Case for a Ukrainian Nuclear Deterrent," *Foreign Affairs* (Summer 1993)

Medalia, Jonathan. *Comprehensive Nuclear Test-Ban Treaty: Updated Safeguards and Net Assessments.* Washington, D.C.: Congressional Research Service, June 3, 2009

Mill, John Stuart. *Essays on Some Unsettled Questions of Political Economy.* London: Longmans, Green, Reader, and Dyer, 1874

Mills, Michael J., Owen B. Toon, Julia Lee-Taylor, and Alan Robock. "Multidecadal Global Cooling and Unprecedented Ozone Loss Following a Regional Nuclear Conflict," *Earth's Future*, Vol. 2, No. 4 (April 2014), pp. 161–76

Minsky, Marvin. *The Society of Mind.* New York: Simon and Schuster, 1988

Minsky, Marvin and Seymour Papert. *Perceptrons: An Introduction to Computational Geometry.* Cambridge, MA: The MIT Press, 1969

Mohan, Vivek and John Villasenor. "Decrypting the Fifth Amendment: The Limits of Self-Incrimination in the Digital Era," *University of Pennsylvania Journal of Constitutional Law Heightened Scrutiny*, Vol. 15 (October 2012), pp. 11–28

Monte, Matthew. *Network Attacks and Exploitation: A Framework.* Indianapolis, IN: John Wiley and Sons, 2015

Moore, Tyler, Richard Clayton, and Ross Anderson. "The Economics of Online Crime," *Journal of Economic Perspectives*, Vol. 23, No. 3 (Summer 2009), pp. 3–20

Moravcsik, Andrew. *The Choice for Europe: Social Purpose and State Power from Messina to Maastricht.* Ithaca, NY: Cornell University Press, 1998

Morgan, Patrick M. *Deterrence.* Beverley Hills, CA: Sage, 1977

——. "Applicability of Traditional Deterrence Concepts and Theory to the Cyber Realm," in *Proceedings of a Workshop on Deterring Cyberattacks: Informing Strategies and Developing Options for U.S. Policy.* Washington, D.C.: National Academies Press, 2010, pp. 55–76

Mueller, John. "Simplicity and the Spook: Terrorism and the Dynamics of Threat Exaggeration," *International Studies Perspectives* (2005).

——. "Think Again: Nuclear Weapons," *Foreign Policy* (December 18, 2009)

Myers, Robert. *Korea in the Cross Currents.* New York: M. E. Sharpe, 2000

National Research Council of the National Academies. *Terrorism and the Electric Power Delivery System.* Washington, D.C.: National Academies Press, 2012

Naughton, John. *A Brief History of the Future: Origins of the Internet.* London: Weidenfeld and Nicolson, 1999

Newsom, David. "Foreign Policy and Academia," *Foreign Policy*, Vol. 101 (Winter 1995)

Njølstad, Olav. *Nuclear Proliferation and International Order: Challenges to the Non-Proliferation Regime.* New York: Routledge, 2011

Nye, Joseph S., Jr. *The Future of Power.* New York: PublicAffairs, 2011

——. "Nuclear Lessons for Cyber Security?" *Strategic Studies Quarterly*, Vol. 5, No. 4 (Winter 2011), pp. 18–38

——. "The Regime Complex for Managing Global Cyber Activities," *Global Commission on Internet Governance*, Issue Paper Series, No. 1 (May 2014)

——. "Deterrence and Dissuasion in Cyberspace," *International Security*, Vol. 41, No. 3 (Winter 2016/2017), pp. 44–71

O'Connor, Damian P. *Between Peace and War: British Defence and the Royal United Services Institute, 1931–2010.* London: Royal United Services Institute, 2011

Ogburn, William, ed. *Technology and International Relations.* Chicago, IL: Chicago University Press, 1949

Oren, Ido. "The Subjectivity of the 'Democratic' Peace: Changing U.S. Perceptions of Imperial Germany," in Michael E. Brown, Sean M. Lynn-Jones, and Steven E. Miller, *Debating the Democratic Peace: An International Security Reader.* Cambridge, MA: The MIT Press, 1996, pp. 263–300

Orlov, Aleksandr. *The Secret History of Stalin's Crimes.* New York: Jarrolds, 1953

Osiander, Andreas. "Sovereignty, International Relations and the Westphalian Myth," *International Organization*, Vol. 55, No. 2 (April 2001), pp. 251–87

Ownes, William A., Kenneth W. Dam, and Herbert S. Lin, eds. *Technology, Policy, Law, and Ethics Regarding U.S. Acquisition and Use of Cyberattack Capabilities.* Washington, D.C.: National Academies Press, 2009

Oye, Kenneth A., ed. *Cooperation Under Anarchy.* Princeton, NJ: Princeton University Press, 1986

Pacepa, Ion Mihai and Ronald Rychlak. *Disinformation: Former Spy Chief Reveals Secret Strategies for Undermining Freedom, Attacking Religion, and Promoting Terrorism.* Washington, D.C.: WND Books, 2013

Paget, François. *Cybercrime and Hacktivism.* Santa Clara, CA: McAfee, 2010

Park, Han S. *North Korea: The Politics of Unconventional Wisdom.* Boulder, CO: Lynne Rienner, 2002

Park, John S. "North Korea, Inc.: Gaining Insights into North Korean Regime Stability from Recent Commercial Activities," United States Institute of Peace Working Paper, Washington, D.C. (May 2009)

Park, John S. and Dong Sun Lee. "North Korea: Existential Deterrence and Diplomatic Leverage," in Muthiah Alagappa, ed., *The Long Shadow: Nuclear Weapons and Security in 21st Century Asia.* Stanford, CA: Stanford University Press, 2008

Pattison, James. *The Morality of Private War: The Challenge of Private Military Companies and Security Companies.* Oxford: Oxford University Press, 2014

Persky, Joseph. "The Ethology of *Homo Economicus*," *Journal of Economic Perspectives*, Vol. 9, No. 2 (Spring 1995)

Poole, Matthew E. and Jason C. Schuette. "Cyber Electronic Warfare. Closing the Operational Seams," *Marine Corps Gazette*, Vol. 99, No. 8 (August 2015), pp. 60–62

Potter, William, ed. *International Nuclear Trade and Nonproliferation: The Challenge of Emerging Suppliers.* Lexington, MA: Lexington Books, 1990

Powell, Robert. *Nuclear Deterrence Theory: The Search for Credibility.* Cambridge: Cambridge University Press, 1990

Powers, Thomas. *Heisenberg's War: The Secret History of the German Bomb.* New York: De Capo Press, 2000

Ramsay, William M. *The Imperial Peace: An Ideal in European History.* Oxford: The Clarendon Press, 1913

Rasteger, Ryan. "How Many Nukes Would It Take to Render Earth Uninhabitable," *Global Zero: A World Without Nuclear Weapons* (July 9, 2015)

Rattray, Gregory J. *Strategic Warfare in Cyberspace.* Cambridge, MA: MIT Press, 2001

Reed, Thomas C. *At the Abyss: An Insider's History of the Cold War.* New York: Random House, 2005

Reus-Smit, Christian. *The Moral Purpose of the State: Culture, Social Identity, and Institutional Rationality in International Relations.* Princeton, N.J.: Princeton University Press, 1999

Reveron, Derek S., ed. *Cyberspace and National Security: Threats, Opportunities, and Power in a Virtual World*. Washington, D.C.: Georgetown University Press, 2012.

Rid, Thomas. "Cyber War Will Not Take Place," *Journal of Strategic Studies*, Vol. 35, No. 1 (February 2012), pp. 5–32

——. "Think Again: Cyberwar," *Foreign Policy*, Vol. 192 (March/April 2012), pp. 80–84

——. *Cyber War Will Not Take Place*. London: C. Hurst and Co., 2013

——. "Attributing Cyber Attacks," *Journal of Strategic Studies* (2015)

——. "All Signs Point to Russia Being Behind the DNC Hack" *Motherboard*. July 25, 2017

Rid, Thomas and Ben Buchanan. "Attributing Cyber Attacks," *Journal of Strategic Studies*, Vol. 38, No. 1 (2014), pp. 4–37

Roberts, Hal and Bruce Etling. "Coordinated DDoS Attack During Russian Duma Elections," *Internet and Democracy Blog*, Berkman Center for Internet and Society, Harvard University (December 8, 2011)

Roesch, Werner. *Bedrohte Schweiz: Die Deutsche Operationsplanungen gegen die Schweiz im Sommer/Herbst 1940 und die Abwehr-Bereitschaft der Armee in Oktober 1940*. Frauenfeld: Huber, 1986

Rogin, Josh. "NSA Chief: Cybercrime Constitutes the 'Greatest Transfer of Wealth in History'," *Foreign Policy* (July 9, 2012)

Rogowski, Ronald. "Institutions as Constraints on Strategic Choice," in David A. Lake and Richard Powell, eds., *Strategic Choice and International Relations*. Princeton, N.J.: Princeton University Press, 1999

Rosecrance, Richard. *The Resurgence of the West: How a Transatlantic Union Can Prevent War and Restore the United States and Europe*. New Haven, CT: Yale University Press, 2013

Roskill, Stephen W. *Naval Policy between the Wars*. London: Walker, 1968

Roustami, Masoud, Farinaz Koushanfar, Jeyavijayan Rajendran, and Ramesh Karri. "Hardware Security: Threat Models and Metrics," *ICCAD '13 Proceedings of the International Conference on Computer-Aided Design, IEEE* (November 18–21, 2013), pp. 819–23

Ruggie, John G. "International Responses to Technology: Concepts and Trends," *International Organization* (Summer 1975), pp. 558–83

——. "Continuity and Transformation in the World Polity: Toward a Neorealist Synthesis," *World Politics*, Vol. 35, No. 2 (January 1983)

Russett, Bruce M. "The Calculus of Deterrence," *Journal of Conflict Resolution*, Vol. 7, No. 2 (June 1963), pp. 97–109

——. *Grasping the Democratic Peace: Principles for a Post-Cold War World*. Princeton, N.J.: Princeton University Press, 1993

Sagan, Scott D. "Why Do States Build Nuclear Weapons? Three Models in Search of a Bomb," *International Security*, Vol. 21, No. 3 (Winter 1996/1997)

——. "The Commitment Trap: Why the United States Should Not Use Nuclear Weapons to Deter Biological and Chemical Weapons Attacks," *International Security*, Vol. 24, No. 4 (Spring 2000), pp. 85–115

Sandee, Michael. *GameOver Zeus: Background on the Badguys and the Backends*. Delft: Fox-IT, July 2015

Sanger, David E. *Confront and Conceal: Obama's Secret Wars and Surprising Use of American Power*. New York: Crown, 2012

Schaefer, Bernd. "North Korean "Adventurism" and China's Long Shadow, 1966–1972," *Cold War International History Project Working Paper*, Woodrow Wilson International Center for Scholars (2004)

Schelling, Thomas C. *The Strategy of Conflict*. Cambridge, MA: Harvard University Press, 1960

——. *Arms and Influence*. New Haven, CT: Yale University Press, 1966

Schelling, Thomas C. and Morton H. Halperin. *Strategy and Arms Control*. Washington, D.C.: Twentieth Century Fund, 1961

Schmitt, Michael N., ed. *Tallinn Manual on the International Law Applicable to Cyber Warfare*. Cambridge: Cambridge University Press, 2013

Schneier, Bruce. "When Does Cyber Spying Become a Cyber Attack," *Defense One* (March 10, 2014)

——. "We Still Don't Know Who Hacked Sony," *Schneier on Security* (January 5, 2015)

Schneier, Bruce. "Someone Is Learning How to Take Down the Internet," *Lawfare* (September 13, 2016)

Schoen, Fletcher and Christopher J. Lamb. *Deception, Disinformation, and Strategic Communications: How One Interagency Group Made a Major Difference.* Washington, D.C.: National Defense University Press, June 2012

Schwartz, Benjamin E. *Right of Boom: What Follows an Untraceable Nuclear Attack?* New York: Overlook Press, 2015

Segal, Adam. "The Code Not Taken: China, the United States, and the Future of Cyber Espionage," *Bulletin of the Atomic Scientists*, Vol. 69, No. 5 (2013), pp. 38–45

——. *The Hacked World Order: How Nations Fight, Trade, Maneuver, and Manipulate in the Digital Age.* New York: PublicAffairs, 2015

Sheldon, Robert and Joe McReynolds. "Civil-Military Integration and Cybersecurity: A Study of Chinese Information Warfare Militias," in Jon R. Lindsay, Tai Ming Cheung, and Derek S. Reveron, eds., *China and Cybersecurity: Espionage, Strategy, and Politics in the Digital Domain.* New York: Oxford University Press, 2015

Sherr, James. "Ukraine and the Black Sea Region: The Russian Military Perspective," in Stephen Blank, ed., *The Russian Military in Contemporary Perspective.* Carlisle, PA: Strategic Studies Institute, U.S. Army War College, forthcoming

Shoemaker, Dan, Anne Kohnke, and Ken Sigler. *A Guide to the National Initiative for Cybersecurity Education (NICE) Cybersecurity Workforce Framework (2.0).* London: CRC Press, 2016

Siboni, Gabi and Zvi Magen. "The Cyber Attack on the Ukrainian Electrical Infrastructure: Another Warning," *INSS Insights*, No. 798 (February 17, 2016)

Simon, Herbert A. *Administrative Behavior: A Study of Human Decision-Making Processes in Administrative Organization.* New York: Macmillan, 1947

Singer, Peter W. *Wired for War: The Robotics Revolution and Conflict in the 21st Century.* New York: Penguin, 2009

Singer, Peter W. and Allan Friedman. *Cybersecurity and Cyberwar: What Everyone Needs to Know.* Oxford: Oxford University Press, 2014

Skolnikoff, Eugene B. *The Elusive Transformation: Science, Technology, and the Evolution of International Politics.* Princeton, N.J.: Princeton University Press, 1993

Slayton, Rebecca. "What Is the Cyber Offense-Defense Balance? Conceptions, Causes, and Assessment," *International Security*, Vol. 41, No. 3 (Winter 2016/2017), pp. 72–109

Smeets, Max. "A Matter of Time: On the Transitory Nature of Cyberweapons," *Journal of Strategic Studies* (February 2017), pp. 1–28

Smith, Merritt R. and Leo Marx, eds. *Does Technology Drive History? The Dilemma of Technological Determinism.* Cambridge, MA: MIT Press, 1994

Snegovaya, Maria. "Executive Summary: Putin's Information Warfare in Ukraine: Soviet Origins of Russia's Hybrid Warfare," Institute for the Study of War (September 2015)

Snyder, Glenn H. *Deterrence and Defense.* Princeton, N.J.: Princeton University Press, 1961

Soldatov, Andrei, and Irina Borogan. *The Red Web: The Struggle Between Russia's Digital Dictators and the New Online Revolutionaries.* New York: PublicAffairs, 2015

Squassoni, Sharon A. *Weapons of Mass Destruction: Trade Between North Korea and Pakistan.* Washington, D.C.: Congressional Research Service, 2006

Steury, Donald P. *Intentions and Capabilities: Estimates on Soviet Strategic Forces, 1950–1983.* Langley, VA: Center for the Study of Intelligence, Central Intelligence Agency, 1996

Stoakes, Geoffrey. *Hitler and the Quest for World Dominion.* Leamington Spa: Berg, 1986

Stoll, Cliff. *The Cuckoo's Egg: Tracking a Spy through the Maze of Computer Espionage.* New York: Doubleday, 1989

Sturtevant, A.H. "Social Implications of the Genetics of Man," *Science*, Vol. 120 (September 10, 1954)

Symantec. *W32.Duqu: The Precursor to the Next Stuxnet*, ver. 1.4 (November 23, 2011)

Szilard, Leo and T. H. Chalmers. "Detection of Neutrons Liberated from Beryllium by Gamma Rays: A New Technique for Inducing Radioactivity," *Nature*, Vol. 134 (September 1934), pp. 494–95

Tabansky, Lior and Itzhak Ben Israel. *Striking with Bits? The IDF and Cyber-Warfare*. Cham: Springer, 2015

Tehranipoor, Mohammad and Farinaz Koushanfar. "A Survey of Hardware Trojan Taxonomy and Detection," *IEEE Design and Test of Computers*, Vol. 27, No. 1 (2010), pp. 10–25

Thomas, Timothy L. "Russia's Reflexive Control Theory and the Military," *Journal of Slavic Military Studies*, Vol. 17, No. 2 (2004)

Thompson, Kenneth. "Reflections on Trusting Trust," *Communication of the ACM*, Vol. 27, No. 8 (August 1984), pp. 761–63

Thucydides, *History of the Peloponnesian War*, trans. Steven Lattimore. Indianapolis, IN: Hackett, 1998

Tipton, Harold F. and Micki Krause, eds. *Information Security Management Handbook*, sixth edition, Vol. 4. New York: Auerbach Publications, 2010

Tor, Uri. "'Cumulative Deterrence' as a New Paradigm for Cyber Deterrence," *Journal of Strategic Studies*, Vol. 40, No. 1 (2017), pp. 92–117

Townsend, Anthony M. "Seoul: Birth of a Broadband Metropolis," *Environment and Planning B: Urban Analytics and City Science*, Vol. 34, No. 3 (2007), pp. 396–413

Turing, Alan M. "On Computable Numbers, with an Application to the *Entscheidungsproblem*," *Proceedings of the London Mathematical Society*, Vol. 2, No. 42 (1937 [delivered to the Society in 1936]), pp. 230–65

Turn, Rein. "Privacy Protection and Security in Transnational Data Processing Systems," *Stanford Journal of International Law*, Vol. 16 (Summer 1980), pp. 67–86

Ulam, Adam B. *Bolsheviks: The Intellectual, Personal and Political History of the Triumph of Communism in Russia*. New York: Macmillan, 1968

——. *Stalin: The Man and His Era*. London: Tauris, 1989

U.S. Cyber Consequences Unit (US-CCU). *Overview by the US-CCU of the Cyber Campaign against Georgia in August 2008*, Special Report, US-CCU (August 2009)

U.S. Defense Science Board. *Report of the Defense Science Board Task Force on Preventing and Defending Against Clandestine Nuclear Attack*. Washington, D.C.: Office of the Under Secretary of Defense for Acquisition, Technology, and Logistics, June 2004

U.S. Department of Defense. *Department of Defense Strategy for Operating in Cyberspace*. Washington, D.C.: U.S. Department of Defense, July 2011

U.S. Senate. *Study of Airpower: Hearings before the Subcommittee on the Air Force of the Committee on Armed Services*. Washington, D.C.: Government Publication Office, 1956

Valeriano, Brandon and Ryan C. Maness. "The Dynamics of Cyber Conflict between Rival Antagonists, 2001–11," *Journal of Peace Research*, Vol. 51, No. 3 (2014).

——. *Cyber War Versus Cyber Realities: Cyber Conflict in the International System*. Oxford: Oxford University Press, 2015

Van Creveld, Martin. *Technology and War: From 2000 B.C. to the Present*. New York: Macmillan, 1989

Van Evera, Stephen. "The Cult of the Offensive and the Origins of the First World War," *International Security*, Vol. 9, No. 1 (Summer 1984)

Venter, H. S. and J. H. P. Eloff. "A Taxonomy of Information Security Technologies," *Computers and Security*, Vol. 22, No. 4 (May 2003), pp. 299–307

Vincent, John. *Human Rights and International Relations: Issues and Reponse*. Cambridge: Cambridge University Press, 1996

Wall, David S. *Cybercrime: The Transformation of Crime in the Information Age*. Cambridge: Polity Press, 2007

Waller, J. Michael. *Strategic Influence: Public Diplomacy, Counterpropaganda, and Political Warfare*. Washington, D.C.: Institute of World Politics Press, 2009

Walt, Stephen M. *Revolution and War*. Ithaca, N.Y.: Cornell University Press, 1996

———. "The Enduring Relevance of the Realist Tradition," in Ira Katznelson and Helen V. Milner, eds., *Political Science: State of the Discipline*. New York: W. W. Norton, 2002

———. "The Relationship between Theory and Policy in International Relations,. *Annual Review of Political Science*, Vol. 8 (2005)

———. "Is the Cyber Threat Overblown?" *Stephen M. Walt* blog, *Foreign Policy* (March 30, 2010)

———. "What Does Stuxnet Tell Us about the Future of Cyber-Warfare?" *Stephen M. Walt* blog, *Foreign Policy* (October 7, 2010)

Waltz, Kenneth N. *Man, the State, and War: A Theoretical Analysis*. New York: Columbia University Press, 1959

———. *Theory of International Politics*. New York: McGraw-Hill, 1979

Waugh, Steven. *Essential Modern World History*. Cheltenham: Thomas Nelson, 2001

Weart, Spencer R. *Never at War: Why Democracies Will Not Fight Each Other*. New Haven, CT: Yale University Press, 1998

Weinberger, Sharon. "Computer Security: Is This the Start of Cyberwarfare?" *Nature*, Vol. 474 (2011), pp. 142–45

Welsh, Jennifer M. "Implementing the 'Responsibility to Protect': Where Expectations Meet Reality," *Ethics and International Affairs*, Vol. 24, No.4 (Winter 2010), pp. 415–30

Wendt, Alexander. *Social Theory of International Politics*. Cambridge: Cambridge University Press, 1999

Whyte, Christopher. "Power and Predation in Cyberspace," *Strategic Studies Quarterly* (Spring 2015), pp. 100–18

———. "Ending Cyber Coercion: Computer Network Attack, Exploitation and the Case of North Korea," *Comparative Strategy*, Vol. 35, No. 2 (July 2016), pp. 93–102

Wight, Martin. *International Theory: The Three Traditions*. London: Leicester University Press, 1991.

Wilson, Geoff and Will Saetren. "Quite Possibly the Dumbest Military Concept Ever: A 'Limited' Nuclear War," *The National Interest* (May 27, 2016)

Wohlstetter, Albert. "The Delicate Balance of Terror," in Henry A. Kissinger, ed., *Problems of National Strategy: A Book of Readings*. New York: Praeger, 1965

Wolfers, Arnold. "'National security' as an Ambiguous Symbol," *Political Science Quarterly*, Vol. 67 (December 1952), pp. 481–502

———. *Discord and Collaboration*. Baltimore, MD: Johns Hopkins Press, 1962

Youngblood, Dawn. "Interdisciplinary Studies and the Bridging Disciplines: A Matter of Process," *Journal of Research Practice*, Vol. 3, No. 2 (2007)

Zumwalt, Elmo R. "Correspondence: An Assessment of the Bomber-Cruise Missile Controversy," *International Security*, Vol. 2, No. 1 (Summer 1977), pp. 47–58

Index